# Vale of Tears

W9-CCD-734

# Vale of Tears

*Revisiting the Canudos Massacre
in Northeastern Brazil, 1893–1897*

Robert M. Levine

UNIVERSITY OF CALIFORNIA PRESS
Berkeley    Los Angeles    London

University of California Press
Berkeley and Los Angeles
University of California Press, Ltd.
London, England
© 1992 by
The Regents of the University of Califoria

First Paperback Printing 1995

Library of Congress Cataloging-in-Publication Data

Levine, Robert M.
    Vale of tears: revisiting the Canudos massacre in northeastern
Brazil, 1893–1897 / Robert M. Levine.
        p.   cm.
    Includes bibliographical references (p.   ) and index.
    ISBN 978-0-520-20343-3
    1. Brazil—History—Canudos Campaign, 1893–1897.   2. Conselheiro,
Antônio, 1828–1897.   3. Cunha, Euclides da. 1866–1909. Sertões.
4. Millennialism—Brazil—History—19th century.   I. Title.
F2537.L475   1992
981′.05—dc20                                                    91-36011

Printed in the United States of America
13  12  11  10  09
9  8  7  6  5  4

The paper used in this publication meets the minimum requirements of
American National Standard for Information Sciences—Permanence of Paper
for Printed Library Materials, ANSI Z39.48–1984. ⊗

*To José Carlos and Alice*

# CONTENTS

# PREFACE

A great number of friends and acquaintances helped me during the course of the research and writing of this book. An unusual and arguably unique collaborative relationship with the staff of the State University of Bahia's Centro de Estudos Euclydes da Cunha (CEEC) in Salvador—headed until November 1989 by Yara Dulce Bandeira de Ataide and Renato Ferraz—provided me with access to documentation being cataloged by the CEEC staff. In return, I visited the Centro on four different occasions, working with its personnel, offering workshops and lectures, collecting materials for a videotaped documentary on Canudos, and discussing in detail plans for further projects emanating from the CEEC's Project Canudos. Renato Ferraz also escorted me and a group of CEEC staff members to the Canudos site, eleven hours from Salvador by truck over impossible roads—the same itinerary covered by Mario Vargas Llosa a year earlier.

José Carlos Sebe Bom Meihy of the University of São Paulo first brought me together with the CEEC team, and worked with me in evaluating materials written by CEEC staff members during his Fulbright sabbatical year in Coral Gables in 1988–89. He also spent time with me in Salvador in December 1989 evaluating my work in progress and making useful comments. In Salvador, I was helped by Prof. José Calasans of the Centro de Estudos Bahianos; Prof. Consuelo Novais Sampaio of the Universidade Federal da Bahia; Prof. Thalez de Azevedo of the Historical and Geographic Association; Consuelo Pondé de Senna of the Arquivo Público; Maria D. de Azevedo Brandão; Mário Cravo Júnior, the eminent sculptor and artist who permitted me to examine and make copies of many of his sketches and other studies of *sertanejo* culture; Mário Cravo Neto (Mariozinho), a superb photographer who knows well the backlands and its people; Elizeu A. Santos at the newspaper *A Tarde*; César Naus; Joana and Didí dos Santos; Kátia M. de Queirós Mattosso; Bert Barickman; Álvaro Pinto Dantas de Carvalho, the custodian of the Baron de Jeremoabo papers; Antônio Marcelino; James C. Riordan; and João Reis. Special acknowledgment goes to M. Conceição Costa e Silva, who helped me find material in various archives and newspaper collections in Salvador.

In other places, the list of individuals to whom I owe thanks includes Carlos and Mary Bakota, in Recife; Eduardo Silva, Nancy Naro, and Jerusa Gonçalves de Araújo of the Casa Rui Barbosa, in Rio de Janeiro; and Janaína Amado, in Goiânia (and Baltimore).

Colleagues in the United States who offered suggestions, commented on drafts of the manuscript, or otherwise lent encouragement include Linda Lewin, Ralph della Cava, Mary Lou Daniel, Martha D. Huggins, Anne-Marie Gill, Dale Graden, Eul-Soo Pang, Gerald M. Greenfield, Iván Jaksić, Todd Diacon, Teresita Martínez-Vergne, Lori Madden, Quélia Quaresma, Warren Dean, Peter Beattie, Paul Vanderwood, Robert Jackson, Charles A. Hale, Joseph L. Love, Nada Massey, and Stanley J. Stein. The willingness of Latin American specialists to share their ideas and to offer constructive criticism is remarkable, and very much appreciated. Nelson Vieira helped me make initial contacts in Salvador. Edward L. Dreyer offered insightful comments about military history. Louise Strauss offered thorough and very helpful editing advice. José Carlos and Alice Bom Meihy kindly edited my manuscript for misplaced Portuguese accents and other gremlins.

My work recognizes the contributions of scholars who have explored aspects of the region before me. These include José Calasans, Maria Isaura Pereira de Queiroz, Walnice Nogueira Galvão, René Ribeiro, Patricia R. Pessar, and Ralph della Cava. Their pioneering studies remain, in my view, the most helpful of any to date. Pereira de Queiroz raises provocative ideas about the social composition of backlands life and about Brazilian messianism; Galvão's work on journalistic coverage of Canudos facilitates examination of Canudos in the national context; Pessar's and Ribeiro's cogent analysis of millenarianism and messianism places Canudos in fertile comparative perspective; and Ralph della Cava's masterful comparison of Padre Cícero and Antônio Conselheiro showed more than twenty years ago how much can be gained by careful research unencumbered by the weight of traditional interpretation.

## TERMINOLOGY

In Brazil, there is no hard-and-fast rule for preferred spelling of names. In the past, individuals frequently used different spellings of their own names at different times in their lives. Scholars today often use Euclydes da Cunha (sometimes Da Cunha), whereas the official name of the city formerly named Cumbe is Euclides da Cunha. Jeremoabo is generally spelled with the modern *J*, not the old *G*. Governor Luiz Vianna's name sometimes appears as Luis Viana; Gilberto Freyre preferred the traditional spelling, not the modern one (Freire). The use of the circumflex in Antônio is optional today. Most names used in the book reflect late nineteenth-century spelling.

Some of the terms typically used by chroniclers and historians to describe the actors in the backlands drama are best left defined but untranslated: *caboclo, jagunço, beato, caatinga*, and so on. Other terms raise problems, but often their use cannot be avoided. It is questionable whether there ever was a Brazilian peasantry, either in the plantation-dominated *zona da mata* or in the *sertão*.[1] Other terms—"rural poor," "lower classes," "elites," "lower orders"—all carry associations borrowed from other cultures and, in any event, are too general to be meaningful. We cannot deny that in spite of relative physical proximity (in a slave-holding society, masters grew accustomed to having slaves and other servile groups nearby), a gulf separated the "traditional families" of the elite from the rest of the population. Nor was there a single or common frame of mind.

When I discuss "official" attitudes, I refer to the attitudes shared by a majority of the elite in the modernizing cities mostly along the Atlantic coast. This viewpoint did not vary significantly along partisan lines; rather, it represented the outlook of a social class that lacked any consciousness of mutual interest to be shared with the mass of the population.[2] What I will attempt to do at least is to define these terms as precisely as possible and within the Bahian context, for this is a study of Canudos as a regional event. All social, class, and ethnic groups' identities in the course of the discussion are to some degree artificial constructs, in part because boundaries dividing one from another are so difficult to apply. In the *sertão* as elsewhere there were, borrowing from the words of a medievalist, "almost infinite gradations, complexities, and mobilities of the kaleidoscope of human society."[3]

Some of the material in this book first appeared in article form in the *Hispanic American Historical Review* (68, no. 3 [August 1988]). Research funding was provided by the Latin American program of the Social Science Research Council (Ford Foundation) for a research fellowship, by the National Endowment for the Humanities' Interpretive Research Program, and by the Graduate School of the University of Miami. A stipend from the Brazilian-American Chamber of Commerce in Miami helped me in the purchase of supplies and some books through its support of Brazilian Studies at the University of Miami.

My deep gratitude goes to my wife and helpmate, Peggy Anne Phillips, for her unstinting support and her useful observations during all phases of this project, and to our small boys, Joey and David, for being themselves.

Coral Gables, Florida

# Introduction:
# The Millenarian Tradition

Until not long ago, Brazilian histories of the decade following the 1889 collapse of the Brazilian monarchy were dominated by a republican viewpoint hostile to groups and influences considered obstacles to what the elite hoped would lead to a new social order patterned after European accomplishments. When a conflict in the remote backlands of Brazil's Northeast erupted and could not be quelled by conventional means, contemporary observers reacted with alarm, offering memorable and comprehensive impressions of the events in language that reflected their anxiety over what they perceived to be their nation's backwardness.

The most influential of these tormented writers was Euclydes da Cunha. His book *Rebellion in the Backlands*, published in 1902 in Portuguese as *Os sertões*, is almost universally considered Brazil's greatest sociohistorical document. It was the first book to convey a detailed sense of the complexity and paradoxical nature of rural Brazilian life.[1] Stefan Zweig, the Austrian writer who found refuge in Brazil in the early 1940s, called *Os sertões* "a great national epic" that offered "a complete psychological picture of the Brazilian soil, the people, and the country, such as has never been achieved with equal insight and psychological comprehension."[2] José Maria Bello proclaimed it a "magisterial" work, one that on first reading seems "florid, pompous, [and] obscure," but on closer examination, "great, rare, of extraordinary merit."[3]

Da Cunha's contribution to Brazilian self-perception was based on two distinctive circumstances: he was one of the few members of the coastal elite to achieve firsthand knowledge of the land and people of the hinterland, and he filtered his observations through the perspective of European social science, including Lambrosian theory about the size and shape of human skulls, Friedrich Rätzel's racist anthropogeography,

Gustave Le Bon's determinism, and especially the racial theories of the
Pole Ludwig Gumplowicz. By reporting his findings to an avid Brazilian
audience terrified by prospects of backland atavism, da Cunha dispelled
some myths about the shadowy, racially mixed men and women of the
*sertão*, but at the same time he created new myths portraying the miscegenated *caboclo* as the backbone of a new Brazilian race.[4]

Da Cunha related the tragic history of Antônio Vicente Mendes Maciel,
known as Antônio Conselheiro (a name derived from the backland way
of addressing lay missionaries), a religious mystic and penitent. Conselheiro wandered the rural Brazilian Northeast for twenty years, preaching against ungodly behavior and rebuilding rural churches and cemeteries that had fallen into disrepair in the forbidding, semiarid interior—a
landscape later described as "corroded" by its austere climate.[5] In 1893,
Conselheiro led a pious group of disciples to Canudos, and in an inaccessible mountain valley in the Bahian *sertão*, on the site of an abandoned
ranch, he founded a community. Although outsiders termed the community "bizarre,"[6] thousands came to it, attracted by Conselheiro's charismatic madness. He promised only sacrifice and hard work and asked the
residents to live according to God's commandments and await the coming
of the millennium, when would come redemption, the Day of Judgment.

Conselheiro's vision inverted the harsh reality of the impoverished
backlands: the weak, strengthened by their faith, would inherit the earth.
Nature would be transformed: rains would come, bringing forth the
earth's bounty. So many men and women streamed out of the settlements
of the *sertão* region and to Conselheiro's community that within two years
the settlement, known by residents as Belo Monte or Canudos, had
become the second largest city in Bahia, which in the late nineteenth
century was Brazil's second most populous state. Indeed, Canudos's size
was staggering for a backland religious refuge: at its height the population was more than one-tenth that of the city of São Paulo in the
mid-1890s.

In reaction, patriarchal backland property owners, stung by the loss
of their usually docile labor force, demanded government intervention.
After fighters loyal to Conselheiro defeated two successive columns of
soldiers sent to capture Canudos's holy leader and disperse the settlement, the Brazilian army itself was ordered to attack Canudos and destroy it. The military assault lasted nearly two years, for it was met with
tenacious defiance. Finally, though, Canudos was circled and, in October
1897, bombarded into submission by heavy artillery. For the first time in
Brazilian history, aided by the new telegraph lines that linked the North
with the more prosperous South, newspapers sent war correspondents
to the front. Their daily dispatches fascinated and alarmed the reading

public: it seemed as if the very republic was on the verge of collapse. The inhabitants of Canudos were portrayed as primitive fanatics, "miserable and superstitious," superhuman in their resistance, and dedicated to the destruction of the paternalistic, civilizing arm of government authority.[7]

Euclydes da Cunha was a disenchanted military officer who in the early 1890s had resigned his commission to pursue a second career as a civil and geological engineer. He was a positivist, a disciple of the French philosopher Auguste Comte. In Latin America—especially in Mexico and in Argentina—positivism had acquired an immense following among elites seeking to modernize their nations under the leadership of the ablest members of society. Comtean positivists rejected religion as superstitious and advocated universal public education. Their doctrine was related to the Benthamism of the 1820s and to social Darwinism, but it also was distinct, rooted in a vision of civilization evolving through three distinct stages: the theological, the metaphysical, and the positive. They rejected the concepts both of aristocracy through birth and of democracy based on equal status, and they believed passionately in reason and in science. Society should, they thought, rely on enlightened leadership by the most capable for the general good. This platonic ideal strongly influenced the creators of the new Brazilian Republic that replaced the monarchy after the 1889 military coup. The Brazilian positivists advocated a moral social policy that would elevate the urban lower classes through social welfare programs—a blueprint for development without social mobilization. Rural problems were another matter, however, and the positivists tended to ignore them. In this sphere, Herbert Spencer's paternalistic social Darwinism more thoroughly influenced da Cunha and the other intellectuals who, as members of a "fragment" society of Europe, chose from among several imported European models those that best fit their needs.[8]

Da Cunha was so much a captive of imported European attitudes that he embraced them even when they ensnared him in contradiction.[9] He accepted European racial doctrines, even though his own observations showed them to be wrong. In Os sertões, he esteems the backland mestizos, lauds them for their adaptability, tenacity, and independence, and designates backland existence as "the vigorous core of our national life." At the same time, however, parroting European theory, he chastises the mestizo's mixed-race origins and considers the mestizo "degenerate . . . lacking the physical energy of his savage ancestors and without the intellectual elevation of his ancestors on the other side."[10] Yet as E. Bradford Burns reminds us, da Cunha was himself a mestizo.[11] Like Raimundo Nina Rodrigues, Machado de Assis, Lima Barreto, and other mixed-race writers and intellectuals who shaped Brazil's self-image during and after the turn of the century, he refused to acknowledge that his own achievements negated the central argument of his disparaging view of the legacy of miscegenation.[12]

Terrified by the specter of rural revolt, da Cunha reported the events of the Canudos conflict as a battle between the forces of civilization and darkness. Canudos tormented him.[13] Although he considered the racially mixed inhabitants of Conselheiro's community to be atavistic and hostile to progress, he also admired their tenacity and bodily strength. This reference to the backlanders' physical prowess touched a nerve, since Brazil's population in 1890 was approximately 15 percent *preto* (black) and 40 percent mestizo or mulatto. Some observers, including Bahia's Raimundo Nina Rodrigues and such visitors as the American naturalist Louis Agassiz, despaired over the fact that such a high percentage of Brazilians were nonwhite, but Euclydes remained optimistic, believing that immigrants from Europe and modern technologies and ideas would allow Brazil to overcome its predisposition to primitivism.[14]

Da Cunha struggled to rise above his ambivalence. He despised the *sertanejos'* seeming aversion to civilization, but because of the Canudenses' strength and endurance, he called them "the bedrock of our race."[15] His experiences at the front were so unsettling to him that after the destruction of Canudos he spent the next five years writing a book based on his field notes and observations. When it was published, *Os sertões* electrified the nation because it shattered the elite's comfortable myth about Brazilian reality.

Perhaps the most remarkable feature of da Cunha's ideas was that, in the final analysis, he accepted the prevailing concepts about biological determinism only in part. In this sense he was similar to Mexico's Justo Sierra, who also wrestled with the realization that Mexico's mixed-race heritage was a principal aspect of its "autonomous personality." Sierra, in fact, refuted Le Bon's theories on the debilitating quality of miscegenation, though he did argue that up to 1889 miscegenation had been the "dynamic [political] factor in our history" and pleaded for European immigrants to Mexico "so as to obtain a cross with the indigenous race, for only European blood can keep the level of civilization . . . from sinking, which would mean regression, not evolution."[16]

Readers of *Os sertões* were shown that the new symbols of Brazilian progress—the burgeoning cities of the coast with their artifacts of material culture imported from abroad—masked the primitive and antisocial impulses still resident in the rural interior. The shock of the Canudos conflict and fears that rebellion would spread to Brazil's cities led politicians to contrive tighter social controls and to reject reforms that might lead the country toward meaningful democracy. Canudos caused those sympathetic to the vision of its leader to fear the ominous combination of church and state working in unison to suppress unorthodox popular expression. Knowingly or not, writers later continued to choose sides, either abiding by da Cunha's negative prescriptions or, more frequently, casting the Canudenses in the role of utopian heroes.[17]

The author of *Rebellion in the Backlands* never answered questions that seem most central: Why did Conselheiro and his followers seek refuge in a remote sanctuary? What led them to risk such extreme deprivation, or to follow a leader whom many called a madman? For da Cunha, a chronicling of the appalling Canudos affair was sufficient, and subsequent writers on Canudos have elected to preserve his romantic emphasis. One, the Englishman R. B. Cunningham Graham, simply appropriated da Cunha's entire story, though without making a single reference to *Os sertões*, which had not yet been translated into English (and would not be until 1944).[18] Mario Vargas Llosa's fictionalized account (published in Portuguese in 1982) was far more literary and original, but it, too, tended toward romanticization.[19]

## SOURCES AND DEFINITIONS

As Eric Van Young has wisely observed, there are almost insuperable obstacles to any meaningful analysis of Latin American rural social conflict and rebellion, especially when the events occurred in earlier times.[20] Much of the problem centers on the sources available to the historian. Moreover, when we generalize about rural folk, we tend to use composite definitions not derived from place-specific data. In my study, I will attempt to avoid this practice as much as possible, drawing instead from available primary and secondary documentation.

Conventional archival materials and other documentation, however, are sparse and in some cases suspect. Surviving records include Conselheiro's two prayer books, written in a flowing, practiced hand and style; about nine-tenths of their texts interpolate prayers and homilies taken directly from the Bible or other liturgical sources. Noemi Soares, Father Alexandre Otten, and others are examining these books in depth to determine exactly what sections were penned by Conselheiro himself (or dictated to his assistant who wrote them out).

A few of the early (pre–*Os sertões*) chronicles about Conselheiro mention letters sent by him or by other Canudos residents to outsiders, but only one source—Favilla Nunes—reproduces or cites any of them.[21] Unfortunately, his commentaries were published serially in *fascículos* (short pamphlets), and only one of them, the third, has survived; although he said he was going to publish at least fifty, none has surfaced to date, despite painstaking efforts to locate them. The army's decision to incinerate Canudos ruined any chance of finding artifacts on the site, and the military records for the campaign (made available only recently by the commander of the Sixth Military Region in Salvador and by the director of the state Military Police) are limited largely to technical specifics about troop supply.

The correspondence and other records stored in the archive of the archdiocese of Salvador, located in the Cúria on the Praça da Sé in that capital city, offer invaluable detail. Documents include parish registers of baptisms and weddings for the backland regions from which most of the *conselheiristas* came, containing data that someday will permit diligent researchers to construct a demographic map of the region: information on family names, legitimacy, skin color, and sometimes places of origin. Other primary materials largely unused by historians heretofore are the letters of the baron of Jeremoabo, which give a comprehensive overview of events, as do the annual reports of Bahia's chief executive and reports of many of the provincial (pre-1889) and state (post-1889) cabinet ministries. Contemporary newspapers offer extensive detail and a sense of the settlement's impact on the region.

A large body of published chronicles, narratives, and studied explanations of Canudos appeared in the first years after the conflagration—capped by *Os sertões* in 1902—but only a few eyewitnesses who actually heard Conselheiro speak described their reactions. Most were predisposed to see in him what they wanted to see: signs of mental imbalance and fanaticism. Almost all of the early sources reflect what I call the *visão do litoral*, a dismissal of the backlanders as primitive fanatics.

Few comprehensive analyses of the actual participants in Conselheiro's religious community have appeared, although some scholars, notably José Calasans, have devoted their careers to piecing together fragments of the puzzle. Only a handful of the authors who have written about Canudos interviewed eyewitnesses, and then mostly much later when memories had dimmed. Because the residents of Canudos and the surrounding area were largely illiterate and lacked knowledge of the world beyond the *sertão*, precise data about the community are hard to come by. In any case, it lasted only four years, in contrast to Padre Cícero's Cariri Valley community in Ceará, which survived intact until his death in the 1930s. Nevertheless, Conselheiro and the bloody military campaigns left an indelible mark on the region: as recently as the early 1980s, when Mario Vargas Llosa visited the region to conduct research for his novel *The War of the End of the World*, many local residents confessed that they were afraid to talk about the "santo Conselheiro"—eight decades after his death in 1897.

In what follows, citations from da Cunha are taken from the masterful English translation of *Os sertões*, *Rebellion in the Backlands*, by Samuel Putnam.[22] Yet I do provide cross-references to the original, using the "didactic" edition published by Editora Cultrix, a useful edition because it reproduces the original maps and illustrations and includes the author's notes as well as a glossary.[23] Moreover, although recent studies tend to rely almost exclusively on da Cunha's account, my study both weighs the contributions of *Os sertões* and examines the evidence provided by other early chroniclers such as José Aras, Dantas Barreto, Manoel Benício, Souza Dantas, Opato Gueiros, Alvim Martins Horcades, Aristides A. Milton, Frei João Evangelista Monte Marciano, Favilla Nunes, Lélis Piedade, Henrique Duque-Estrada de Macedo Soares, José Américo Camillo Souza Velho, and César Gama.

Another difficulty with which researchers must deal involves the significant lack of microstudies on the backland region. On occasion, therefore, I do cite studies written about rural or small-town life elsewhere in the region or even in another part of the country—not to suggest that conditions were the same but to allow for valuable parallels and suggest continuities.

*Millenarianism* refers to the quest for total, imminent, ultimate, this-worldly, collective salvation. The term as used in this study refers to social movements seeking massive and radical change in accord with a predetermined divine plan. Members often reject the existing social order and withdraw from it. At times, violence erupts in the form of assaults by believers on established authorities—or, as in Canudos, by the established authorities on the millenarian community. In the Christian millenarian tradition, which in turn is rooted in Persian Zoroastrianism, Jewish apocalyptic literature, and the New Testament writings of Saint John, Christ is expected to reappear in the guise of a warrior, establish his kingdom, and reign for a thousand years. *Messianic* movements predict that universal salvation will occur through the enthroning of a messiah. In Christianity, then, millenarian movements are by definition messianic as well.[24]

Most histories of the Canudos conflict preserve Euclydes da Cunha's *visão do litoral*, his assumption that the Canudenses refused to accept the republic because they feared progress. Exaggeration and hysteria shaped the way Brazilians viewed events at that time. The young republic craved a Manichaean explanation of Canudos in order to build national unity and deflect embarrassment from the armed forces, who displayed flagrant ineptitude at all levels during the four campaigns against Conselheiro's followers. As a result, some claim that the topic of Canudos has become sacrosanct because Brazilians needed to reassure themselves that the assault and eventual massacre were necessary for the preservation of the realm. Da Cunha and his contemporaries unconsciously (or perhaps deliberately) cloaked their accounts in patriotic colors, just as writers on the left in later decades portrayed Canudos as a heroic cell of political resistance against oppression. Neither interpretation contributes much to an understanding of the lives and motivations of the men and women who followed Conselheiro to his holy site. Nor does either permit analysis of Canudos as a dynamic phenomenon both religious and political in nature.

My aim in this book is twofold: to penetrate the worldview of Canudos in its broadest dimensions—at the local, state, regional, and national levels; and to understand Conselheiro's movement and his vision on their own terms. To the extent possible, my study reconstructs the cultural, economic, and political meaning of Canudos from the perspective of its actors: the Canudenses themselves, the region's and nation's traditional elites, the representatives of the state political apparatus, the officers and soldiers sent to disperse and destroy Conselheiro's community, and the regular and secular Catholic clergy who found themselves trapped in the web of Conselheiro's life and influence.

My study employs a wide spectrum of archival and other sources and, as well, draws on the work of specialists who have broken new ground on questions ranging from peasant societies and culture (Clifford Geertz, Shepard Forman, Candace Slater, Ronald H. Chilcote) to Catholic theology (Alexandre Otten) to literary criticism (Walnice Galvão, Marlisse Meyer, Flora Süssekind) to millenarianism and messianism (René Ribeiro, Janaína Amado). The title, *Vale of Tears*, is borrowed with permission from José Carlos Sebe Bom Meihy's *livre docência* thesis at the University of São Paulo, which explores the fate of the underprivileged during the nineteenth and twentieth centuries in Taubaté in the state of São Paulo's Paraíba Valley.

A final comment. I have come to believe that, on certain occasions, both sides in a conflict are right, from each side's perspective. This occurs especially in cases of prolonged hostilities where each belligerent act is interpreted by the adversary as evidence of its own righteousness and the other's malevolence. Combatants inevitably see everything— from the history of the conflict, to its conduct, to all questions of right and wrong—through unique lenses, shaped by how they have been taught to see. Each side denigrates the other's view and rationalizes its own prejudices, especially if the conflict is fueled by nationalism or by other emotionally charged issues. The action of the enemy cannot help but yield self-fufilled prophecies, simply because the reasons for the friction can be viewed from only one side: the perspective of the adversary remains inevitably unfathomable. As examples, I would point to many electoral campaigns, to the American Civil War, the Israeli-Palestinian conflict, and, unquestionably, Canudos.

Antônio Conselheiro scorned and distrusted those who did not hold his moral and religious principles, just as, on the other side, Jeremoabo and his compatriots in the agro-commercial elite despised and feared Conselheiro's unyielding stubbornness. The tendency to hold obdurately to one's position is reinforced, of course, by life experience and cannot be dismissed casually, especially when large issues are at stake. In the case of Canudos, the elite's predisposition to disparage rural behavior was exacerbated by the political usefulness of interpreting events in exaggerated terms. To coastal observers, Conselheiro represented fanaticism, dissidence, and manipulation of rural folk for whom they felt pity mixed with disgust. Because the *conselheiristas* were attacked and not vice versa, our compassion tends to extend to them (perhaps also because we romanticize the courage they showed in choosing life in Canudos), but the heroic-nationalist cloak in which Canudos as an event has been wrapped has not permitted this sympathy officially. It is telling, therefore, that Brazil will mark the centenary of Canudos in 1997, the anniversary of its annihilation, and not in 1993, the anniversary of the settlement's birth.

Conselheiro's four-year ascendancy between 1893 and 1897 brought major social upheaval to the *sertão*. It caused economic dislocation, profoundly disturbed the Catholic hierarchy, and created political turmoil. His movement—its mystical spirituality combined with a commitment to the needy and to the faithful—like other movements of messianic figures in history, created polarities: true Catholicism and the Antichrist; the moral and immoral; the humble, faithful, and austere against the rich and cynically powerful. Conselheiro proposed no less than a return to the austerity, antieroticism, and the patriarchal mentality of what he imagined to be the heritage of the original church.[25]

Conselheiro's striking appeal to backlanders is explainable in part by the fact that, historically, Luso-Brazilian culture frequently embraced eruptions of messianic expression, but the appeal of Canudos was not exclusively, or even primarily, messianic. Rather, the faithful backlanders who moved their belongings to Canudos to live under the special guidance of Conselheiro had a variety of motivations. Foremost, perhaps, they saw in him a powerful lay religious leader in the folk-Catholic tradition of the region. Indeed, in some ways the missionary priests of France who, following the publication in 1891 of the encyclical *Rerum Novarum*, devoted their energies to working among the poor can be regarded as Conselheiro's counterparts. Although, unlike Conselheiro, these priests were never personally persecuted, their activities were curtailed in 1901, repudiated by the Vatican.[26]

## GOALS

This study is an attempt to interpret Canudos in several ways: by reexamining the causes and consequences of its settlement; by analyzing the events in the backlands both as a local phenomenon and in terms of state and national perceptions; by exploring the motives of the participants and of those threatened by its success; by seeking to comprehend the collective world of Canudos and the role of its leader, Antônio Conselheiro, his theology, and his motivation. As much as possible, my goal is to examine Canudos from the perspective of those caught up in its élan. This study is not calculatedly revisionist; instead, drawing upon a broader resource base than most previous studies, it reinterprets Canudos and its place in Brazilian history.

Six chapters follow. The first situates Canudos as an event within a national context and examines the outlook of Brazil's coastal urban elites, that is, the *visão do litoral*. Euclydes da Cunha came out of this milieu; his eloquent writings on Canudos helped reshape how Brazilians perceived the faceless residents of the hinterland and how they interpreted the implications of a country divided (in the elite view) into backward and modern populations. Chapter 2, in counterpoint, looks at the world of the rural backlands: its landscape, social structure, and economic institutions. Chapter 3 examines in detail the city of Belo Monte (Canudos) and the man who created it, Antônio Conselheiro. Chapter 4 reexamines the story of the armed conflict and Canudos's destruction. Chapter 5 probes Conselheiro's theology and his vision of man's worldly role. The sixth and concluding chapter considers Canudos as a millenarian movement, thus closing the circle of inquiry.

# ONE

# Canudos and the *Visão do Litoral*: An Overview

The early 1890s were a powerfully disturbing time for Brazilians aware of their nation's history and its uncertain transition from monarchy to republic. Republican government came to Brazil following a little-resisted military coup on November 15, 1889—nearly seven decades after most of its neighbors had made the change. Legislation separating church and state established secular primacy, and the army, assuming the mantle of defender of national unity, ruled dictatorially from 1889 to 1894. Much of the nation was mired in economic stagnation and chronic impoverishment. Streams of migrants were on the move in search of regular employment and sustenance, but few gained either. Brazilian landowners, considering mixed-race rural people unwilling to work hard and incapable of being productive, attempted through government-subsidized colonization schemes to recruit agricultural workers from northern Europe, though in the end most of those who came were from Italy, Spain, and Portugal.

Past historians characterize the republic's political birth as a minor event: one authoritarian regime replaced another, and ordinary people, referred to contemptuously as "beast-like," were unaffected.[1] "This State is not a national entity," wrote the liberal republican Alberto Sales, brother of the president, in 1901; "this country is not a society; these folk are not a people. Our countrymen are not citizens."[2] Others, particularly foreigners attentive to Brazil's unfulfilled opportunities for national development, lauded the overthrow of the monarchy: in 1889 the London

Part of this chapter has previously appeared in *Hispanic American Historical Review* 68, no. 3 (August 1988): 525–72; another part has been published in *The Americas* 49, no. 2 (October 1991).

*11*

*Statesman* called the emperor's exile the most important event in the
world. More recently, economic historians have considered the transition from empire to republic to be the natural consequence of the abolition of Brazilian slavery in 1888, and the cornerstone of the establishment of the "bourgeois state."[3]

Unsettling changes were accelerating worldwide, but in Brazil the
slow pace of industrialization forestalled the momentous transforma-
tions affecting city life in Western Europe and the United States. Still,
new technology and new ideas challenging the nineteenth-century or-
thodoxies were filtering in from abroad to coastal cities at a quickened
pace. Even agriculture, at the heart of the oligarchy's traditional hold on
power, was changing. Within the space of a decade and a half (from the
early 1880s to the mid-1890s), centralized refineries supplanted the
centuries-old system of mills driven by water or animal power. The east
coast's sugar plantation economy became permanently transformed, especially in Pernambuco, Alagoas, Rio de Janeiro, and Bahia. Railroad
networks and improved ports, built with foreign capital, sharply lowered
the cost of transporting export staples to markets.[4]

The accelerating changes were disruptive, and they did not proceed
smoothly. Coffee culture in the Southwest, an area that had absorbed
much of the migratory stream, was soon experiencing overproduction.
Northeastern plantations hired fewer workers as rates paid for sugar
and cacao stagnated or fell. Prices of staple foods such as corn, beans,
and rice almost tripled.[5] Warehouses erected at railroad hubs supplanted the market system in rural towns and altered trading patterns.
More people, many from outside the traditional aristocracy, were able to
make fortunes from these innovations, thus disrupting the status quo
and destabilizing daily life. Foreign investment poured in. Oligarchic
hegemony was undermined as cycles of boom and bust occurred, fueled
by speculation and deflationary pressures.[6]

As elsewhere in the hemisphere, the crude forms of government that
had prevailed since at least the 1870s gave way to more pragmatic and
nuanced prescriptions for national progress. These approaches tended
to combine nineteenth-century economic liberalism with measures designed to stifle popular expression and block social mobilization. Brazilian
politicians agreed to ignore rural problems by keeping power in the hands
of the traditional landed oligarchy and its clients.[7] One consequence was
an assault on autonomous folk societies; Canudos was one of these victims
of Europeanized "progress" imposed by the nation's coastal elites.[8]

A campaign for republicanism emerged in the Center-South of the
country, especially in São Paulo. There, the powerful coffee planters
and their clients sought the power to levy taxes, build independent militias, obtain foreign loans to finance infrastructure development and

modernization, and subsidize the immigration of Europeans to replace the old slave labor force, now diminished in size since the forced cessation of the African slave trade at mid-century under pressure from Great Britain. Thus emerged the main argument for replacing the monarchy with a federal republic: imperial centralization, rooted in the tradition of Portuguese absolutism, was hindering economic progress. The monarchy had been protected by the old plantocracy, the imperial bureaucracy, and the church, but in the end conflict over slave abolition and church-state relations began to dissolve old alliances.

The 1889 fall of the centralized monarchy ushered in an era of extreme federalism. Each of the former provinces, now states, could tax its exports, raise its own armed forces, and, to the limits of prevailing fiscal resources, pursue its own construction of railroads, roads, port facilities, and urban improvements. As a consequence, the dynamic units of the federation, all without exception in the south (Rio Grande do Sul, Minas Gerais, and especially São Paulo with its expanding coffee frontier), jumped ahead in material growth and political power while the rest of the country languished. The state that lost the most in national influence as a measure of its shriveled economic base was Bahia. Its large population brought few political benefits because representative government had little value in practice. Throughout the 1890s, while the Bahian political elite became splintered by partisan infighting, the southeastern elite grew strong, and united state republican parties began reaping the benefits of the new federal system. In this framework, the national government did little more than arbitrate, sometimes lending its support to an oligarchic faction, at other times negotiating directly with local bosses, the interior *coronéis*, who in Bahia and the backlands of the Northeast were so powerful that throughout the region on both sides of the São Francisco River "nations of coronéis" were said to flourish.[9]

A major issue in the early years of the republic was the fiscal system. Bitter Constituent Assembly debates over the basis of taxation under the federation exemplified the precarious nature of the early republican consensus. The provisional government's bill specified revenue categories for the union and the states, requiring that federal needs should prevail in cases of dispute. For example, Rio Grande do Sul's Júlio de Castilhos and his federalist faction opposed the taxation bill and demanded that all sources of revenue not specifically earmarked for the federal government be given to the states. The government's bill was approved by seventy-three, with fifty-three opposed, thus preventing, in the words of Bahia's Rui Barbosa, "anarchy" and "inevitable bankruptcy." Yet at the same time, the taxation rights of the municipalities remained unspecified; municipal revenues were to depend on the strictures of the individual states, without uniform criteria.[10] Thus, in states governed by a split elite, incumbent political machines could punish localities where opposition politicians held power by withholding revenues or limiting the kinds of taxing powers (taxes on urban buildings, fines and indemnities) permitted to municipal authorities. In the last decade of the 1800s, the issue of municipal revenue remained particularly acrimonious in Bahia, a state rent by factionalism.

When Canudos began to take shape as a settlement in the remote interior of Bahia, Marshal Floriano Peixoto, who succeeded Marshal Deodoro da Fonseca as military president, was still in power. Only in 1894 did Peixoto turn power over to a civilian, São Paulo's Prudente de Morais. Floriano's legacy was one of authoritarian rule and bloody repression, especially in the South. Despite a severe economic depression, however, Prudente embarked on an ambitious program of reconstruction and urban development. But in this the entire Northeast was forgotten: not all things changed. The propertied class continued to expect that certain rights would accrue to those holding the reins of power. Thus, political parties served as vehicles for winning elections and holding on to the spoils of office.[11]

The transition to the republic did not benefit the bulk of the population. Only a tiny percentage could vote. Elections were frequently rigged or manipulated by party machines. Challenges on ideological grounds were equated with lack of patriotism, or worse. In any case, opposition political associations recruited members from the same social and economic circles as those in power. Increasingly, too, dissenters faced intimidation, physical violence, and deportation if they were not native-born. Judges applied differential justice, reserving the harshest punishments for dissenters belonging to the less privileged classes. The system of education remained inadequate, even at the primary level. Although political factions adopted liberal and even revolutionary names and symbols, most acted in little harmony with the principles they espoused. The antimonarchy radical clubs in the 1870s demanded universal suffrage and freedom of initiative, but in 1889, when the emperor sailed into exile, most of their members allied with former members of the imperial Liberal and Conservative parties to form the new republican state political machines, which were as antidemocratic as their predecessors. Even members of the abolitionist movement abandoned, after emancipation, the cause of the ex-bondsmen, who fared badly despite their new freedom.

Brazil's republican constitution, written largely by Bahian senator Rui Barbosa, had been modeled selectively on the Constitution of the United States (it failed to include many guarantees of personal liberty). The mostly Paulista founders of the Brazilian Republican party had studied carefully the writings of Thomas Jefferson, Alexander Hamilton, and James Madison; Quintino Bocaiúva, a founder and editor-in-chief of the newspaper *A República* and the author in 1870 of the Republican man ifesto, had lived in New York City in 1866–67, seeking emigrants to Brazil as an agent of the Imperial Immigration Ministry. National progress, it was expected, would follow liberal-constitutional reform, but the new government at the same time rejected the complementary model of a state composed of citizens holding legal and political rights, directly served by the state.[12] The monarchy's collapse did not in any way change the elites' implacable consensus that broad public participation in government was unthinkable and that the mere existence of autonomous movements not subject to state control was antithetical to the national interest. What eventually triumphed in the Brazilian Republic was a bland and asocial liberalism, an imitation of the political system of the United States without meaningful defense of individual rights or any commitment to public education or other mechanisms to prepare the population for citizenship. Urban growth and the impact of technological modernization offered to some young men outside the traditional aristocracy opportunities for advancement, but real change was blocked by the continued preeminence of the landed elite. Adoption of a federal system pushed the weaker rural states further into the periphery. Forward-looking citizens, in Emília Viotti da Costa's words, "continued to judge patronage from the point of view of liberalism and to judge liberalism from the point of view of patronage."[13] The state advanced the interests of the propertied, who entrenched themselves by forming and manipulating intricate networks (*panelinhas*) of family members, allies, and clients.[14]

Economic development and social change—exemplified by the tardy but dramatic act of abolishing slavery (May 13, 1888)—generated dissatisfaction but posed no threat to the status quo. The most dynamic reformers of the 1890s followed Auguste Comte's advocacy of patriarchal social hierarchy and the view that "freedom is a right but equality a myth." These positivists were no revolutionaries. Following Comte's warnings, they abhorred the libertarian excesses of the French Revolution and linked the idea of progress to the concept of imposed harmony in society. Social engineers were the new elite who would replace the "reformers identified with the Brazilian oligarchies."[15] European observers concurred: they lamented the exile of the Emperor, but hailed the new republican policies of progressive economic liberalism which promised to increase commerce.[16]

◇ ◇ ◇

Canudos was located in the remote northeastern Brazilian interior known generally as the "backlands" or *sertão*. This region was afflicted by a severe climate and generally forbidding terrain. The word *sertão* came from the term meaning a "large desert." For the seafaring Portuguese, all inland parts of the Terra Incognita were considered places with dark and sinister qualities.[17] Mention of the *sertão* conjured up images of backwardness and inhospitableness of place and people, although on the whole the dry climate was neither intolerable nor oppressive. Backland residents were not peasants like the sedentary rural peoples of the Andean highlands or Middle America, where the term "peasant" is used mostly to describe poor families with little freedom or independence, living and working on land once communally shared but now either divided into *minifundia* (units too small to yield profit) or organized into larger properties owned by others.[18] Most rural backlanders lived as renters or sharecroppers under miserable conditions, but they retained a limited freedom of movement and a grudging spirit of self-reliance.[19] Before 1893, few outsiders passed through the Bahian *sertão* except en route to the São Francisco River eighty miles to the north.

Canudos grew precipitously and contained more than five thousand mud-and-wattle huts scattered in close proximity below a ring of hills and low mountains. Its population of 25,000 (at its height in 1895 probably closer to 35,000) made it the largest urban site in Bahia after Salvador, the capital, 435 miles distant to the southeast. Canudos drained labor across two states, from the Rio Real in southern Sergipe to Inhambupe in Bahia.[20] Between 1893 and 1897, the community formed the basis of a popular movement that outsiders considered backward but that was vigorous and pragmatically adapted to the region's limitations—a pious, religious community organized and dominated by the orthodox lay Catholic mystic Antônio Conselheiro.

Popular movements often are seen as collective expressions of demand for social change or as struggles to resist change that has already taken place.[21] Both modes of analysis are useful in the case of Canudos. I propose, however, that an understanding of the events at Canudos may be best accomplished by placing the settlement's history in the context of its environment and times. This approach will be useful for cutting through the polemical, romanticized, and embellished generalizations that characterize traditional studies of Brazil's rural population; moreover, it will dispel the stereotype of the backlanders as crazed fanatics and introduce the possibility that they were spiritual men and women captivated by a compelling leader whose motivations in seeking a refuge from hostile adversaries were in strong measure pragmatic, stemming from external pressures and perceived possibilities. The term "Canudos," therefore, in this volume means much more than a place; it includes the people, ideas, and events that, though created in the 1890s in this place, were acknowledged far beyond its borders.[22]

1. Euclydes da Cunha, ca. 1900. Anonymous studio photograph. Courtesy Fundação Casa Rui Barbosa, Rio de Janeiro.

## CANUDOS

By far the most influential traditional study about Canudos was that of Euclydes da Cunha (Fig. 1). When his work, *Os sertões*, was published in 1902, it at once became the basis for the official interpretation of Canudos's meaning. Not that da Cunha's observations were singular; there had been an array of other voices, some dating from the first days of the creation of Conselheiro's community, and all sharing the outlook I term the *visão do litoral*. Brazilian intellectuals since at least the early 1870s had worried about the backlands and its mixed-race populations—mostly illiterate *caboclos* (those having white, African, and Indian blood) deemed by outsiders to be ignorant and superstitious, since most practiced a deeply felt and often austere form of Catholic observance.[23] This assessment was not uniform, of course; residents of the burgeoning southern cities probably rarely thought about the destitute North at all. Yet on the whole, given that during the empire intellectuals tended to receive similar educations, a collective *visão do litoral* may be said to have been present, hostile to perceived rural backwardness.

*Os sertões*'s most lasting impact was that it interjected Brazil's disregarded common people, the *povo*, into national consciousness as half-crazed fanatics. For at least half a century after the book's appearance, mainstream Brazilian historians applauded da Cunha's explanation of Canudos as being the result of geography, climate, and race.[24] The publication of *Os sertões* marked Brazil's intellectual coming of age; as such it became a sacred text that was compared to Euripides and called "the Bible of Brazilian nationality," leaving da Cunha's interpretation of Canudos virtually untouchable.[25]

The details related by da Cunha in brilliant descriptive prose seem incredible. Most of the events actually did happen in Canudos, though he sometimes inserted incidents that occurred elsewhere. After all, da Cunha was there only briefly at the end. His depictions are colored by his anguished personal view of what he saw as the terrible fanaticism of the *conselheiristas*. The story is told so vividly that many readers consider it a novel, not factual, especially since the treatment is inflamed by the author's fervor and his exceptional talent for epic description.

Euclydes Rodrigues Pimenta da Cunha was born in 1866 on Fazenda Saudade, a farm in Cantagalo, Santa Rita do Rio Negro, in rural Rio de Janeiro province. His parents were from Portuguese and Bahian backland ancestry; his father, Manuel Rodrigues Pimenta da Cunha, was of mestizo stock. The young Euclydes's mixed-race ancestry was more pronounced in his skin color and facial features than was the case with his brothers, but he grew up in a favored environment and did not lack opportunities to advance. When he was three, however, his mother, Eudóxia Moreira da Cunha, died. According to some, her death was a morbid influence.[26] The father declined to take responsibility for raising his sons, and they were shifted about among relatives. At one point Euclydes lived with his paternal grandparents in Salvador, where he attended the Colégio Bahia and the Carneiro Ribeiro School, both reserved for children of the second-level elite.[27] He wrote poetry and was attracted to natural science. His understanding of religion came from his high school teachers, who were Salesian fathers. The Salesian order combined conservatism on political issues with an emphasis on material and technical progress. His Salesian training, then, can be considered as the probable grounding for what amounted to his conversion to positivism in his *colégio* years.

One of his teachers at the Colégio Aquino in Rio de Janeiro was Benjamin Constant Botelho de Magalhães (1836–81), a republican and abolitionist leader and Comtean ideologue. In his youth, Constant had elected to study military engineering, but he also devoured the writings of intellectuals revered by positivists in the heady decade of the 1880s, such as Herbert Spencer, Henry T. Buckle, Hippolyte A. Taine, Lord James Bryce, Charles Darwin, Comte Georges Vacher de Lapouge, and, at the time, the two leading commentators on race and mass society, Ludwig Gumplowicz and Comte Arthur de Gobineau.[28] Some later observers said that members of the elite who studied with Constant or who read European political philosophy in fact devoted little time to the endeavor; Brazilian positivism, they charged, was half-baked and ill digested.[29] In any event, in da Cunha's case, his biologic determinism became tempered, perhaps by his *mulato* appearance, by his confrontation with the interior, and by the remarkable adaptability of the backlanders to their antagonistic environment. More than many of his contemporaries, he modified at least some of his positivistic ideas because of his observations of Brazilian conditions.

In 1884 he enrolled at the Polytechnic School of Rio to study civil engineering, but he transferred two years later to the War College, where he earned his military commission. Most of his colleagues in the officer corps shared the same *déformation professionelle*, a view of reality based on professional training and elite upbringing. Da Cunha's thinking, however, continued to evolve: he spent years before and after Canudos agonizing over Brazil's singularity and in the end began to see strength in what others dismissed gratuitously as embarrassing. Although sections of *Os sertões* reflect the racism of Nina Rodrigues, Sílvio Romero, and their contemporaries, his conviction that the *sertanejo* represented "the very core of our nationality" remained the crux of his argument.[30]

His observations both during and after his schooling taught him that life was too wondrous to spend being confined to the discipline of a military career. Unstable, tremulous, and a militant republican, as a cadet at the War College in 1888 he intemperately threw down his sword in the presence of the war minister, whereupon he was forced to abandon his commission. Only the fact that Euclydes's father-in-law was an army general likely prevented this belligerent act from earning the young man severe punishment.[31]

Although he eventually gained reinstatement in rank, he never felt comfortable as a soldier. Indeed, his personality is described as having been antimilitaristic, not pacifist; he considered war illogical and wasteful and to have "the stigma of the original banditry behind it."[32] He wrote newspaper columns for a while, under the pseudonym of "Proudhon," then returned to the Polytechnic School for two years. He was there when the republic was proclaimed. His mentor, Benjamin Constant, helped him reenter the army as a lieutenant, and during the 1893 naval rebellion he worked building trenches and sanitary works. After an uneven career, he left the army again in 1896 to become a civil engineer, but when the Canudos conflict deepened a year later and the third military expedition failed, he was asked to accompany the war minister to the front in order to send home dispatches for the *Estado de São Paulo*.[33]

Five years later, in 1902, he published his masterpiece. The first edition sold out in two months and went into several printings, followed by new editions in 1903, 1905, and 1911.[34] At age thirty-seven, da Cunha was elevated to national celebrity. Not entirely relishing this sudden fame, he returned to his career as engineer and surveyor. Then, in 1909, he was fatally shot by an army officer, Dilermando de Assis, the lover of his estranged wife and presumably the father of one of the so-called da Cunha children. At the time of his death, Euclydes da Cunha was working on a second manuscript, to be titled *Paraíso perdido*, or "Paradise Lost." He was forty-three, and his towering place in Brazilian literature was sealed.[35] More than thirty-five editions of *Os sertões* have appeared since the first small printing sold out. Total sales in Portuguese have reached 750,000—a remarkable number given Brazil's low literacy rate.

Even though his analysis of Canudos overshadowed all published writings by others during and after the conflict, he was in the vicinity of the front only during the last third of the fighting, and much of this time was spent in Monte Santo, a half-day's march from Canudos. As an invited guest of the army chief of staff, he tended to reflect the official line in his reports, minimizing the brutality being committed against the *conselheirista* enemy. The *Jornal do Commércio*'s Manoel Benício witnessed much more than da Cunha, yet his book describing what he saw attracted relatively little attention when it was published in 1898, three years before da Cunha's book created a national uproar.[36]

Da Cunha was no apologist for the military, however. One reason for the great appeal of *Os sertões* was its ambivalence, including its dual portrait of the backlanders as savages fighting mightily for a sacred cause. This view differed considerably from that of his fellow reporters, the seeds having been sown early in 1897 when da Cunha published two successive articles under the same title, "A nossa Vendéia" (Our Vendée), referring to the appalling slaughter of rural promonarchy stalwarts following the French Revolution, in the newspaper *O Estado de São Paulo*. In both works, he paid more attention to the harsh environmental conditions of the backlands than to the combatants. Da Cunha saw Canudos's founding in 1893 to be a striking counterrevolutionary challenge to the 1889 republic, exactly paralleling the Vendée's 1793 challenge to the French Revolution of 1789—and in each instance, coming exactly one hundred years later. This theme was later borrowed by Brazilian historians. The republic, wrote José Maria Bello in 1940,

> was battling against desperate reactionary opposition, even as the armed forces of the French Revolution, victorious on all European fronts, had hurled themselves against the Chouans of Brittany. As a matter of fact, though the men of the period did not think so, the Canudos affair was much more modest. The differences between the Catholic, realistic Chouans and Conselheiro's fanatics were as great as those between the physical geography of the Vendée and that of the backlands of the Brazilian Northeast.[37]

Bello, an influential amateur narrative historian who was the governor of Pernambuco before being exiled in the 1930 coup, swallowed da Cunha's characterizations without questioning them. Yet da Cunha had slighted the universal aspects of the French Revolution, viewing it simply as a national, purely political event.[38] In any event, when he began to write about Canudos, his ideas were still forming. In the first of these Vendée articles the backland rebels were hardly described at all. Only in his second article did they come to life. And not until the appearance of *Os sertões* did he find in them any elements of courage and tenacity worthy of praise.

Overall, da Cunha's contributions were several. He explained the background of the conflict not only in human terms but also in terms of the region's geomorphological, climatic, and demographic history. By the time his book appeared in print, the author's anguish over what he had seen had flowered into a troubled ambivalence over what he considered to be a crude backland peasantry, the Brazilian racial question, and the resolute struggle of the faithful settlers. The elevation of *Os sertões* to an instant national classic carried a significant liability: many readers tended to gloss over the author's frequent qualification of his "two Brazils" theme, ignoring da Cunha's dissatisfaction with the mechanistic division of Brazil into citified coast and primitive backlands. Da Cunha, Richard M. Morse reminds us, offered a pathology of *Brazil*, not merely of the *sertão*.[39]

That his own views changed rapidly is illustrated by the language he used to describe the backlanders loyal to Conselheiro. In the first of his 1897 Vendée articles he mostly called them *sertanejos*. The strongest noun he used was *tabaréu*, or rustic, analogous to the *caipira* of São

Paulo's Paraíba Valley. The second newspaper piece used the term *ja-gunço* in italics to accentuate its peculiar nature (in the 1890s, the word *jagunço* was synonymous with the word *cangaceiro*, a hired gunman, often a bandit). When *Os sertões* appeared half a decade later, da Cunha's "jagunço" was without italics, yet preserved were his inconclusive feelings about the figure he described as a "Hercules-Quasimodo."

For da Cunha, the Brazilian army's confrontation with the backlanders did seem analogous to the Romans fighting the barbarians. Yet he was not all disparaging. He stood in awe of the ingenious ways in which the *jagunços* fought for their lives and cause.[40] He also pitied them, and the confrontation unnerved him to the point of depression. Retreating to a tiny wooden shack in his birthplace in rural Rio de Janeiro, he wrote his book as a "cry of protest" against the "act of madness" carried out by the republican government.[41] Da Cunha and other unflinching positivists were dismayed by continuing military factionalism and by the alleged monarchist plots hatched after the birth of the republic; they lamented the failure of Brazilians to endorse nationalistic goals. Thus, two varieties of scapegoats were created: the faceless backland rebels and, in their own midst, the impassioned but harmless advocates of monarchist restoration.[42]

## MONARCHISTS, ANTIMONARCHISTS, AND THE NEWS

Monarchists, of course, did seek the return of the imperial system under which Brazil had been governed successfully during most of the nineteenth century. The emperor's role as arbiter among elite groups, who held the same outlook on life but whose interests conflicted on specific issues, had satisfied most members of the upper classes.[43] The advent of the republic did not displace this attitude, and as strife among its political factions as well as between civilians and military officers continued unabated after 1889, some came to believe more boldly than ever that Brazil should turn back the clock and restore the royal house of Bragança. However, although their position was stated forcefully enough in the strident monarchist press, few monarchists acted on their predilections.

There were several reasons why the stories about Canudos traumatized the nation whereas news of other military campaigns and regional revolts—including the navy rebellion of 1893 and the bloody southern civil war through 1895—left the public unmoved. Dispatches from Canudos were the first to be sent via telegraph, the vehicle by which republican politicians finally consolidated the power of the federal administration. Because each dispatch was subject to rigorous military censorship, only a one-sided view was transmitted. That Canudos was distortedly painted as a monarchist political plot only heightened its psychological impact. Jacobins and others seeking strong government measures to wipe out enduring promonarchist sentiment seized the opportunity that Canudos provided to eulogize the heroic role of the military and to justify strong-arm methods to suppress dissidence.

The Jacobin movement, led by a rabid opponent of the monarchy, Antônio da Silva Jardim, started out by embracing the concept of popular democracy, in the spirit of the ancient Greeks and the French Revolution. But they were quickly rebuffed by the *povo*, the common people. For example, to gather a crowd, Lopes Trovão, a Jacobin politician and conspirator in the 1889 Republican coup, had men stand in the street with *cachaça* to gather passersby.[44] The Jacobin wing of the Republicans, which sought radical restructuring of the political system along nationalist lines, led the invective against Canudos, using the antimonarchist cause as a battering ram against the still-fragile Republican administration. The last-minute conversion of empire-era politicians to republicanism in the wake of the 1889 coup yielded a divided republican movement and, in many ways, lent new energy to the monarchists who *after* the fall of Dom Pedro II, in limited circles, enjoyed more vitality than before the promulgation of the republic. Before the coup, defenders of the status quo had felt no compulsion to defend monarchy as a political system; under the hated republic, however, monarchists mobilized advocacy of restoration, even if such hopes were farfetched.[45]

Thus Canudos functioned as the flash point for Brazil's last battle between monarchism and republicanism. The first republican decade witnessed regionalist insurrection; nasty rivalries between the states, the newly autonomous units of the federation; and economic depression after mid-decade. In this context, the tales of military incompetence and supposed monarchist fanaticism that surfaced seemed to threaten the very fabric of the national government. Most of the allegations were fabricated, of course, but that did not make the threat seem any less real: officials as influential as General Artur Oscar Andrade Guimarães, commander of the Second Military District and leader of the fourth and final expedition against Canudos, blandly distributed to reporters copies of forged letters attesting that monarchist leaders were using the summer residence of the ousted monarch in Petrópolis as their base for plotting to overthrow the republic. This typified the inflamed atmosphere engendered by the conflict: General Oscar willingly fed the anxiety by spreading rumors to the opposition and by offering to reporters his political interpretation of events. If he did so out of personal ambition, his plan failed, for the military disasters only diminished Oscar's prestige and led to the firing of the minister of war by Prudente, who struggled to maintain the upper hand.[46]

Highlighted by the universal fascination with stories about crazed religious fanatics, the Canudos conflict flooded the press, invading not only editorials, columns, and news dispatches, but even feature stories and humor. For the first time in Brazil, newspapers were used to create a sense of public panic. Canudos accounts appeared daily, almost always on the first page; indeed, the story was the first ever to receive daily coverage in the Brazilian press.[47] More than a dozen major newspapers sent war correspondents to the front and ran daily columns reporting events. In contrast, during the barely concluded civil war in Rio Grande do Sul there had been hardly any press coverage at all. Something about Canudos provoked anxiety, which would be soothed only by evidence that Canudos had been destroyed and that a new political arrangement would return Brazil to the conservative outlook, if not the political system, of the empire.[48]

To politically conscious citizens, especially after the unexpected initial military setbacks at Canudos, the news of the ferocity of the backland insurrection threatened all that the modernizing republic represented. Worse, Canudos signaled a radical departure from the supposedly pacific legacy of Brazil's past.[49] Newspaper accounts from the front continually painted the enemy as cunning fanatics. Nearly every politician in Brazil joined in the war of words, caught up in the frenzy. The press thus became the major arena in which the conflict was played out, involving not only the dozens of daily and weekly newspapers and magazines in the larger cities, but also the business offices and typesetting shops owned by controversial publishers, especially of monarchist bent. In nineteenth-century Brazil, overall rates of literacy were low, but journalistic activity was intense, with nearly every political faction disseminating its point of view through one or more periodicals. In 1897, the year of the final Canudos military campaign, twenty-nine *new* newspapers were established in the federal capital. Nearly seven hundred newspapers were published in Bahia during the course of the century, and even the tiny backland hamlet of Curralinho boasted nine.[50] Most newspapers did not survive long, but for every one that died a quick death, others appeared in its place.

Some of the more ephemeral journals were satiric broadsheets, wickedly provocative. Under the young republic, monarchist and antimonarchist editors habitually exchanged insults and invective. Some were comic: Salvador's *A Bahia* at one point began to refer to President Prudente de Morais as a *maragabirigunço*, a hybrid word playing on Prudente's nickname, *O biriba* (meaning a rustic), the partisan federalist *maragatos* embroiled in the revolt in Rio Grande, and *jagunço* (one of the backland herdsmen who formed the bulk of Conselheiro's armed forces). Other barbs were less innocent; personal attacks of the crudest and most violent sort were the order of the day. A number of newspapers printed falsified (and sardonically mocking) articles attributed to Antônio Conselheiro, including a supposed "Manifesto" in which the mystic, in uneducated language, boasted of selling 500 réis' worth of beef jerky in Canudos for "5 nikelis de tustão sem cara do imperadó" ("5 nickels without the emperor's face," that is, a worthless sum).[51]

Salvador's *Diário de Notícias* published without further explanation a monarchist manifesto, "Credo de Antônio Conselheiro"—not likely written by him, but consistent with his monarchist sentiments.[52] Across Brazil, any published reference to Canudos or Conselheiro generated sales; as a result, editors ran almost anything on the subject, authentic or not, to spur circulation. Retail shops in Salvador featured Conselheiro's name or references to the Canudos campaign freely in their advertising broadsides. Even advertisements for shoes and clothing worked in references to the arrival of the federal armed forces.[53] Newspapers across Brazil used the Canudos episode to introduce sensational reportage of a kind never before seen in the country, which, despite prolific journalism, had a tradition of rather staid coverage.

With the stimulation of the press, the monarchist-republican conflict became a severe strain on the national government. The leading monarchist voice was that of Eduardo Prado, of the influential Prado clan of São Paulo.[54] He crusaded in print against what he termed the republic's "financial pathology" and its electoral corruption. Reaching the end of his patience in October 1896, São Paulo governor Manuel Ferraz de Campos Salles (and president of Brazil, 1898–1902) decided to crush the state Monarchist party. While, he said, he "never gave importance to restorationist pretensions," he now feared that monarchist agitation would harm São Paulo's efforts to raise new foreign loans. Campos Salles warned that he would "hurl the police" on the monarchists and "not permit them to have more than the slightest liberty of movement."[55] Police invaded private homes to break up peaceful monarchist meetings and were ordered to obstruct public rallies. Eduardo Prado was a primary target.

By January 1897, antimonarchist invective and attacks on the Prudente regime so heated the atmosphere that some newspaper editors stridently advocated "elimination" of "political enemies." At precisely this point, Rio de Janeiro's *Gazeta de Notícias*, on January 30, printed the text of a telegram from a correspondent in Salvador, reporting on the "bloody Canudos drama" and stating baldly that the Conde d'Eu, Princess Isabel's publicly despised husband, had provided funds to Conselheiro's rebels to open an insurrectionary military front aimed at monarchist restoration.[56] Given that the republican forces were faring very badly, the timing of the allegation, however absurd, could not have been worse. Outraged monarchists protested vehemently, but to no avail. A regionalist dimension was involved here as well: the progress-minded South was predisposed to view the North as retrograde, and urban Brazilians, for their part, were prepared to believe all manner of fantastic things about the backlands.

It is now suspected that the killing of the flamboyant federal commander Colonel Antônio Moreira César during the third military campaign in early 1897 resulted not from *jagunço* gunfire but from shots fired by his own troops, who hated him.[57] The shocking news of the officer's death reached the city of São Paulo five days later, on a Sunday. Steered by politicians, public opinion turned its wrath against the monarchist cause. The governor advised against violence but told the crowd milling outside his official residence that Moreira César's death would have to be avenged. The mob proceeded to the nearby offices of the *Correio Paulistano*, shouting insults and threats, and stormed the building, unhindered by mounted militiamen stationed there to prevent trouble. Cadets at Rio de Janeiro's military academy mutinied, remaining defiant until the government surrounded the academy with soldiers and moved naval units into place. Troops were dispatched to take similar precautions at the military academy in Fortaleza, and civilian patriotic battalions were dissolved.[58]

Republicans recommenced their attacks on Coronel Gentil de Castro, the editor of the monarchist *Liberdade. A República* accused the editor of sending arms and money to Canudos in the name of "monarchist chieftains" and warned that he was instigating national treason. On February 9, 1897, shortly after dawn, a group of men began to attack the building that housed *Liberdade* and *Gazeta da Tarde*. When employees inside used carbines stored in the newspaper offices to fire warning shots, the assault ceased, but recriminations on both sides continued for days. Stirred up by the press and by the steady flow of alarming reports via coastal steamer and telegraph of government losses at the Canudos front, the crisis reached a fever pitch. Meanwhile, republican leaders as highly placed as Campos Salles coyly used every federal setback to stir up antimonarchist feeling. "It seems to me," he commented, "that simple yokels or fanatics, no matter how numerous, could not completely rout a force organized, prepared for war, and commanded by a leader of the most solid prestige and proven capacity."[59] At the same time, the vice-president continued to maneuver against the president, blaming Prudente, in a speech to the Clube Militar (Military Club), with having failed to heed the army's warnings to mobilize quickly against the monarchist threat.

The Rio de Janeiro police commander ordered his men not to defend the offices of monarchist newspapers under attack. Policemen, in fact, joined the mobs on Rua do Ouvidor, Rua do Sacramento, and several side streets, looting and burning the offices and typesetting facilities of the capital city's three leading monarchist newspapers, *Gazeta da Tarde*, de Castro's *Liberdade*, and *Apóstolo*. Vandals then turned to da Castro's elegant house, where they smashed furniture, carried off paintings, and overturned drawers in search of compromising documents or letters. When a torrential rain dampened the mob, it eventually dispersed. The following morning, de Castro attempted to flee by train, but he was followed and, at the São Francisco Xavier station, killed by a gunshot as he sat in his compartment waiting for the train to depart.[60]

News of the shooting inflamed the capital even further. President Prudente locked the doors of his palace and took no steps to quiet the atmosphere. The editor of the monarchist newspaper *Apóstolo*, Padre Scaligero Maravalho, along with his attorney, sought police protection but were denied it. "Death lists" with names of known monarchists were circulated, even to hospitals so that treatment could be refused.[61] Government officials and police cavalry stood by and watched buildings burn on the Largo de São Francisco de Paula. Some monarchists were driven into exile or hiding after the destruction of *O Commércio*. Writing under pseudonyms, Eduardo Prado bitterly blamed the republican administration both for the regime's defeats at Canudos and for the convulsive atmosphere being stirred up in the press. The statements of such national figures as General Artur Oscar de Andrade Guimarães, the commander of the fourth expedition against Canudos, were to blame as well; he wrote to opposition newspapers hinting bluntly at monarchist complicity in training the *jagunços* and in supplying them. The progovernment *O Estado de São Paulo*, moreover, published manufactured evidence linking Prado to the Canudos conspiracy.[62] In all this lay an irony of the highest magnitude: the fighting in the backlands, trumpeted as a severe threat to civilization, triggered brutal attacks in the very heart of that "civilization"—Rio de Janeiro and São Paulo.

Asked soon afterward why the antimonarchist riots had occurred, the president replied that the reaction had been provoked as a display of "patriotic exaltation of the national soul."[63] Euclydes da Cunha later observed "a certain similarity" between the Rua do Ouvidor bonfires of newspaper offices and Canudos, "one equaling the other in savagery." He added: "Backlands lawlessness was precipitately making its entrance into history; and the Canudos revolt, when all is said, was little more than symptomatic of a malady which, by no means confined to a corner of Baía, was spreading to the capitals of the seaboard. The man of the backlands, that rude, leather-clad figure, had partners in crime who were, possibly, even more dangerous."[64]

Based on the Canudos events, two principal interpretations of 1890s

Brazil emerged. One, the republican version, emphasized the reformist acts that had carried forward political modernization: abolition, the 1891 Constitution, separation of church and state, the creation of a stable civilian regime, and victory over dissidence, from Canudos to the antivaccination riots of 1904 and beyond. The other, a far more pessimistic analysis, doubted Brazil's capacity to overcome its legacy of backwardness and racial mixture. These interpretations gelled during or immediately after the period when the *conselheiristas* appeared able to hold out almost at will. "It is puerile," the mulatto professor of forensic medicine Raimundo Nina Rodrigues wrote in his scholarly analysis of Canudos, "to expect that the [*sertanejo*] will ever be able to understand that the republican federation carries within itself the guarantee of future political unity."[65]

Some intellectuals agonized over Canudos, and a few directed blame at the government. César Zama, a Bahian partisan of Governor Luiz Vianna, published under a pseudonym a vehement analysis of how Conselheiro had been misunderstood and falsely libeled.[66] Bahia's eloquent Senator Barbosa, who had labeled the Canudenses "idiots and galley slaves," now called them his "clients" and pledged, in a speech written but never delivered, to ask for habeas corpus for the dead. Barbosa also attacked the army's killing of its prisoners and blamed "Brazilian indifference" for not having understood the truth about the backlands.[67] As the nominal spokesman for Bahian interests at the national level, he apparently did not want to sully his reputation by defending in public a cause that had so obviously lost.[68] Self-styled political "realists" accepted the bloody cost of perhaps thirty thousand dead and cited the lesson of the conflict to justify their support for the "politics of the governors," which would tighten the mechanisms for social control by ceding absolute power to the rural *coronéis*.

The overwhelming opinion expressed following the destruction of Canudos, to be sure, approved da Cunha's idea of the irrevocable duality of Brazilian society between backlands and coast. As a Spencerian positivist, da Cunha was troubled long before Canudos by the question of national progress "stained" by Brazil's miscegenated population. At the same time, he considered his work not a defense of the *sertanejo* but an attack on the barbarity of the "civilized" leaders of the nation. All his writings—not only *Os sertões*—pilloried the arrogance and incompetence of civilian and military officials. In one of his daily dispatches from the front, in 1897, he told the story of a young *jagunço* defender captured and taken to Salvador, where military officers and reporters interrogated him, expecting to hear rubbish about Conselheiro's miracles or other tall tales. When the youth calmly responded that he had never heard of any miracles, they pressed him, asking what the holy man had promised to convince his followers to die for him. The reply was simple and direct: "To save our souls."[69]

The racial character of the uprising permitted the elite to justify cold-blooded execution of the surviving male residents of Canudos; it also prevented the movement from attaining the same glorification as that bestowed posthumously on the heroes of the 1789 independence-seeking *Inconfidência Mineira*.[70] To rationalize the massacre of the Canudos population and the decision to wipe the village from the face of the earth (not that they admitted any need to justify their position), chroniclers claimed evidence of the antediluvian and even psychotic factors underlying the settlement of this place of refuge. Their depictions of Conselheiro as a threat to the republic seemed as credible to members of the region's elite as the patriarch's saintliness did to simple residents of backland hamlets and towns. Canudos entered the Brazilian consciousness as a fearful symbol. Intellectuals of the left later saw the movement as a heroic grassroots rebellion against feudalism—it was, in the words of Abguar Bastos, "one of the most stupendous manifestations of human courage in Brazil," as well as one of the bloodiest episodes in the nation's history, a resistance more heroic than Troy's or Verdun's;[71] yet most Brazilian intellectuals condoned da Cunha's interpretation, viewing the conflict as a dystopian symbol of primitive impulses of backward peasants manipulated by a false messiah.

## CONSELHEIRO AND THE CHURCH

The mysterious Antônio Conselheiro, whose captivating presence and message somehow enticed thousands of backland men and women to abruptly abandon their residences and come with him in search of refuge and guidance, also played a major part in the refinement of the *visão do litoral* that da Cunha's writing spawned. Euclydes da Cunha's Conselheiro was not the same Antônio Vicente Mendes Maciel who started out as a debt-ridden teacher of Portuguese and arithmetic in rural Ceará. What can be pieced together from the historical record of Conselheiro's life and career stands in sharp contrast to the picture of the reckless, malevolent, antisocial zealot painted by da Cunha. But if Brazil needed a cathartic image by which to rationalize the suppression of rural dissidence, Conselheiro, because of his stubbornness as well as his charisma, delivered himself outright to the Jacobins and others eager to launch Brazil on the path of civilizing advancement.

Brazil's Catholic church fathers shared a version of the *visão do litoral* with other elites, even though church relations with the state were difficult during the closing years of the empire. Careers in the church, as well as in the armed forces and the foreign service, were considered very prestigious, and more than a few young Brazilian men entered the priesthood with the same conservative attitudes as other youths following secular callings. The church was well aware of the Vatican's renewed emphasis on administrative reform and its instructions to cast out elements of superstition and heterodoxy that had taken hold over time; shortages of clergy willing to minister to the poor in remote parishes had left many rural Brazilian Catholics, especially in the *sertão*, virtually on their own.

Although he was welcomed by some overworked backland priests, Conselheiro became a thorn in the side of the church from the 1870s through the early 1890s, thus stirring the church hierarchy to action. Not only was his presence—if not his theology—a major irritant, but he also railed against the new republican state, which the institutional church had grudgingly accepted. Bahia, exuberantly imbued with Afro-Brazilian cult overtones in the nominal Catholicism of its coastal black population and given to dour penitential rituals in the interior, was a ripe target for church sternness.[72]

The Brazilian Roman Catholic church initiated a comprehensive program of episcopal reform in 1883, seeking to improve the quality of the clergy and, in the backlands, to combat Protestants, Masons, and spiritists. The hierarchy maneuvered aggressively to deny independent tendencies and to cast out parties or canons willing to cooperate with the liberal state, especially secularism. More important for Latin America, it demanded restoration of traditional liturgical practices, seeking to root out previously tolerated local and even syncretistic variations. Individual bishops were subject to greater papal authority. Ultramontane concerns, in fact, were responsible for large numbers of foreign priests being sent to the Brazilian Northeast.[73]

The archdiocese of Salvador, which supervised the Canudos region, sought repeatedly to reorganize and to implement the new directives. The effort, however, was severely handicapped by staffing problems; in particular, during the critical decade and a half up to 1894, the archdiocese functioned virtually without an archbishop.[74] Dom Luiz dos Santos, selected because of his reputation for toughness in Fortaleza, where he had founded the Ceará Seminary, was extremely reluctant to assume the position because of ill health. Thus, almost as soon as he arrived in Salvador to be invested, he pleaded to be relieved of his duties; in 1893 he traveled to Rio de Janeiro to ask permission to resign, which was denied. Shortly afterward he was stricken with paralysis, whereupon he went to Ceará for treatment, spending nearly two years there before returning to Bahia. In the meantime, Monsignor Manoel dos Santos Pereira, his associate, handled day-to-day administrative affairs. Dom Luiz's other assistant was a newly arrived Italian priest who understood virtually nothing about Brazil; thus, Msgr. Santos Pereira enjoyed almost a free hand through 1890, when Dom Luiz died. Divisions within the church hierarchy prevented a new archbishop from taking office until 1894. Yet that man, Dom Jerônymo Tomé, moved quickly to consolidate his authority and was the official responsible for sending the Italian Capuchin mission to visit Canudos. From that point on, the church lobbied forcefully for the government to intervene, thereby hammering another nail into Conselheiro's coffin.

The main goal for the Brazilian church during the late 1880s and early 1890s was the intent, originating in Rome, that bishops reassert control over parishes and curtail heterodoxy. Ironically, though, the deeply felt religious expression of faith that outsiders labeled "mystical" and "fanatical" represented a continuation of a spiritual revival among both laity and rural clergy begun in the 1860s. The church, having thrown in its lot with a policy of political accommodation and realizing that its relatively meager resources and shortage of priests blocked any meaningful attempt to reassert its influence among the mass of the population, concentrated its attention on the urban elite—focusing especially on educational and charitable concerns. Sharing common values with the littoral elite, the hierarchy joined the campaign to destroy Conselheiro's sanctuary.

In Bahia, church fathers, comfortably seated in Salvador but financially embarrassed, could do little for their flock in the remote interior. In 1887, 124 of the state's 190 parishes lacked a full-time or permanent priest. Even civil officials worried about the consequences of this state of affairs.[75] Although nominal observance of Catholic ritual continued unabated without priestly supervision, such compliance tended to take on a life of its own. Pious backland residents traveled long distances on pilgrimages to religious shrines on patron saints' days, sometimes at Christmas, and during Holy Week, but most rarely encountered priests, some never in their lives. Once every three or four years, vicars or their deputies visited central locations, usually *fazendas*, offering mass and celebrating communal baptisms and weddings, though some visits were canceled and not rescheduled. Most newly trained priests pulled strings to permit them to remain in the capital city or on the coast; eighty parishes, most in the remote interior, were served by no clergy whatever.

As a consequence, church officials encouraged evangelical preaching missions to coincide with the circuit-riding visits by parish priests to remote parts of the diocese. The purpose was to combat secularization and deviance from standard ritual and to extend to remote areas a well-disciplined clerical presence.[76] Results were mixed. Ultimately, the initiative was dropped for lack of personnel whom rural parishioners could understand, since most of the priests available for the missions were foreigners. Interestingly, the concept of public preaching, the principal basis of Antônio Conselheiro's reputation in the region, was introduced by the institutional church precisely as a gesture to engage the backland population. Also, after 1892 Vatican policy toward Brazil resembled policy toward the French Republic. In that year, Pope Leo XIII's encyclical *Au milieu des sollicitudes* opened the way for a rapprochement with the latter, just as in Brazil the church moved to acquiesce to the separation of church and state and, tacitly, to support the government. Where policies differed greatly was with respect to the preceding encyclical, *Rerum Novarum*, which called on Catholics to concern themselves with the social welfare of workers. In France, the hierarchy ignored these instructions, but at the lower ranks clergy who came to be called "democratic priests" engaged in missionary activity among the poor, going further, in the words of Alfred Cobban, "than respectable society was willing to accept."[77] The handful of state legislators and others who considered Conselheiro harmless and who applauded his ministry saw him in the same way that French liberals saw the priests who devoted their lives to the poor.

The long-standing conflict between Brazil's two major seminaries—the one in Fortaleza (Ceará), the other in Olinda (Pernambuco)—now came under the shadow of ultramontanism, the Vatican's determined campaign led by Pius IX (1846–78) and his successor, Leo XIII (1878–97), to centralize control under stronger papal authority in matters of ecclesiastical government and doctrine.[78] The Brazilian ultramontanist campaign gave ecclesiastical authorities in Salvador all the justification they needed to side against those local vicars who had counseled toleration of Antônio Conselheiro and in favor of those who urged his removal as a potentially seditious element. This struggle, tellingly, was played out in the context of the old division between priests educated at the two rival seminaries. In Fortaleza, seminarians—especially during the tenure of long-term director Padre Chevalier—were considered more likely to enforce discipline in their parishes than graduates of the Olinda seminary, whose administrators, because of pragmatic considerations, often disregarded temporal and liturgical transgressions. Many Bahian priests, for example, lived in open relationships with women and were labeled by Padre Cícero, a Fortaleza graduate, as the "worst [priests] in Brazil."[79]

In quick order, the Olinda-trained clergy were forced to retreat from their relaxed behavior. Some were removed from positions of importance; others discreetly decided to follow the more austere precepts of the Fortaleza school. The hierarchy considered this a victory, yet in real terms it meant that the church would have to stand still further from its dispersed backland congregations and from the nominally Catholic Afro-Brazilian population on the coast. The papal initiative encouraged *ad limina* visits for discipline, and refractory bishops were frequently called to Rome. From the perspective of the Roman Curia, ultramontanism yielded higher spiritual earnestness and intellectual and professional caliber from church personnel, but "not always a thorough grasp of contemporary needs and trends."[80] In Brazil, the change resulted in the arrival of freshly minted missionary clergy, many from Italy, Belgium, and Germany, including some who would play a major role in examining Conselheiro's settlement and measuring it by the new, more stringent rules imposed on Catholics.

Even though the backland population received virtually no formal religious instruction, piety rarely wavered. From time to time frustrated parishioners had petitioned in vain for a priest—as, for example, three thousand residents of Boqueirão in 1817, saying that they were "abandoned and helpless"[81]—but their wishes were rarely granted. Wandering missionaries filled the breach during the first half of the century to some extent, especially in more remote and impoverished areas. Sometimes the missionaries traveled alone; more frequently they worked in teams. Franciscans, Redentorists, Jesuits, and German and Italian Capuchins all followed a similar pattern. Visitations lasted twelve days, starting each day as early as two hours before daybreak and continuing in marathon prayer sessions that culminated with confessions, the levying of penitential acts, and administration of sacraments.

By the 1850s, more was needed. The decline in the number and influence of regular clergy (religious orders), as well as a continued drop in the numbers of secular priests willing to accept assignment to the interior, severely limited the influence of the institutional church. Pombal, a strategic population center and the second oldest parish in the region, had no vicar for the thirteen years from 1843 to 1856, or again from 1877 to 1895, a span of eighteen years. Because the church stressed spiritual salvation, not social change, when it did maintain a presence in certain locales, its priests only defended and reinforced the status quo.[82]

By the late nineteenth century, religiosity in the backlands was expressed in forms that differed significantly from those in regions with a more traditional church presence, such as Minas and the Rio de Janeiro–Espírito Santo–São Paulo triangle. Although in the *sertão* the formal liturgy and sacramental practices were always within the bounds of accepted Roman Catholic tradition—even in Canudos after Conselheiro's settlement was established—the spiritual context was greatly different. There, the penitential, Sebastianist, and potentially millenarian atmosphere provided the perfect setting in which an austere but charismatic religious seer could recruit simple people to follow him to a community that was subversive only in the most technical sense of the term.

Antônio Conselheiro, the target of the *visão do litoral*, was a product of his unique backland religious environment. Since colonial days, the São Francisco Valley had been known for the powerful influence of flagellant penitential brotherhoods. The backland population, largely self-instructed in its Catholicism, tended to blend everyday stoicism and resignation with messianic hopes. It sanctioned an apocalyptic view of life and the cult of personal saints. The *beatos* (lay persons living as though members of a religious order, following consecration by a curate) and other late nineteenth-century wanderers were in fact laymen in religious garb.[83] They offered quasi-sacramental services and combined moral and practical advice with fire and brimstone millenarian allegories, becoming, in the words of a present-day cleric, "an institutionalized form of popular religion."[84] Herein lay the gist of the clash between the "modern" and "backward" cultures involved in the Canudos conflict: the characteristics that coastal observers disapproved of and scorned were the very ones that brought vitality to Conselheiro's followers. Da Cunha's disparaging descriptions of the "mud-walled Troy of the *jagunços*" identify the elements that prove that Canudos was a viable society whose residents sought "patriarchal principles of government."[85] He wrote in *Os sertões*:

> Not being blood brothers, the inhabitants found a moral consanguinity which gave them the exact appearance of a *clan*, with their chieftain's will as the supreme law, while justice lay in his irrevocable decisions. Canudos, indeed, was a stereotype of the dubious form of social organization that prevailed among the earliest barbarian tribes. The simple sertanejo, upon setting foot in the place, became another being, a stern and fearless fanatic. He absorbed the collective psychosis. . .[86]

## THE NATIONAL DIMENSION

Nationwide the transition from monarchy to republic was not easy, especially in Bahia. We have noted that although the last years of the empire witnessed a boom in the Center-South, in the northeastern states the economy remained stagnant. From Ceará to southern Bahia, the changes set off by the abolition of slavery and the beginning of a new military regime a year later alarmed the elite, already apprehensive because in 1889 Bahia's exports had fallen to levels not seen since 1850. Most prominent members of the Liberal and the Conservative parties in Bahia opposed the inauguration of a republic, insisting that a change would aggravate the economic crisis. The last president of the province, Liberal José Luis de Almeida Couto, refused the invitation of Marshal

Deodoro da Fonseca to continue in office because in his view the Bahian people were still staunchly loyal to the monarchy. Salvador's municipal council voted to reject the national military dictatorship and reaffirmed its devotion to the monarchy: it accepted the republic only after the imperial family sailed for European exile. Business and commercial leaders worried that republican rhetoric about expanded political participation and social justice threatened "anarchy and danger."[87]

Worse, the state political system immediately fragmented. In 1892, deputies to the legislature were elected from thirteen different parties. Reluctant converts to the new order, the so-called eleventh-hour republicans, formed a short-lived alliance with the Catholic party. The first governor's Republican party splintered and fell from power; there was even a minuscule Workers' party, which called for higher wages and more outlays for education. The state Federal Republican party (PRF) took two years to organize effectively; when it did, opposition groups aligned into a bloc powerful enough to counter most government initiatives. Even after 1896, by which time it had consolidated its hold on the political apparatus, Bahia's incumbent party did not hold the state firmly, in contrast to the experience of most other state republican parties in the Northeast and elsewhere. The Canudos turmoil forced Bahian representatives to take the defensive and to waste political capital in countering the allegations that Bahia was secretly monarchist.[88]

Salvador, the state capital, was inundated in 1890 by rural migrants— freed slaves, many infirm or otherwise unable to work, and backlanders pummeled by the severe drought that spanned the transition from empire to republic. The head of the provincial government expressed concern, as another backlands winter passed without rain, that the *sertão* had been reduced to a "lamentable" state.[89] Not only was Salvador inundated by thousands of homeless migrants, but ex-slaves and other rural people swelled the population of the Recôncavo (the rich agricultural zone beyond the capital, Salvador) as well, without any real hopes for work. Influential members of the elite were so convinced that these Brazilians could not be gainfully employed that they approved plans for a special bond issue to pay (in pounds sterling) £5.15.8 each for up to twenty-five thousand European agricultural colonists to be brought to the state.[90] The state police force was so underfunded that sixteen hundred men and officers were asked to maintain order in all of Bahia's 120 *municípios*. Yet soldiers' wages were 1.6 milréis a day—less than thirty cents, the same as a stonecutter's assistant earned[91]—barely enough to pay for a family's food, in a region where prices were higher than in the South. The state did nothing for drought relief except authorize special funds that local authorities could use to hire temporary workers, simply to provide jobs. Ironically, the most frequent use of the funds in the mid-1890s was for the building of new cemeteries.[92]

Bad times reinforced the sullen mood of the elite and caused angry infighting in the new state legislature. Bahia's federal delegation, badly divided, was unable to gain benefits for its constituency, which gravely weakened Bahia's traditional political clout. The state's police force, though nominally the largest, was in effective strength inferior to that of Rio Grande do Sul and, by 1896, São Paulo. Only 2.4 percent of Bahia's population voted in state elections through 1906 (and only 2.7 percent through 1930).[93] Some Bahian *municípios* in the 1890s had fewer than fifty registered voters, and eleven had none at all.

At the national level, control remained in the hands of the military and their allies. Their co-conspirators in the 1889 coup, the true republicans, shared administrative power, but their ranks were thin and they lacked experience (much like their Argentine counterparts in the Radical Civic Union some years later). The Brazilian republicans were soon caught in the civilian-military tensions of the early 1890s. Unresolved frictions accompanying (and surviving) the fall of the Bragança dynasty in 1889 and the military rule led to vengeful acts of repression against monarchists, who were labeled traitors.

Inflammatory rhetoric, at times followed by strong-arm repression, characterized political life. From the 1870s, republicans had berated the imperial regime, referring to Pedro II as "Pedro Banana" and blaming the monarchy for national backwardness. The criticism was apt in some ways, but not in others. For example, the government had spent pathetically little on public education, but it invested large sums to develop the country's infrastructure. Still, republicans reviled not only the monarch, but the fierce centralizing policies of the monarchy as well. Eduardo Prado's attack on the republican government's pro-U.S. foreign policy, *A ilusão americana*, published in 1892, was at once banned, and distributed copies were seized by the police.[94]

Many national problems remained unresolved. These included, but were not limited to, a severe lack of confidence in Brazil among foreign investors, regionalist conflict, and angry divisiveness within the armed forces. Prudente de Morais Barros, who assumed office in November 1894 as the first civilian president, was a São Paulo lawyer closely connected to coffee producers and exporters.[95] He soon took steps to increase state economic intervention in order to rescue planters hit by falling coffee prices, and to meet the pressing costs of servicing Brazil's foreign debt.[96] Economic troubles in the mid-1890s, affected by international factors, domestic scandal, and reckless speculation, resulted in the bursting of the investment bubble known as the Encilhamento, thus worsening the crisis. The boom, as Steven C. Topik put it, created republican millionaires but few products. The milréis lost half its value between 1892 and 1897, causing, according to an official report issued by the Bahia governor's office, "panic" and (here, as if mocking Antônio Conselheiro) "the sense that the world was going to end."[97]

Other fiscal woes afflicted the national government under the republic as well. Exports fell, thus limiting the federation's capacity to float new loans. Inflation and economic chaos followed. Agricultural crisis in the Brazilian Northeast had been building since the mid-1870s, caused by falling commodity prices and the region's inability to sell to foreign markets. Further upheavals and instability arose from structural imbalance in the mainstay economy.[98] In Bahia, the long decline in sugar cane revenue speeded up after the 1870s, spurred by incomplete and uneven modernization, the upheaval in the labor market, and the terrible droughts of 1866–68 and 1877–80, which drained both fiscal and human resources from the region. There had been electoral violence in 1868 and 1871, as well as bloody clan warfare in the backland municipalities of Monte Santo, Itapicurú, and elsewhere. These feuds further harmed the regional economy, weakened by steady economic decline and shaken by the nationwide depression of the early 1890s.[99] Runaway inflation caused consumer prices to spiral. The state economy was buffeted further by the effects of the Encilhamento, by agricultural stagnation in the Recôncavo and the coastal South, and by a drop in mineral production in the Lavras Diamantinhas region. Cacao and tobacco exports fell. In the *sertão*, even formerly independent cowherds reverted to marginal activities, selling goat hides and working for pitiful wages on the ranches of large landowners. Bankrupt agriculturalists sold or abandoned their land and moved to cities. The collapse of the Encilhamento discredited the model of organized capitalism and damaged Brazil's foreign credit. It signaled the failure to create a national capital market, and raised fears about the viability of the Brazilian federation itself.[100]

The extreme federalism of the 1891 Constitution heightened political stress by conferring unprecedented power on the stronger states, thereby attenuating the symbolic authority of the federal government in a country where the sense of nationhood was weak to begin with. One traumatic confrontation followed another: a naval revolt in Rio de Janeiro in 1893; in the same year, the so-called secession of Canudos, alleged to be part of a centrally directed plot financed by monarchists; and the civil war in Rio Grande do Sul, which persisted until 1895. To republicans, it was urgent that these fires be put out immediately, lest national consolidation be imperiled. Republican politicians were especially concerned that they not give the impression that they were, in the words of São Paulo governor Manuel Ferraz de Campos Salles, "unable to control their own government."[101]

When Prudente went in for surgery in November 1896, the federal government fell into the hands of Vice-President Manoel Vitorino Pereira, who, furthering his own ambitions, moved immediately to ally himself with military dissidents and make personnel changes hostile to Prudente. Just two weeks after Prudente's operation, the acting president fired the war minister. In response, Prudente, weeks earlier than his physicians counseled he should, hurried back from his convalescence and took charge again. Barely a few days later, news of the crushing defeat of the army's third military expedition against Canudos and the death of its commanding officer hit the press, triggering violent antimonarchist outbursts. Opposition newspapers fanned the flames of emotion by arguing recklessly and vociferously that the rebels were in fact being financed by monarchists. Rio de Janeiro's *A República* alleged that arms were being channeled through Minas Gerais, believed to be a monarchist stronghold, and shipped via the São Francisco River to Canudos.[102]

Against this background, Canudos could not have existed at a worse time. Rumors of plans for a Jacobin coup to restore Floriano's policies under a radical and nationalist dictatorship surfaced almost daily. Republican party boss and fellow Paulista Francisco Glicério broke with Prudente over mutinies by military school cadets at several locations, creating a deep schism within the Federal Republican party. City residents felt the sting of higher prices, the result, ultimately, of the fall in coffee export revenues. All over Brazil, rapid urban growth created new tensions and pressures, especially as unskilled rural migrants flocked to the cities. The characterization of Canudos as a monarchist "rebellion" heightened the feeling of panic.[103]

The irregularly published, discordant, and violently nationalistic newspaper *O Jacobino* (Rio de Janeiro) praised Floriano's patriotism and demanded that Prudente rehire large numbers of Florianists who had been fired from their government jobs, ostensibly to cut expenditures. Jacobins incited military discontent and hinted at the need for a coup d'état. Members of the powerful Military Club published an antimonarchist pact, pledging to defend the republic against changes "menaced by subversive groups" and linking the "destinies of the Republic" to the officers' "military honor." Pressured, state and federal officials in 1896 agreed to dismantle Canudos. This task proved arduous, much more difficult than anyone could have imagined. The humiliating defeat of the first two relatively small expeditions sent out to subdue Conselheiro, followed by the rout of the massive third military expedition, led to calls by radicals in major cities for a national crusade against the enemies of the republic and for a general mobilization.[104] Canudos stood for autonomy; therefore, in the eyes of most Republicans, it had to be destroyed.

Canudos was the last example of publicly expressed monarchist sentiment and of Florianist hard-line agitation.[105] When the recuperating president, barely able to stand, rode by train from his residence in the mountains above Rio de Janeiro to retrieve his presidency from his hostile vice-president, amid rumors of new attacks on newspapers and government agencies, some opposition politicians (including Tobias Monteiro, who wrote for the *Jornal do Comércio*, and Senator Rui Barbosa) hastily left the capital. Barbosa journeyed to his home city of Salvador, where he delivered two stormy speeches against Jacobinism but disparaged the rebels and called Canudos "a matter for the police." General Oscar, a hero in the fight against the federalist insurgents in Rio Grande do Sul, was named commander of the fourth expedition against Canudos.

Voices of moderation were stilled. In the backlands, however, popular religious expression continued unabated. In Juazeiro, in Ceará's Cariri Valley, veneration of the defrocked miracle-working priest Cícero Romão Batista began to take on imposing proportions in the mid-1890s, showing that the willingness of backland men and women to follow a charismatic leader was not limited to Canudos.[106] In reaction to anticipated Jacobinist counterrebellion, and to smash the Canudos "menace," incumbent governments in northern states mobilized their militias, even though these were poorly equipped and made up largely of untrained recruits. When, after the loss of thousands of lives over many months, word arrived finally that Canudos had fallen to the commander of the bloody fourth military expedition, on October 5, 1897, the resulting patriotic euphoria finally permitted the government to take credit, but the traumatized young republic's façade of harmonious national progress was shattered. It is telling that in his valedictory Order of the Day on October 6, 1897, General Artur Oscar de Andrade Guimarães did not call the defeated *conselheiristas* bandits or fanatics. Rather, in an uncanny statement of respect, he reminded his listeners that "both sides in the conflict"—the legalist troops and their opponents—had been "steadfast in their political ideals."[107] The victorious troops severed Conselheiro's head from his disinterred body and displayed it on parade along every major city on the northeastern coast. In spite of this conclusion, Jacobin voices continued to assail Prudente. *O Jacobino*'s editor, consumed by venom, blasted "the corrupting and unpatriotic policies of this sickly imbecile called Prudente de Morais . . . [who is attempting to annihilate the army, part of] the plan of restoring the monarchy . . . with the entire knowledge and frank protection" of the president.[108]

The final scene was played on November 5, 1897, when a soldier, Marcelino Bispo, a passionate Florianist (later described by historian José Maria Bello as a "young half-breed soldier from the North"), mounted the reviewing stand at a parade honoring troops returning from the backlands and tried to assassinate Prudente de Morais.[109] In the struggle, the war minister, Marshal Bittencourt, was stabbed to death while attempting to protect the president. Martial law was imposed. At the official inquiry, the soldier implicated *O Jacobino*'s editor, Deocleciano Martyr, with having enlisted him to kill Prudente as part of a larger conspiracy that included officer members of the Military Club. The police report named the vice-president and other leading politicians as principals, but Prudente hesitated to arrest them, though mobs were allowed to destroy the offices of *O Jacobino*.

The foiled assassination of the president broke the opposition, rallying support to the president and defusing the crisis. The radical Jacobins were silenced and never again regained their momentum, whereas the failure of the monarchists to defend themselves reduced their cause to the status of a curiosity. Just as in France in the 1890s, the old right ceased to be a political force in Brazilian life. Public anger gave Prudente justification for shutting down the prestigious Military Club, called the "fortress of Brazil's glories," the chief extramilitary voice of high military officers. It would remain closed until well into the next presidential regime. The "rebellion in the backlands" thus brought the republican government closer to collapse than anyone might have suspected.

Raymundo Faoro has argued that the Prudente de Morais administration represented the defining moment of the republic, and that Canudos was the central event influencing the kind of government Brazil would have under civilian rule.[110] The national controversy that accompanied the Canudos rebellion and massacre signaled attitudinal, if not structural, change in Brazilian life. Press coverage of the four military campaigns yielded outrage as well as bewilderment at the rebels' inexplicable ability to resist and at the army's ineptitude—a particularly acute shock given the Brazilian penchant in the late 1800s for romanticizing the supposed invincibility of its military establishment. What transpired at Canudos appalled the vicarious bystanders in the coastal cities, who followed the news of the campaign in the newspapers. While the battle was still being waged, politicians like Rui Barbosa insulted the Canudenses, but soon after it ended expressions changed to disgust over the excesses of the conflict.[111] Seen as animals during the resistance, on the day of Canudos's capitulation the victims were called "brothers" and "Brazilians" by military officers. Dead, the *conselheiristas* were afforded the same heroic benedictions as the fallen legalist soldiers, who days earlier so eagerly had slit the throats of their captives.

## THE NORTHEAST REGION

In the Bahian *sertão*, the cruelest drought occurred between 1888 and 1892, exactly during the anxious transition from monarchy to republic, a time when no one knew the extent to which the newly autonomous states would be able to provide financial assistance to afflicted areas. As it turned out, under federalism precisely those states that could least afford to proffer drought relief were those hardest hit. In the Bahian case, landowners in the drought regions had less political influence than planters on the coast, and virtually no state aid came their way. Da Cunha was joined by a generation of northeastern writers, some before *Os sertões*, some after, who brought the crisis to national attention.[112] Without meaningful resolution, northeastern politicians had argued for decades for massive drought relief to ameliorate the unproductivity of the region. The republican regime's persistent economic difficulties undermined further efforts by the federal government to consolidate its authority. This sense of being under constant siege, then, contributed to the sensitivity of political officials to the Canudos threat. Conditions were worse in the North, where unprecedented population instability, triggered by the quickening drought cycle, the end of slavery, and the shift of productive power from the Northeast to the Center-South, heightened the effects of the depression.

The repercussions of the severe and prolonged periodic droughts were drastic. In the first and last three decades of the nineteenth century, periods when unusually low rainfall was a worldwide phenomenon, drought caused unusually adverse consequences for agriculture and human lives.[113] The Brazilian backlands were especially hard hit in the second part of the century, for three main reasons: there were virtually no facilities for storage of water or irrigation; mounting population in the region made suffering more acute; and the lure of coastal cities made migration more attractive, causing demographic dislocations and heightening regional tensions.

Difficult environmental conditions, especially due to the devastating droughts of the mid- and late nineteenth centuries, shaped how Brazilians thought about the northeast region. Gerald M. Greenfield has shown that the very concept of a "Northeast" emerged relatively late, much after the empire's fall in 1889. The term conjured up images of deprivation, backwardness, economic stagnation, and negative racial stereotypes.[114] Southerners readily accepted explanations of backland uprisings and Canudos as evidence of Luddite fanaticism. The Northeast's political and economic decline occurred during a time of growing elite divergence and of "increasingly sharp North-South dialogue with regard to questions of national development," especially over such infrastructural priorities as railroads, reservoirs, and agricultural credits.[115] Before Canudos, even educated Brazilians not from the Northeast hardly thought about such places as the backlands at all. The bloody conflict changed all that, creating a formula of backwardness and fanat-

icism that was crystallized in da Cunha's writings but was evident as early
as the first newspaper dispatches from Bahia in 1893 and 1894 about the
growth of Conselheiro's community.

The attitudes and erroneous suppositions of educated coastal Brazilians about life in the rural hinterlands only exacerbated the shock of
news about the army's inability to subdue Conselheiro's *jagunços*. Although stereotypes of the rural poor included images of resistance to
authority and latent violence, at the same time coastal dwellers sub-
scribed to the long-standing myth that, even in the Northeast, the period
after 1850 represented a kind of nonviolent golden age.[116] In reality, the
region was swept by both urban and rural conflict between 1850 and
1900, including food riots in Salvador and slave revolts in the interior:
no fewer than fifty-nine violent conflicts were enumerated by the provincial Ministry of Justice through 1889, and undoubtedly many others
went unreported. Major outlaw gangs roamed the backlands. Among
them was one in the 1860s headed by David José dos Santos—known
locally as the "terror of the county"—operating out of Jeremoabo.[117]
(The Jeremoabo region, in fact, produced more violent gangs, or
*quadrilhas*, than any other part of Bahia.) Nor did the government's
victory over Canudos mean any cessation of politically linked violence.
The 1899 municipal elections pitted anti-incumbent interests against
Governor Luiz Vianna's allies, just as before, with the usual attendant
beatings, attacks on commercial establishments, and murders.[118]

Because they aimed their actions against the dominant classes of the
region, bandits in a way balanced the dominance of powerful landowners and others in the backlands. But *sertão* brigands did not help the
poor—regardless of the Robin Hood myth wishfully appropriated by
some commentators. The bandits stole everything they could: cattle,
jewelry, agricultural implements, guns, food, even holy images from
churches.[119] Some *quadrilhas* not only rustled cattle and committed
armed robberies; they also attacked tax revenue agencies. The police, in
turn, frequently lashed out in frustration, making arbitrary arrests and
casting suspicions on *sertanejos* generally. Insurrections, when they occurred, inevitably led to suppression. Although when mobs looted warehouses or food stores, the quickest among them could make away with
what they wanted, once the police arrived mass imprisonments followed,
and sometimes judges fined entire populations to pay for damages.

Conditioned by centuries of obligation, the Brazilian rural poor were
intimidated and dominated by the landowners and their politician
clients.[120] Perhaps because of this sense of helplessness vis-à-vis secular
power, many revolts took on a millenarian character, sometimes rooted
in mystical visions or notions of divine revenge; in the end, however,
these charismatic movements left no more of a mark on the mass of the

rural population than folktales, which eventually became half-legend, half-myth. Historically, insurrectionary leaders had fared poorly: like Conselheiro, two of the major rebels in earlier centuries—Zumbí in the seventeenth and Tiradentes in the eighteenth (followed by Lampião in the twentieth)—had their heads severed and displayed on pikes by forces representing the law.[121]

In the mid–nineteenth century, certainly less than 5 percent and probably less than 1 percent of the rural population owned land.[122] The persistence of slavery and the smooth transition from colony to monarchy influenced nineteenth-century Brazilian life. The author Machado de Assis, one of the few mulattoes accepted as a member of the elite, complained with unconscious irony in 1876 that "[we] are what came over in Columbus's Caravel."[123] Safely conservative, Brazil avoided the worst forms of Spanish American *caudillismo* (strongman rule) and the terribly destructive forces of racial civil war; power remained distributed within a narrow spectrum of interlocking elites.

As far as most of the population was concerned, the substitution of republic for monarchy had little impact. In contrast, Catholic France, for example, witnessed the implementation of compulsory education in 1883, which in turn led to the ascendancy of village schoolteachers and a new prominent role for public education. This was accompanied by a decline in the importance of the village priest, whose old-fashioned and sometimes narrow methods were no longer as appreciated as they had been traditionally. In Brazil, no such change appeared even on the horizon. Only seven hundred primary schools functioned in the entire nation; the secretary of public instruction complained that another thirteen hundred were urgently needed, but to no avail: they could not be built for lack of funds and qualified teachers.

The region in which Conselheiro preached contributed thousands of families to Canudos. In 1894, hardly a town or hamlet in the region had a school with more than fifty children enrolled, and many had fewer than twenty-five.[124] The elite's resistance to finding new sources of tax revenue doomed any hope for real change. In 1896 the largest single source of state income came from the sale of tax stamps (as befitted a society mired in bureaucracy), followed by duties on property transfer, professional and business license fees, and export duties. There were no real estate or land taxes, virtually no levies of any kind in rural areas, and no assessments on income or inheritance. All improvements had to be funded through bond issues and annual foreign loans, which in the first decade of the republic were floated to yield sums greater than all combined sources of income.[125]

Under the empire, lack of provincial autonomy reinforced the influence of the agricultural elite across Brazil. Even the adoption of federalism under the republic did not change the system right away. As Richard Graham aptly points out, "liberalism" in Brazil principally meant favoring local elites over national ones.[126] Very few members of the oligarchy, their lands largely clustered on the outskirts of the city of Salvador and along the southern coast, cared very much about deprivation in the hinterlands. For these people, the *sertão* was extremely remote. Although some modernizing influences—fiscal reforms, an expanded railroad network, telegraph communications, and resulting improvements in the infrastructures of towns—had begun to penetrate the rural interior during the late empire and especially after the proclamation of the republic, most aspects of life there remained unchanged.

The ferocity that Canudos defenders displayed should not have surprised astute onlookers familiar with the region's history. The conflict followed hard on a good half-dozen years of violent events after the proclamation of the Provisional Government in 1889, including coups, countercoups, the civil war in the South, a naval revolt, the Jacobin challenge to the imperial ruling class, martial law, cold-blooded repression, and economic adventurism leading to boom and bust. There had been intellectual rebellion as well. Euclydes da Cunha himself was a product, if not a member (he was born in 1866), of the 1870s generation, infused with a determination for national regeneration. His positivism and training at the Escola Militar, known as a "bastion of [the 1870] generation's worldview," caused him to be dismayed by the failure of the early republic to fulfill its promise.[127]

## THE *VISÃO DO LITORAL*

Unlike the Spaniards, who located their major settlements inland, the Portuguese, in the words of Frei Vicente do Salvador, "scraped along the seacoast like crabs."[128] For their administrative capitals, they favored cities overlooking the sea. The royal city of Salvador was founded in 1549 on an escarpment towering above the azure waters of the vast Bay of All Saints. It functioned both as the focal point of the captaincy-general of Bahia and as the capital of Brazil until 1763, when the royal administration was transferred to Rio de Janeiro—also a colonial-era metropolis nestled in mountains overlooking a large expanse of water. Salvador followed the two-level pattern of Lisbon, Porto, Olinda-Recife, Luanda, Macao in China, and the seafaring cities of classical Greece. The Portuguese sought hillsides for fortification, in exchange gaining hemmed-in cities with narrow, twisting streets (*ladeiras*) and crowded buildings (Fig. 2). The conditions of early settlement in turn shaped attitudes. Unlike Spanish-American creoles, upper-class but born in the New World and increasingly resentful of metropolitan domination, the

2. Urban Street Scene, Salvador, Bahia, ca. 1897. Anonymous photograph. Courtesy Fundação Casa Rui Barbosa, Rio de Janeiro.

descendants of Brazil's aristocratic families sooner or later shed strong identity with the Portuguese crown and adjusted to the Brazilian environment, in which there was little Portuguese presence.

As the decades and then the centuries passed, the evolution of Brazil's coastal cities was influenced by the Portuguese colonial system, which, unlike the Spanish system, did not seek to create elaborate colonial administrative centers on the model of the metropolis. Brazilian cities developed more on the order of trading entrepôts and places of residence for high-placed colonial families. In time, as plantations and ranches began to spread deeper into the hinterland, and after the discovery of gold and other valuable export commodities opened up parts of the vast Brazilian interior, a new stratum of wealthy and influential clans established themselves in cities: absentee *fazendeiros* and other landowners content to leave their properties in the hands of overseers in preference for living in the city, with its more stylish life and proximity to Europe. After independence, still others joined this urban upper class: high-level bureaucrats; *letrados* (university-trained lawyers, scribes, notaries, and others using skills of literacy); foreign-born engineers and technicians, some of whom stayed and married into decadent planter families eager for infusions of capital and entrepreneurship; merchants; and the successors to the old social elite, members of the titled nobility, the church, and the armed forces. Brazilian cities became places of stark contrasts between the wealthy—the "better families," as they were called—and their slaves and servants. Most people in Portuguese America, as in France and elsewhere in Europe, lived in towns. Some urban residents were European immigrants or their descendants; others were *gente de cor*, freeborn or freed *mulatos* and blacks, who worked side by side with slaves imported from Portuguese Africa.[129]

Brazilians had no clear-cut break with Portugal. Separation from Lisbon was achieved in 1822 not through violent insurrection but through imperial dynastic politics, whereby the Portuguese emperor, returning home, left his Brazilian colony in the hands of his Bragança heirs, Pedro I and then Pedro II. Before 1822, most urban elites strongly favored a continuance of the monarchy. When independence fell their way, they worked to maintain the substance of the old system, based on social linkages cemented by marriage, patronage, and ties of commerce, friendship, and mutual interest.[130] Some of the less privileged intellectuals, influenced by the ideas of the French Revolution, favored a sharp break with monarchy, but the elites, their strength rooted in the flourishing extractive economy, relegated these disaffected romantics to marginal status. Some of these intellectuals took refuge in Freemasonry and later became Comtean positivists, followers of the doctrine popularized in France that called for republican government run by a dictatorship of the "elect," men selected for their capacities and powers of reason who would lead the nation to material progress through industrialization.

Republicanism took shape in Brazil in a formal way only in 1870. Through most of the nineteenth century, Brazilian elites were content to watch their country being opened up by foreigners, whom imperial bureaucrats had invited to build railroads, bridges, canals, city sewage-disposal systems, and aqueducts. To promote the feeling of progress in the tropics, they also built broad boulevards, opera houses, and elegant mansions for the rich. Manufacturing, on the whole, did not fit into this equation; as a result, cities lacked a proletariat (in the European sense), although immigrants to the Center-South from southern Europe and migrants from the impoverished Brazilian Northeast did supplant the earlier urban work force of slaves and freedmen, mostly as manual laborers and craftsmen.

Even with this model, problems caused by strife within ruling circles and increasing popular political mobilization were compounded by imperial Brazil's lack of many of the attributes of a modern nation.[131] The educational system, for example, served only a tiny portion of the population. There were but four university faculties in all of Brazil: two medical schools (in Rio de Janeiro and Salvador) and two schools of law (in Pernambuco and São Paulo). All were relatively small, each graduating no more than a few dozen *bacharéis* (baccalaureates) every year. Standards were low, with students required only to memorize the curriculum and recite it back on examinations. Still, *bacharel* status guaranteed acceptance into the elite. Most university students, of course, already came from the "better" families, although a tiny number of orphans and others demonstrating unusual talent were able to attend as well. On taking their degrees, graduates usually entered the imperial bureaucracy. Outside of the military academies, a few of which offered sound training, especially in engineering, the nation had no other sources of higher schooling.

Urban Brazilians from the "better families" kept abreast of European fashion and political developments, yet they remained content to maintain colonial-era institutions. The slave trade flourished well into the 1840s, when British pressure forced its end, though Brazil's economy remained dependent on slavery (only abolished in 1888) and cheap, semicoerced labor throughout the century. Elites, moreover, thought it necessary to import European comforts and progress for their tropical setting. This attitude became defined in the *visão do litoral*, an urban outlook that deprecated rural life as rustic and primitive and reflected embarrassment at the fact that Brazil was overwhelmingly populated by *gente de cor*, especially in the hinterlands.

The still-rudimentary transportation system and huge distances between cities preserved the great differences from region to region, but most members of the upper class related to their social inferiors and to the rural world in general in a unified way. Contributing to this consistency in outlook was the imperial practice of elite circulation, in which young graduates were typically assigned to far-flung locations at the beginning of their careers, often in secondary urban centers in the interior. As they rose in the bureaucracy, they were relocated again and again until finally they ended up in a major coastal city or in the city of their birth in a position at the top of their career scale, perhaps as provincial president (governor) or as a high-level magistrate.[132]

The Roman Catholic church played a preeminent role in Brazilian life. Moreover, given its historical role as the transmitter of church policy from Rome and Brazil's ecclesiastical centers to the Catholic population, it played a major role in shaping the *visão do litoral*. Catholic observances filled the calendar, and family life revolved around sacramental ceremonies marking every event from birth to death. The open spaces in front of and adjacent to church buildings served as meeting places for the whole community—women as well as men—in contrast to taverns, where men congregated to drink *cachaça* and to interact socially.[133] In the urban world of Salvador, too, religious brotherhoods, corporations, and confraternities exercised such philanthropic and charitable functions as administering orphanages, asylums, and hospitals.

During the colonial period, much of this work had been performed by nonparochial groups, including the Santa Casa de Misericórdia, the Orders of Saint Francis and Saint Dominic, and the Carmelites. Lay associations played important roles as well. In Salvador, for instance, a brotherhood composed of blacks, the Society of Our Lady of the Rosary, was elevated in 1889 to the category of Third Brotherhood by Salvador's archbishop and thereby admitted to the status of a favored institution. Governed by boards elected annually, religious brotherhoods organized the religious festivals, provided social assistance, executed wills, and administered the estates of the deceased.[134]

The dissimilarities between institutional Catholicism in the more affluent neighborhoods of the capital and the understaffed, often unenthusiastic church apparatus in poorer locales were sharp, and they shaped variant religious attitudes and practices. It was not that the lower-class folk were less faithful or less observant, but their lives were touched much less frequently by any clerical personnel except overworked parish priests. The contrast was even greater in the *sertão*. Few rural backlanders entered the priesthood, so the clergy in the region were often foreign-born, sometimes had only rudimentary Portuguese, and were not linked by family ties to the powerful local families.

Ecclesiastical reform after 1870 affected the institutional role of the Roman Catholic Church significantly. Now parish churches began to devote more attention to what form worship took. Newly trained clergy were encouraged to be ardent, evangelical, and assertive. Reform and the new emphasis on orthodox discipline bred rigidity and impatience with syncretistic forms of religious expression.[135] Priests, a large number of whom were foreign-born, no longer were willing to tolerate the religious subculture, which was flourishing. Brazil's bishops made peace with the republican government, even following the removal of church jurisdiction over marriages and burials; indeed, church officials not only shared but contributed to the hardening of emphasis on urban issues and benign neglect for the rural interior.

There was no single *visão do litoral*, of course. Urban life in Brazil's South, especially in Rio de Janeiro, the imperial capital, and in burgeoning São Paulo, tended to embrace frequent change and to be influenced by a greater population flux. In the North and Northeast, change came more slowly. The upper classes on the coast, whether in Salvador, Recife, Natal, Fortaleza, or any of the other primary cities, all held a similar view of the hinterland. Their negative attitude was exacerbated by increasing population density in the *sertão*, which was driving greater num-

3. Mass celebrating victory of the "legal forces" at Canudos, Salvador, October 1897. Conçalves Studio. Courtesy Instituto Geográfico e Histórico da Bahia, Salvador.

bers of miserable backlanders to the coast; this meant, to urban observers, the threat of epidemic disease, not to mention unemployment and poverty. By the closing decades of the century, officials were erecting barricades on roads leading into their cities, interning drought refugees in camps and denying them entrance.

Early photographs epitomize the outlook of nineteenth-century urban Brazilians. The first daguerrotype studios (run mostly by Europeans) date from the 1840s and 1850s, opened in response to the new craze for "scientific" portraits.[136] By the century's last decade, the craze had mostly died down, but photographers still earned their living producing keepsake images of brides, communion celebrants, family members, and sometimes the dead in their coffins, especially children. Occasionally they took their equipment outdoors on special assignments or in search of subjects with commercial interest (Fig. 3). In Salvador, photographer Flávio de Barros captured the commotion in the city streets when federal troops arrived destined for the fourth expedition to the front, and he accompanied them on their trek into the *sertão*. After the destruction of Canudos, copies of his photographs were displayed throughout Brazil. Although most scenes were carefully posed, some were spontaneous. Officials found them extremely useful for bringing alive the threat posed by the "primitive and superstitious" backlanders.[137]

## THE BAHIAN ELITE AND URBAN CULTURE

The outlook and nature of Bahia's elite is relevant to establishing the *visão do litoral*, even though the man who later became known as Antônio Conselheiro was born and raised in the backlands of neighboring Ceará. Yet Canudos was located in Bahia; therefore, that state's government and bureaucracy—with its littoral attitudes—had to deal with the problem. Conselheiro, moreover, spent the greatest part of his ministry in Bahia, and Bahian officials arrested him on trumped-up charges and extradited him from the state. Finally, because his refuge at Canudos—which he sometimes called Belo Monte—was located within state limits, it was the Bahian political apparatus that first debated whether Canudos should be tolerated and then took steps to destroy it.

Although Bahia's elite was traditionally confined to a small number of families, it was augmented by the monarchy's granting of nonhereditary titles of nobility to 986 men and women, 113 of whom were Bahians.[138] Most were ennobled for their economic prominence or for special political or military service to the empire. The new presence of barons and viscounts, almost all white Brazilians from families considered "good" if not necessarily eminent, and the prizing not only of lineage but also of political acumen, entrepreneurship, and agrobusiness, created an upper class considerably different in composition from the narrowly based landed elite of most of Spanish America. Brazil's nineteenth-century elite, in other words, mixed profit-oriented "gentry" and status-oriented "aristocracy." Confounding matters further, there were, at least until after the Paraguayan War, coexisting exogamous and endogamous patterns of marriage, high incidences of illegitimacy among even the "best" families, overlapping kinship, and the practice of elopement or bride abduction (*rapto*). (Interestingly, *rapto* represented an aggressive challenge to traditional patriarchal authority, almost always with the consent of the woman. *Rapto* rendered the woman unfit for marriage to her father's candidate through the loss of her virginity, and unmarriageable to any man except the one with whom she had eloped.)[139]

Even though, as Pareto and Mosca argue, elite kinship and network are the bane of the institutionalized state, Bahia's endogamous upper class successfully co-opted the state, at least during the lifetime of the empire.[140] More than two-thirds of the Bahian-born nobility remained at home, where they tended to marry within their own limited circle. This situation prevailed well into the closing years of the century, by which time endogamy, which, facilitated by the small size of the dominant elite, had traditionally protected family groups against challengers beyond kin bounds, was no longer practical.[141]

Other members of the Bahian elite (dubbed *fluminenses*, meaning residents of Rio de Janeiro) used Rio as the base for political and administrative careers, where they took their places in the emerging national elite. They preferred to marry outside Bahian family clans, mostly because of their desire to gain economic or political advantage.[142] Throughout the upper classes, women generally submitted, willingly or not, to having their marriage partners arranged for them. Upper-class women endured homebound lives, more often than not condemned to isolation, constant scrutiny, and boredom owing to a masculine obsession with female fidelity. Two-thirds of the Bahian *fluminense* expatriates—principally those following administrative careers that took them to other provinces—married non-Bahian women, a third of whom were daughters of foreigners, mostly Portuguese-born.

The waning years of the empire also saw a surge of new noble titles, sometimes awarded in lieu of indemnification to slaveholders.[143] Beyond the very top level of nobles, aristocratic planters, and imperial politicians, the boundaries of the upper class included minor branches comprising descendants of colonial-era landowners and those who married into these family clans. By 1890, a majority of the most powerful families no longer resided in the rural plantation zones, but in Salvador, the capital. There was a small urban upper-middle sector, made up of the families of businessmen, many of whom were foreign-born—German, French, Belgian, Italian, English—as the late nineteenth- and early twentieth-century membership rosters of the commercial associations of virtually every northeastern city attest.

Lawyers and government officials invariably came from the "traditional" Brazilian families, although their life-styles depended to a certain extent on the quality of their connections to these families. Not all members of the urban intermediate sector, especially those wholly dependent on wages, lived well, compared to the much more comfortable echelon of families with wealth derived from inheritances, rents, and agricultural properties.

The oligarchy not only controlled the reins of government; it also distributed power based on an internal patriarchal family structure.[144] Following the overthrow of the monarchy, each state organized its own Republican party, which included a handful of true republicans but mostly last-minute adherents. Dissident factions formed offshoots and, in a few cases, managed to take over power at the state level. Divisions almost always followed splits within regional and local clan factions, and represented no differences whatever in policy or social outlook. Incumbency at the state level allowed one to negotiate with the federal government for favors and, in turn, to dispense patronage to allies and clients within state borders.

Most of Salvador's leading merchants were sugar brokers who also traded in slaves. Indeed, Salvador thrived both as Brazil's major slave entrepôt (the sea passage from Luanda took forty days, ten less than the voyage across the Atlantic to Rio de Janeiro) and as a distribution center for sugar, tobacco, and hides from the interior. The waters of the Bay (Bahia) of All Saints were traversed by boats of all sizes and descriptions, carrying goods to and from the larger islands in the bay, the port of Salvador, and the towns on inlets within the bay stretching into the surrounding Recôncavo. Salvador was the chief whaling station in the South Atlantic, the seat of a high court, and the main port of trade with Portugal and West Africa.[145] A great windlass hauled cargo between the port and the town proper, on the escarpment overlooking the sound. Yet although the bay offered a secure port for active commerce, it was too wide for military defense; as a result, Bahia had long been subject to attack by privateers and foreign navies.[146]

The 1872 imperial census enumerated 108,139 residents in the capital, the large majority mixed-race or black. Officials estimated the city's 1897 population to be 180,000, "occupied for the most part in commerce and industry."[147] A port city and shipping nexus, Salvador functioned as the commercial hub for the entire middle portion of the country south of Recife and north of Rio de Janeiro. Some 600 to 650 ships flying flags representing the entire Western world entered and left the docks annually. Imports were unloaded from ships that plied the Atlantic trade as well as ones coming from the provinces of the South, especially those that produced jerked beef, or *charque*. Salvador, in fact, functioned as the metropolis for the entire hinterland beyond the Recôncavo, although it lacked banking capital and therefore exercised a kind of clan-based political hegemony not backed by economic resources.

Officially sanctioned religiosity in all parts of Bahia centered on the preeminence of Catholic saints. In Salvador, nearly every residence contained a small oratory or niche for plaster replicas of Jesus and individual saints and, almost invariably, a straw rose of Jericho. Each of the dozens of saints was given a specific function. Santo Antônio intervened in behalf of family misfortunes; Santo Raimundo helped oversee childbirth; São Sebastião provided protection and a mystical link to the Portuguese homeland. Salvadorean blacks favored an even richer panoply of saints and images, imbuing the imagery of Catholic saints with deep-seated African spiritist personalities and cults of Dahomeyan and Yoruban derivation—orthodox African rites such as *candomblé*, which predominated in Bahia; the single-divinity cult *xangô*, especially popular in Recife; and the Brazilianized *macumba*, most common in Rio de Janeiro. All together, these yielded a galaxy of ways to gain intercession from the gods of water, fire, and the earth. Sorcerers (*feiticeiros*)—shadowy practitioners of black arts, hired to cast magic spells against enemies from all social levels—were as common in the city as tailors, shoemakers, or carpenters.[148]

Salvador, more than any other Brazilian site, not only provided a stable environment for the preservation of Afro-Brazilian spiritism in general, but it also proved fertile ground for the survival of openly African sects—Gantois, Opó Afinjá, and others. In syncretistic cults, Jehovah took on the personage of the long-bearded Olurun, the monarch of the heavens, brother to Odin and Zeus. Xangô, the Yoruban god of thunder and lightning, was merged with Saint Jerome; Naná, the mother of the *orixás*, was Saint Anne; Ogun, the god of the hunt, became Saint Anthony in Bahia and Saint George elsewhere in Brazil. Each god/saint enjoyed special powers, and each had its own characteristics.[149] The exception to the syncretistic duality was Nosso Senhor do Bonfim— not a saint, but the city's guardian spirit, more powerful than any single saint, and openly celebrated, if not worshipped officially.[150]

Members of the elite from other regions of Brazil viewed Bahia's African coloration with suspicion and tended to denigrate the richly African flavor of Bahian popular culture, which they considered too influential in urban domesticity and family life. The "maternal" dominance of spiritist celebration was distrusted, as contrasted with the "masculine" nature of traditional rural life, the open sky, Portuguese Catholicism, and republican politics. Bahians, it was said, had "feminized" African culture, transforming the "manly" cult of Nosso Senhor do Bonfim into the annual festival of Nossa Senhora (Our Lady) do Bonfim, ruled by white-clad, dark-hued Baianas who performed profane burlesques of religion, merrymaking, and samba.[151] "Negroes love color," pontificated European visitor Hakon Mielche, "and there is no better setting for large glass beads and cheap shiny silks than the coffee-color of a negro's skin."[152]

The reputation that Salvador and the Recôncavo had as a center of slave life was so great that even members of the city's nineteenth-century commercial and political elite, who in turn were closely related to the great landowners and *senhores de engenho* (sugar plantation owners), were stigmatized in national opinion for purportedly having been stained by the brush of miscegenation. Bahia was the home of the "white *mulato* and the black *doutor*" ("doctor," a term used for any educated person). Some families were *branco de dinheiro*, or "white by money," according to popular gossip (and hardening prejudice) in the South.[153]

That the elite might have slave or Indian antecedents in their genealogical closets made Bahians squirm, but as a rule admission to the elite remained closed, not only to nonwhites but to virtually anyone not connected by blood or marriage to the region's agricultural barons. An attempt by the United States to appoint a black consul to Salvador raised

a "tropical hurricane" of protests.[154] Pedigree was important, even for
whites. Consider the case of Conselheiro João Rodriguez Chaves, named
forty-fourth president of Bahia in 1884, a native of Paraíba and a *bacharel* from Olinda Law School. When he died in 1899, his obituary
noted that he was director of the new Bahian law faculty and that he had
died in "the most absolute and honorable penury," leaving for his survivors an "insignificant pittance." What had counted among his peers
was his *formação*—an ambiguous (but generally understood) notion combining "ancestry" and "upbringing" as primary factors in one's social
acceptability."[155]

Bahia's elites overlooked another characteristic of local life: the penchant among the area's slaves for revolt. Collective slave resistance
reached a peak between 1807 and 1835, intensifying the already con-
flictive relationship between whites and blacks in the Bahian capital,
where whites were outnumbered three to one, and in the Recôncavo, out
of the capital, where they made up an even smaller fraction of the
population. Worsening conditions after a sustained recovery and boom
in the sugar export economy from the late eighteenth century to the
early 1820s cast the region into economic depression, which was coupled
with severe climatic extremes in the hinterlands. After Brazilian independence in 1822, moreover, Portuguese merchants fled Bahia in large
numbers. It thus became extremely difficult for slave families to be
maintained and for free blacks to earn a living.[156] Racial tensions were
the inevitable result.

The most sizable mutiny, in 1835, was carried out by literate Islamic
Nagôs, most of whom lived in the basements of their masters' city residences. Following this rebellion, manumitted blacks were deported
wholesale to Africa, and those who remained were no longer permitted
to rent houses. Not only did officials outlaw the Muslim religion, but
they declared that African-born blacks—which defined most slaves in
Bahia—"must never be considered Brazilian citizens and enjoy the guarantees offered by the constitution."[157] As economic conditions continued to deteriorate, race relations in the capital city as well as in the
Recôncavo remained tense, even after abolition.

It is difficult to enumerate Bahia's overall population at the time of
Canudos because Brazil's 1890 census was flawed, distorted by virtually
every state government to assure a better share of congressional reap-
portionment. The practice was old. Ever since the early days of the
empire, administrators had been required to submit detailed annual
reports to their superiors, who in turn incorporated this information
into their own reports, up to the level of provincial president [governor];
as a matter of course, then, officials at all levels doctored statistics or
fabricated them to show anything from declining crime in their juris-

dictions to healthy fiscal balance sheets. The 1872 census, which counted 9,930,478 inhabitants nationwide, is considered to have been more reliable, if incomplete.

The data of Favilla Nunes (as likely accurate as any others) show the province of Bahia in 1888 to have 1,821,083 inhabitants, an aggregate increase of 24 percent over sixteen years. The Brazilian population was booming at an annual growth rate exceeding 2 percent. While Bahia remained the second most populous state after Minas Gerais, its growth was 5 percent *less* than the average for Brazil as a whole between 1872 and the empire's last year.[158] Once the colonial capital and locus of the captaincy's major urban and ecclesiastical center, Bahia by the end of the nineteenth century languished, attracting few internal migrants or foreign settlers. In contrast to southern Brazil, the failure of efforts to recruit European agricultural settlers for Bahia through official schemes contributed to a decline in agricultural development, and it had few other resources to attract immigrants. Thus, as a percentage of the total, Bahia's European-born population dropped by half between 1872 and 1890.[159]

Although its national importance had greatly diminished by the 1890s, Salvador continued to play an important role in trade, still serving as the main export port for tobacco, hemp, hides, cacao, coconuts, and other products of the coast and Recôncavo. Exports exceeded imports by a small percentage. Goods entering the port were handled by sixty-four import houses, twenty-five of which specialized in cloth shipped from Britain. The export business, in turn, was, in keeping with the national pattern of the late 1800s, dominated by foreigners. Only one of the eleven licensed exporters in Salvador was a Brazilian national; the others were German, English, and American—though most of these businessmen had settled more or less permanently in Brazil, even if they had not applied for citizenship. Nearly a thousand retail stores dotted the city, including bazaars selling used furniture and clothing and seven bookstores. Salvador boasted 123 industrial shops, most of them small with the exception of some sugar refineries, textile mills, and two shoe works. The largest factory, Companhia Progresso Industrial, had eight hundred employees.[160]

Only southern Bahia's cacao region avoided the overall economic decline of the 1890s, chiefly because prices for cacao on the world market rose during this period and planters were able to profit from cheaper labor costs because of an influx of migrants driven from the *sertão* by drought.[161] In the rest of the state, economic growth lagged. Business failures associated with the heated speculation of the Encilhamento slowed exports, halted credit, and drove down wages. Currency devaluation to half of 1892 levels had a deadening effect on investment. The boom caused by the presence of troops and the importation of great quantities of materials and food for the first two military campaigns against Canudos was relatively short-lived. By late 1897 prices for cacao and sugar had dropped to such an extent that transportation costs were higher than the prices offered by brokers. Two by-products were a sharp decline in available housing and an increase beyond ten hours in the urban workday. Probably more than any of their counterparts in the other states, Bahia's elites faced the Canudos conflict with anxiety, trepidation, and a fear that if the rebellion was not put down soon, the area's already diminishing political importance would shrink even further.

Always insecure over the rest of Brazil's whispers that Bahia's leading families had intermixed too much with the *gente de cor* during the heyday of slavery, the Bahians seized the conflict as a way to demonstrate their commitment to continued progress on the European model. State officials paid large sums to publish ornate display books and to mount boastful exhibitions at both national and international expositions, including Paris (1867), Vienna (1873), St. Petersburg (1884), Philadelphia (1896), and Paris (1889).[162] Just as local politicians worried that Conselheiro's magnetism would cost them potential voters as well as rural hands, the republican clique knew that a prolonged impasse would only further erode their position. Both assessments proved to be accurate. Canudos did create economic havoc in the backlands, and once the conflict ended, the incumbent state political party lost power and, a year later, dissolved.[163]

## PATRIMONIALISM AND POLITICS

Throughout most of Latin America, and certainly under the slow-to-change Brazilian empire, the means by which justice was administered revealed a dual system of treatment for citizens, a legacy of the colonial era. Unlike the English practice of debating law in open court, which made it subject to public scrutiny, and unlike the two-tiered system of England and France, which permitted private individuals to file formal charges in court, Latin American procedure found judges sitting behind closed doors, reviewing all evidence in writing, and passing sentence in kind. In short, the judiciary functioned implicitly as a tool for social control, not social justice. Until the republican constitution of 1891 formally disestablished the Roman Catholic religion, the church provided legalistic functions: priests mediated disputes for parishioners, and bishops oversaw public morality, acting, for example, to interdict or censor books and theatrical productions not considered proper. Until 1891, the church also handled the registry of births, deaths, and marriages. Even before mid-century, parish records show that stamps and fees charged for the proper registration of nuptials—in order to meet legal requirements for inheritance of property—cost the equivalent of two months of daily wages, a steep sum indeed for all but the most affluent members of society.[164]

Brazilian reformers had achieved a measure of popular legal participation during the first three decades of independence, but then conservative reaction set in, and the system was closed again. Because most Latin American nations, Brazil included, lacked civil and criminal codes before the late nineteenth century, law enforcement permitted extreme arbitrariness in the treatment of the accused. The application of law involved a curious duality: namely, maintaining "the coexistence of Justinian rigidity with the flexibility of regional and customary practices."[165] Judges, members of the elite and graduates of the prestigious law schools of the nineteenth century, operated strictly within the confines of the clan-based patronage system. Even in the case of appeals, the prevailing tendency was to respect local decisions—regardless of whether these were based more on realities of local power relationships than on abstract justice. Nor was there any public accountability of police or judicial officials.[166] The oligarchy was too inbred for that.

Especially in the Northeast, but throughout Brazil in the closing years of the nineteenth century, state institutions were closely linked to what Linda Lewin terms "indispensable, informal structures maintained by bonds of kinship, political friendship, and personal association."[167] The transition from monarchy to republic was uneventful. A major innovation of the 1891 Constitution was the transfer of responsibility for public education to state *municípios*, but in the Bahian case the change yielded no improvement: there were simply no municipal resources for schools. The state of Bahia maintained only two public schools that provided vocational training: the Escola Normal for teachers and the four-year Mechanical Trade School. Schoolteachers were paid miserably, and in some cases salaries went unpaid for months and even years for lack of funds.[168] The vast majority of poor children received no instruction at all.

Lack of individual freedom was greatest at the local level, owing to a strict, unwritten agreement giving final authority to members of the elite whose business it was to maintain social control. This authority extended not only to the administration of justice, which made judicial and police arbitrariness acceptable, but to economic life as well. Employers received full license to hire and fire, to set wages, and to stamp out trouble among malcontents. This patrimonialism—a legacy of colonial-era privilege—reinforced the notion of common interest and social bonding among the elite. As time passed, administrative functions were increasingly taken over by the growing bureaucracy, but traditional clientelism survived, having burrowed deeply into the system. The population remained divided into two groups: the "traditional classes," as the elite was frequently called, and the *povo*, a term for "common people" but, especially in the Brazilian Northeast, connoting racial miscegenation and untrustworthiness. Both the judicial system and the marketplace were governed by a tacit understanding that the common people had to be kept in line for their own good. Political differences reflected not genuine disputes over ideology or social outlook but rivalries between factions of the elite jockeying for hegemony. The system applied differing kinds of justice. All members of the elite saw the *povo* in the same way: at best, they were simple and docile, like children; at worst, they were unstable and superstitious, and potentially dangerous. Although there was much infighting within the elite—often bitter and even violent—individuals were ostracized only if they contravened accepted social behavior. Political labels during the nineteenth century in Brazil were mostly window dressing for clan-based interests. The cliché "For friends, anything; for enemies, the law" summed up the way society functioned.

Regional variations did exist.[169] For Bahia as well as Pernambuco, its rival to the north, each passing decade during the nineteenth century saw a waning of power and influence, owing to the slow but steady shift of hegemony to the provinces of the Center-South, especially Rio de Janeiro, Minas Gerais, and, in the closing years of the century, São Paulo and Rio Grande do Sul. By 1890, Bahia had slipped to second-rank influence; it was still Brazil's second most populous state, however, and so its legislative *bancada* was large, if no longer centrally powerful.[170] Even Rui Barbosa, Bahia's great contribution to the political world of the early republic, did practically nothing for his home state; nor did he seem to care about its drift.

Many factors contributed to the decline of the region's fortunes. The modernization of sugar cane production redistributed power from the traditional landowning class to the smaller numbers of agro-industrialists who managed to secure foreign loans to build mechanized refining mills. The southern states, meanwhile, buoyed by the growing international demand for coffee, found themselves much more able to secure foreign loans. In the Northeast, foreign capital went mainly to improving transportation and shipping facilities to aid exports. Few improvements accompanied the expansion of railroad track, in contrast to the South, where more dynamic provincial (and state) governments brought in large numbers of foreign immigrants and, in many cases, gave them plots of land for cultivation.[171]

In southern Brazil, although the hinterland remained impoverished and even the subsidized immigrants struggled against an exploitative system of tenancy, variety in economic development gradually brought some measure of prosperity. From Bahia north, stagnation led to decline. The republic's federalism rewarded the more dynamic states and relegated the rest to the status of near pariahs. Political arrangements remained ossified; in fact, stable civilian government on the national level was achieved at the turn of the century only at the cost of restoring, in the Northeast, the old hegemony of *coronéis* and clan oligarchies.

By the end of the empire, the Northeast seemed to be dozing as the South flourished. Still, the traditional elites remained passive, and their malaise drove out individuals with the most initiative and creativity. By the 1890s, the leading southern states were spending more on education and public improvements than Bahia and Pernambuco were allocating to their entire annual budgets combined. The smaller northeastern states—Sergipe, Alagoas, Paraíba, Rio Grande do Norte—fared even worse under the federation. On the one hand, then, the region was being buffeted by forces for change: abolition and its aftermath; demographic pressures; and efforts by the state bureaucracy to penetrate rural zones to collect taxes, recruit soldiers, and control elections. On the other hand, the near bankruptcy of the weakest states tied the hands of politicians fiscally and made them more vulnerable to pressures from traditional interests, even if they were neither progressive nor dedicated to the general welfare. A vicious cycle of state penury coupled with in-fighting for reduced spoils at the local level characterized the political system as the 1890s ended.

## DA CUNHA'S REPORTING

In Brazil commentators have tended to give currency to the *visão do litoral* without reading *Os sertões* carefully or attempting to see it in the light of the attitudes and fears of its day.[172] The book laments the tragedy of the Canudos conflict, but it also eulogizes the strength and determination of the Canudenses and their fellow backlanders. More than any other writer probing the causes of conflict in Brazilian life, da Cunha profoundly affected how Brazilians came to wrestle with the question of the nation's destiny. His characterization of the *jagunço* as a primitive "bronzed titan," a stubborn obstacle to the littoral cities' quest to imitate the grandeur and sophistication of Europe, shocked readers of both his dispatches from the front and *Os sertões*, forcing them to the depressing realization that what the elites had elected to ignore—the real condition of the mass of the nation's population—posed a latent threat to the nation's headlong rush to superficial modernity.

Da Cunha's reporting was much more than a gathering of *petits faits vrais*. Like Zola, who, before writing his novel *Germinal*, descended into the mines at Anzin in 1884 to see for himself the terrible conditions of coal miners' lives,[173] da Cunha internalized his subject to such a degree that he remained tormented for the rest of his unhappy life. But whereas in France Hugo and other socially conscious critics achieved some measure of political influence, da Cunha's leverage was neutralized by his popular lionization, by his own unhappy end, and by the failure of Brazilian society to attack any of the terrible circumstances he exposed. Still, the legacy of the backland tragedy persisted even after public fascination with it had subsided.

In his view of the backlanders, da Cunha drew on the notion of progress adopted in both Europe and North America in the second part of the nineteenth century.[174] Sensitive to the suffering he saw during the final military assaults on Canudos and to the brutality exhibited on both sides, da Cunha reflected in his account his dualist view of Brazilian society as irrevocably divided between the archaic primitivism of the backlands and the progressive culture of the coastal cities. This view of Canudos frightened coastal Brazilians, who knew, deep down, that the material progress of the capital cities and the façade of civic modernity symbolized by the new republican form of government were more show than substance. Ambivalence tormented him: while he deeply respected the perseverance of the rural peasants, he also accepted the prevailing belief that they were racially inferior. Influenced by the appeal of Comtean positivism to science and its loathing of superstition and backwardness, he believed that the republic was threatened by Conselheiro's stubborn resistance to the new order, embracing as it did nostalgia for the empire. Dismayed by military factionalism and monarchist plots after the republic's birth, internecine jockeying among the states, and severe economic depression in the early 1890s, da Cunha and others of like mind thus came to see Canudos as a challenge to the new civilian government, a threat, even, to the nation itself.

His epic narrative was painstakingly written and rewritten in the five years following the destruction of Canudos. On the one hand, it was a political statement of anger and revolt. On the other, it was a personal declaration, written at a crisis point in the author's career, a means, perhaps, for the failed military officer to purge the upheaval he had witnessed from his mind. In his writing and research he was aided by others, including the engineer and regional historian Teodoro Sampaio and academicians Francisco Escobar and Lúcio de Mendonça. Strangely, da Cunha had trouble finding a publisher for his long and angry narrative, written, as Joaquim Nabuco put it, "with a stiletto."[175] Yet within a year following the appearance of *Os sertões*, Euclydes da Cunha, the soul-searching critic of the republic's Vendée, was voted into both the Instituto Histórico e Geográfico Brasileiro (the Brazilian Historical and Geographical Institute, a stronghold of traditionalism founded by Emperor Dom Pedro II) and the august, self-important Brazilian Academy of Letters. After some brief carping, critics rushed to lionize the military engineer and amateur historian who acknowledged that he had been waiting with a "schoolboy's" fear for approval.[176]

## REAPPRAISAL AND PURPOSE

Several new emphases emerge from a reappraisal of the historical record.[177] Although Brazilian society accepted the interpretation of Conselheiro-as-devil, and of Canudos as a fearsome threat, grounds for doing so were few. In twenty years of wandering through the northeastern backlands, up until the destruction of Canudos itself, Antônio Conselheiro exercised the role of a dedicated lay missionary who counseled against civic and religious disobedience. He had intense feelings about social justice and personally opposed slavery. His followers were not aberrant primitives mesmerized by religious superstition, as chroniclers insisted, but a heterogeneous community whose members included emancipated slaves (*crioulos*), Indian-Caucasian *mamelucos*, rural sharecroppers, people from small towns, and a few linked by family ties to leading elite networks on the coast.

Most rural backlanders lived at the subsistence level, raising garden crops on land with access to water owned by others. Some performed farm labor or worked as herders for local landlords. Religion touched nearly every aspect of their lives. Some individuals imposed penitential restrictions on themselves, and many fasted through much of the day. For Conselheiro and his closest followers, Canudos represented an earthly "vale of tears," a transitory passage awaiting the final judgment and the coming of the end of the world. It is perhaps no wonder that Conselheiro's rhetoric, which borrowed heavily from Padre Couto's popular *Missão abreviada para despertar os descuidados, converter os pecadores e sustentar o fructo das missões* (Short missal to awake the careless, convert the sinners, and sustain the work of the missions)[178] and contained numerous apocalyptic references, disturbed outsiders seeking evidence of more orthodox religious practices in the community.

Among Canudenses were a thousand or so backland men who had been *vaqueiros*; some may have been army or police deserters as well, and some had been fugitive slaves or bondsmen before emancipation. Da Cunha and others gave them the pejorative collective name *jagunços*, meaning both "a race of mestizos . . . virile and adventurous" and "incoherent, uneven, and turbulent [in] character."[179] The term delved into the national psyche and for years came to be used for backlanders of any vocation—though even in Canudos only a small number of people (Conselheiro's bodyguards and some of his fighters) were true *jagunços*. During the military conflict, the name was used generically for Conselheiro's fighters: tenacious rural ruffians quick to become violent. It could also be used sympathetically; the children in Conselheiro's settlement were dubbed *jaguncinhos* (little *jagunços*), as if they had been raised by wolves or Satan-worshippers.

From these ranks Conselheiro drew his fighters, who were invariably skilled with rifles and knives and had an uncannily intimate knowledge of the topography. Although they resembled the *gaúchos* of the southern pampas, the backlanders herded their cattle in great, open spaces and were more at the mercy of the rocky, sun-baked terrain, epizootic cattle infections, alternate flood and drought, and the need constantly to defend themselves against marauding cattle thieves. While da Cunha considered the backland *jagunços* "less theatrically heroic . . . stronger and more dangerous" than their *gaúcho* counterparts on the southern frontier,[180] these differences were likely exaggerated. Both groups of leather-clad cowboys brought a savage resilience to battle, showed little regard for their lives, and were without equal as army cavalrymen and foot soldiers. An important difference that da Cunha did not mention was that the *gaúchos* lived in a more abundant environment and could thrive by hunting wild cattle—though this was changing in Rio Grande do Sul by the late 1890s with the introduction of barbed wire, which facilitated livestock herding. Significantly, da Cunha characterized the entire *sertanejo* population as pastoralists, although most of the population lived from sedentary agriculture or petty commerce.

The men and women who made up Conselheiro's legions were diverse, hailing equally from the rural and urban portions of the region—including the Recôncavo, the towns of Alagoinhas and Esplanada in the *tabuleiro* region near the coast, and *sertão* hamlets several hundred miles distant in western Pernambuco and Paraíba—and representing a broad spectrum of ethnic and economic origins. Rural folk from neighboring towns comprised the majority; although mainly *caboclos*, the residents of Canudos represented a much broader socioethnic spectrum than conventionally believed. Their towns were not indolent; the *sertanejos* were not, as residents of the coast believed, all as miserable as beggars.[181]

Canudos quickly became an irritant, but it hardly posed a real threat to the republic. Until the settlement was attacked by soldiers and earmarked for destruction, it coexisted peacefully with its neighbors. While some twenty-five thousand people flocked to Canudos, hundreds of thousands more in the region did not and showed no inclination to do so. In the end, Canudos was a victim of circumstance: its birth and explosive growth fatally coincided with the opportunity to mount a propaganda campaign depicting a monarchist plot. Following the carnage, jingoism shored up the shaky civilian government and, under the weight of carefully orchestrated patriotism, facilitated consolidation of what became known as the "politics of the governors"—a brokered arrangement that gave the strongest states in the federation unprecedented power—and alliances between state machines and *coronéis*, through which the agro-commercial oligarchy secured unopposed control of rural Brazil.

Nor was Canudos unique as a site of local resistance to authority except in its scale. The monarchy's fall in 1889 was accompanied by an increase in both rural intransigence and urban discord, a situation that unnerved the affluent and politically conscious sector of urban society. The republic was not especially popular among rural landowners either, with the exception of some local elites in the southern states. Disorganization characterized all levels of government, from the *municípios* to the federal capital, and the old two-party system of the empire—which for all its failings had at least run smoothly—lay in shambles. State parties now dominated, but they remained largely divided along traditional lines based on local, clan-based rivalries. Then, too, there were the "eleventh-hour Republicans," old political hands who had finally seen the light and at the last minute had become nominal republican converts as a strategy of political survival.

Most control resided in the hands of the army and the southern veterans of the antimonarchy struggle. For the first time since their movement's formal origin in 1870, these republicans emerged in positions of power, but because they lacked experience they soon became caught in the civilian-military tensions of the early 1890s. Stung by the interstate conflict over tax revenues and other benefits and vulnerable to journalistic bombast, they cringed at revelations of cracks in the already shaky edifice of order, progress, and stability.

Conselheiro acted to establish a refuge in the mountains, defended by bodyguards, only after he and a band of followers were set upon by the Bahian state police in 1893, sent to arrest him after he stirred up anti-republican sentiment at the weekly *feira* at Bom Conselho. While his acts were provocative, they did not constitute an isolated event; similar incidents were recorded in the towns of Lençóes, Lavras Diamantinhas, and Jequié, and elsewhere mobs attacked and looted entire backland villages—something Conselheiro's followers never did.

The pretext for the October 1896 order to attack Conselheiro's followers, thus igniting the military conflict that would end in the destruction of Conselheiro's pious city, was, in da Cunha's own word, "trifling." Conselheiro had ordered, and paid for, a supply of lumber to build a new church from the river town of Juazeiro north of Canudos; when it was not delivered according to contract, the local magistrate, who years before had clashed with Conselheiro's followers in another town, Bom

Conselho, requested protection from the governor in case the Canudenses unleashed their anger.

The subsequent clash at Uauá, in which Conselheiro's men unexpectedly prevailed, disturbed members of the elite and heightened discussion of the danger posed by the sect. As the months passed, reports began filtering out of the region about the settlement's phenomenal growth, its seemingly bizarre religious practices, and its antirepublicanism. For the construction of Canudos's second church, one onlooker reported, men and women *conselheiristas* hauled stone, wood, and other construction materials a distance of twenty-two miles in a cart loaned by a local landowner. Conselheiro had evidently turned down the use of oxen on the grounds that the suffering demanded of his followers in pulling the wagon would test their religious faith.[182] Newspapermen, foreign priests, some (not all) members of the elite, some (not all) local vicars, and numerous contemporary chroniclers and eyewitnesses called the *conselheiristas* "madmen, criminals, ex-slaves, and, most of all, religious fanatics." This was the view, reinforced by da Cunha's haunting and brilliant narrative, that Brazilians came to embrace in order to rationalize the stunning brutality of 1896–97 when the settlement was crushed.

Maciel/Conselheiro was a product of his environment and his times. He followed in the footsteps of others. Although more successful in his itinerant mission than others were in theirs, he emphatically did not exploit the fact that some considered him a saint or the Bom Jesus. His sermons frequently borrowed apocalyptic themes from standard liturgical sources, notably the *Missão abreviada*. He fulminated against the republic because of its adoption of civil marriage, and at one point he publicly witnessed (and possibly instigated) the burning of republican tax notices. Still, this defiant act was part of a statewide political campaign of opposition; he was but one of many who performed identical acts. And, though a monarchist, Conselheiro withheld approval of the monarchy when in the 1870s it acted aggressively to weaken the power of outspoken bishops during the so-called Religious Question crisis.

Canudos was remote but never isolated, a fact that allowed it to survive economically. Conselheiro not only required that the Canudenses do hard agricultural work, but he also contracted out day laborers to neighboring ranches. He relied on resources donated by admirers and sent out his followers to ask for contributions of money and materials, chiefly for use on the new church. But virtually none of these facts was acknowledged by the settlement's enemies, who relentlessly hammered away at what they called the fanaticism of Conselheiro and his followers.

The attempt of Canudenses to retreat to a sanctuary beyond the menacing, intruding arm of modernizing Brazil generated tangible fears about the ability of the republic to survive, yet Canudos was only one of many "disturbances" and mass uprisings in Brazilian history. The 1893–97 conflict, seen through this prism, was part of a longstanding confrontation between rural Brazilians and the increasingly powerful state. Canudos confirmed the elite's underlying, if unspoken, dread that the backwardness of the rural population would doom all attempts to rebuild Brazil on a European model. It also revealed the fragility of the First Republic and the brutal lengths to which its officials would go to crush discord. Canudos left an indelible legacy to Brazil, but a contrary one. A symbol of the clash between urban rationality and rural "backwardness," the Canudos movement has frequently been recalled as a war against not just progress but the ideological cement holding together the republic.

For decades afterward, many Brazilians still considered the Canudos tragedy to have been a rebellion of dangerous fanatics, just as most contemporaries did. Warnings of evil pervaded virtually every written record, including the "orders of the day" of state and federal military contingents, in which officers made sure their men would not forget that they were combatting the forces of the devil.[183] The fact that Canudos residents gladly accepted Spartan rules as their way to serve God and that the community functioned smoothly, offering succor to the faithful in ways never before available, is ignored. Scholars who have classified movements of protest and resistance, too, have tended to accept the premise of the 1890s *visão do litoral* that Canudos represented a fanatical movement motivated by millenarian ideology. In some measure, of course, Canudos did constitute "a primitive, barbarian social collectivity," at least in the sense that coastal Brazilians defined "barbarian" and "primitive." Yet many of the stories told about Canudos were accepted without verification, such as the allegation that newcomers turned over some 90 percent of what they brought with them. Further, in that change came to only those backlanders who migrated to find better opportunities, the 1893–96 flight to Canudos may be seen not as a retreat to a primitive, fanatical utopia but as a desperate, yet eminently practical, collective decision to escape intolerable conditions. In that case, the formation of Canudos as a settlement should be seen as a precursor to the great migratory waves that occurred decades later, and not as a retrogressive withdrawal from coastal-inspired progress, as it has been depicted.

The purpose of this study is to reexamine the context of Conselheiro's mud-hut Jerusalem and to reevaluate the validity of labeling Canudos as a fearsome threat. The next chapters focus on the Canudos region, Conselheiro's new Jerusalem, and that community's response to the exogenous threat to its existence.[184]

# TWO

# The Backlands

Vast in territorial breadth although only the sixth largest Brazilian state, Bahia is almost four times the size of Portugal, and larger than the combined land areas of Denmark, Belgium, Holland, Switzerland, Portugal, Romania, and Greece. Its coastline is exceeded in length only by that of the enormous state of Pará. In the 1890s, swift coastal vessels took from sixty-four to seventy hours to reach the nation's capital, Rio de Janeiro. Inland travel was even more arduous. The only way to get to the coast from any point beyond the *tabuleiro* region was on horseback; in the *sertão*, travelers had to trek to the winding São Francisco River, where they then caught boats to the mouth of the river beyond Penedo in Alagoas, halfway between Maceió and Aracajú, for transfer to coastal packets (Maps 1 and 2).[1]

On the coast, sugar plantations in the northern part of the state and cacao plantations south of the capital lent a flavor of abundance to the towns that served as trading and distribution centers. In the backlands, by contrast, villages were scanty and unimpressive, despite some growth resulting from expanded technology (the telegraph, railroads) and bureaucracy (tax collectors, schools, agencies of state banks). Mail and telegraph service nominally reached every *vila* (small town) in the state, although government reports noted that the backland postal service was entirely untrustworthy: mail sacks were frequently stolen and post offices looted.[2]

Life in the plantation zone had changed little since colonial times. The landed aristocracy and their families occupied the top of the hierarchical ladder; most of the rest of the population, whether recently emancipated from slavery or long free, were at the bottom, with a small layer of artisans, shopkeepers, and petty officials in the middle, living mostly in

Map 1. Brazil in 1893.

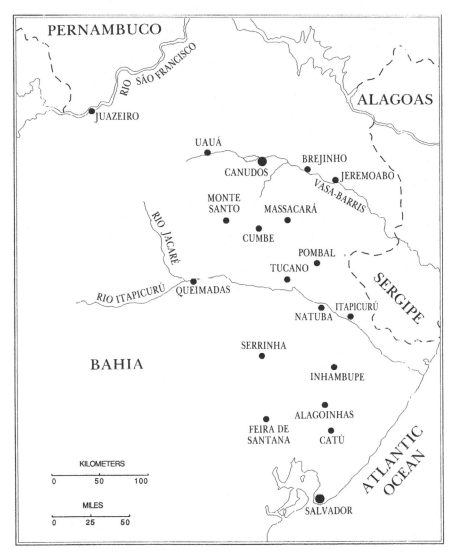

PERNAMBUCO

RIO SÃO FRANCISCO

JUAZEIRO

ALAGOAS

UAUÁ

BREJINHO

CANUDOS

JEREMOABO

VASA-BARRIS

MONTE
SANTO

MASSACARÁ

RIO JACARÉ

CUMBE

POMBAL

TUCANO

SERGIPE

RIO ITAPICURÚ

QUEIMADAS

NATUBA

ITAPICURÚ

SERRINHA

BAHIA

INHAMBUPE

ALAGOINHAS

FEIRA DE
SANTANA

CATÚ

ATLANTIC
OCEAN

KILOMETERS

0        50        100

MILES

0     25     50

SALVADOR

Map 2. Canudos Region, 1893–97.

the small towns dotting the countryside. The vast majority of the population never attended school and were officially classified as illiterate.
More than anywhere else in Bahia, the residents of this region tended to
be either black or *mulato*. Officials, predisposed to consider these populations as troublesome, devoted little effort to improving conditions.

Settlement of the interior had followed the search for wealth. Portuguese military excursions from Olinda and Salvador, initially accompanying missionaries seeking to situate permanent missions across the Indian frontier, but also in pursuit of silver and gold, explored the interior
of Bahia, following the Jequitinhonha, Paraguassú, Itapicurú, and Real
rivers inland from the Atlantic slope.[3] By land, *bandeirantes de gado*
(herdsmen adventurers) laid down cattle trails, which crisscrossed the
lands of the high *sertão* centuries later, providing access to the site of
Conselheiro's settlement. Indian labor had been sought ever since Governor Mem de Sá in the late sixteenth century defeated the tribes near
the Recôncavo and cleared the land for sugar cultivation. Slavers, including brutal *bandeirantes* from São Paulo contracted by Bahian governors, launched excursions inland for new Indian labor, and gradually
the frontier moved westward beyond the *tabuleiros* into the backlands.[4]
The earliest mission villages, the antecedents of later rural towns and
population centers, maintained armed defenses against attacks from
hostile Indian raiders. Cattle always accompanied conquest, since they
were a mobile food supply, and herds became the main source of commercial income in the hinterland. Unlike cultivated farming, cattle raising necessitated a relatively small labor supply, a fact that contributed to
the region's general abundance of available workers despite its sparse
population.

Once the resistance of the indigenous Tupis was broken, commercial
ranches spread to the interior, but the early efforts to pacify Indians
generally failed. Many tribes died out; others fled. Indeed, most of
the tribes in the region perished within decades: the Amoipiras, Tocós,
Sapoiás, Paiaias, Moritises, Sequakirinhens, Borcas, Separenhenupãs,
Mongurus, Boimés, Caimbés, coastal Kiriris, inland Kariris—all lumped
together by the Portuguese as *tapuias*, the Tupi word for savages. Some
Indians were coerced into the service of cattle barons, who treated them
so badly that mission priests fought a constant battle against the local
landowners. Franciscans, Jesuits, and hooded French (and later Italian)
Capuchins all established missions to protect those Indians who voluntarily moved in to the religious communities.[5] Missionaries employing
*caboclo* guides swept the middle and lower São Francisco River valley,
first dispersing the indigenous population across a swath of land that
extended as far away as the Cabrobó region of the captaincy of Pernambuco, then rounding them up to live in mission *aldeias* (native settle-

ments). Some villages, like the French Capuchin Missão de Roldas, established in 1671 for Tuxá peoples, were located in the backland *caatinga*, scrub that was regularly burned by ranchers to provide pasturage.[6] By 1700 virtually no Brazilindians other than those in missions remained in the Bahian hinterland.

Jesuits organized their *aldeiamentos* along the same lines as their villages in Paraguay. Each was run by two priests, who provided instruction in catechism as well as in cultivation techniques and domestic housekeeping, in an effort to ease the transition from seminomadic life to sedentary agriculture. Jesuit missions were established along the coast in the 1550s and extended into the hinterland in subsequent decades. One of the first *aldeias* was Nossa Senhora da Conceição de Natuba (1662; modern Souré). While most of the older residents lived there grudgingly and refused to learn the catechism, the younger males did study the Catholic religion. (Girls apparently were not offered instruction.) All were baptized and, in the words of a visiting priest, "prepared for salvation."[7] A second Jesuit mission in Massacará thrived until the order's expulsion from Brazil in 1759, part of the marquis of Pombal's effort to restore the hegemony of the crown. Capuchins then took over the missionization program, expanding their ministrations to the larger population.[8] Some native people drifted away, but a few communities down to the late nineteenth century and beyond kept the indigenous culture distinctly alive, as in the case of the annual *sábado dos caboclos*, when priests permitted Indians to carry out their own rituals in the church and to ring the chapel bells "in aboriginal rhythms."[9]

Further *entradas* (forays into the interior) during the late seventeenth century established Capuchin missions in Itapicurú and in Jeremoabo. Most of the new villages were on land originally ceded by crown grant to the first Garcia d'Ávila, the founder of the Casa da Torre, a tower-shaped fortified house on Tatuapera Bay thirteen leagues north of Salvador. More interested in raising cattle than in prospecting for minerals, the Garcia d'Ávila family acquired title to much of the Bahian, Pernambucan, and Piauian *sertão*, seeking land grants in distant Ceará as well. By the early eighteenth century they were the largest landowning family in Brazil, holding title to more than 340 square leagues on the banks of the São Francisco and its tributaries.[10]

Once the land was theirs, the Garcia d'Ávila clan, the colonial antecedents of the landowners of the Canudos region, clashed with the church, accusing the missionary priests of enslaving their Indian charges. In 1669, the ranchers allied with the Garcia d'Ávilas and launched armed attacks against the missions, destroying churches and seeking to expel resident Jesuits and, along the São Francisco, French Capuchins. The conflict subsided, but in the following decade, Leonor Pereira Marinho, the widow of Francisco Dias Garcia d'Ávila and now the head of the clan, ordered renewed military attacks on the Jesuit communities.

The Portuguese crown did little to resolve the situation, although, seeking to ensure continued mission revenues, it did issue a 1700 decree granting one square league to each mission for sustaining the native population. Measured in eight directions, this land grant formed an octagon with a total area of 12,230 hectares. Yet landowners complained bitterly that the priests were simply forming rival *fazendas* for their own profit. Certainly, the missionaries did consider the Indians lazy, and they sought to teach discipline and the work ethic; the charge that the priests were enslaving the Indians may even have been effectively true. In any case, the *fazendeiros* simply took matters into their own hands and rounded up mission Indians to work their cattle drives.[11] No one argued publicly that Indians should not be forced to work. After 1690, the gold rush in Minas further destabilized the mission villages, which became subject to frequent raids for draft labor.

Many of the cattle drives ended up in Jeremoabo, established as a military district in 1697 to put down tribal uprisings. The missionary villages of the Bahian backlands—Jeremoabo, Inhambupe, Natuba (Souré), Pajehú, Nossa Senhora de Pilar, and a host of others bordering the future site of Canudos to the north[12]—enjoyed close ties with the other northeastern provinces. Subsequent decades saw a flurry of new activity owing to the gold rush: the backlands of the high *sertão* saw an influx of adventurers, immigrants, cattle producers, merchants, and slaves. The *sertão* filled with ranches, though population density remained low. The total of religious missions diminished in proportion to the growing numbers of new settlers; by 1758, only thirty-five remained functioning.

Even fifty years earlier, Jeremoabo was inhabited by a racially mixed population, whose antecedents included runaway slaves and fugitive Indians (*canhemboras*). In 1702, the district was subdued at the request of the vicar of Itapicurú by a regiment of troops maintained privately by Garcia d'Ávila interests.[13] Some 3,070 pagan souls were baptized in a mass conversion. Such cooperation on the part of the church and secular authorities was not always the rule, of course. Usually, the decades-old conflict between missionaries and landowners continued. Bad feelings increased even more after the Jesuit expulsion, when Italian Capuchins and Franciscans wrestled over control. Mission priests angrily complained of continued abuses by landowners. A case in point was Domingos Sertão, whose vast holding, Sobrado, contained more than fifty cattle ranches at the convergence of the northern provinces of Ceará, Piauí, Pernambuco, and Bahia. He used catechized Indians to hunt and subdue so-called *Índios de curso* (wandering Indians), considered prone to bad behavior because they were "undomesticated." Sometimes entire tribes were forced by aggressive landowners into serfdom.[14]

Missionaries whose purpose it was to learn Indian languages in order to make catechism instruction more effective were precursors, in a way, of the later itinerant backland religious travelers. A former professor and vice-rector of the Olinda (Pernambuco) Seminary, Padre João de Barros, took a permanent leave and journeyed through the backlands during the late 1690s, studying Indian speech and translating religious texts. But Pombal's decrees, as we have seen, doomed the Jesuit missions.

Civil administrative divisions now replaced the parish structures as the centers of urban growth. *Vilas* were established to provide judicial functions over wide areas, overlapping with *freguesias*, religious districts counted in numbers of "souls" (excluding children under the age of seven, pagans, and nonbaptized slaves). In the eighteenth century, at the height of the São Francisco region's importance as supplier to the mining regions, the backland population was larger than during the next century. Construction funds for churches came from a combination of sources, mostly from the archdiocese in Salvador, as well as from popular subscription. Large sums of money, however, did not guarantee quality work. The new Jeremoabo church, near collapse, had to be abandoned less than fifty years after it was consecrated; thereafter, masses were celebrated in an adjacent shed.

Jeremoabo's sixth vicar, José de Souza Pereira, reported in 1754 that only five of the parish's permanent adult residents were "white"; the rest were *pardos* (dark mulattoes), mestizos, Indians, and blacks, the last two groups being legally exempt from parochial jurisdiction. All buildings but the vicarage and one other house in the *freguesia* (religious district) had straw roofs. Jeremoabo, seventy leagues in length, contained only 152 *fazendas* and *sítios* (small farmsteads), most with two or three personal slaves; rarely did a *fazenda* contain more than twenty people. The great majority of the farm plots were seasonally dry; they lacked wells, or even watering holes for the animals, and rainwater was collected in pots. The parish's dozen large *fazendas*, in contrast, bordered on one or another of the locale's small rivers—the Jeremoabo, the Vasa-Barris, and Massacará—and so were privileged in having a constant source of water. Nevertheless, stretches of desolate and mostly arid land separated each *fazenda* and *sítio*. About three thousand men, women, and children lived within the borders of the 35,000-square-mile parish. With the exception of twelve *fazendas* owned outright, everyone in Jeremoabo lived as *foreiros* (tenant renters) or squatters on Casa da Torre land.

Vicar Souza Pereira expressed a dismal opinion of the parish and of his flock. His account was very reminiscent of da Cunha's observations nearly two hundred years later. Squatters live in "moral indolence," he wrote; except for the dozen landowners, women, and slaves, the rest were "lazy." Anarchy prevailed: many of the men were fugitives and troublemakers, "bandits within their own houses." They committed "incredible" misdeeds against upright folk. "Every day sees injuries, hateful acts, and evil deeds. Jeremoabo has the worst reputation of any *freguesia* in Brazil. Just the mention of its name conjures up a sense of fear. The locals deny both the parish and the nation; those who have to pass through the region do so with great reluctance, as if they are entering a region of enemies likely to attack them and their cattle and horses."[15]

Exaggeration or no, the vicar's opinions seemed borne out by the history of his predecessors. The first parish priest lasted only one month before he fled; the second never left his house without armed slaves at his side. The third, fourth, and fifth departed hastily. Only the sixth, Souza Pereira, stayed longer, but he "suffered" and was "ignored by the population." On the last night of Christmas, he wrote, twenty armed men invaded the church during mass and shouted insults at the priest, who had dared issue a list of residents who did not take confession during the previous year. There was an economic reason behind the bad relations between the priest and his congregation: government subsidies had been curtailed, and priests were required to impose a levy on persons taking sacraments.[16]

The achievement of Brazilian independence seventy years later brought little change to the high backlands, although inheritance laws and the lack of incentives to maintain enormous holdings led gradually to a more diverse pattern of property ownership. Most land in the Bahian *sertão* remained firmly in the hands of the heirs of the Garcia d'Ávila clan. Imperial policy made more land available for purchase during the nineteenth century, mostly in the intermediate *tabuleiros* and in the *sertão*. But backland water rights were tenaciously guarded by the traditional landowners. In any case land was rarely surveyed. The chief basis for land claims resided in possession, which could change hastily over time.

The precarious legal status of landholding and the common practice of adjudication by force exacerbated conflicts among landowners. Rivalries and competing claims contributed, in turn, to political cleavages pitting one set of claimants against another. To preserve their legal rights to the land and to hinder unwanted squatters, owners rented out portions or allowed relatives or clients long-term use. While *rendeiros* (sharecroppers) were granted notarized deeds defining their rights to the land, *moradores* (renters) lived under more precarious informal agreements. The sharecroppers often had closer personal ties to the owners than the renters, but were vulnerable to the weaknesses of the patron-client system and could be turned out without recourse if political or economic circumstances abruptly changed. Lowest on the scale were the day laborers (*jornaleiros*), who could find work only when the landowners needed extra help and who had no means to grow even subsistence crops.[17] Some lived under conditions worse than slaves: bondsmen, being capital assets for their owners, were more valuable when young and healthy.

General economic stagnation and a consistently low standard of living in the *sertão* meant that few backland families were well off. Most lived harsh lives, devoid of luxury, deficient in diet. Even large landowners were not especially comfortable. For people without land, access to political influence or legal rights to use another's land did not significantly improve the quality of life. In this sense, backland life differed little from rural life in the Transvaal, or Russia, or Mediterranean Europe—in short, in much of the precapitalist world.

The basic social and economic unit in the *sertão* was the same as in most rural sites worldwide in the late nineteenth century—"a rural household of (essentially) subsistence producers bound by intimate ties of kinship."[18] Indeed, however hard life might be, backlanders always found ways to help their own relatives. Nevertheless, life was difficult. Even when armed bandits were kept at bay, rural residents might be victimized by confidence artists and *poseurs* who tricked them out of their meager savings. Policemen were in short supply: in 1870, only 283 rural gendarmes and National Guardsmen patrolled the entire backland region of Bahia, clearly an insufficient number—as landowners fiercely pointed out—given the rampant lawlessness. Officials admitted in the public record that portions of the backlands were in the control of outlaws such as Cecílio Pereira de Carvalho, whose gang invaded towns on horseback and shot residents indiscriminately.[19] Most of the sixty-one backland jails were private houses rented by the authorities, who lamented that criminals could escape from them with ease.[20]

Under the empire, the *município* emerged as the most important administrative unit at the provincial level. Local interests constantly lobbied to create new *municípios*—not merely to reduce large distances for administrative efficiency, but simply to create bureaucratic sinecures for clients and relatives. Also, they made political hegemony easier. For example, Monte Santo (1837), Tucano (1837), Ribeira do Pombal (1837), Santo Antônio da Glória (1840), and Nossa Senhora de Cumbe (1881) were new *municípios* carved out of the original territory of Jeremoabo and its colonial subdivisions. These administrative areas were sparsely settled: indeed, the population of the entire region probably did not exceed ten thousand through the early nineteenth century. Most *muni-cípio* residents lived in hamletlike clusters of mud huts, given the jurid-ical designation of *arraial*.

The population of the *sertão* was transitory, and grew much more slowly than the populations of regions nearer the coast, owing to out-migration from the drought-afflicted hinterlands. Many of these mi-grants were sickly, hungry, or infected with disease. Inoculation pro-grams against smallpox were suspended for long periods for lack of vaccine, even during epidemics.[21] Relief commissions arranged hand-outs of clothing and at times supplies of seed, for planting when the rains returned. Railroad and coastal freight lines shipped emergency supplies of food, mostly dried beef, manioc (cassava), corn, and beans, without charge.[22] Some permanent residents opposed such charity, fear-ing that the region would be inundated by migrants seeking welfare maintenance. But in the end, the aid was never enough anyway.

Bahia's backlands remained relatively isolated even after the partial penetration of the railroad. To reach the Vasa-Barris Valley, the traveler would pass through the fertile Recôncavo, the site of Brazil's earliest sugar cane plantations, prized for its rich *massapê* soil. Life in the Recôncavo was comfortable for those who owned land: the region was dotted with large and small farms, most worked by slaves. An 1865 photograph by Camillo Vedani shows a newly constructed farmhouse, part of a Recôncavo *fazenda*, surrounded by a wooden picket fence (Fig. 4). The *fazendeiro* poses with a book as his wife and child sit in their finery. The house is whitewashed and has a tiled roof; its windows are fitted with glass. The tree-shaded property looks more like a rural *sítio* a century later than a working agricultural property at the height of the empire.

In the backlands, in contrast, although the landowners and regional bosses enjoyed the same near-absolute power over the local population as their plantation counterparts, the rich and powerful did not live sig-nificantly better in terms of material comfort than those they dominated. In places controlled by absentee landowners, where virtually all resi-dents shared a kind of generalized poverty, society was rudimentarily structured along vaguely egalitarian lines. Geographic isolation ren-dered this effect even more striking.[23]

## THE CANUDOS REGION AND ITS CULTURE

Brazilians, it is safe to say, knew next to nothing about the bleak region of the Vasa-Barris and Itapicurú river valleys in northern Bahia before the first newspaper notices about Antônio Conselheiro began to appear in the late 1870s. The Canudos "war" of 1896–97 reversed this neglect,

1. Recôncavo *fazenda*, ca. 1865. Photograph by Camillo Vedani. Courtesy Gilberto Ferrez.

of course, and the backlands were suddenly stripped bare before national scrutiny. More than any of the reporters who tapped in their stories via telegraph, Euclydes da Cunha's gift for vivid descriptions—of landscapes as well as of men—branded the *sertão* on the nation's consciousness. Although his cause-and-effect reasoning and his premises about the influence of harsh conditions on what he believed to be inherent genetic inferiorities in the backland population are no longer fashionable, the fact that he was a trained scientist well read in history and the new social science disciplines makes his descriptions of the region come alive.

Canudos lay within the Grão Mogul Range, a convulsive, cordillera-like upland region characterized by granite spurs, hillocks, valleys, canyons, depressions, and other "sculptural effects." The Bahian backlands in which Antônio Conselheiro oversaw the growth of his refuge were mountainous, harsh, and, to visitors from the coast, primitive, but the area was not and never had been entirely isolated. Known during colonial days as the "high," the "Bahian," or the "San Franciscan" *sertão*, the territory was populated by Europeans in the early sixteenth century. Indeed, their cattle drives and raids to capture Indian slaves in the remote interior of the Northeast were arguably as important historically as those of the more widely known *bandeiras* (groups of adventurers) who invaded the São Paulo hinterland in the Center-South. As in the São Paulo region, every aspect of the early development of the Northeast during the first two centuries of colonization was directly connected to "the expropriation, exploitation, and destruction of indigenous populations."[24]

On Map 2, Canudos seems relatively close to both the coast and the navigable São Francisco River to the north. But nineteenth-century travelers were limited to trekking on foot or horseback, an arduous journey from any established population center. Even today, on the terrible unpaved and rutted backland roads, the trip to the Canudos region from Salvador takes eleven hours, longer during the brief rainy season.

Yet the distance was not onerous, even a century ago. In the 1880s, railroad construction in the province of Bahia, financed by imperial bonds sold abroad, extended the Estrada de Ferro São Francisco (São Francisco Railroad) from Salvador through the coastal region to Serrinha via Alagoinhas, covering more than half the distance to Canudos and passing through *municípios* regularly visited by Conselheiro. By 1888, a secondary line reached Timbó, beyond Entre Rios, almost at the Sergipe border. When Conselheiro preached in tiny Saco, a hamlet tucked away between Timbó and Vila do Conde (modern Altamira), two thousand men and women, mostly blacks, assembled in the square; while they may not have been able to afford the train fare, many likely found Saco by following the tracks.[25]

Consider the 1861 photograph shown in Figure 5, by the Englishman Benjamin R. Mulock, who operated a studio in Salvador.[26] The image shows the village of Santana do Catú, one of the first places in the *tabuleiro* region to be reached by the railroad. Taken as publicity for the rail company's London office, the photograph depicts the effect of sudden prosperity. Structures on both sides of what would eventually be the main street are under construction, and several are of two stories, something unheard of in the backlands before that time. Cattle still graze where they always had before the train arrived; now, though, things would change in this town, less than forty miles from Salvador, which until the coming of the railroad had been wild and inaccessible.

Traveling beyond, in the region of the Paraguassú River, one entered a transitional landscape dotted by small lakes and rising abruptly to a low, steep-edged plateau, an expanse known in Bahia as the *tabuleiro* region, also known as the "coastal *praia*."[27] Here, rainfall is fairly regular during the early months of the year. Some places, like Monte Santo and Alagoinhas, though culturally and by tradition backlands, were actually part of the *praia-tabuleiro* zone and not subject to severe drought.

5. Santana do Catú, 1861. Photograph by Benjamin R. Mulock. Courtesy Gilberto Ferrez.

When the *sertão* actually begins, after the town of Euclides da Cunha (formerly Cumbe, renamed for the author after his death), the change is abrupt. Mud, if there has been rain, suddenly becomes dust, and the air shimmers in the low humidity. The terrain becomes even more rocky and mountainous. It has been noted that the word *sertão* comes from the old Portuguese term for the region, *desertão*, an immense desert, although it is not a desert at all. Canudos and its surrounding region, in fact, were well served by seasonal rivers and so in most years were far more habitable than reaches of the *sertão* further north and west in Ceará, Rio Grande do Norte, and Pernambuco. There, productivity was limited to lethargic livestock raising and impoverished dirt farming sunk, as Richard M. Morse puts it, in "atony."[28]

For Conselheiro's followers who settled there, Canudos's physical location was fortunate. The high backlands were bounded by rivers: the powerful São Francisco, forming a semicircle to one side; the sinuous Itapicurú on the other; and, parallel to the others, also dropping to the coast prodigiously, the Vasa-Barris, called the Irapiranga by the Tapuias. The arrival of heavy rains during a few months of the year and the permeable and easily dissected soil created a "chaotic drainage system" that contributed to the land's wild appearance. In *Os sertões* da

Cunha, a geologist as well as an engineer, speaks of the "martyrdom of the earth":

> There is the extreme dryness of the air, which in summertime, through nocturnal radiation, leads to the instantaneous loss of absorbed heat by rocks exposed to the sun's rays, subjecting them to a sudden rise and fall of temperature; whence a play of dilations and contractions that is disjunctive in effect lays them open along the planes of least resistance. . . . The forces that work upon the earth attack both its inner contexture and its surface, with no letup in the process of demolition, one following the other with unvarying cadence in the course of the only two seasons that the region knows . . . In the crude light of day here in the backlands, these exceedingly rugged hills shed about them a most ardent glow, and they glitter, darkly and dazzlingly.[29]

The starkness of the topography, in fact, led da Cunha to speculate that life in the region had, at some distant point after the American continent emerged from the vast Cretaceous ocean, been "sudden[ly] assaulted and extinguished by the turbulent energies of a cataclysm."[30] Thousands of years later, but still in prehistory, Neolithic tribes lived in the region, making clay pots and formulating a system of lapidary design possibly linked to patterns of artisanship indigenous to other parts of the hemisphere.[31] But points of contact diminished and then vanished entirely, and the backlands assumed its modern quality of seeming loneliness and impenetrability.

Rarely did the population of interior towns exceed a few thousand. Officials stationed inland—usually at the start or end of their careers—tried to imitate the flavor of city life, establishing amateur music and literary societies, sporting clubs, and the like. Most such organizations were merely ceremonial, given to flowery rhetoric and lacking any sustained activities. Churches badly needed repairs; some had been abandoned altogether for lack of resources, the raising of which, under the empire, was the responsibility of the provincial administration.

Visitors described local folk as "docile" and thirsting for evangelical guidance. Eighty to ninety percent of residents could neither read nor write, and virtually no funds were allocated for schools. Taxation on land was either nonexistent or so insignificant as to be useless.[32] Backland populations, even in town centers, were buffeted by continuing struggles over landownership and power, often waged between clans divided for decades or even centuries by blood feuds. Officials were concerned that potentially fertile properties were left unattended by absentee landowners while large numbers of rural inhabitants remained landless. The frequent droughts in the region were considered the cause for the "habitual laziness" of residents, especially—warned Bahia's chief executive official in 1870—in the region around Inhambupe, Itapicurú, Pombal, Monte Santo, and Jeremoabo.[33]

Within the backlands—the largest ecological zone in the Northeast, 49 percent of the total area—the "inner" or "high" *sertão*, the heart of Antônio Conselheiro's ministry, constitutes the driest portion. There, not only is rainfall sparse (less than twenty-three inches a year), but it is capricious as well, often staying away for two or three years, other times falling all at once in torrents that quickly run off the caked, flinty soil. Temperatures hover in the nineties (Fahrenheit) year round. While the dry heat is more bearable here than on the humid coast, the broiling sun beats down fiercely. High evaporation eliminates much of what rain does fall. In the 1800s, visitors to the high *sertão* often expressed shock at the misery of the inhabitants' lives. The backlands, a priest noted, was nothing but a "vast hospital." *Sertanejos* "are more nerves than muscles," said a physician: almost always fasting, working entire days in the sun without food, riding leagues on empty stomachs.[34]

Dozens of famished men would sit aimlessly near slaughterhouses—pariahs with no hope of eating meat. Travelers lamented the fate of widows, abandoned to their own devices and often unable to provide food for their families. Filth abounded. Rates of infant mortality—when authorities bothered to determine statistics—were invariably found to be "astoundingly high." In good years, children in squatter families were fortunate to be able to eat a glutinous porridge made of pulverized manioc meal larded with goat fat. In every public place travelers saw beggars with deformed limbs, men and women blinded from trachoma, and shrunken children with festering infections and repugnant maladies.

As might be expected, people's physiological development in the northeastern hinterland was poor in comparison to more prosperous regions. Four decades after Canudos, men in the backlands averaged 5'2" in height (a full two inches less than the average height of slaves imported into the colonial United States), and women were between 4'9" and 5'0". Backland women, moreover, menstruated earlier (at twelve years) than the national average, and 55 percent married by the age of fifteen.[35] In 1916, a writer from nearby Paraíba described backland residents as suffering from illiteracy, subjugation, and "anemia, starvation, and semi-barbarization."[36] This assessment is borne out in an anonymous photograph taken roughly at the time of the Canudos conflict (Fig. 6). The *vaqueiros* with their horses seem faithful to da Cunha's description: short men, stooped, like knights, wearing leathery suits of armor. A sickly dog cowers behind a horse's legs (domestic animals in this part of Brazil that were not raised for food were usually unhealthy, for they rarely had enough to eat).

The rough terrain and seeming isolation of the Bahian backlands

6. Backland cowboys, or *vaqueiros*; they wear broad-brimmed leather hats, jackets, and leg coverings, also of roughly cured hide. Anonymous photograph. Courtesy Biblioteca Nacional, Rio de Janeiro, and Gilberto Ferrez.

provided a stage for outsiders to traverse, some escaping more parched locales further inland, others motivated in their wandering by a personal sense of religious mission.[37] The backland inhabitants were varied racially and ethnically, not homogeneous as a reading of da Cunha and other writers would suggest. Tiny settlements of ex-slaves (*crioulos*), including former fugitives, dotted the landscape. Some communities were made up mostly of Brazilianized descendants of local tribes, in some cases relatively pure-blooded, in others highly miscegenated.

One locale in the Canudos region looked much the same as another. The city of Bom Conselho, for example, fifteen leagues from Jeremoabo near the Sergipe border in the north and connected to Alagoinhas by the Itapicurú road, consisted of two hundred houses. Described in official records as being "indifferently built," the houses were usually constructed of mud hardened on wooden frames and covered by woven palm fronds; often openings on the sides substituted for windows and doors. *Agregado* families (those living by favor on another's land) typically owned one piece of furniture: a bed on which parents and young children slept together. Three or four large stones served as a cooking stove. Most structures faced a long street adjacent to the chapel, with about twenty commercial houses clustered near the site of the weekly market. Lack of potable water arrested further development; during most of the year, residents had to use rainwater collected in a public tank. There were two elementary schools—one with thirty boys, the other with twenty-six girls—both described as being in a state of terrible disrepair, and neither having books or even enough chairs.

Capim Grosso, on the right bank of the São Francisco twenty leagues from Juazeiro, boasted "plastered houses one story high," a few with glass windows, and two squares, Mercado ("Market") and "Wagner"—so named not in honor of the composer but after the owner of the buildings on the square, a merchant of German origin. Bom Conselho benefited from its location at the confluence of rural roads linking Sergipe, Alagoas, and Pernambuco. As a result, it possessed a house in which its municipal council met, and a boisterous *feira*, or outdoor market, was held there, attended by people from the entire surrounding area.[38]

"Indifferently built" dwellings notwithstanding, a closer examination of the condition of backland *municípios* suggests that da Cunha and contemporary chroniclers missed signs of vitality and agricultural diversity, factors that may explain how Canudos was able to support its astonishingly large population. The backlands were not a desert, even if scorching heat and lack of water in the places where they encamped gave battle correspondents a sense of hell.

Conselheiro's sanctuary attracted thousands of pilgrims from Inhambupe, Alagoinhas, Itapicurú, Souré (Natuba), Tucano, and Monte Santo. Inhambupe consisted of clusters of buildings in "terrible shape" (some 293 of the 5,189 houses were so decrepit that they had been abandoned), a barracks for soldiers, and a "decent" municipal building; the main event in the town was the weekly market, which had a reputation for abundant produce. In nondrought years the land around the village produced tobacco, which was shipped to market in Salvador via the railroad in Alagoinhas. There were four schools, two of which were in the neighboring hamlet of Aporá. (Schools were a vital sign of relative prosperity, since they were funded mostly from municipal revenues.) Adjoining *fazendas* raised cattle, horses, mules, goats, and sheep and grew manioc, corn, and French beans.

The 1872 census paints an interesting picture of the *comarca* (a judicial district, smaller than a *município*) of Inhambupe, even then a major backland population center with 22,004 residents.[39] Every soul in Inhambupe save one was counted as a Roman Catholic. All but 154 (12 Portuguese, 9 Italians, 3 Germans, a Frenchman—the latter three nationalities likely priests—and 129 Africans, all slaves) were Brazilian-born. Some 13 percent of the adult population was literate (excluding slaves, none of whom could read or write). Less than 10 percent of free school-age children attended school. Virtually all residents of Inhambupe lived in the countryside. The occupational data confirm that the population of the town proper must have been tiny. All together, Inhambupe's elite—its public officials, lawyers, clergymen, teachers, and shopkeepers—numbered fewer than two hundred (Table 1). There was only a token force of police and soldiers: in the backlands justice was usually taken care of by *jagunços* employed by landowners.

Women's occupations are not explicitly indicated in the census. Presumably, many of the "seamstresses" (over thirteen hundred were counted—a remarkably spurious number) and domestic servants worked as prostitutes as well, not a census category. No grouping was included for housewives; were some wives then listed as seamstresses? It seems unlikely. In the countryside, some of the agricultural laborers must have been women. Indeed, whatever their occupation, the women worked as hard as their men, and they bore and raised children as well. The small percentage of children in Inhambupe points up another characteristic of the nineteenth century: the low rate of survival. In modern, developed societies, children under eighteen make up about half of the population; in Inhambupe in 1872, even if children who worked as early

TABLE 1.   Census Count by Occupation for
Inhambupe, Bahia, 1872

| | |
|---|---|
| Pharmacists | 1 |
| Lawyers | 2 |
| Notaries | 2 |
| Physicians | 3 |
| Soldiers | 6 |
| Police | 8 |
| Secular clergy | 9 |
| Public employees | 11 |
| Teachers | 17 |
| Day workers | 190 |
| Commercial employees | 259 |
| Domestic servants | 276 |
| Artisans | 505 |
| Slaves without occupations* | 542 |
| Seamstresses | 1,343 |
| Agricultural slaves | 3,015 |
| No occupation (including children) | 3,682 |
| "Capitalists and property owners" | 4,859 |
| Agricultural laborers | 7,274 |

*Includes slave children
SOURCE: Recenseamento, Província da Bahia, Comarca do Inhambupe, Município de Santo Antonio de Alagoinhas, 1872, Arquivo Público do Estado da Bahia, Salvador.

as ten or eleven were counted in the census as agriculturalists or domestic servants, they still represented only some 20–40 percent of the total population. Late nineteenth-century Inhambupe was overwhelmingly rural. There was no manufacturing or food processing, no transportation sector, no professional construction industry. Most families built their own houses, just as the women made all of their clothing by hand—even those not employed as "seamstresses."

Houses in Itapicurú, on the sandy left bank of the river of the same name, stood twenty leagues from Alagoinhas and seven from the village of Souré, with their mud-caked walls and roofs of rough ceramic tile. Many residences were in disrepair and nearly falling down. Such was the state of the jail, which was so dilapidated that prisoners escaped with ease. There was no public sanitation anywhere in the area. Animal wastes littered the streets and were used, untreated, as fertilizer. Human feces were simply dumped outdoors.

The land in and around Itapicurú was fertile and well watered. Its soil produced corn, rice, beans, tobacco, and sugar cane, and the Itapicurú Valley was hospitable to raising cattle and swine. Several thermal springs bubbled up, important sources of water. In contrast, Monte Santo's rocky soil yielded fewer crops, but the town supported crafts (shops manufacturing hammocks) and some tanneries. It also housed a jail, whose guards lived with their prisoners because they could not afford housing. Souré's houses were whitewashed and sparsely furnished, but with glass windows; the hamlet had a cemetery in good repair (work had been initiated by Conselheiro himself), two schools, and a small public square with a stand for the Saturday market, the only local commerce.

Reactions to the backlands among travelers varied widely according to individual outlook and motivation. Officials of incumbent administrations lauded the region's dry climate as healthy, praised recent improvements, and saw things through the rose-colored lenses of chamber of commerce publicists. Less subjective visitors saw the same things differently. For example, the *vila* of Jeremoabo, wrote Durval Vieira de Aguiar in 1882, is a "stagnant, insipid" place, hemmed in by mountains; it "completely lacks decent buildings" and is populated by "common people, orderly, but poor and ignorant, effectively without either commerce or industry" save two or three tiny shops selling dry goods and "a few rude bars selling cane liquor (*cachaça*)."[40]

If a nineteenth-century rural middle class can be said to have existed in the Bahian *sertão*, it mainly comprised the few renters (*foreiros*) living on *fazendeiro* land, some of whom owned a few slaves, and a handful of artisans and merchants residing in rural towns.[41] Tucano, for example, to those looking for signs of progress, boasted solidly built plastered houses—some more than a story high—ten streets, three squares, three schools in the *município*, sheep ranches, weaving establishments, a railroad

station on the line to Serrinha, thermal springs, and a grotto.[42] Vieira de
Aguiar, however, found that the same place offered a bleak visage.
Tucano's agricultural output, he wrote, was "extremely insignificant"; its
produce wretched; its livestock decimated by the drought and lack of
pasturage, "as empty of vegetation as if the ground had been swept with
a broom. . . . Commerce," he continued, "is nonexistent. . . . The village
is small, and the jail, housed in the military barrack, *happily* closed."[43]

Residents of smaller rural villages included merchants, retired military personnel, innkeepers, prostitutes, and, in the larger towns, schoolteachers and private tutors. Educators were mostly women, although
some (including the young Antônio Vicente Maciel) were men employed
by landowning families or who started up small schools. Distances between rich and poor in such places were much less extreme than in the
coastal cities, with their fashionable aristocracy. Well-to-do families of
the backlands consumed monotonous foods not much more refined
than what their employees ate. Rich and needy alike shared significant
common cultural ground.[44]

Although backland towns offered few comforts, and residents could
rarely aspire to owning their own land, *sertanejos* retained more social and
economic independence than inhabitants of the coastal strip, where slavery and plantation agriculture had been prevalent. Throughout Bahia,
as in most parts of the world, traditional village culture was strongest
where the poor and the economically marginalized were materially dependent on the more powerful members of local society.[45] For this reason, the Bahian seaboard may be said to have supported a traditional
peasantry, whether they continued to live on the land or resettled in
urban circumstances. In the *tabuleiro* region and in the *sertão* itself, however, even the poorest citizens enjoyed forms of independence—freedom
of movement, availability of land for sharecropping, contractual relations
with ranchers and landowners—that did not foster docile behavior.

The open-air *feiras*—held too frequently to be explained by economic
need alone—exemplified the relatively high degree of give-and-take in
backland life (Fig. 7). For one thing, *feiras* permitted unaffected interaction.[46] In a society such as Brazil's, where virtually all of what anthropologists call "public space" was not communal at all but dominated by
private interests exercising power and prestige,[47] the *feira* was the exception: it was open to all. Moving from place to place on a fixed weekly
schedule (the largest towns claimed Saturdays), the markets were places
of trade, display, barter, socializing, and entertainment for the entire
region. Like the Levantine bazaar, the *sertão*'s *feiras* were laboratories for
interpersonal exchange, in addition to being vital to the local economy.[48]
*Feirantes* (professional hawkers) erected wooden platforms or tables;
part-time sellers, mostly women, sat on straw mats or squatted on the

7. Backland *feira*, location unknown, ca. 1890. Anonymous photograph. Cour
tesy Instituto Geográfico e Histórico da Bahia, Salvador. This *feira*, like most,
took up virtually the entire town square. Its location was probably in the *tabuleiro*
region near the coast.

ground. They sold food (goat cheese, guava paste, onions and garlic,
cakes of *rapadura* [brown sugar], dried meat), baskets, small tools, kerosene, cane liquor, even guns.

Backland *feiras* introduced the earliest municipal activities in places
otherwise devoid of amenities—places more like the proto-towns of England from before the Norman Conquest, consisting essentially of clusters of buildings.[49] In the *sertão*, virtually everyone in the vicinity attended the *feira* at least briefly on market day: herders; itinerant
repairmen able to mend shoes, metal pots, or harnesses and saddles;
cowboys needing equipment; men riding to town to carouse and drink;
used furniture dealers; horse traders—"a vast field," in the words of
Clifford Geertz, "of petty traders and craftsmen, working the intimately
known corners of commercial life in a weakly joined system of multiple
units . . . none of them well standardized [and therefore putting] an
enormous premium on interpersonal exchange skills."[50]

*Feira*-connected activities may have accounted for half or more of the
employed labor force of the region. At nearly every market one could find
card sharks, gamblers, and shell game artists; men selling caged birds;
potters; *cordel* troubadours selling chapbooks reproduced by means of

primitive presses onto rough paper; people giving poetry readings or performing music; and, of course, prostitutes. In some larger and more populous markets or when circuses came to town, setting up on the *feira* grounds, there would be shows by magicians and escape artists, as well as carnival entertainment ranging from displays of animal freaks to sword and fire eating. A religious dimension was evident as well: preachers came to *feiras*, and missionaries, and peddlers hawking icons. Everything came together at the market site in a free and colorful mix of rude language, bargaining, supplication, pickpocketing, and mingling.

The relatively close-knit fabric of coastal society was replaced in the backlands, at least to a degree, by the culture of backlands Catholicism. The *sertanejo* population rarely saw parish clergy but were ministered to instead by evangelical missionaries, *beatos*, lay preachers, healers, and, in the mid-1890s, by Antônio Conselheiro. The fact that religious influence in the hinterlands was focused on itinerants and makeshift arrangements only accentuated the backland tradition of freer individual choice, and it may have made it easier for backland families to pick up and follow Conselheiro to his protected sanctuary.

Northeasterners believed that failure to accept one's circumstances would result in suffering and misfortune, the consequence of divine retribution.[51] In one community, during a period of excessive rainfall in which farmers lost their entire crops of beans, anthropologist Patricia R. Pessar discovered that most local residents attributed the calamity to the fact that "a man down the road" had earlier cursed God for "neglecting to send rain."[52] Given this attitude, it is not surprising that backlanders viewed individual saints as protectors, or patrons. They also stressed the fatherly nature of God: dispensing protection and benevolence but also stern punishment, just as the landowner-patron did in his traditional role. At the same time, however, saints were feared. Misfortunes—disease, ill luck, devastating weather—were blamed on individuals' misdeeds. Because saints were thought to be at times punitive (in the tradition of the Golden Legend [*Legenda áurea*], dating back to twelfth-century France and Italy),[53] the backlands were filled with shrines to which devout souls came, often under hardship and sometimes crawling on bloodied knees, to make *promessas*, or penitential vows—sometimes in order to thank a saint for a favorable personal intervention, more often to plead for help or to beg forgiveness. The penitential tradition helped shape the singular nature of Catholicism as practiced by the rural poor: vows were made directly to Jesus (not to God) or to a saint on a quid pro quo basis. As a result, the faith of humble backlanders was often tinged with fear; without much hope of official aid, for priests were rarely available in rural communities, they had to negotiate not only with the world, but with the devil, whose presence was always felt, and the supernatural as well.

Despite the spirit of personal autonomy in their region, rural backlanders, lacking strong horizontal groupings within their own communities, were socially limited to vertical patron-client relationships with the elite,[54] and those relationships were growing increasingly intrusive as economic development, accompanied by a need for greater specialization, spread. The abrupt transition from monarchy to republic brought new pressures to bear. And in the religious sphere—always of paramount importance to devout backlanders—from Rome (and then Fortaleza and Salvador) came neo-orthodox reform and hierarchical displeasure at the role of lay Catholic *beatos* and other itinerants.

More active government apparatuses at the national and local levels, even before the advent of the republic, touched individual lives in a number of ways. Backland men were now subject to forced military recruitment under an 1874 law that made them legally subject to an impressment lottery at virtually any time. Upon promulgation of the statute, angry crowds attacked draft registration offices and burned registration records across Minas province and the entire Northeast. In Ponte Nova, Minas, a mob of sixty women "armed with clubs" invaded the church where the draft commission sat, seized the enlistment records, ripped them up, and threw the pieces into the holy water font and the town square's fountain. Recruitment drives were halted after enlistment commissioners received personal threats. In Muritiba, Bahia, draft officials requested militia protection to deal with "seditious movements" seeking to stop forced impressment.[55] Eventually, the authorities stopped trying to enforce the draft lottery because it created more trouble than it was worth. Instead they revived the old and equally unsavory army press gangs, which rounded up unwilling recruits in periodic sweeps.

Changes occurred in the form (if not the substance) of limited political mobilization when suffrage was extended to literate male adults following the removal of property qualifications for voting. The greatest changes in people's lives, however, were occasioned by regional commercial development. By the 1870s railroads linked the hamlets and villages of the Jeremoabo-Juazeiro region of the high *sertão*, in the midst of which Conselheiro in 1893 would establish his millenarian community.[56] By-products of the region's pastoral economy—mostly hides and tallow—were shipped to the coast or farther into the interior via the São Francisco River.

The railroad not only forged new links to the coast, but it also brought changes to the backland way of life. In a region where the only foreigners had been occasional missionary priests, now the railroad managers and engineers, as well as many of the construction workers, were immigrants. A thousand workers came from Sardinia and Italy proper, mainly Turin, virtually all of them men, recruited in Europe by agents of the railroad company. Some returned to Italy, but most stayed, adding to the population mix in the region.[57]

Proponents of economic development and modernization saw the railroad as a critical, even mystical emblem of progress, but backlanders were at first terrified by what they saw. To them, the iron locomotives followed by boxcars were evil, potentially instruments of oppression, and proof that the end of the world was imminent.[58] Hamlets that were little more than dots on the map—Parafuso, Peripéri, Muritiba, Olaria—now became linked to the capital by railroad track. Although there was no rush of development, as in the Center-South (investment remained limited, and regional agriculture, at least in the region north of Salvador, did not yield high-demand goods like cacao or coffee, produce that fueled boom times to the south), the transition zone between coast and backlands in Bahia was brought into greater contact with the littoral cities. The psychological isolation of the backlands may not have been reduced, but the outside world was now closer than ever before.

The expanded reach of government also reduced opportunities for tax evasion. Improved commerce, and the opportunity to tax *feira* proceeds, brought about the regulation of commercial exchanges. Antônio Conselheiro once angrily defended a woman who could not pay the license fee that would permit her to sell her meager wares. Efforts of provincial governments to institute standardized weights and measures—less to prevent customer cheating than to regularize licensing and tax levies—led to a series of violent *feira* riots, the so-called Quebra Quilos (Smash-the-Kilo-Scales) movement, which affected at least seventy-eight markets in the backlands of Pernambuco, Rio Grande do Norte, Alagoas, and Paraíba in 1874 and 1875. Backland participants in these riots, of course, were portrayed as primitives terrified of modern scientific innovations; yet one could also praise them for figuring out that uniform weights and measures would inevitably lead to a higher tax burden. Examination of the tax records in the affected *municípios*, in fact, reveals that between 1870 and 1875 new taxes were created or raised in two out of every three *municípios* after standardized weights were introduced.[59]

The range of *feira* products broadened as improved transportation and new warehousing facilities permitted brokers and city-based merchants to penetrate the backland economy. This expansion ultimately doomed most of the smaller *feiras*, victims of larger and more permanent facilities at railroad hubs that did business every day in bulk orders.

Veterinary services came to the permanent markets as well; whereas previously cowboys had had to rely on patent remedies, now they could buy real medicines for *toque* (carbuncles) and other cattle ailments. Still, through the late nineteenth century the traditional system of floating, one-day *feiras* managed to survive in the backlands. From its origins along the cattle trails through its refinement as an entrepôt serving a radius of perhaps twenty miles, the *feira* functioned as a mechanism for the production and exchange of goods and services—in short, it was a true economic system.[60]

## THE WORLD OF THE BACKLANDS

At least until Canudos erupted in 1896–97, people rarely thought much about the northeastern backlands. When they did, it was usually with scorn. Just as southern elites thought of their northern counterparts as having been "tarred" by the brush of miscegenation, *cariocas* and *mineiros* told their share of jokes imputing African ancestry to *baianos*. Backlanders were less likely to be considered Caucasian, in the contemporary social-cum-biological use of the term, and more likely to be labeled mestizos; they were considered "white" by census takers and by society only if their economic status or family pedigree merited. Antônio Vicente Maciel offers a case in point: his father, a medium-complexioned mestizo, was considered "white" and of "good family" because of his economic status, but only by local chroniclers. Writers from Rio de Janeiro and São Paulo, always aware of the "darker" nature of Brazil's North, dismissed him as the "*caboclo* Messiah."[61] *Caboclos* made up the large majority, but in no manner were they the only inhabitants of the backland region.

The family-based oligarchic system operated in much the same way across Brazil, but in the Northeast its tenacity mounted in proportion to declining economic fortunes. While elites there were not notably affluent, they wielded immense power. The empire's lack of interest in the region led to almost complete dependence on local elites for effective provincial administration. As a result, corruption, venality, and political rivalry were at least as bad and probably worse than elsewhere in Brazil, though the financial stakes were relatively smaller because it was easier to become rich on the coast. Government was flawed by the fact that under the empire, just as before and after, most appointments were sinecures created to generate political loyalty. Interior residents feared landowners and hated the tax-wielding apparatus of state and *seigneur* alike. This situation would prove propitious in 1893 and 1894, when word about the establishment of Conselheiro's refuge spread with the speed of lightning.[62]

The realization that economic disparities in Brazil were widening, with the continued decline of sugar even as industry and commerce prospered in the South, fostered tension among northeastern landowners: lack of capital for loans, they complained, was forcing them to rely on "usury" and to sell their slaves. In 1871, Bahian planters sent a petition with over four hundred signatures to the imperial government asking for agricultural credit, but to no avail.[63] In the three most powerful units of the Brazilian "First" or "Old Republic" (1889–1930)—São Paulo, Minas Gerais, and Rio Grande do Sul—the national government was largely controlled by, and in turn served, local elite interests.[64] Edgard Carone has identified a "geography of oligarchy," with personalistic ties that were tightest in Brazil's most underdeveloped regions and with underdevelopment and poverty that were often accompanied by a near monopoly on clan power.[65] Even during the shifting political conditions of the late 1880s and early 1890s, patrimonialism—whereby those in power, through patronage and clientelism, distributed influence to relatives and clients—governed regional life.[66]

Land use, a basic factor in social stratification, changed little in the interior as the decades progressed. Because of the sparse population density, each family had to raise at least a minimum of subsistence crops, even in the driest regions. Until railroads arrived in the mid to late nineteenth century, the sense of isolation deeply affected *sertanejo* life. Self-sufficiency was necessary for survival, although not even the remotest areas lost touch with the market system. Because prices in the hinterland were usually lower than on the coast, interior commerce was able to remain competitive. *Vaqueiros* fared somewhat better than sharecroppers and other agricultural tenants; still, *fazendeiros* continued to exercise considerable power.[67] Whereas in Europe, better transportation led to more effective famine relief in the late eighteenth and early nineteenth centuries, in Brazil, little changed over time. Nothing was done to combat the mounting toll from drought. Landowners and their politician clients were consequently less willing to tolerate what they considered threats to the status quo. Canudos could not have come along at a worse moment from the perspective of the regional land-labor relationship.

The Portuguese crown had granted *sesmarias*, vast tracts of land up to six leagues—more than twenty-two miles—in depth to single individuals. Members of some families, notably the Garcia d'Ávila clan, acquired holdings of two hundred leagues or more in Bahia. Expansion was rapid: by 1584, ranches occupied the territory halfway between Salvador and the São Francisco River, some of them jumping provincial borders to occupy riverbeds on both sides of fertile waterways. In the early eighteenth century, two families nominally possessed the greater part of Bahia, although they did not act on this control. By the 1750s, while urban centers were still small (Jeremoabo had only 252 inhabitants in 1759), census data showed that the entire Bahian *sertão* had more people—almost 80,000—than the economically declining sugar zone of the Recôncavo adjacent to Salvador, with 60,000. Nevertheless, *sertanejos* lived at such distances from one another that few families were within a day's horseback ride from any neighbors or village.

Into the nineteenth century, as much as 80 percent of arable land held by *fazendeiros* and ranchers went unused except to graze livestock. Climate and topography were the determining factors: because of the aridity of the land, at least 10 hectares were required to support one head of cattle.[68] Small commercial farm plots worked by independent agriculturalists were concentrated mostly in oasis (*brejo*) locations at higher elevations with adequate rainfall and, in the *sertão*, along seasonal streams. Backland ranchers ignored subsistence farmers, concentrating instead on livestock.

Cowhands displayed well-honed skills that permitted them to nurture their herds under harsh and often exceptionally dry conditions. As part of their job, they subjugated Brazilindians, squatters, and anyone else they found, forcing them to work for the landlords.[69] Ranches expanded through the building of new corrals and contracting of work. Most hands had to perform all tasks themselves, although a few men earned reputations for particular kinds of expertise—such as the *curandeiros de rasto*, self-taught veterinarians. These pragmatic men sometimes performed wonders, not unlike the herbalists and other healers many relied on in the absence of physicians and licensed pharmacists in the remote interior.[70]

Raising crops without acquiring tenant status or paying rent to landowners was difficult in the backlands, especially since access to potable water was so limited. Squatters occasionally banded together to plant subsistence crops, but they were usually evicted from the land after a few seasons. Life was rigorous. The untimely periodic droughts devastated entire *municípios*, forcing tens of thousands to flee the *sertão* in search of refuge. Experience, however, taught that little succor would come from governments, which usually interned migrants, impressed males into militia service, and prevented families from entering city limits. Almost every backlander lived a stressful and uncertain life.

After 1889, Bahia, now a relatively weak member of the national federation, saw the *praia* zone and the *sertão* increasingly invaded by market forces and by the arm of state government, which under federalism had to seek revenue locally. These conditions introduced, in turn, new stresses and antagonisms into lower-class life, which were expressed not only economically, but culturally as well. Some backlanders maintained their traditional independence, even at the cost of further marginality and ultimate destitution. Others migrated to the less remote watered backland oases that supported small agricultural and pastoral activities, thus becoming more like traditional renters and therefore more dependent on landowners. Many of the families caught up in these difficult transitions in the early and mid-1890s may have found Conselheiro's community a viable alternative, promising stability in exchange for rigid personal conformity.

In the Bahian hinterland beyond the Recôncavo, the *município*, though the lowest administrative unit in the political system, enjoyed virtual autonomy. The dominant figure was usually the *coronel*, who was often the major landowner in the area or his client. (The military-sounding title originated in the fact that some of the first backland *coronéis* had been commanders of National Guard brigades or regiments when that body was created in 1831. There was no necessary connection to National Guard service, however. Some local bosses simply appropriated the title; other were granted it out of custom.) Rival *coronéis* often vied for power, with the victorious one allying himself with the incumbent regime at the provincial or state level. Rural politics was long dominated by this fierce and sometimes deadly tug-of-war between competing factions, each demanding utter loyalty from subordinates and from the population at large.

Ordinary people, of course, were excluded from this mutually profitable exchange between coastal political machines and rural local chieftains. As Victor Nunes Leal and others have demonstrated, not only did the system link public power and the decadent social influence of these men, but it also spawned a host of pernicious subsets of corruption: *mandonismo* (dominant rule), nepotism, voter swindles backed by violence, and the disorganization of local public services.[71]

*Coronelismo* functioned as a means of assuring political control over a private domain, enforced through what Joseph L. Love terms "a graded series of inducements and threats ranging from political patronage to murder."[72] The height of *coronel* power came during the First Republic, when incumbent state officials granted unlimited license to client *coronéis* in exchange for votes, guaranteed through fraud at the ballot boxes. *Coronéis* usually controlled the election of local judges. This influence, together with the power to name the local police chief, meant that crimes committed by the incumbent faction could go unpunished while members of the opposition suffered from the whims and capriciousness of the administrators of justice.

Most *coronéis* owned agricultural businesses or ranches, but some were merchants, bureaucrats, and even priests.[73] They exercised power by means of clan-based networks and alliances, and frequently kept gangs of *capangas* (thugs) to enforce discipline. This patriarchal power base was hallowed in the region, having preceded even the establishment of formal colonial government in 1549; it was perpetuated through kinship bonds and fine-tuned through a system of rewards (the distribution of parcels of land, for example) and punishments. In the *sertão*, however, because the social distance between the backland elite and the rest of the population was less than in the coastal sugar-growing zone, the *coronel* acted more as a "first among equals" than as a patriarch, even though his power over his domain was in some ways nearly absolute.[74]

Some bosses exercised their power behind the scenes, acting through surrogates. Others affected more flamboyant postures, sometimes holding higher office—even deputy or senator—while simultaneously operating their *município* as personal fiefdoms. The chief executive officer of each *município* was the *intendente*, elected in off-years as a practical measure to permit the state government to exert political pressure and retain a measure of control. Local ruling families headed by individual *coronéis* dominated municipal politics, controlling elections through a combination of manipulation and coercion.

The political game evolved its own glossary of terms for fraudulent balloting practices: *fantasmas* (ghost voters), *fósforos* ("match sticks"), *bicos de pena* (falsified voting rolls based on fictitious names).[75] Ballot boxes were stuffed, hijacked at gunpoint, or simply "lost." In electoral years, citizens were termed the "herd," like sheep or goats. The system flourished not only because few believed that the common people could be trusted to behave independently, but also because the *coronéis* headed the most powerful families in a region where patrimonialism had dominated for centuries. The system was considered natural.

The violent side of the *coronel* system was exacerbated by the fact that backland culture placed inordinate emphasis on personal honor. The smallest event could be taken as an offense, with redress possible only by physical means; long-term grudges between political factions and family clans were common. These characteristics of backland culture weighed most heavily on women, who were expected to remain devout, passive, and deferential toward their fathers and husbands. Men, in turn, were expected to defend their own honor at all times and to exhibit extraordinary sensitivity to possible slights to female family members. The masculinity complex led to constant harassment of females by males, often involving beatings, especially when the men were inebriated, as they were frequently.[76]

Men in the backlands normally carried arms, usually sheathed knives, though bellicosity was more prevalent in towns than in the countryside, since men engaged in agriculture or stock raising tended to be surrounded by their kin and behaved more soberly. Violence in the name of honor or revenge was endemic to Brazilian life, and feuds and clan warfare often lasted generations. Euclydes da Cunha himself was killed in a duel, as was his son. "Violence," a historian of rural life wrote, "was a routine form of adjusting local relationships."[77] The line between co-operation and physical violence was thin, often dependent on changing conditions. Although the instinct was to help, in times of hardship neighbors might put their own interests first. The fluid, unstable atmosphere was governed by unwritten rules and exaggerated sensibilities. According to Pereira de Queiroz, "The family patterns of mutual assistance, respect for older people, strengthening of the solidarity between relatives, conjugal fidelity, virginity of the unmarried girl, just like the help given by the better off to the underprivileged, persisted only as values, but were not followed in real behavior."[78]

The insecurities generated by the backland code—the need to protect personal honor, the intimidating presence of the *coronel* system, the pressures of economic hardship, the efforts by the Catholic church to drive out unorthodox practices, the new republican strictures requiring civil marriages and stripping the church of its former control over registration of births and deaths—must have contributed to the willingness of rural men and women in the 1890s to follow Antônio Conselheiro to his theocratic sanctuary.

The exaggerated morality demanded by Conselheiro contrasted sharply with backland tolerance of vices practiced for generations. Cane alcohol (*cachaça* or, more colloquially, *pinga*) played a major role in the day-to-day life of the backlands. Many became addicted as teenagers when they first took jobs, for some patrons paid partly in currency and partly in drink. Straight *pinga* was consumed in large quantities everywhere: at family gatherings, at festivals, at the end of the market day. Many men worked in an alcoholic stupor. Some vicars were notorious for their drunkenness.[79] Large quantities of Jacaré, Januária, and other brands of cane liquor, packed in wooden boxes, were shipped up and down the São Francisco River, though in poorer areas the population made do with home-distilled liquor. Alcohol, which was easy to ship, facilitated frontier commerce: in an economy where money was scarce, popular consumer products like tobacco and alcohol were almost as important as currency in trade.

In one sense, Conselheiro's moral stance against distilled alcohol was impractical. Alcohol may have become important because brackish backland water supplies were often contaminated with bacteria. *Sertanejos* drank as little water as possible, for good reason. *Cachaça* was not an ineffective curative; in addition to being used internally for medicinal purposes, it was applied externally to counter infection. Heavy drinking was also popular because it provided a release from the hardships of rural life. Although some became addicted to it, for many it probably provided more benefits than liabilities.

Public backland morality did not tolerate women who drank, but regional lore related dozens of tales of tipsy women filling the air with curses and of inebriated brides at their weddings.[80] Men and women both consumed tobacco whenever they could obtain it. Men rolled their own cigarettes; women preferred pipes. Prostitution was endemic, owing to the blunt fact that unmarried, illiterate women or women whose husbands had died or abandoned them had no other means of sustaining themselves. On one occasion, an official of the Bahian state police ordered an economic census in the town of Rumo, in the *município* of Xique-Xique. His report counted nine hundred prostitutes among fifteen hundred lower-class women.[81] If the number is accurate, this must have been rough territory, a backland Sodom and Gomorrah. Xique-Xique's town center was invaded by bandits in 1882 and left in ruins after being looted and set aflame, the residents finding refuge in the hamlet of Barra and the town authorities fleeing to Remanso, at a greater distance.[82]

Increased state sovereignty under the federal republic and the corresponding need to raise revenue internally amplified pressures for administrative centralization, which was undertaken by state political machines. These entities were usually organized along lines of rural-urban alliances: landowners and other *coronéis* maintained near-absolute control in their zones of influence in exchange for state support in the form of fiscal resources and favorable decisions on such matters as capital fund outlays, routes of rail construction, loans, and the use of state police troops when necessary. State officials publicly admitted their helplessness to deal with the "bandits and thugs" who swept through the interior, leaving "devastation" in their wake.[83] Instead they looked away, permitting the *coronéis* to maintain order any way they wished. In return, the local bosses allied to the incumbent machine delivered votes by means of fraud and iron-fisted intimidation and provided dutiful tribute when requested. In the final analysis, the state governor served essentially as a broker between rural bosses and the president of the republic.[84]

## THE UNDERCLASS

Most common people, overwhelmingly illiterate and unable either to acquire land or to gain meaningful education or training, coped by following the unwritten rules of the game. Although they lived in physical proximity to the *gente decente*, as the "good people" of the oligarchy were known, they rarely had much personal contact. Intermediary agents—policemen, priests, overseers, foremen—dealt with them directly. As time passed, population growth increased competition for food and pasturage, lowering the quality of life even further in the region. The system demanded docility and constantly threatened violence to dissidents. Anyone perceived as even a potential troublemaker was treated roughly. In the 1890s, towns and cities passed ordinances requiring that beggars be licensed, evidently a measure to insure that itinerants and other nuisances could be easily run out of town. Although the paternalistic overlay of the system permitted the oligarchy to see itself in a charitable light, as bureaucracies grew and the state came to play a great role in daily life measures to preserve social control grew ever tighter.

Mendicants were tolerated only if they posed no threat. Young men—especially emancipated slaves—were regularly impressed into military service at the state and federal levels, to keep them out of trouble and to provide recruits for militia and armed forces. Members of the *povo*, lacking formal access to the courts, were arrested arbitrarily and routinely brutalized by the police. The darker one's skin color, the more likely that one would receive harsh treatment. The rare few who managed to achieve upward mobility within this system were mostly new arrivals to urban places, young men pursuing economic opportunities. The key to acceptance was to learn the system and play by its rules, adopting both the vocabulary of the elite and its outlook.[85]

Plantation monoculture dominated rural Brazil from southern Paraná to the northern coast and linked agrarian production to the nineteenth-century export market. The plantations were also the loci of patriarchal power over the local population. Planter control remained largely unchecked by outside authority. Inefficient in terms of output (a function of high transport costs and the low state of technology), the plantation system kept labor costs low by using slaves or free laborers and by profiting from high mobility among the landless, who were easily attracted by word of mouth when work became available.

Slaves remained at the center of plantation life; not only did they perform day-to-day agricultural tasks, but they also served as bodyguards, artisans, craftsmen, domestics, and even hired-out laborers. Free laborers found it virtually impossible to acquire land, although further back in the hinterland—and especially in Pernambuco's transitional *agreste*, between the humid coast and the backlands—some farmers managed to buy small plots and so formed the nexus of a smallholding class. The vast majority passed their lives as squatters or sharecroppers, or as drifters, constantly looking for work, despite the fact that the plantation system discouraged mobility in order to preserve the labor supply.

World market conditions hastened the declining competitiveness of Brazilian sugar. Shipping was subject to cyclical fluctuations, and after

1880 big shipping interests, achieving economies of scale by using larger vessels, gained oligopolistic control.[86] By the 1880s, provincial governments were using loan guarantees to construct mechanized refineries, *engenhos centrais* (centralized plantations) and their successors, *usinas*, large sugar factories that by the turn of the century dominated the still-shrinking export market. Controlled by either powerful family clans or city-based corporations, the *usinas* established themselves as the most powerful socioeconomic institutions in the countryside. Hungry for land, *usinas* bought up dozens of nearby *engenhos* and relegated the formerly independent class of *senhores de engenhos* to the status of cane supplier. Because *usinas* needed unskilled, cheap seasonal labor, they rejected tenancy arrangements as inefficient. Politically powerful, the emerging agro-industrial elite moved to guarantee a captive and docile labor force by squeezing the peasantry and integrating it into the export sector.

The complaint of the 1820s about "labor scarcity" gave way after abolition to complaints about the "labor problem," the supposedly unreliable, lazy, and obstinate free labor force. The interminable pattern of droughts only worsened matters. When the rains did not come, families who usually lived as squatters or renters fled to less parched areas, either to the oasislike *brejos* in the *caatinga* or to the coast. When this occurred, labor scarcities did result, a problem for ranchers who needed to keep their cattle alive.

Even in nondrought years, however, the perception that there was a permanent labor shortage in the backlands before the 1890s was rarely accurate. Although population density was much lower than on the coast, the *sertão* was not underpopulated. The elites, though, believing what they wanted to believe, pressured public officials in the last quarter of the nineteenth century to turn to broad-based forms of intimidation and repression, with tactics ranging from dragnets of the countryside to impress idle peasants into military service to the establishment of forced labor pools in the guise of rehabilitation centers and disciplinary schools.

Landowners acted to preserve their advantages. The 1871 Free Womb Law, passed by the imperial parliament, stipulated that free slave children would remain in the service of their mother's master until the age of twenty-one, thus preserving the skeleton of a slave mode of production even as the nation moved toward emancipation. Provincial legislators bound employees of low status (*criados*, a category that included servants and workers in public places) to their employers through contracts filed with the local police. Vagrants, defined under the Penal Code as persons lacking a fixed residence or an "honest" occupation or means of support, or otherwise judged socially undesirable, were required to sign a legal pledge (*termo de bem viver*) promising to seek employment under penalty of three years' imprisonment if arrested again for idleness. Vagrant children were sent to disciplinary work houses until they reached legal maturity.

During the waning years of slavery in the 1870s and 1880s, nonslaves constituted about 60 percent of the rural population, with another 20 percent classified simply as "without occupation." Changing regional economic fortunes produced internal cycles of prosperity and depression, but because the overall economic system remained firmly neocolonial after independence, the potential social impact of agricultural diversification was minimized and patterns of exploitation remained constant.

Landless folk were known as *agregados* (retainers), a disparaging term suggesting rootlessness. Slave or free, the rural labor force was captive and dependent, largely because planters preferred to cling to the trappings of aristocracy rather than risk social upheaval through efforts to modernize. The survival of slavery until 1888 reinforced the traditional Brazilian distaste for manual labor, based on the association between slavery and work. When news of the final decree of abolition on May 13, 1888, reached the interior, blacks converged in towns to celebrate. Hundreds flocked to the church in Bom Jesus da Lapa (known among blacks as Lenibé-Furamê), where for eight days they celebrated in Carnivalesque fashion.[87] Nevertheless, regional attitudes changed little. Emancipation only led to planter demands for new vagrancy laws and the enlargement of police powers, though, despite fears of the "servile horde," police reports for 1889 and 1890 nationwide show no statistical increase in crime.

Across Brazil, land continued to rise in value, especially as modern transportation and technology encouraged large-scale agriculture. Other Latin American nations may have been struggling with what Torcuato Di Tella called the "highly mobilizable and menacing mass," but Brazil seemed comparatively rooted in stability.[88] Although latifundia dominated at one end of the scale, most agrarian properties were unproductive minifundia units, usually short of water. Yet despite these otherwise classic preconditions of social instability,[89] the system remained intact. One reason may have been the general malaise in which backlanders lived, with millions affected by infection or by malnutrition.

Physician Belisário Pena, who traveled throughout the backlands a decade after *Os sertões* was published, examined thousands of rural men, women, and children. He found a litany of medical horrors: snail disease, anemia, paralysis, deformities, spasticity, tumors, eczema, congenital retardation, leprosy, smallpox, rabies, and elephantiasis.[90] Brazil's infant mortality rate stood among the highest in the world. In the absence of trained physicians, charlatans migrated inland, setting up "medical" clinics and offices. One, a "Dr. Félix," had been a mule handler for Recife Tramways before he opened his backland clinic.[91] Fortunately, few people likely suffered at his hands, since only a handful could afford his fee.

Elites responded to these circumstances with demands for tighter measures of social control. As soon as abolition was effected, landowners, complaining that the vagrancy statutes were unenforceable, clamored for tougher penalties for public idleness. Groups of overseers and cattlemen gathered at Escada, Pernambuco, in 1874, to hear a paper on the subject of requiring freedmen to work without wages (the paper, however, never materialized). An angry planter demanded at the 1878 Recife Agricultural Congress that the government create "a severe police regime . . . to which all individuals without trade or craft be subjected."[92] Officials reactivated some of the refugee holding camps established during the 1877–79 drought, designating them agricultural colonies. There was also a broadening of all the extralegal definitions of vagrancy, a term applied not only to drunks, beggars, and misfits but to all persons judged capable of working who did not do so.

As police powers grew, society worried less about disguising its intent through euphemisms. An orphans' home in neighboring Pernambuco, the Colônia Izabel, established with the stated goal of providing moral and religious training as well as instruction in the arts, industry, and agriculture, was converted in the succeeding decade into an industrial reform school, renamed the Escola Industrial Frei Caneca. Politicians congratulated themselves on their social responsibility, even as their actions reinforced the image of the poor as miserable and ignorant. Officials called for new jails, asylums for beggars, correctional schools for minors, and penal colonies for incorrigibles. Without these institutions, Pernambuco's governor warned, criminals and ex-convicts would reenter society lacking work habits and so return to a life of crime.[93] An 1899 decree provided for a new agricultural reformatory for adults and a training school for delinquents. This law also permitted individuals and associations to set up their own agricultural penal colonies, thus saving the state the maintenance expenses and delivering coercive powers directly into the hands of those who had clamored for them.

More and more public land was taken over by large landowners. The number of slaves diminished as the century wore on, and sharecropping arrangements became more specialized. Small farmers never flourished, particularly in the backlands, where almost all land having access to water was held by large, often absentee, landowners. A new agricultural category emerged at the end of the colonial period: the *morador*, a resident sharecropper obliged to pay rent in both produce and labor in exchange for the right to live on land and grow garden crops. This arrangement offered protection but pulled tighter the knot of social dependency.


## STRATEGIES FOR COPING

Throughout Brazil the rural poor adopted new forms of tenancy depending on local conditions and needs. Sharecroppers, or *parceiros*, constituted a sizable portion of the rural labor force. When prices were low, coffee planters traded land use rights for labor, but when they rose tenants were forced to work as wage laborers and were charged rent. In the cacao region of southern Bahia, planters leased uncleared land for periods of five or six years to tenants, who, though allowed to grow temporary crops, had to plant cacao trees to be handed over at maturity. Thus owners freed themselves from the obligation to pay wages; moreover, they could give land in distant, inaccessible places to the tenant to clear. Such arrangements usually denied the sharecropper the right to live near his grove, but forced him to travel each day from his shack near the landowner's dwelling.

In the southern pampas, the cowboy *gaúchos* fared better, although observers noted with amazement that it was possible to starve in Rio Grande do Sul in the 1890s. Relatively well nourished (their diet included ample beef), although illiterate, the cattle workers were usually treated well by local ranchers, who used them as shock troops in the violent internecine wars of the region and who protected them from military press gangs and other intrusions. Traditionally they had had added leverage in being able to subsist as wild cattle hunters or as rustlers, but the spread of barbed wire by the 1890s sharply reduced these options.[94] Lack of access to capital or credit, moreover, limited opportunities for ranch hands to acquire land or to climb the social ladder.

In the Amazon, especially after 1870, rubber plantations employed thousands of Indians and *caboclos* from the drought-ridden North and Northeast as latex gatherers. Working conditions were appalling: many rubber workers never left the jungle alive. The poor lived in *palafitas*, insect- and vermin-infested stilt houses perched at water's edge. Although the term *caboclo* in the Amazon region was used originally to designate Indian-European mestizos, in time Japanese, Chinese, and Koreans as well as blacks also entered the ethnic melting pot. Long impoverished and stereotyped as unteachable in European ways, the Amazon *caboclo* continued to be victimized by the commercialization of jungle agriculture. Used to slash-and-burn horticulture, fishing, hunting and gathering, the rural work force of the Amazon was drafted into forced labor brigades to supply the extractive raw materials for the so-called commercial pyramid that integrated the region into the global market system after the turn of the century.[95]

At the same time, the indigenous population shrank, devastated by the diseases brought during decades of intrusions by slave hunters, prospectors, and missionaries. Births declined, expectant mothers died; starvation induced amenorrhea, preventing conception.[96] In the mid-1800s, the dissolution of some commercial ties with the Amazon Valley had increased *caboclo* autonomy, but local elites, centered in the jungle towns of Belém do Pará, Santarém, and Manaus, had quickly tightened their control by using the system of credit and debt and by lowering wages whenever possible. In contrast to the decline of the native population in the Amazon, for decades tens of thousands of hapless backlanders streamed to the region, mostly from the even more destitute Northeast. The post-1870 rubber boom set into motion long-term migration into the region, even though by 1912 prices for latex had collapsed.

Rubber profits brought latifundia to large areas of the Amazon Valley for the first time; concurrently, local subsistence agriculture declined. As a result, food had to be imported almost continuously, despite the region's fertility, its still relatively sparse population, and its natural wealth. When rubber prices collapsed, the boomtowns emptied, leaving the agricultural laborers imported during better times unprotected. Some large properties were sold off, and the Amazon Valley returned to its former state of isolated poverty. The *caboclos* turned to manioc cultivation as well as hunting and gathering for sustenance.

In central Brazil, *foreiros* rented marginal lands from planters and in addition were required to perform corvée labor during planting and harvest seasons. *Meieros* rented land in return for a share, often fixed, of their crops—a risky proposition in the face of potential ecological calamities such as drought, floods, or insect infestations. *Meieros* also had to cede grazing rights to landowners on demand. The *meiação* system originated in the coffee-growing Paraíba Valley and then spread to central Minas (where it helped to cushion the impact of the agricultural depression beginning in 1897) as well as to the interior of São Paulo.[97]

In the Northeast's transitional *agreste*, the semiarid band separating the backlands from the humid coastal zone, *foreiros* clustered in cotton-cultivating regions. Cattle raising initially predominated throughout the region, but in time—as early as the eighteenth century—squatters and renters began to appear. Traditionally known as the "poor man's crop," cotton was normally grown in combination with beans, corn, manioc, and other staples. This practice brought some degree of economic diversity and stability to *foreiros*, many of whom managed to acquire small pieces of land during boom years in the mid–nineteenth century when cotton prices peaked. Yet the new imperial land law of 1850, which made acquisition of title possible *only* through formal purchase, drove up land prices and squeezed out squatters and renters seeking eventually to buy land.

Ultimately, few *agregados* of any category ever managed to buy land except when it was too infertile or unproductive to interest large land-holders. The Center-South and South offered some exceptions, mostly cases of foreign immigrants who came as *colonos* (land colonists) and who after one or two generations became vegetable farmers. Native-born *colonos* rarely fared as well. Even in the relatively prosperous farming regions of southern Brazil, nearly half of rural family incomes went for food. Tenants earning daily wages who fell short in their quotas to the property owner were regularly fined, often in amounts ranging up to two days' pay per week.[98]

The oldest type of free rural laborer in Brazil was the *intruso* (intruder), a migratory squatter who usurped uncultivated public and private lands for his own use as early as the seventeenth century. These laborers took advantage of the best work or sharecropping arrangements offered to them. Differing from the *corumbás*, seasonal migrants who followed the harvest cycle, returning home when climatic conditions there improved, the *intrusos* represented a mobile supply of unskilled labor that depressed rural wages, thus tightening the economic noose around the necks of the *agregados* who stayed put. Then as later, the abundance of labor during both upswings and downturns in longer economic cycles permitted the land tenure system to function despite its unstable characteristics.

Migrants who trekked from one rural area to another in search of religious salvation were still another component of the rural poor. The rise of Padre Cícero Romão Batista's Ceará hamlet of Juazeiro as a mecca for thousands of impoverished pilgrims, especially following Vatican condemnation of Juazeiro's "miracles" in 1894, offers a case in point. Lacking church approval, the stream of pilgrimages became spontaneous and unorganized, drawing rural folk from the interior of Maranhão, Bahia, Pernambuco, Piauí, Rio Grande do Norte, Paraíba, and especially Ceará itself, despite the fact that would-be pilgrims were informed only by word of mouth, mostly through the networking mechanisms of the market towns. Ralph della Cava points out that the greatest number of devotees came from the distant São Francisco region of Alagoas.[99]

Before 1894, pilgrims to Padre Cícero's holy city in Ceará had been drawn from all social classes, but Rome's intervention drove away the more affluent, yielding a narrower migrant stream of the landless, the infirm, and the abandoned. Juazeiro offered more than religious faith. Padre Cícero himself dispensed commonsense advice, including simple hygienic information, which, when effective, was taken by believers as evidence of his miraculous powers. To critics, Juazeiro's pathetic population housed only fanatics, sinners, and criminals. But the pilgrims saw themselves as the padre's godchildren; he was their protector. In fact, the saintly priest offered little more than a compelling form of paternalism to a disoriented population nurtured on the *patrão* system.[100]

In the western portion of the Bahian *sertão* began Brazil's cattle region, stretching from southern Mato Grosso and Minas provinces north into Bahia, Goiás, Pará, Maranhão, and across the northeastern backlands. This was the realm of the *vaqueiros*, usually *caboclos*, who drove their stock each year on great cattle drives to slaughterhouses near the most important markets. These vending sites—Campina Grande in Paraíba, Feira de Santana in Bahia, and Petrolina, Garanhuns, and Caruarú in Pernambuco, among others—evolved as secondary urban centers, each providing complex services and developing its own satellite network of food supply. While most of the weekly *feiras* remained barter centers and places where country folk could sell their wares, once railroads linked the eastern portion of the agricultural and pastoral zone to the port in the 1860s, the expanding market towns became significant distribution hubs, points of contact with the coast. Unlike in Pernambuco, in Bahia not a single market hub developed even remotely near the backlands. Bahia's Estrada de Ferro Salvador–São Francisco, a British-financed railroad, transformed the seaboard, though not beyond, since the railroad reached only to Timbó and Alagoinhas in the *tabuleiro* zone (see Map 2), leaving the interior without railroad service.[101] The reason was mostly that this region produced nothing for export whose prices would be enhanced by cheaper transportation. Hides could be delivered by mule and did not spoil quickly. Nothing else in the backlands appealed to would-be investors or developers.

## CUSTOMS AND PRACTICES

We have seen that rural backlanders fell into different categories depending on their relationship to the elite and its control of the land. The ubiquitous *moradores* were present in the *sertão*, though in smaller numbers than on the coastal strip. There were also *meieros* and day workers, tenants who performed manual labor in lieu of rent. In his study of the Ceará *sertão*, Billy Jaynes Chandler observes that with the end of slavery the number of *moradores* grew, for some had been landowners but lost their property to the ravages of drought, the impact of which worsened with each decade as the population of the region increased. Throughout Brazil, the *morador* could be expelled at any time without compensation. After the promulgation of the republic, conditions for *moradores* deteriorated even further, since the poorer states, pressed to find sources of revenue, began to introduce taxes on land; property owners then passed on the levies to their tenants in the form of higher rents either in cash or in produce.[102]

Backland cowhands enjoyed the highest status among the lower classes, measured by the fact that they worked according to contracts that gave them use of a pasture (*roçado*), total freedom over their herds, and sometimes ownership of every fourth calf born. Thus some *vaqueiros* should have been able to rise out of their social class and become ranchers themselves, but the extent of such mobility is unknown. Northeastern cowboys had even greater freedom than their southern counterparts, for while in the nineteenth century southern ranchers lived on or near their lands, most northern *fazendeiros* resided in coastal cities; some never even saw their properties or spoke with the hired men who bred, cared for, and sold their cattle. The cowhands, in turn, lived most of their lives on the same piece of land, to which they returned after following the dusty cycle of the cattle drives.

Unlike southern Brazil by the 1890s, where barbed wire and tree-lined streams curbed wandering cattle, in the Northeast there were few fences. Da Cunha retells the (probably apocryphal) story of cattle sometimes being returned years after they had wandered off, identified by their still-decipherable brand. We also know that renegade backland cowboys, and even *jagunços* from Conselheiro's settlement, stole livestock. The enforceability of the *vaqueiro* code probably was not very high, though there always was a certain truth to the adage that "when you live outside the law you must be honest."[103]

By mid-century, a new group of planters and pastoralists, some of them European immigrants attracted by one of the province's colonization schemes, managed to gain a small degree of autonomy, in contrast to the hapless *caboclo* sharecroppers, few of whom ever really improved their lot. Agricultural colonists could buy government land for the equivalent of a daily skilled wage per square meter, but acquiring decent land with clear title necessitated influence and often bribery of various levels of officials. Most of the immigrants were from northern Portugal, though there was a strong secondary stream from Italy and Sardinia; many came to Bahia on Italian ships from Naples, Palermo, Trieste, and Genoa (forty-seven such ships docked at Salvador between June 1837 and July 1839 alone), and thousands more came as railroad workers in the 1850s and 1860s.[104] Few on the coast knew or cared about this immigration: the *visão do litoral* still held that the residents of the rural Northeast were all *caboclos*.

Roderick Barman shows that the immigrants did not have to compete with slaves, who amounted to less than one-tenth of the work force beyond the coast; moreover, they were able to ride the cotton boom of the mid–nineteenth century and profit from it. A kind of migrant elite, these men and women were known as *matutos*, a colloquial term for country rustics analogous to *caipira* in the South, *guasca* in Rio Grande do Sul, or *catingueiro*, an inhabitant of the backland *caatinga* region. The *matutos* preserved their Portuguese peasant traits, especially their devout Catholicism, whereas *caboclos* and blacks usually embraced syncretistic spiritism derived from Bantu and Yoruba religion. African-derived spiritism was strongest in the coastal slaveholding regions of monocultural agriculture and to some degree farther beyond, in pockets inhabited by former slaves and their descendants.

Spiritism, practiced mostly in cities but also to some extent in the interior, among certain elites, assumed three distinct forms in late nineteenth-century Brazil. One portion of the upper classes practiced European mesmerism, which emphasized mediumistic healing, reincarnation, and individual self-control.[105] In regions where slaves were most numerous (in Bahia, mostly along the coast as well as in the capital) the African-derived cults flourished. Cult worship penetrated the *sertão* only weakly, though *matutos* did borrow from the Bantu-Yoruba panoply of spirits, especially the *orixás* invested with healing powers. Rather, in the hinterland folk religious practices and totems derived largely from Amerindian beliefs, mostly animistic: anthropomorphic hawks, jaguars, turtles, songbirds, and wandering supernatural personages—werewolves, headless she-mules, the devil in all guises; *boitatás*, beings able to protect or to destroy pasturage; *caaporas*, mounted demons that crossed the plains on moonlit nights; and the diabolic *sací*, which attacked tardy travelers on Good Friday eves.[106]

Folk belief in supernatural intervention reduced the need in the region for political and legal means of social control. In Brazil, rural inhabitants believed that misfortune resulted from a failure to accept one's predestined lot in life; suffering in the form of droughts or disease was thus viewed as divine retribution, and political subjugation was similarly accepted, usually without protest. Backlanders expected punishment when they did not fulfill duties (*obrigações*) to the saints or to God after petitioning for assistance through a vow (*promessa*).[107] This is not to say that the faithful faced life with complete resignation. They fought hard to surmount obstacles, wrestling with the earth even as they called on individual saints to mediate between the secular and sacred worlds. Existence involved constantly restating one's faith in the power and goodness of personal deities.

Backland women prayed constantly for divine intervention, groveling on dirt floors and chanting for salvation while their men blotted out their travails with alcohol. We have noted the strenuous devotion to particular saints. The saints were believed not only to cure disease but also to cause afflictions, which then could be removed only through vows and pilgrimages to specified shrines or holy places believed to be inhabited by the particular saint's presence. Men and women offered heroic vows in exchange for favors; when the vows failed, the pious blamed themselves and pledged self-denial and suffering. For many humble men and women, even daily devotions were expressed with astonishing concentration and fervor.

Prayers and pilgrimages were habits, ways of expressing intense wishes. Such acts had medieval roots in the Iberian peninsula. Offerings—food products, knitted pieces of clothing, candles, rosaries of wood or *uricuri* shells, carved wax relics, and the more elaborate ex-voto images, sculpted representations of injured or deformed body parts—were left at pilgrimage shrines, part of a personal transaction between supplicant and saint. These offerings were not only mechanistic gestures, but they permitted anxiety and heavy emotion to be released. Da Cunha attributed one fetishistic rite to Conselheiro himself: the "kissing" of the images at the end of the long, drawn-out daily prayer service in Belo Monte, after those present had "run the gamut of litanies, said all the rosaries, and intoned all the rhyming benedicites." Starting with Pious Anthony, the altar boy, then taken up by Conselheiro and finally by every congregant in turn, each crucifix, saint's image, veronica, and cross in the church would be passed from hand to hand, from mouth to mouth, accompanied by "the indistinct drone of half-stammered exhortations" and "stifled exclamations of the throng."[108] Such graphic descriptions dismayed city readers and reinforced their discomfort about backland life.

Flagellant practices—*imitatio Christi*—introduced by Jesuits and Franciscans in the sixteenth century, survived and took on a life of their own in many backland communities, where they became focal points for group associations. More than anything else, this strong penitential tradition explains the passivity with which Canudos residents accepted their lot. People were thin because their diet was restricted, but also because of the *culto de fome*, the almost continual fasting undertaken as a penitential act to mortify the body. Everyday backland religious practices contained aggressive elements as well. *Ermitães* (shrine hermits), in exchange for payment, incanted "black" prayers, casting spells against enemies in a Catholicized variant of coastal *quimbanda* (cult spiritism).[109]

Rural and urban poor alike frequently used marijuana—variously called *diamba*, *rafi*, *maconha*, or *fumo d'Angola*—especially in the São Francisco region and on the northeast coast.[110] Herbalists knew about other, more powerful mind-altering substances as well and probably introduced them to communal ceremonies and occasions. Healers also prescribed natural remedies: salt for healing and apotropaic rites, boxwood, the poisonous seed of the cashew fruit (for cathartic ends, not nature worship).[111] Then there were miracles and miraculous sightings, usually experienced after the unexplained restoration of health, often following a pilgrimage to a religious shrine.[112] Claims of miracles were part of the popular cultural system and were often welcomed by the church. The commotion raised by miracles provided a respite from the monotony of everyday life in "remote, patriarchal communities" and brought instant prestige and importance to the humble sufferer able to attest to the miraculous.[113]

Denigrated for their "mestizo religion" and for their heritage of "a multitude of extravagant superstitions which are no longer to be found along the seaboard," backlanders' behavior only confirmed the prejudices of their detractors. They were ridiculed as being prolific. Rural families often ran to more than a dozen children. One woman, forty years of age, was said to have borne thirty children, of whom eleven survived.[114]

Reactions to hardship varied, but remained consistent with the stoic "vale of tears" outlook on life. Although day-to-day hardship was accepted, when a long-standing condition changed abruptly, local inhabitants would mobilize spontaneously in protest. This was true of the Quebra-Quilo eruptions in much of the rural interior Northeast, when the government introduced new regulations that effectively challenged the traditional way of doing business at the weekly markets. The rioters, it could be argued, smashed the weighing machines not in Luddite ignorance, but precisely because they understood that the regulations, however "fair" to consumers, would bring new government control. What coastal officials deemed reformist and progress-minded, the backlanders saw as a violation of their autonomy.[115] Individuals, however, whether rich or poor, were not thought to have the right to complain about their own condition, because whatever was, was God's design.

Some of the region's superstitions and taboos were more lighthearted but nonetheless influential and prevalent. Backlanders refused to marry on Sundays, and girls marrying on Sant'Ana Day, July 26, it was believed, risked dying in childbirth. The marriage partner who got into bed first, it was said, would determine the sex of the first child; the one who left the bed before the other in the morning would be the first to die. Wedding parties (even in austere Canudos) were greeted with rifle shots into the air, fireworks, *vivas*, and elaborate feasting. One prescription, that a banquet be held no matter how humble the bride and groom, gave even the poorest members of the community something a bit special in their lives.

Backland townspeople, though more circumspect and formally Roman Catholic in their outward behavior, also clung to old beliefs about magic and miracles.[116] Throughout the region, women carried fetishes and amulets with their rosary beads and crucifixes. Simple folk carried out elaborate penitential vows to erase infirmities or spells of misfortune. In the Bahian *sertão* south of the São Francisco River, residents practiced rites linked to a death cult first developed in the early 1700s, in which initiates performed acts of flagellation for seven-year periods.[117] People sought countermagic (*juju*) and healing ceremonies (*catimbó*) to complement natural remedies. *Catimbó*, a form of white magic, involved ingestion of "holy smoke," singing, and the shaking of hand rattles (*maracás*) harboring protective healing entities.

Outsiders, as might be expected, found such practices to be atavism at its worst, the result of a "miscegenation of beliefs." Secular positivists leaped to identify such influences as remnants of the inquisitorial religious fervor exported three centuries earlier from Portugal. Because in the backlands time had "stood still—[backland] society ha[d] not been affected by the general evolutionary movement of the human race"—it was easy enough to dismiss *sertanejo* religious practices as extravagant superstitions, "stigmata of . . . [an] underdeveloped mentality." This attitude was reinforced by the fact that under the empire, folk medicine was tolerated as "just another part of slave and *caboclo* culture," but under the 1890 republican Criminal Code, spiritism, *catimbó*, homeopathy, and all "natural medicine" were prohibited, with prison and fines promised to transgressors.

The backland *matutos* were closely influenced by the neo-orthodox Catholic revival and therefore, unlike most other rural groups, were linked institutionally to the outside world. A portion of the *matutos'* traditional independence, however, disappeared after 1900 when they were increasingly drafted for corvée labor (*sujeição*) on *fazendas*, an obligation arising out of uncollected debts to landowners. With their new *agregado* status, their reputation declined. *Matutos* came to be seen as "degenerate," men who lived by *vadiagem*—"hanging out" and making do day to day.[118]

Yet backland rural inhabitants were seen in a relatively better light than the *caboclos* of the coastal plantation zone. To some extent, this image reflected the elite's prejudices on the subject of race. "The *sertanejo*," the president of the Brazilian Academy of Letters later wrote, "lacks Negro blood; rather, he is a product of Portuguese genes mixed with Indian blood and conditioned by the environment. . . . There is less ignorance and primitivism there," he added, "a legacy of the[se people's] pastoral activities and the wide and deep resource of natural decency."[119] More recent (and more scientific) studies have revealed that the black presence in the backlands was greater than originally thought, especially in isolated places sought out by fugitive slaves or other migrating blacks in the nineteenth century and earlier. An anthropologist working in the Potengi-Encruzilhada region in the São Francisco Valley noted the use of words of African origin and classified three-quarters of the local inhabitants as *pardos*.[120] Another investigator claimed to have found the remnants of a runaway African encampment (*quilombo*) in the Serra de Borborema in neighboring Paraíba.[121]

## THE CULTURE OF SILENCE

Squatters lived in fear, not only of natural calamity but also of random violence. Individual landowners were often warm and supportive, especially given the paternalistic tradition; many looked the other way when times were bad and permitted favored squatters to use small tracts of land rent free. Gregório Bezerra describes how, as a six-year-old child toiling in the fields, a *senhor de engenho* offered him two days' wages even though he had until shortly before been too sick to work.[122] Few rural poor, however, could count on such charity. Long-term distress reinforced the strong fatalism of those who watched in silence as garden plants perished and soil washed away in floods. Such bad times forced destitute people to eat rats, lizards, unripe bananas, and rotten sugar cane. Children worked as early as four or five years of age, their stomachs often too swollen from hunger to digest the lumpy manioc gruel fed to them. When the poor fell ill they called on *curandeiros*, who prescribed noxious mixtures of herbs, tobacco, animal droppings, and minerals; wounds were washed with urine. Animals that caused accidents were slaughtered or sold, regardless of the economic consequences, to exorcise their evil spirits.

Some behavior patterns may have followed from mechanisms of coping. Backlanders often affected exaggerated deferential postures, avoiding eye contact or walking with heads bent downward when in the presence of superiors. Speech took on a cringing manner that suggested, in the words of an observer, a combination of degradation and suppressed revolt: "They have the impression of being stripped of their humanity, constantly spitting in nervousness, stooped, awkward."[123] Rustics observed laughing or singing were assumed to be drunk on *pinga*. Perhaps they were expressing high spirits—without any aid from cane alcohol.[124]

Even though frightened and, in the eyes of sophisticates, superstitious and fanatic, the poor found ways of avoiding or even defying conventionally expected behavior. Contrary to the opinion of many early ethnologists and subsequent historians, superstition was naturalist if not rationalist in inspiration, serving as it did the need to find explanations and to aid psychological escapism.[125] Magic and popular forms of faith provided a sense of self-definition and brought relief. Secret practices, drawn from formal Catholicism but heretical in the distorted forms they

assumed, allowed practitioners to take refuge in the comfort of person-
alized ritual, ritual that evolved away from a church presence. Not that
"naive faith" was in all places truly religious. Emphases varied over time
and from place to place. Sometimes practices for penitential healing
predominated; at other times piety might center on efforts to exorcise
the presence of the devil. In locales with a variety of economic zones,
classes, and racial groups, religious observances varied.

We should remember that Enlightenment confidence in the essential
rationality and natural virtue of man was shaken only with the rise of
modern psychiatry, which showed anxiety and uncertainty about the
world to be a universal if not desirable human trait. In the nineteenth
century, thoughtful Brazilians were still attempting to erase the stigma
of primitivism and, less publicly discussed, of racial miscegenation.[126]
Proponents of radical rationalism—in Brazil, led by the secular positivists, for whom Euclydes da Cunha was a vanguard activist—distrusted
the lower orders, most of whom were dark-complexioned. This fact was
further evidence to the positivists of racial degeneracy. If Brazil's adoption of such modern attributes as republicanism, rational positivism, and
modern values in the closing decades of the nineteenth century meant
real change among urban elites, in the countryside old ways of viewing
the world survived and flared up in seemingly self-destructive ways,
notably in the behavior of men like Antônio Conselheiro.

◇  ◇  ◇

Despite the harsh trials suffered by the backland faithful, their fervent
prayers seemed to be answered when in good years rain fell and the earth
bloomed. The poor accepted the bounty as an undeserved gift from
Providence. Families gathered together and returned to abandoned
homesteads. To buy seed and supplies, backlanders took credit from
landowners, further feeding the cycle of debt obligation. Men, women,
and children worked the land. Women cleaned the rudimentary farming
utensils and mill machinery as well, pounded manioc tubers into meal,
and sewed clothing from rough cloth. In good years they also embroi-
dered apparel for festivities and made gifts for the Christmas season. In
these bountiful times, rural families ate decently, subsisting on bananas,
rice, beans, tripe, jerked meat, salted cod, coffee, and sometimes bread—a
protein-rich diet, if deficient in certain vitamins and heavy in carbohydrates. In hard times, of course, most of the protein vanished. While the
harsh climate required that men consume up to three thousand calories
per day, rural workers received 20 percent less, mostly in starches; the
average annual allotment of meat was only 62 grams. In drought years,

intake shrank to less than one thousand calories per day, with terrible effects, especially on children and pregnant women.[127]

The poorest, of course, never ate much more than *farinha* and some rice. Food taboos contributed to malnutrition as well. Cow's milk in some areas, even when available, was often excluded from the diet, even for children no longer nursing.[128] Moreover, landowners rarely allowed tenants to eat indigenous fruits (coconuts, bananas, *cajú* fruit, passion fruit), which often grew uncultivated all around; these restrictions may well have caused the odd ways in which local residents consumed fruits, when they did at all (eating bananas by squeezing them rather than by peeling them, for example, as if eating them surreptitiously). Charity and self-sacrifice were characteristic traits of the poor, who ended most sentences with "Se Deus quiser" (If God wills), the mainstay of the rural vocabulary. No matter how badly a family fared, it shared its resources with distant relatives or neighbors in greater need. Traveling with their gravely ill mother, the Bezerra family was given refuge at a shack where the inhabitants had only rotten sweet potatoes to eat; yet they shared them, and gave up their single bed to the dying stranger.

The breakdown of a rural tenant's harvest illustrates how things worked on the land. Allowed to grow manioc on a local *fazenda*, one family produced at season's end fifty-four sacks of 60 kilos each. Twenty-seven sacks were turned over to the *patrão* as rent; three were bartered for provisions (soap, salt, beans, kerosene); eight were kept for family use; six were given to other *agregado* families in exchange for the women's backbreaking work of grinding the tubers into meal; and the remaining ten were sold as profit. In addition, some sacks might be reserved for the *mutirão*, a form of reciprocal communal labor in which residents would pool their resources to work clearing land or building a house for a member of the community.

Although in the high *sertão* there is little evidence to show that the *mutirão* functioned as an important institution—there, families tended to seclude themselves from their neighbors and to fend for themselves, even during droughts—recollections of such voluntary group labor in the coastal plantation zone emphasize the good humor and camaraderie of the participants. Nevertheless, the work was deadly serious, often performed to put a roof over a family's head or to forestall violence from the *patrão* for failure to perform contracted tasks. As many as 150 or 200 men and boys worked in shifts around the clock on such *mutirão* projects as building water storage tanks or dwellings. Fed food and cigars by their women, they kept in good humor by singing or stepping rhythmically to music. Meals were served "Indian file" to workers, an uncharacteristic form of social intercourse for rural *caboclos* who usually ate alone, hunched on the ground in silence. Spirits were kept lubricated with *pinga*, drunk neat or mixed with passion fruit juice. Drunkenness resulted frequently, and often small disputes exploded into violent fights.[129]

Backlanders' clothing was as rudimentary as their housing. The poor nearly always went shoeless, like slaves. Men wore shirts and trousers of coarse cotton muslin and straw hats. Often they wore nothing but a kind of waist-apron made from burlap sacking, or flung over their shoulders like a poncho. Women and children wore long cotton shirts reaching to their knees or formless dresses. Boys did not wear trousers until adolescence, and then only if their families could buy cloth.

## CYCLES OF VIOLENCE

Out of the many, occasionally overlapping, groups of people who inhabited the rural interior, some general traits may be noted. First, the continued presence of large groups of squatters and *agregados* may be attributed to the fact that land in Brazil, though always cheap, was difficult to obtain for most members of society. Thus rural Brazil contrasted sharply with rural Europe, for example, where, as in the case of France, peasants managed to acquire land and thereafter cloaked themselves in a strong conservatism rooted in the desire to anchor themselves more firmly to their own plot of soil.[130]

The northeastern *agregado* made few demands, accepting a relationship borrowed from feudalism even though rooted in a capitalistic system. The *agregado* way of life embarrassed educated Brazilians, who contrasted backland behavior unfavorably with that of the free *colonos* of Italian, German, and Japanese stock recruited to southern Brazil through government subsidies. Oliveira Vianna, the conservative historian, praised the foreign-born *colonos* for seeking to establish themselves as small proprietors, salaried workers, or share tenants; *agregados*, however, he described with contempt:

> They live in rude huts located on small dispersed plots that are scattered about the great house on the hill to which they are oriented and which dominate them. From the fertile land they extract, almost without work, sufficient game, fruits, and cereals to live a frugal and indolent life. They represent a type of small, self-sufficing producer vegetating at the side of the large *fazendeiro* producer.[131]

Rural *agregados* were thus entrapped by the needs and demands of the landowning elite. Bernard Siegel explains:

> Regardless of the region, each peasant type is a variation of the rural *caboclo*. Each has a status in a traditional set of interpersonal relationships whose structure is determined by the nature of the economic activity to

which he is devoted. The form which these take varies from region to region and from economic activity to economic activity. All of these various regional arrangements are, broadly speaking, similar.[132]

The bond linking the backlander to the larger economic system remained constant, despite the fact that the pastoral economy offered laborers more freedom than workers on coastal plantations. Independent cowhands often raised cattle owned by others for up to a year before an agent came to count the herd and pay the tenant for his services. Coastal Brazilians did not know what to make of such people. The Bahian *jagunço*, wrote Aristides Milton, a newspaper editor, "lives in habitual lawlessness, on his own terms."[133] This view was relatively new. Before Canudos, *jagunços* were considered to be unsophisticated but harmless. During and after the conflict, however, the connotation of the term changed sharply. Urban residents of the backlands now mocked cowhands who came into town, calling them "monkeys" and "dog killers."[134]

Da Cunha, as ever, was typically ambivalent. He described the *sertanejo* as a member of a backward race separated from the coast not by an ocean but by three centuries of barbarism; but he also described him as a contradictory figure, slouched one minute, animated the next. He added a political connotation: "Your jagunço," he said, "is quite as inapt at understanding the republican form of government as he is the constitutional monarchy. Both to him are abstractions, beyond the reach of his intelligence."[135] Further:

> One alights from the train, walks a few hundred yards between rows of squat houses, and forthwith finds himself, at the edge of the village square—in the backlands. For this is in reality the point where two societies meet, each one wholly alien to the other. The leather-clad vaqueiro will emerge from the caatinga, make his way into the ugly-looking settlement, and halt his nag beside the rails where natives of the seaboard pass, unaware of his existence.[136]

The *caboclo*, da Cunha concluded, using the term as a synonym for *jagunço*, "is almost always an unbalanced type . . . degenerate . . . lacking the physical energy of his savage ancestors and without the intellectual elevation of his ancestors on the other side." His mind is "unstable, restless, inconstant, flaring one moment and the next moment extinguished, the victim of the fatality of biologic laws."[137] Armed *jagunços* riding through the backlands in packs of as many as three hundred were more feared than the underpaid, usually poorly equipped, and ineptly led state police. More than one governor renewed his forces with *jagunços* impressed into service—at least until most of the would-be soldiers deserted—creating units before which rural residents cowered in apprehension.

Da Cunha's powerful imagery, coupled with his stylized nineteenth-century prose, distances him from most present-day readers. But his descriptions of *sertão* life were for the most part accurate. Everything we know about the backlands confirms that life was very harsh. Propertyless backland *caboclos*, terrorized by bandits and police alike, were forced to pay for protection by providing food and, to bandits, ammunition. Both outlaw bands and government forces dragged men away and impressed them into involuntary service. The Jeremoabo police chief explained to his superiors in 1871 that endemic hunger in his district was increasing sympathy for the bandit *quadrilhas* (gangs), who provided food and provisions to local residents in exchange for protection.[138] The common people enjoyed few if any rights. Provincial laws permitted the police to hold anyone without formal charge, even if only for being suspected of having the inclination to commit a crime or for being vagrants, beggars, prostitutes, drunks, or threats to public order and quiet.

Landowners, merchants, clergymen, and officials always sat at the top of the rural pyramid, set apart by their great power and privilege, their links to the outside, their wealth, and their mutual interrelationships. In a hypothetical rural *município* of fifteen thousand persons in 1890, perhaps five hundred occupied the first two tiers: the powerful, plus a second level, somewhat more heterogeneous, comprising lesser merchants, bureaucrats, businessmen, and their families. This group's lifestyle—education for its children, its patina of cultured, urbane behavior—more closely resembled that of the coast than that of the hinterland. A third level of perhaps three or four thousand men and women would take in the rest of the population centered in the county seat as well as the upper echelons of the rural folk: the smallholders, muleteers, craftsmen, independent *vaqueiros*, and specialized agricultural workers—in all, a sort of lesser bourgeoisie, its membership determined by regularity of employment. Insecurity, not abject misery, distinguished this group and probably accounted for its deep conservatism, rooted in a fear of sliding into the group below.

The final group, characterized by more or less permanent hardship, took in the remaining 70 or so percent of the local population. Relatively most fortunate were the tenants who had access to land, though they lived under conditions of near indigence; the least stable were the odd-jobbers, beggars, and vagrants. The landless earned no wages and so were excluded from the market economy. The rural poor faced constant, contradictory pressures: pressures to stay put (the *patrão* system, help from kinsmen, debt servitude, vagrancy laws) as well as pressures to move (the search for a plot of land or for employment; the need to flee harassment or natural disaster).

Even the diseases of the rural poor and their symptoms—lethargy caused by parasites, impaired vision, nervous disorders, spasticity caused by aglastoma, chronic underweight—fed stereotypes of unreliability and lack of stamina. Physical infirmities seemed evidence of moral weaknesses; moreover, it was suspected that the wiry, rail-thin, stooped *caboclos* were shiftless and could not be counted on. Yet the generalized landowners' fear that the poor would refuse to perform the work of slaves after abolition proved groundless. Despite the allure of outmigration, made progressively easier by improvements in transportation, most backlanders remained in or near their birthplaces throughout their lives, accepting whatever conditions were imposed on them. The exodus of thousands of backlanders to Canudos in 1893–97 was remarkable, and many others in the closing decades of the nineteenth century did migrate to the coast and beyond the region; but in all, the population remained stable, bolstered by a constantly high rate of childbirth.

Not all of the factors detrimental to the landless poor resulted from deliberate acts by landowners. Some planters, especially in the North, themselves progressively impoverished by modernized agriculture and the attendant trend toward land concentration, befriended the needy whenever they could. As regional markets evolved, crops previously grown for subsistence—corn, beans, manioc—became increasingly commercialized. This situation benefited small family farmers, who now had no need to hire workers, but it also encouraged larger landowners to cancel tenancy arrangements and switch to large-scale planting methods. In this way, the poorest rural inhabitants fell victim to the very fact of economic progress.

Modernization led to downward social mobility and stripped thousands of rural workers of their livelihood—especially sugar mill workers, cane transporters, peddlers, and seasonal agricultural laborers. Labor-saving technologies imported to agricultural areas at great cost halved the work force, and the slack was apparently not taken up by other economic activities.

Despite repressive measures on the part of landowners to control the rural labor force and maintain its docility, the dislocations of economic change in the nineteenth century only prompted a further broadening of definitions of lawlessness. Arrests of marginalized rural workers increased steadily after 1860. The incidence of brutality, moreover, peaked during times of stress, especially in periods of forced military recruitment and drought. Bands of men frequently attacked jails and troop caravans to free recruits who had been impressed forcibly into militia or army service, though news of such incidents, as of the looting of food markets, was usually suppressed. Along the highly populated northeastern coastal plantation zone, interpersonal violence and crime,

including murder, also increased noticeably after 1890, coincidental
with the final stage of sugar mill modernization. In the backlands, too,
arrests increased, if less dramatically.

Violence, as has been noted, was institutionalized both at work and in
the home. Young girls and women lived in constant fear of rape, not
only by males of their own or lower classes, but by landowners, their
overseers, and the landowner's sons. Folklore claims that backland bandits branded their initials on the shoulders or breasts of their victims.
Once abused, girls usually became outcasts; yet impoverished mothers
were known to offer their virgin daughters in desperation for a few
coins at local markets.

Cruelty surfaced frequently. An illustrative tale survives from the
sugar-growing region of the coast north of Bahia. An elderly mill owner
sold his business and departed for the city. When the new owner caught
a *caboclo* squatter chewing on a stick of cane, he had the culprit brought
in. Although the wrongdoer meekly protested that eating cane had
never been a crime in the region before, the *patrão* remained unmoved:
he ordered the victim stripped, lashed to stakes, and covered with mo-
lasses, to be trampled by grazing cattle. At the end of the day witnesses
who were forced to watch said that the man's skin had been reduced to
a "paste of meat." He then was tied to a tree, and by the next morning
he had died, his body a "festering ant hive."[139]

Those who earned their livelihood in occupations that involved contact with others always ran the risk of being victimized. These included
men and women working as domestics, servants, bodyguards, and, in the
small towns, shopkeepers, odd-jobbers, craftsmen, musicians, and prostitutes. Two independent types of peddler traveled the countryside,
bringing, in small ways, the outside world to even the most remote
agricultural habitations: itinerant peddlers, who carried their wares on
their backs; and muleteers (*almocreves*), nearly twenty thousand strong in
the 1870s in the Northeast alone, considered with *vaqueiros* to be the elite
of the rural lower class because they carried firearms and were often
accompanied by slaves or hired servants. Both groups frequently engaged in brawls, drank heavily, and sometimes terrorized females left at
home while male family members were at work. The penetration of the
interior by railroads and ultimately by highways, however, doomed the
*almocreves*, who, deprived of their traditional livelihood, drifted further
into the hinterland or became unemployed. Still others, men who came
to the towns from rural areas, became day workers and were marched or
transported by cart to the fields. These hired hands, although free from
tenancy obligations, occupied the lowest rungs of the social ladder; they
were miserably paid (they were usually assessed for their transportation)
and were only engaged when needed.

Clearly, the conditions under which the largely uncomplaining rural poor of the region lived were perpetuated by the principle of "shared poverty" and by the patron-client relation, whereby the patterns of domination and submission, as Clifford Geertz has shown, were accepted as God's design.[140] Backland Catholicism inured the faithful to accept their roles in rural society; at the same time, it provided the logic—the meanings, directions, and guidelines—by which these men and women reacted when the world as they knew it seemed threatened. The downfall of the monarchy, the abolition of slavery, and the introduction of change to the region raised tensions and spread anxiety as parts of the old system crumbled.

Political power in rural Brazil remained in the hands of a small number of families whose power stemmed from landownership. Brazil functioned as a "patrimonial state"; the political elites, both under the empire and after, were mainly concerned with holding onto office and rewarding themselves and their clients with the booty of patronage. Under the republic, members of the liberal professions—lawyers, journalists, even engineers and teachers—were subject to these power brokers' whims, often becoming caught in the cross fire between feuding clans or political factions. In the rural Northeast, and especially in the backlands, the *coronelismo* system and powerful landowners like the baron of Jeremoabo preserved the arrangement whereby patriarchal values (loyalty, hospitality to one's allies, respect for authority) were reinforced by poverty, latifundary monoculture, coerced labor, and *compadrío*, political patronage and favoritism.[141]

Into this world came the pietist Antônio Conselheiro, to observers from the *litoral* "a second-century heresiarch in the modern world."[142] The fact that modernity was invading even the backlands had disrupted the older and slower patterns by which inhabitants related both to the land and to the hierarchies of power that controlled their lives. By 1893, the legends about Conselheiro's promises of a new Jerusalem, of a protected, holy settlement in which the faithful could await the final Coming, were well known throughout the hinterland. As he marched due north from Tucano to Canudos, believers joined him. They did not, we are told, make any inquiries as to where they were going. To da Cunha, Canudos became the "objectivization of a tremendous insanity."[143] To those who followed Conselheiro, their pilgrimage held the promise of peace, a strenuous but exhilarating release from the growing uncertainties and torments of backland misery.

# THREE

# New Jerusalem

*"Quem tem que morrer, não chora" ("He who must die, sheds no tears")*
NINETEENTH-CENTURY *SERTÃO* SAYING

Antônio Vicente Mendes Maciel was born on March 13, 1830, in Santo Antônio de Quixeramobim, deep in the Ceará backlands 140 miles from the coast.[1] His grandparents were *vaqueiros*. His father, Vicente, considered by some a semivisionary and iconoclast, achieved a rare feat for a backlander born into a family of cowherders: he became a shopkeeper and, eventually, a successful businessman with several "good houses" on Quixeramobim's square, the town's prime location for commerce. At the same time, though, he was a difficult man. Partially deaf, he was known for his distrustful eye and his introverted way of dealing with people. He was also a man of few words and an alcoholic. His first wife hid whatever extra money she had so that Vicente would not squander it in drinking sprees.

Vicente's first marriage ended disastrously: he deserted his wife after cudgeling her so savagely that she almost died. His second wife, Maria Maciel (usually known as Maria Chana), imposed strict religious discipline within her household. Punishments were frequent. Gradually, Vicente's fortunes began to slip away, a situation he dealt with by becoming more morose and by staying away from his family in sullen bouts of inebriety.[2]

As a child, Antônio was shy and studious. He appeared wan and pallid, for he spent much of his time indoors, working for his father. He was of typical northeastern stature, rawboned, with black eyes and an aquiline nose, and he had small hands and feet.[3] The boy's complexion was tawny (*moreno*), a feature later attributed to partial Calabaça Indian ancestry. It is indicative of the wide latitude in the application of racial descriptions in nineteenth-century Brazil that his birth certificate listed Antônio as *pardo*, but chroniclers who saw him generally referred to him as "white"; this was also the description presented to Salvador's arch-bishop, Dom Luiz, by the visiting Italian Capuchin Frei João Evangelista in 1895.[4] Antônio had two younger sisters, Francesca and Maria. By the time he was ready to enter school, his prospective life course would have been considered conventional for the only son in a small-town family (which today we would call middle class), although psychologically he must have been affected by his father's frequent abusiveness. By modern standards, his home life was unhealthy, influenced by his father's de-clining economic status—the result of bad investments and of his drink-ing—and a lack of affection at home combined with harsh religiosity practiced as a kind of penitence.[5] To compound the boy's already un-happy situation, his mother, Maria Joaquina de Nascimento, died when the boy was only six.

Antônio's first formal instruction came from his father, who wanted him to become a priest. After a year or two, however, the boy entered a school run by Professor Manuel Antônio Ferreira Nobre, where he stud-ied arithmetic, geography, Portuguese, French, and Latin. Some of his schoolmates later took their places in the regional elite, including Major Eufrásio Nogueira, police chief in Quixeramobim, and João Brígido dos Santos, a newspaperman, lawyer, and polemicist.[6] Local inhabitants con-sidered the Mendes Maciel clan a "good family"; in the language of the day, it belonged to the "conservative classes," though it was not partic-ularly wealthy.

Since 1833, members of the Maciel clan who lived in the backlands between Quixeramobim and Tamboril had been engaged in a dispute with the more dominant and affluent Araújos, relatives of even more powerful landowning clans in the region. Despite the odds against them, the Maciéis had initiated a bloody feud against their rivals, over a minor incident (in the eyes of the authorities if not of the principals) in which the Maciéis were blamed for robberies on an Araújo's property without clear evidence. Being the *senhores de barraco e cutelo* in the region—the dominant elite, "lords of life and death"—the Araújos took justice into their own hands, deciding to make an example of the Maciéis, who thus far had enjoyed a reputation for being "sturdy . . . truthful and obliging."[7]

Antônio's grandfather, Miguel, became one of several Maciéis who, along with the head of the clan, Antônio Maciel, paid with their lives. The men were tricked by police in the pay of the Araújos: in Boa Via-gem, a village between Quixeramobim and Tamboril, they surrendered upon being offered amnesty, only to be arrested, manacled, and beaten to death. An uncle, Miguel Carlos, escaped, allegedly even though he had been handcuffed and his legs bound beneath his horse. The Araújos pursued him, but he slipped away and took refuge at his sister's house, where he hid in a shack overgrown by *oiticica* boughs.[8] When Araújo's hired assassins arrived, they shot the sister and set fire to the shelter, from which Miguel Carlos was shooting. Legend tells that the victim momentarily put out the flames, jumped over his dead sister's body, and rushed his assailants with only a rifle and a long knife. After a skirmish he again broke away and disappeared into the wilderness. Some time later, the Maciéis struck back, killing an Araújo bridegroom as he approached the church with his bride. The blood feud then spread until it enveloped all the clan members on both sides, for more than a generation.[9]

Antônio Mendes Maciel himself is not known to have participated in any of the hostilities.[10] When his father married again in 1836, soon after Maria Chana's death, Vicente brawled frequently with his new wife and beat her.[11] In 1855, Vicente died; by then the steady decline in the family's economic fortunes had only been worsened by overspeculation.[12] Now twenty-five years old and responsible for four unmarried younger sisters (two of them half-sisters), Antônio inherited little, for most of his father's assets went to pay off debts. He took over his father's business and filed papers to back the remaining loans with a mortgage. In 1857, he married his fifteen-year-old cousin, Brasilina Laurentina de Lima, the daughter of Francisca Maciel, his father's sister. Although she had grown up in the town of Quixeramobim, where there were good schools, Brasilina never learned to read or write. Contemporaries said that the girl's mother, who moved in with the couple, had once been a prostitute. This reputation came not from evidence, but from the fact that she had a quick tongue, like her daughter, and was considered by the dour residents of Quixeramobim to be lacking in the deferential air that community demanded of "good" women.[13]

Still in debt, Antônio—now known as Maciel—mortgaged his house and liquidated his father's remaining assets in order to become a tutor in Portuguese, arithmetic, and geometry at Fazenda Tigre, some leagues from Quixeramobim. In 1859, he worked as a shop clerk, then opened a dry goods store in Tamboril and, soon thereafter, another in Campo Grande. Both went bankrupt. He worked as a cashier in a store owned by Major Domingos Saboia, a merchant-coronel in Campo Grande; in Ipu, he tried to earn money as a *requerente*, a kind of nonlicensed lawyer, taking simple cases in the tribunal. He and Brasilina likely had a child in 1859, though firm evidence is lacking.[14] A second child was born in Tamboril in 1860. There, Brasilina had an affair with one João de Melo, a *furriel* (a noncommissioned soldier intermediate in rank between corporal and sergeant) in the Ceará militia, and ran away with him. (Later on she deserted de Melo as well, ending her days as a beggar in the streets of Sobral.)[15] A year or so after his wife's departure, Maciel abandoned the children to the care of Brasilina's mother. The backland code of honor gave him little choice in this unhappy situation: he could either avenge himself by killing his wife and her lover, or he could do nothing and suffer endless humiliation. In the end, flight proved a third option.

Maciel's financial fortunes and presumably his emotional state continued to falter; nevertheless, he struggled to reassert himself within the system, now working as a traveling salesman (selling, among other things, *cachaça*, which later in Canudos he prohibited as sinful). He relocated to Crato, became an itinerant peddler, and took to accompanying evangelical missionaries who preached at the weekly *feira*. We know little further about his life during the 1860s, although there is some evidence that his personality continued to change. Once, at Paus Branco, on the Crato-Cariri road, he stopped to visit one of his sisters and furiously attacked his brother-in-law. He was spared a prison sentence only because, when the police arrived, the relative refused to press charges.[16]

Between 1862 and 1863, in Santa Quitéria, he met a woman known as Joana Imaginária, an artisan who crafted and sold saint's images. A child—presumably his third—was born, Joaquim Aprígio. (Manoel Benício in 1898 offered an alternative scenario: that Antônio had fathered Joana's child during an extramarital relationship *before* Brasilina left him, thus justifying her dalliance and departure with the soldier; but this version is undocumented.)[17] Then we lose track of him (though for fewer years than da Cunha suggests). During 1867 and 1868 he likely worked as a salesman, wandering from town to town in the outback. He stayed in Várzea da Pedra from 1869 to 1871, but when an old creditor in Quixeramobim sued him for unpaid debts, he left, only to reemerge in São Mateus, Ceará, in 1872. The following year he arrived in Assarí, where he met the Villanova brothers, Antônio and Honório, who later would establish shops in Canudos. By this time he was surviving mostly on charity, living the life of a penitent. In these years, too, he surely heard Padre Ibiapina, the renowned missionary from Ceará who preached against vanity (and who during his sermons burned items of women's clothing, for effect).

Maciel now left Ceará for Pernambuco and Sergipe, and in 1874 he emerged in the high *sertão* of Bahia, where he became known as "Brother Antônio" or "Antônio dos Mares" (Fig. 8). The evolution of the names by which Conselheiro was known is interesting. As a boy he was called Antônio Vicente; as a young adult, Maciel. At the outset of his lay ministry he was known as Irmão (Brother) Antônio, then, variously, as Antônio dos Mares, Santo Antônio dos Mares, Santo Antônio Aparecido, and, finally, by the mid-1870s, as Antônio Conselheiro. This last title signified that he was considered not merely a *beato* but a wise counselor, a nineteenth-century title that few religious men in the backlands attained. Whereas *beatos*, who were formally consecrated as such by par-

8. Antônio Conselheiro. Woodcut, widely circulated in the Northeast, early 1890s. Courtesy Instituto Geográfico e Histórico da Bahia, Salvador.

ish priests, begged for alms for the poor, *conselheiros* preached and extended advice about spiritual as well as secular problems, such as difficult marriages or disobedient children. Both *conselheiros* and *beatos* were common in the backlands, a region otherwise extremely understaffed by regular clergy.

Maciel continued to roam the *sertão* of Bahia, Pernambuco, and Sergipe, following in the well-trodden paths of lay penitential pilgrims. He visited the old Capuchin missions, thereby earning a following among the scattered remnants of the region's Brazilindian population. He became gaunt, fasted regularly to extreme lengths, and slept little. He walked through the backlands from town to town, asking permission to preach and warn local residents of the need to repent, in exchange offering to rebuild dilapidated walls of churches and cemeteries fallen into disrepair.[18] The first parish curate to request guidance from his superiors following such a request was the vicar of Nossa Senhora de Conceição de Aporá, Padre João José Barbosa. The reply specified that Conselheiro could stay and work if he did not preach, a condition that Conselheiro rejected; in turn, Padre Barbosa condemned the itinerant missionary as "disobedient."[19] So began two decades of conflict with church authorities, though on many other occasions local representatives of the church responded much more warmly.

Usually when Conselheiro entered a hamlet or village, townspeople offered him a place to sleep, and he took alms when he needed to eat. Occasionally he would stop at a *fazenda*, where he would preach to the rural inhabitants of the surrounding area. (After Canudos was founded in 1893, the owners of two ranches where he had stopped years earlier— the *fazendas* Ouricuri and Buri—reportedly sold them and went to join Conselheiro.)[20] Of all the acts Conselheiro performed, his work mending and enlarging cemeteries may have had the greatest impact on local residents and on parish clergy. Burial was an extremely important rite for backland society; sometimes families sold nearly all of their possessions to pay for the funeral of a loved one, or to buy a plot in a more prestigious location, since cemeteries were rigorously segregated according to family status. Occasionally patrons or *coronéis* would pay for interment, but usually families had to bear funeral expenses themselves. One reason for the need to rebuild cemetery walls was that population growth necessitated cemetery expansion; another was the high mortality rate, especially among children, due to the severe droughts in the region. Local churches were too poor to hire laborers to do the work. In addition, the dead were often interred in the walls themselves, but after two years, unless fees were paid, their bones were removed to ossuaries. Thus, by enlarging cemeteries, which provided more room for permanent burial, Conselheiro paid respect to the dead and, perhaps, lowered burial charges.

In the course of his wanderings, Conselheiro also designed and constructed cisterns to hold water, chapels, and even small churches, aided by parishioners who worked without wages and by disciples who followed him. His first known project was to rebuild the small Rainha dos Anjos chapel in Itapicurú in 1874, the first of twenty-five churches he would adopt during his lifetime. When he entered a populated area, usually accompanied by a ragtag band of mendicants, the event created astonishment. Virtually all regular activity ceased as the curious strained to watch and then to listen. When he built, from scratch, a church in Dendê (later Crisópolis), villagers carried wood from Fazenda Genipapo, a half day away.[21] Over the doorway, he carved an inscription that may still be read today: "Só Deus é Grande" (God alone is great). He supervised construction by day and preached in the evenings in the public square, surrounded by small bonfires that warmed the chilly night air and attracted passersby. Word about the stern but compassionate penitent quickly circulated throughout the region.

There is concrete evidence of Maciel's presence in the Pernambuco backlands during 1873 and 1874, still wandering and performing the tasks of a penitential hermit and rebuilding churches and cemeteries.[22] By this time, coastal archdioceses in Olinda and Salvador had virtually stopped sending new priests to backland villages: there were simply too few recruits. More and more, the church relied on foreign missionaries, such as the Lazarites who visited Monte Santo, Saúde, Urubú, and even the moribund Canudos *fazenda* in 1877. Conselheiro's appeal during these years may have stemmed more from the fact that the region was starved for a religious presence than from his mystical or charismatic powers. His austere Catholicism was characterized by a brooding spirituality and message of devout responsibility. For example, he attacked the institutional church for not enforcing clerical celibacy, although later, in Canudos, he looked the other way when Cumbe's Padre Sabino, the father of ten children, came to offer sacraments.[23] Those who heard Maciel during this time offered different characterizations: some said that he was confused, almost incoherent; but most marveled at his ability to hold audiences enthralled.

Local residents of the backlands found him a spellbinding orator, with a sonorous voice that he projected in rhythmic cadences. His sermons, a survivor of Canudos later said, although delivered in quiet tones, caused his listeners to feel "as if they were flying up to the clouds."[24] Later analysts criticized his emphasis on frugality and penitential redemption as "primitive" or rural "folk" Catholicism, but no evidence suggests that Conselheiro advocated heresy or even digressed significantly from the Catholic precepts common to the region. Although some of his prophecies were enigmatic, he mostly spoke of things that touched the lives and concerns of hinterlanders: debts, morality, the government, and individual destiny. When the republican 1891 Constitution was enacted, he lashed out at it, reviling the provisions on separation of church and state, civil marriage, and registry of births and deaths. Shaken by the forced exile of the old monarch, Pedro II, he fulminated against the republican regime as a personification of the Antichrist.

His mission, even his dress, emulated the tradition of Brazilian seventeenth-century lay religious *ermitães*. These were solitary penitential wanderers who, because of the lack of priests in remote areas, were often treated by backlanders as representatives of the church. *Ermitães* resembled missionaries: they wore robes of heavy indigo cloth with a rope knotted at the waist, and they walked barefoot or in crude leather sandals. Remaining unshaven and unshorn, they covered their long, unkempt hair with a hat. Sometimes, on a string around his neck, an *ermitão* wore a small reliquary box containing small saints' images, scapulars, and relics. They prayed for long hours each day and lived on alms collected in return for special prayers or advice.[25]

Maciel, it is obvious, followed in the footsteps of earlier *ermitães*. Lay and clerical missions were already proven avenues by which individuals could garner considerable followings in the backlands. The practice of rebuilding churches, chapels, and cemeteries, moreover, was a clearly enunciated church policy, initiated in the region in the 1860s to improve ecclesiastical property and to reach out to the lower classes. José Antônio Maria de Ibiapina was the most prominent precursor. A Cearense whose father was executed in 1825 for participating in the failed republican Confederation of the Equator, Ibiapina entered the priesthood in 1853 at the age of forty-seven, having already served as a *pro bono* lawyer in Recife for four years, in the National Assembly in Rio de Janeiro, and as a municipal judge in Quixeramobim. As a priest, he embarked on a career in which he functioned as the first "modern" northeastern-born Brazilian missionary.[26]

Padre Ibiapina spent the years between 1862 and 1883 walking through the six provinces of the backlands, where he earned widespread fame as a holy man. He founded at least twenty-two *casas de caridade* for abandoned and orphaned girls, and preached against the "sins" of government.[27] Like Antônio Conselheiro, he commented on politics: he believed that God was good but that society had entered into a state of dissolution, and that Masons—including the Prussian chancellor Otto von Bismarck—represented the Antichrist. To Ibiapina, Jesus Christ was a "Jesuit against the forces of the devil and a Brazilian Saint Vincent of charity to help the miserable."[28] Yet Ibiapina's and Conselheiro's visions were not cut from entirely the same cloth. After all, Ibiapina was an ordained priest and Conselheiro was not. Ibiapina's Mary was the Virgin of the Sacred Heart, loving and charitable according to the characterization of the hierarchical church. Conselheiro, in contrast, spoke of "Nossa Senhora das Dores," Our Lady of Sorrows, the suffering mother-figure of backland tradition.

There were other *conselheiro* precursors. One was the Pernambucan Conselheiro Guedes, who dressed in a Carmelite habit and was the father of a brood of children, who walked with him. Another was Conselheiro Francisco (Francisco Maria de Jesus), a "jovial *cabra*" (mulatto) who helped build a church in Cumbe near Canudos and who exercised priestly functions: he supposedly traveled to Canudos every two weeks to say mass.[29] During the mid-1880s, at least two "false *conselheiros*" wandered the backlands in imitation of Maciel. One, Luís Ribeiro da Silva, was a former *beato* who wandered away from his mentor's band and who established his own holy site, to which other pilgrims came. Another, Francisco Conselheiro, imitated his namesake and former mentor in every way, dressing like him, preaching, and caring for cemeteries.[30] There may have been several dozen other imitators.

No imitator, but an extraordinarily successful and charismatic priest considered a sainted holy man by his followers, was Padre Cícero Romão Batista. He had had a perfectly conventional chaplaincy between 1872 and 1889 in the Carirí Valley in Ceará, but deviated from orthodoxy after he participated in an alleged miracle, whereby the host being administered to a *beata* in Juazeiro turned into the blood of Christ. Clerics other than Padre Cícero publicized and exploited the event, organizing pilgrimages to the site from all over the Northeast. By the time Antônio Conselheiro established Canudos, some hundreds of pilgrims had settled at the Cearense Juazeiro, residents of another holy city that lasted more than fifty years despite Cícero's suspension from priestly orders in 1892.[31]

During the late nineteenth century, changes in the Northeast's ecclesiastical organization began to affect how priests related to backland parishioners. New dioceses were created, for the most part served by secular priests from São Paulo and Minas Gerais. These men took steps to refurbish rundown ecclesiastical properties (thereby signaling, Ralph della Cava notes, outward reform),[32] and they established two new seminaries in Ceará, one in Fortaleza (1864) and the other in Crato (1875), to train new priests recruited from the region. The leading figure was Dom Luiz Antônio dos Santos, named Ceará's first bishop in 1861 and elevated to archbishop of Salvador in 1880. Under Dom Luiz's leadership, the Ceará seminaries turned out zealous graduates, in keeping with attitudes then emanating from Rome of hostility to Protestantism, Masonry, positivism, and secularism. Yet there were still not enough priests to go around, and relations between Brazilian-born priests and the augmented number of European priests staffing the seminaries and working as backland missionaries remained tense.[33]

By the mid-1870s, Maciel's fame as "Antônio Conselheiro" had been established. The title of "counselor" was apt, because he did not offer sacraments. Rather, he preached and dispensed legal and moral advice, always with the approval of the authorities. First making a courtesy call to the local priest, if there was one, the emaciated missionary set himself up in the public square, doing repair work by day, taking small meals when offered, preaching at night, but mostly reposing in silence. In March 1876, a local policeman complained to superior authorities that Conselheiro was a threat to public order (the first such complaint), but no action was taken.[34] Sometimes, as in 1882 in Nova Souré and 1887 in Vila do Conde, village priests asked the police to expel the unwelcome visitor from their parishes. In the first instance, Monsignor Santos Pereira, in the name of the archbishop, responded with a circular letter advising all parish priests not to cooperate with Conselheiro, and to go to the civil authorities if the missionary refused to behave appropriately. He also proscribed laymen from preaching. But there was no effective way of enforcing these admonishments, short of driving Conselheiro out of town physically or calling in the police.

A second pastoral letter, dated November 10, 1886, directed priests to warn their congregations against Conselheiro. A few local priests, friendly to Conselheiro, refused, but most complied, making Conselheiro's work more difficult in the period that followed. The episode in Vila do Conde ignited when small boys threw buckets of water, stones, and other objects at Conselheiro, until finally the people who had given him shelter intervened. The vicar, Rodolfo Duarte Guimarães, took to calling him "the untitled Antônio Conselheiro." Conselheiro shrugged off the slight, but when he crossed the Itapicurú River to preach in Vila Velha, *jagunços* attacked the vicar's house and forced him to flee for protection to a nearby ranch.[35]

Consistent with lay backland traditions established long before, handfuls of *beatos* consecrated by Conselheiro or by friendly local priests wandered with the missionary across the dusty wilderness trails. The women among them likely included former prostitutes (as Samuel Putnam observes, they were expiating their sins by penance), but the only evidence of this is da Cunha's reference to the fact that *some* of the women at Belo Monte were "old maids," the backlands term for loose women.[36]

Conselheiro in person in effect mirrored observers' prejudices. Those who came expecting to see a fanatic commented on his unkempt appearance and his otherworldliness. They noted his pilgrim's clothing, his air of grim austerity, and his unconcern with worldly goods; they commented with wonder that he was said to sleep only one or two hours a night, usually on the ground without a blanket. His sermons, delivered from makeshift platforms covered by leafy bowers, usually erected in the public square, mingled Latin quotations and excerpts from the *Hours of Mary* and the *Missão abreviada*, the prayerbook commonly used during the late nineteenth century by lay Catholics performing the work of missionaries.

Conselheiro would begin with a few sentences in Latin, which had the effect of mystifying his listeners and establishing his authority (in this respect he resembled backland priests, who performed similarly, especially when they first arrived in a locale). Sometimes he stared for long minutes, as if in a trance. Many of his imprecations were practical: he castigated unchristian employers who cheated their workers, and employees who stole. Undoubtedly, the spellbinding behavior only enhanced his sermons. Da Cunha's description illustrates the *visão do litoral* view:

> Sparing of gestures, he would speak for a long time, eyes downcast, without looking his audience in the face as they stood there overwhelmed by this endless flow of jargon, the tiring lilt of nonsense. He was, however, it would appear, concerned with the effect produced by this or that outstanding phrase. He would enunciate it, then pause, raise his head, sud-

denly lift his eyelids, and one would then have a glimpse of his extremely black and sparkling eyes, his gaze—a dazzling flash. No one dared look at him then. His listeners would succumb, would drop their gaze in turn, fascinated by the strange power of hypnotism exerted over them by this awful form of insanity.[37]

Others, either disinterested or predisposed to see him in a positive light, marveled at his kindness and his concern for victims of political wrongdoing and police arbitrariness.[38] Some said that he was "saintly" and "prophetlike."[39] Occasionally he was joined in his pilgrimage by missionaries sent by the church from Europe. Sometimes they preached with him; at other times they listened silently. Although Conselheiro did speak against Masonry, Protestantism, and secularism, mostly he preached penitence, morality, righteousness, and devotion. No specific sermons against slavery are recorded, but we know from his writings that he opposed the institution and that after emancipation hundreds of freed slaves flocked to hear him, and later many followed him to Canudos. Sometimes his audiences in remote towns surpassed two or three thousand, a startlingly high number for the backlands. As soon as he finished, the crowds would melt away in an instant.

By the early 1890s Conselheiro had visited dozens of backland population centers in Bahia, Pernambuco, Alagoas, Ceará, and Sergipe, as well as some towns beyond the *sertão*—in the *tabuleiro* region and even on the coast, as when he visited Vila do Conde in 1887. Times were harsh; the cycle of periodic drought had intensified, with an ever-widening impact on the local economy, and his presence caused stress among landowners and officials, even though his crowds were never unruly. Conselheiro remained as much an ascetic as ever; many times he nearly died after a prolonged fast. His face was described as lifeless and rigid as a mask, "at once unseeing and unsmiling; eyelids drooping over deep-sunken sockets," his garb suggesting the "general aspect of a disinterred corpse." But crowds thronged about him, and he was greeted by "the ovations . . . of frightened believers and terror-struck pious women."[40] Da Cunha's description of the missionary's growing and awe-inspiring charisma was probably quite accurate:

> There was probably not a town or city in which he had not made his appearance. Alagoinhas, Inhambupe, Bom Conselho, Geremoabo, Cumbe, Mucambo, Massacará, Pombal, Monte Santo, Tucano, and other places had beheld him approaching, accompanied by his riffraff band of the faithful. And in nearly all these towns he left some mark of his passage: here the ruined walls of a cemetery had been rebuilt; there a church had been repaired; and farther on a chapel had been erected, with a display of fine artistry always.[41]

During 1890 or 1891, Conselheiro, now on the defensive, settled a number of his followers on two abandoned *fazendas*, Dendê de Cima and Dendê de Baixo, 135 miles north of Salvador. They planted crops, began to raise goats and chickens, dug a cistern, and erected a church. The settlement, known as Bom Jesus, prospered, and later grew into the urban center of the *município* of Crisópolis.[42] Conselheiro moved on; the effort to build a refuge where he would actually live with his flock came a few years later.

His decision to settle at Canudos in the Vasa-Barris Valley was the direct consequence of an attack on him and his followers by the Bahian state police at Masseté (later renamed Tucano) early in 1893. In that year, he commenced preaching about a holy land, deep in the backlands. The response was remarkable and immediate. Streams of people—individuals, whole families, eventually entire portions of neighboring localities—followed him to Canudos, leaving their homes, sometimes selling their property for whatever it would bring, and carrying their possessions, their furniture, their portable altars to the new colony. Outsiders scoffed, calling the settlement "sinister," a "monstrous *urbs*," a "colossal weed patch," an "aggregation of clay huts," a "city of ruins."[43]

Most of those who left their homes to live in Conselheiro's austere community had little to lose; even so, migrating to a new locale required bravery, since few backlanders ever permanently left their place of birth except in dire necessity. And in any case, not all his followers were poor or dark-skinned, as da Cunha claimed. Some were "white" women from "good families"; a few even brought money, jewelry, and other valuable possessions with them.[44] Piety, more than any other element, linked the inhabitants of the holy city. The merchant Antônio Vilanova remarked that when Conselheiro preached, a throng of some five thousand listened raptly—"the same number as listened to Jesus Christ."[45]

The sudden exodus of hundreds and then thousands of families within the short span from mid-1893 through 1895 jolted local *fazendeiros* and their clients. Every hamlet and municipality from Itabiana and Entre-Rios to the São Francisco portion of the Bahian *sertão* saw contingents of pilgrims leave. Again, da Cunha's description was a tour de force, patently untrue except in the narrowest sense of the *visão do litoral*. Always ready to stamp the believers as fanatics, da Cunha described the Canudos settlement as "the objectivization of a tremendous insanity. A living document whose implications were not to be evaded, a piece of direct corpus delicti evidence on the aberrations of a populace . . . with the fervor of the mad."[46]

The truth is that few joined Conselheiro capriciously or because they were seduced by a crazed magician. Backlanders knew their immediate region intimately; they probably had heard that Canudos was fertile, and they likely had some sense of Conselheiro's good relations with at least some local *coronéis*. They were, of course, attracted by the hypnotic aura of his preachments. But residence in Canudos did not require religious "rebirth" or any form of conversion to a messianic creed. *Conselheiristas* had always tried to live according to backland Catholicism; Canudos simply provided reinforcement and encouragement, however harsh the results seemed to outsiders. Once in Canudos, some adopted more stringent forms of observance, while others did not. Several things did *not* happen: there was no enforced standard of communal behavior, religious or otherwise, even though Conselheiro constantly reminded his congregants of their obligation to live according to God's laws. There was no drunkenness, no prostitution, no hunger caused by lack of food. Canudos's inhabitants never suspended their rational understanding of the realities of backland life. Those who wanted to remained in constant touch with neighboring communities; they came and went at will. People visited Canudos, did their business, and left. Many *conselheiristas* worked outside the community every day. They were not prisoners. They came to Canudos to preserve their Catholicism, not to exchange it for a cult or deviant sect.

The chroniclers of the *visão do litoral* considered Conselheiro a manipulator and charlatan. Yet in contrast to Padre Cícero, who did not object to others publicizing his miracle and who skillfully enlisted political allies as well as a personal following, Maciel behaved unpretentiously to a fault. He often chided penitents who genuflected before him, remarking, "I am a Maciel by name and a Conselheiro only in my heart." He did permit the curious to follow him around, and he did not dissuade them from addressing him as "my father." Even during the military attacks on Canudos he mostly devoted himself to building the community's new church and to penitential prayer. He never claimed miraculous powers. He was no "cunning devil," as some journalists tried to picture him.[47] His political passivity, including his lack of attention to forging alliances that might offer protection to his community, was a major reason for Canudos's fall.

The first published reference to Conselheiro appeared in *O Rabudo*, an odd weekly political satire sheet published in newspaper format in the town of Estância, Sergipe, in 1874.[48] The article, which filled half of the paper's four pages, did nothing but ridicule Maciel. The penitential dress of the preacher, it said, who had the appearance of "the most debased figure in the world," indicated that he had committed some crime or was fleeing from justice. Nevertheless, the piece concluded by acknowledging the power of "Antônio dos Mares" to draw crowds "in fabulous numbers," and stated that he was currently engaged in building a "temple" in Rainha dos Anjos, Bahia.[49] At about the same time, in the mid-1870s, landowners began complaining privately about a "massive exodus to Canudos."[50] Two years later, Conselheiro was mentioned in the Bahian press as an ascetic with "great influence over our ignorant and simple peasants of the lower classes."[51] A story was told that in the absence of the vicar in Natuba, Bahia, Conselheiro gathered stones to rebuild the church. When the prelate returned, however, he ordered the work halted because he had not been consulted and Conselheiro had "taken" stones that did not belong to him. Conselheiro left, and the church remained unfinished.[52]

In February 1882, a letter from Archbishop Dom Luiz Antônio dos Santos declaring Conselheiro persona non grata went out to parish priests in the archdiocese. Rural priests were now caught up in the bishops' effort to preserve their authority. Significantly, the church never condemned Conselheiro's religious practices or his theology. He was always orthodox in his Catholicism, and he continued to enjoy good relations with some local clergy, who gave him free access to their churches and, in many cases, publicly commended his efforts to repair church property. Priests in several localities ignored the archbishop's order against lay preachers. Cumbe's Padre Sabino, for example, became a friend of Conselheiro and an ardent defender of Belo Monte. Oral tradition in the region holds that Moreira César, commander of the third expedition against Canudos, was so angered by Sabino's outspokenness that he ordered the priest arrested for sedition.[53] Like many other backland priests, Sabino lived in a monogamous relationship with a woman who bore him children, behavior that did not endear him to the reform-minded hierarchy (even though priests hostile to Conselheiro, including the state senator and vicar of Itapicurú, Cônego Agripino da Silva Borges, were themselves known to have fathered children as well).[54]

Priests assigned to the arduous task of serving backland districts varied widely in their judgment of Conselheiro.[55] Some were friendly. "The devout Antônio, vulgarly known as Antônio Conselheiro, arrived here and asked my permission to pray nightly in public," wrote the vicar of Inhambupe, Antônio Porfírio Ramos, to the archbishop. Since it was raining in torrents, "I permitted him to pray inside the parish church. . . . I can guarantee," he concluded, "that in investigating his doctrine, I found nothing more than the true word of God. His [Conselheiro's] life is no less than a veritable penitence."[56]

Others feared and distrusted Conselheiro and assailed priests known to be sympathetic to him. At the parish level, Conselheiro's most ardent detractor was Father Júlio Fiorentini, an Italian-born Capuchin missionary who had come to the diocese in 1881 and who was zealous, devoted, and well educated.[57] In early 1886 he mounted a letter-writing cam-

paign, accusing the mystic of evildoing; at one point he even alleged that
Conselheiro was a heretic, a "wolf in sheep's clothing."[58] He wrote to
Cônego Miranda in Salvador: "He is bad. You need to know all of the
facts." He is "sustained and protected" by Vigário Agripino and the vicar
of Aporá, Padre José de Araújo Pereira Cavalcanti.[59]

> He is a heretic. I refuse to give sacraments to his followers, but they go to
> Padre José. Many people either have these padres baptize their children or
> rebaptize them if they were baptized by me or another priest Conselheiro
> does not like. His followers pay these priests large sums of money—they are
> bought off. They pay for baptisms, weddings . . . it is scandalous. . . . Padre
> José marries anyone without permission [the church normally checked for
> collateral descendants, etc.]. People are convinced that Antônio Conse-
> lheiro is God and that José is the only priest authorized to speak for him.

To cap things off, he wrote, "His followers say that you [Cônego Mi-
randa] are a Mason and a Protestant."[60]

On September 9, 1886, Padre Fiorentini sent a shocking letter to the
archbishop, which was never discussed publicly and was neither confirmed nor denied by any subsequent investigation. Conselheiro has
bred such fanaticism, the priest wrote, that, reportedly, a sick man in this
parish "has been drinking, as medicine, Conselheiro's urine and eating
the man's excrement."[61] That a reform-minded vicar of the church genuinely believed that Antônio Conselheiro was capable of generating such
monomania and reckless emotions illustrates the seriousness of the hierarchy's growing conviction that the penitent's harmful influence must
be countered.

The earliest known attempt to interdict Conselheiro's activities coincided with the decision by the most authoritative local landowner in
Bahia's northeast, the future baron of Jeremoabo Cícero Dantas Martins, in collusion with the archbishop of Salvador, to neutralize Conselheiro's rising influence. Jeremoabo's career epitomizes the intricacies of
the region's interlocking elite networks. Not only was he one of Bahia's
most powerful local *coronéis*, with Itapicurú as his political base, but his
marriage into the Costa Pinto family of Santo Amaro in the Recôncavo
brought him into the sugar aristocracy as well: he became the son-in-law
of the count of Sergimirim and nephew-in-law of the Liberal prime
minister, Sousa Dantas. Dantas Martins's barony was granted in 1880 for
his part in financing the province's first sugar refinery, the Engenho
Central do Bom Jardim in the Recôncavo, in which he was a partner,
presumably through his wife's share of land. The refinery was sold in
1891, after which time Jeremoabo directed his interests to his backland
fiefdom.[62] By then he, more than any other *fazendeiro* in the region,

stood to lose from Conselheiro's ascendancy over the local population, and he became an implacable adversary, carrying his enmity to the political arena.

We can only speculate on whether Martins had a hand in the first effort to rid the region of Conselheiro. Claims that backlanders were beginning to refer to him as a "messiah" and reports of ever larger bands of followers led to Conselheiro's arrest in Itapicurú, the baron's principal dependency, in June 1876. Although Jeremoabo was in Rio de Janeiro at the time, as a member of Bahia's parliamentary delegation, he kept in close touch with Itapicurú. The events leading up to Conselheiro's arrest and imprisonment, as we might expect, have been embellished indiscriminately, but a close reading of the sources reveals the facts.

Conselheiro often timed his appearances in urban centers to coincide with important saints' days. According to tradition, he arrived in Itapicurú on a Tuesday, Saint Anthony's Day. The police chief, Boaventura da Silva Caldas ("seu Boa"), was a close friend of the baron's as well as a fellow member of the Conservative party. Initially, Caldas dealt patiently with the petty disturbances created by the missionary's presence. Neighbors complained of the noisy late-night prayer gatherings in the unoccupied house borrowed by Conselheiro and his disciples; characteristically, Conselheiro's *beatos* answered angrily, but Conselheiro calmly overruled them, saying that his followers would cause no further disturbances.

The situation worsened when the vicar, Agripino da Silva Borges, demanded that the police chief bar Conselheiro from speaking in public. Agripino, one of the most capable churchmen in the region and an ally of the Liberal opposition bloc, the *gonçalvistas*, knew that by challenging Conselheiro he could embarrass Jeremoabo as well. Soon after lodging his complaint, however, Agripino made peace with Conselheiro, who offered to repair the vicar's church. Relations between the two men quickly improved, forming the basis for years of friendship.[63]

In the meantime, the police chief found further reason to protest Conselheiro's presence. Distracted, local residents had stopped buying goods from the town's main store—owned, as it happened, by Chief Caldas, who wrote to Jeremoabo that Conselheiro was "diverting the behavior of the population."[64] Jeremoabo then intervened personally, demanding that the provincial government seize Conselheiro. Forewarned, Conselheiro and his flock exited Itapicurú and crossed the Real River into Sergipe, beyond the jurisdiction of the Bahian militia, where they stayed until tempers cooled.

A few months later, Conselheiro crossed back into Bahia, invited by

Father Agripino to serve as godfather for children baptized by the prelate.[65] An important institution in the rural interior, *compadrío*, the godparent system, functioned as a vital form of co-parentage, building interpersonal ties as strong as blood relationships in a region where the need for personal protection was so critical. Since at least the medieval Council of Munich in 813, however, parents had been forbidden to serve as godparents to their own children. Many therefore named local land-owners or other important patrons, while others listed the Virgin Mary as *madrinha* and sometimes Bom Jesus as *padrinho*. Now, though, dozens asked Conselheiro, a living saintly man, to attend the baptisms of their children and to honor the child with his promise of protection. The baptism records indicate that persons from all social tiers of the back-land population accepted Conselheiro without hesitation. From 1880 through 1892 he attended and was listed as godfather at ninety-two baptisms in Itapicurú de Cima alone. In nearly half these cases, the godmother named was "Nossa Senhora" (the Virgin Mary).[66]

Conselheiro then proceeded to visit other towns in the Bahian *sertão*, and in Aporá, in June 1875, he requested formal permission to preach in exchange for repairing the local Lazarist cemetery. Aporá's tempo-rary vicar, João José Barbosa, however, contacted the archdiocese in Salvador and refused permission. Conselheiro left without completing any work. He then moved on to Aracá, Esperados, Caatinga, and Cumbe, to which Padre Barbosa responded by demanding police action; provincial authorities, however, demurred on the grounds that they could not spare the manpower. It is telling that the larger issue of Con-selheiro's relationship with the church was never really resolved. In some places Conselheiro was opposed by local authorities but supported by the clergy; elsewhere the opposite was the case; and sometimes clerics attacked one another over tolerating (or not tolerating) Conselheiro, complaining bitterly in letters to superiors.[67]

Through early 1876, officials, including clerics in Salvador's archdi-ocese, seemed willing to let Conselheiro proceed and took no steps to curtail his activities, even when requested to do so at the local level. But in late May of that year, when demands for action against Conselheiro accelerated, Bahia's police chief, Dr. João Bernardo de Magalhães, promised the bishop in writing that he would "take the necessary steps to incarcerate Antônio Conselheiro." The police chief added that he was convinced that the missionary was provoking trouble among the rural clergy and causing general instability in the region.[68] On June 6, An-tônio Maciel was arrested in Itapicurú, on the preposterous charge that he had murdered his mother and wife in Ceará some years before. He offered no resistance and counseled his supporters not to interfere.

Conselheiro and one of his closest disciples, Paulo José da Rosa, were then locked in the local jail to await a contingent of fifteen policemen to transport them to Salvador.

The public prosecutor asked that Conselheiro be transferred to Ceará, the letter of extradition noting that the accused was a bad influence among the "ignorant folk" of Itapicurú and that he had shown disrespect to the local vicar. Even if he is not found to be a criminal, the document concluded, it would be wise "not to permit him to return here," since that would "provoke disagreeable results among the fanatics angered by the arrest of their idol."[69] On the way to Salvador the missionary had been forced to walk (until the company reached a railroad station at Alago-inhas), and, in leg and wrist irons, he was badly beaten by soldiers. Upon arrival in Salvador the two men spent three days in jail and then were led through the streets, to the taunts of onlookers, to another facility among a larger group of prisoners. Conselheiro was then placed in manacles and taken to the coastal steamboat *Pernambuco*, accompanied by two guards, and, a week later, was delivered to Quixeramobim.[70]

No sooner did he arrive than it was verified that his mother had died when he was a child and that his estranged wife was still living. Not a single person came forward to testify against him. The charges were dismissed, although the soldiers who had accompanied him from Bahia to Ceará did get in one last beating.[71] Freed, he spoke bitterly to by-standers in the courthouse, but he refused to file a formal complaint about his treatment, saying that "Christ had suffered worse." He then returned to the Bahian backlands and Sergipe and again took up his old work of rebuilding ruined churches and adobe cemetery walls.[72]

Conselheiro's fame spread fast after his arrest and release, fueled in part by other reasons as well. From February 1877 to May 1880, the devastation of what became known as the Great Drought sent hundreds of thousands of refugees from five northeastern provinces fleeing across the *sertão* in the direction of the Atlantic or to the Amazon. Sixty-four thousand died from epidemic disease in Fortaleza in 1878–79 alone.[73] The desperate situation sharpened tensions and made many people more receptive to drastic solutions in the fight to survive. In the midst of this volatile atmosphere, the monarchy entered its last decade. Chattel slaveholding, which in 1872 had stubbornly survived even in the *tabuleiro* and *sertão*, suddenly virtually disappeared in the Northeast beyond the coast. The practice was no longer economically viable, owing to the lack of new sources of slaves, the uncompetitiveness of sugar producers in the face of mounting foreign competition, and the fact that slaves went for higher prices in the prosperous South. In 1863, one-fifth of all male workers in Souré were slaves, mostly used in ranching and agricultural chores. In 1872, there were 17,235 registered slaves in the larger region from which Canudos later drew population, including a good number in the immediate vicinity of Souré and Jeremoabo.[74] As slavery declined, landowners turned for labor to *caboclos* and emancipated slaves who stayed in the region. Given that many of Canudos's residents were of very dark skin—not *caboclos*, as outside chronicles generalized—it is highly likely that many slaves freed by abolition (1888) were among those who joined Conselheiro's sanctuary.

## CANUDOS SEEN THROUGH HOSTILE EYES

In spite of the legends that grew up around him, Conselheiro did not dwell on miracles in his sermons, only faith and hard work. He did not usurp sacerdotal functions, nor did he perform healing or provide medicine.[75] Some of his followers called him "Bom Jesus Conselheiro," emphasizing the suffering aspect of Christ, although we do not know that he ever encouraged use of that appellation. Conselheiro never asserted that he had been sent from God, or that he was a prophet: he remained within the boundaries of formal Roman Catholicism as a lay preacher and *beato*. His works were performed in the name of the church and in the service of local priests.

Outsiders were predisposed to see what they wanted to see. The journalist and writer Sílvio Romero, fresh from Recife Law School and newly appointed prosecuting attorney in the town of Estância, referred in a tract published after the establishment of Canudos to its "army of believers committing depredations of all kinds." In the mid-1870s, Conselheiro had wandered through Lagarto, Romero's birthplace in Sergipe, and obviously made an impression. Usually friendly to manifestations of local folk culture, Romero had been repelled by the "dour fanatic" who detested ostentation and who forbade the women in his flock to use hair combs and wool shawls, ordering them to burn possessions representing personal vanity.[76]

Once at a weekly outdoor market, Conselheiro was said to have been present when an old *curuca* (crone) attempted to seat herself to sell a straw mat. When the municipal fee collector demanded that she pay more than the value of her merchandise for the right to sell, she began to cry out and sob, drawing a crowd. In a sermon that evening Conselheiro referred to the old woman's plight and chastised the republic for trying to deliver the people back into slavery.[77]

Few allegations appearing in print and in rumor about Conselheiro were based either on meetings with him or on observation of his works, however. One exception was the experience of Durval Vieira de Aguiar, a lieutenant-colonel in the Bahian state police and at one time its commanding officer. Vieira de Aguiar ran into Conselheiro in Cumbe, in about 1882. Conselheiro was starting work on a new church, having completed a chapel in Mucambo (today Olindina). The colonel described Conselheiro as "short, emaciated, swarthy, with dark hair and a long beard, dressed in a beltless blue tunic, living alone in an empty house, where he is attended to by *beatas* with food." Vieira de Aguiar watched Conselheiro dispense advice and pronounce homilies and sermons. The local population flocked to hear him, listening raptly. The colonel noted that the local vicars earned handsomely from the baptisms, marriages, festivals, novenas, and every other kind of service rendered by the church, while Conselheiro "earned nothing."[78]

A second personal encounter was related by Dr. Genes Martins Fontes, a judge in nearby Monte Santo in the early 1890s and a political client of Jeremoabo's, to whom he owed his post. As a student at Recife Law School in 1881, he had come across Conselheiro during a trip to Sergipe. Like Vieira de Aguiar, he described Conselheiro's long, unkempt hair and his skin-and-bones appearance; he also noted his dirty hands and body lice. Conselheiro, he observed, wore an expression of indefiniteness, "characteristic of mystics and dreamers." Martins Fontes came away marked by the encounter.[79] Some years later, as a magistrate, he wrote again to a newspaper, this time remarking on how dramatically Conselheiro had changed. The mystic, he said, now clearly exuded an air of leadership and seemed capable of "dominating multitudes."[80] Martins Fontes, it seems, was not the only member of the elite to consider Conselheiro a troublemaker after initial doubts.

Cícero Dantas Martins, baron of Jeremoabo, also met Conselheiro personally and recorded his impressions. A prodigious correspondent, he exchanged hundreds of letters with relatives and cronies, many of whom were shaken by what they saw happening around them. A letter from a cousin, José Américo, dated February 28, 1894, captures the vehemence and revulsion with which the landowning elite viewed Conselheiro's movement:

> Today things aren't what they used to be. . . . [We have to contend with] that damned "Conselheiro Antônio," who is exercising more power now than the first Napoleon. I no longer feel Brazilian: the worst offense a man can commit is to call me a Brazilian subject. I am thinking about naturalizing myself African. We will soon see this *sertão* confiscated by [Conselheiro] and his people, who now number more than 16,000, all miserable ex-slaves and criminals from every province, without a single one who is a human being; [Conselheiro is] imposing his own laws, raising an army of soldiers, and doing anything he wishes.[81]

Jeremoabo's own letters reveal similar attitudes. Not only was he the leading landowner in Itapicurú—where, more than any other place in the *sertão*, Conselheiro stayed for long periods of time—but he had also been the leading *coronel* in the region around Canudos since the late empire. Before that, as noted, his interests were centered farther east, in the humid sugar-growing region around the Recôncavo.[82] A Conservative party stalwart, after the fall of the monarchy in 1889 he had joined the new state branch of the Partido Republicano Federal, the PRF-Bahia, together with other *coronéis* led by José Gonçalves da Silva. Gonçalves, a landowner and *coronel* from the municipality of Bomfim, served briefly as president of the new state until he was ousted by Salvador's federal garrison in 1891 after he backed President Deodoro da Fonseca's coup attempt. When the PRF split apart in 1893 over issues of patronage and internal power, Dantas Martins became a principal founder of a new opposition party loyal to Gonçalves, the Partido Republicano Constitucional (PRC), which had its power base in the interior.[83] Canudos was settled in that same year.

Jeremoabo was initially tolerant of Conselheiro, but grew less so when Conselheiro's influence over the local population became evident. As we have seen, in 1887 Itapicurú's police chief, one of the baron's clients, had petitioned Salvador to take steps against the "fanatic." After the Republican party schism, Conselheiro's lieutenants looked for protection to the faction headed by former Conservative leader Luiz Vianna, possibly expecting that party to gain control of the state assembly and the governorship. We do not know if meetings were ever held, or whether Vianna's partisans considered Conselheiro's followers to be *fósforos*, that is, potential votes to be delivered on demand as payment for local autonomy. Conselheiro himself likely remained aloof, but the defense he received in the state legislature strongly suggests that contacts were made. We do know that such arrangements were part of regional political culture in all portions of republican Brazil. We also know that the *vianista* faction burned *gonçalvista* tax edicts publicly, to symbolize its implacable opposition to those measures. Conselheiro's defiance of the republic may easily be seen as just such an act.

Conselheiro's flock was thus caught up in the generations-old factional struggles of the Brazilian oligarchy. Canudos was only one of several contemporary points of political instability in Bahia. Anti-gonçalvista tax decree bonfires occurred in 1893 and again in 1894, not only in Bom Conselho but elsewhere in the state, in Itapicurú, Souré, and Amparo.[84] At the same time that Conselheiro was constructing his mountainous retreat, the city of Lençóes had been attacked by *sertanejo* bandits, ruffians were threatening nearby Lavras Diamantinhas, the village of Mendes Brito was under siege by a mob, and the town of Jequié reportedly witnessed numerous violent crimes. What was not said publicly but was known by anyone familiar with backland life was that for decades the rural population had hated the police, who were undisciplined, poorly paid, and often permitted to run rampant and terrorize individuals and entire villages.

Vianna was the son of the party chieftain of Casa Nova in the *município* of Juazeiro on the São Francisco River. He took his law degree at Recife in 1869 and became a protégé of João Maurício Vanderlei, Baron Cotegipe. As an entry-level judge in 1889, he became notorious for corruption. When the empire fell he became the speaker of the state senate, the main founder of the PRF-Bahia, and city boss of Salvador, the state capital. His public works programs were riddled with instances of political favoritism, and he made free use of violence to quell any opposition. But opposition *coronéis*, especially in Ilhéus, Lavras Diamantinhas, and the *sertão*, resisted his efforts to dominate the state; Vianna was thus unable to aid his partisan allies in the backlands. His opponents also launched a barrage of charges that he was exploiting Conselheiro's movement for his own ends.[85]

Canudos precipitated stormy arguments in the Bahian Chamber of Deputies beginning in 1894, when the town's population had grown to more than fourteen thousand. These conflicts subsided only at the end of the final military campaign three years later. What is obvious from the debate is that supporters and enemies of Conselheiro divided along clear party lines: *gonçalvistas* allied with Jeremoabo and other *coronéis* from the regions losing population to Canudos demanded swift intervention, while others staunchly defended, if not Conselheiro himself, at least his acolytes' right to live undisturbed. Indeed, the debate proceeded along exactly the same lines as later controversies about religious communities elsewhere (most specifically, Padre Cícero's community in Ceará), thus demonstrating, if nothing else, that Canudos was not unique in the history of the region.

The anti-Conselheiro voices raised the usual charges that he was "either insane or [a] criminal," that he reigned as "an absolute monarch," and that his sway over his hapless flock was "nauseating." Conselheiro not only prays and rebuilds cemeteries, Deputy Antônio Bahia da Silva Aragão charged, but he is also organizing batallions, armed to the teeth, that are manned by criminals and fugitives from every prison in the state.[86] What is remarkable about the exchange between the deputies is how well informed the discussants were; clearly, Canudos was not the remote and evil place later depicted by da Cunha, but a settlement well integrated into the life of the region. To a question from a neutral deputy asking how the residents of Belo Monte fed themselves, Deputy Bahia da Silva responded that some of Conselheiro's followers had sold their property and turned the proceeds over to the community. An ally of Bahia da Silva's, also a resident of the state capital, Deputy Manoel Ubaldino do

Nascimento Assis, speculated that Conselheiro must be enjoying political influence; any man with a following as large as his, he said, has to have played his cards in the last senatorial election, given the *sertão* tradition of using everyone's votes.[87] In a statement preceding a colorful allegation that Conselheiro's forces included "Indians armed with bows and arrows," the *gonçalvista* spokesman linked Canudos, in an aside, to the statewide "resistance to tax payments" in April 1894, thus contradicting the Jacobin insistence that Canudos constituted a singular threat.[88]

To all this the anti-Gonçalves opposition responded with equal vehemence. Antônio Conselheiro, shouted the Federalist deputy José Justino (to mixed applause and new objections), is not only not a pariah, but he enjoys the support of the local curates.[89] Nothing Conselheiro has said contradicts Christ's religion, he continued, to which another *vianista* deputy, Antônio Joaquim Pires de Carvalho e Albuquerque, added, raising a tumult of objections from the floor: "Nowadays Antônio Conselheiro is superior in moral virtue to our own clergy." "I doubt," commented Deputy Hermelino Leão, a priest and a protégé of Senator Rui Barbosa at the state level, "that Conselheiro preaches subversive doctrines."[90]

Thwarted by the *vianistas*, Jeremoabo and his allies temporarily abandoned their efforts to force the state to intervene (even though the *gonçalvistas* controlled the senate) and instead turned their attention to other partisan disputes. By the time Vianna took power and was inaugurated as governor in May 1896, conditions had changed. Now, having consolidated his hegemony over Salvador, he no longer needed a backland base and could afford to listen with sympathy to the continuing demands for action from backland *fazendeiros*, even if they were not members of his own party. This switch was politically astute, in that it effectively co-opted Jeremoabo and his allies, who had been directly pressuring the federal government to act. Backland elites now, for the first time, stood together behind the antimonarchist colors, thus raising an issue that had been entirely absent from the debate during the previous two years.

This new alliance of *sertão* bosses and political interests in the incumbent state administration permitted Vianna to act unimpeded by factionalism, at least over this important issue; thus, faced with the new barrage of calls to destroy the "seditious backland cell,"[91] anyone who might still want to defend Conselheiro and his followers fell silent. The switch, of course, was entirely pragmatic. Although Vianna had never sympathized with Conselheiro, his initial reluctance to move against Belo Monte had been a political decision calculated to irritate Jeremoabo's dissident PRC. Ironically, Vianna's belated intervention against Canudos, an obvious effort to recoup his prestige among rural landowners, failed. His own explanation, during the final campaign in August 1897, was to claim that he had acted to soothe "the worries and fears" of regional agricultural interests, not to fight monarchism.[92] When his municipal candidate in Salvador lost in 1901, he refused to capitulate, and as a result President Campos Salles intervened with troops, exiling Vianna to Paris.[93]

The church, too, had continued its pressures to neutralize Conselheiro's influence. Dom Luiz Antônio dos Santos, the founder of the zealous Ceará seminaries, opposed Conselheiro from the moment the curate was invested as Salvador's archbishop in 1880. Seven years later, amid otherwise strained church-state relations, Dom Luiz personally warned the provincial chief of the "subversive" presence of Conselheiro, who was said to be "doing great harm to the church and to the state" and "distracting the common people from performing their daily tasks." For this disruption, the cleric averred, Conselheiro should be incarcerated in the state mental hospital as a religious fanatic.[94] For the time being, however, provincial officials were reluctant to take such drastic action.

It is clear that the conventional view that Conselheiro was opposed because of his antirepublicanism is misleading. Da Cunha's desire to paint Conselheiro as a revolutionary fanatic obscures the primary source of Conselheiro's dissatisfaction with the new constitution, which was equally opposed by the Catholic church hierarchy and local parish priests throughout the backlands—namely, the republic's enactment of compulsory civil marriage and the secularization of cemeteries. Conselheiro also bitterly objected to the 1891 Marriage Act, which was interpreted (incorrectly) by some Catholics as banning marriages between first cousins. Since such marriages were frequent in the backlands, and since many more northeasterners had been married in church only, people feared that such unions would in the future or even retroactively be invalidated, thus jeopardizing inheritance plans within families and placing rural couples in disgrace for not having been properly wed.[95]

The 1893 Bom Conselho rally, at which Conselheiro reputedly oversaw the burning of tax edicts in the town square, was considered to have been a turning point because it represented a sharp break with the republican order. According to *Os sertões*, Conselheiro "gathered the people and, amid seditious cries and noisy demonstrations, had them make a bonfire of the bulletin boards in the public square."[96] What da Cunha did not report was that municipal taxes in Bahia were no higher or lower during the early republic than they had been during the empire, and that the exercise was probably an act of political partisanship, not treason.[97] Conselheiro's action, the only illegal aspect of which was destruction of public property, probably had more than its desired effect: it gave his enemies a pretext to demand retaliation. All other allegations of Conselheiro's active opposition to the republic, to the point of advocating civil disobedience, were based on hearsay and were, in all probability, false.

The Bom Conselho events followed closely on the schism in the ruling state Republican party. Conselheiro's tax edict bonfire may have been a show of loyalty for Vianna, who was now temporarily out of power after having lost his assembly majority. Similarly, the act of ordering a contingent of thirty soldiers from the state police to intercept Conselheiro and a few hundred followers on the Monte Santo road was probably an attempt by Vianna's assembly opponents—now in the majority—to punish "their enemy's backland ally." (Ironically, they employed the same tactic for which Vianna would gain a reputation later: use of state police as personal *jagunços*.) Nor was the clash between Conselheiro's followers and police at Masseté in 1893 a singular occurrence: troops were sent out to Belmonte and Canavieiras in the southern portion of the state to aid Vianna supporters there against local *coronéis*, but in both cases the badly led expeditionary units were defeated.[98] Observers, then, should not have been as shocked as they claimed to be when Conselheiro's men also prevailed against uniformed soldiers.

The police met Conselheiro and his followers on the Monte Santo road near Masseté, a "sterile and forsaken tract of land between Tucano and Cumbe, in the vicinity of the Ovó Mountains."[99] When the troop commander discovered that Conselheiro had his own weapon-carrying soldiers, he ordered his men to fire into the group of "beggarly penitents." The bodyguards, however, fired back and routed their adversaries, at which point the commanding officer was the first to turn tail and run. News of the rout shocked state officials; after all, the province of Bahia spent considerable sums on its police force, more than for all levels of public education combined.[100] Seemingly oblivious, Conselheiro marched straight north, following the trails that would take his band to Canudos, where they would be better protected from the influence of Jeremoabo and the other regional *coronéis*.[101]

Meanwhile, pro-Vianna spokesmen strenuously protested that Conselheiro was not a threat and that he should be left alone. When word of the Masseté incident reached Durval Vieira de Aguiar, he wrote to the *Jornal de Notícias* in Salvador avowing that Conselheiro was no dangerous agitator but merely a simple, deeply religious missionary seeking to be of help by building and rebuilding temples and cemeteries.[102] Another citizen, Maximiano José Ribeiro, a commercial employee in Salvador writing to the same newspaper three days later, reported that he had spent some time in conversation with Conselheiro in Bom Jesus (Crisópolis) and that Conselheiro, rather than offering personal advice, had referred him to the regular church representative in the parish, the vicar of Itapicurú.[103] Continued political infighting and victory for Vianna's party in 1896 meant that for the time being Canudos was not threatened, and all the while its reputation as a haven for the faithful continued to grow.

Yet ominous clouds hovered on the horizon. From 1893 through Vianna's inauguration as governor in May 1896, almost all public mention of Conselheiro and his followers was negative except for the debate within the legislature, which the press mostly ignored. Journalist clients of Gonçalves da Silva railed against the "pernicious monarchist cell."[104] The Masseté clash was reported in the federal Chamber of Deputies in Rio de Janeiro, and Bahia's gonçalvista acting governor, Dr. Rodrigues Lima, demanded that Brazilian chief of state Floriano Peixoto avenge the attack on the police.

## THE HOLY CITY

Title to the land on which Conselheiro's settlement was established was held by the baroness de São Francisco do Conde, whose main lands were in the Bahian Recôncavo. A niece of Jeremoabo, she was unwilling to spend the resources needed to develop the abandoned Canudos *fazenda* or to attempt to close down the settlement. Jeremoabo complained bitterly but to no avail. Her reasons for failing to develop her lands are unknown, and indeed would be hard to guess. The district of Santo Antônio das Queimadas, which included Cumbe, Canudos, and a dozen other hamlets, contained only 3,360 souls, some slaves, almost all illiterate, before Conselheiro's coming, yet it was well watered by rivers and potentially fertile.

The highest peak was the *morro* (mount) called Favella, which could be used as a lookout to spot any arrivals to the settlement. When Conselheiro arrived, there were about five hundred mud-thatched wooden shanties scattered in the vicinity, and the manor house had been left in ruins.[105] (One merchant, Captain Jesuíno Lima, claimed later that he had been driven out by Conselheiro's *jagunços*, which may have been true.) Conselheiro, almost as soon as his personal aides found shelter for him, withdrew into a passive state, emerging only to work on the new church and to preach. He left the defense of the community to his Catholic Guard, and his personal needs to his Santa Companhia, the circle of *beatas* who hovered around him protectively. Later, after the hostilities began, he was moved to a more secure house, called the "Sanctuary," where armed guards stood four-hour shifts around the clock.

Seemingly unaffected by the growing tension, Conselheiro exerted a calming influence on his followers when he mingled with them. His main daily activities involved rebuilding the old church, planning a cemetery, and building Canudos's new church, which was never to be completed. Work on the original church was completed in late 1893, and it was reconsecrated by Cumbe's Padre Sabino to the accompaniment of music and rockets fired into the air.[106] The celebration confirms one aspect of Conselheiro's personality: once established in Belo Monte, the name he sometimes used for Canudos, he seems to have relaxed his strict standards of austerity, at least for his followers. The fireworks display on São João's (Saint John's) Day was likely the most impressive ever held in the region.

Outsiders, of course, saw Canudos in a very unsavory light. In 1876, a delegation of Lazarite priests, accompanied by the vicar of Cumbe, had visited. One later described the idle population there as made up of people "armed to the teeth . . . whose sole occupation, almost, consisted in drinking brandy and smoking certain strange clay pipes with stems a yard long."[107] The initial few hundred settlers who trekked with Conselheiro through the wilderness worked to construct mud-brick houses and to plant and raise goats and horses. They followed in the hallowed Brazilian tradition of pilgrims, but with a difference: they came to the holy city to stay, not to make *promessas* and then return to their homes. We cannot know to what extent Conselheiro's charisma was responsible for these astonishing decisions. Nor do we have evidence that within the short life span of the community, its residents constructed a "master legend" or community-held interpretation of their faith. Surviving folk tales communicated orally in the Northeast make it clear that each person took Antônio Conselheiro for his or her personal patron—always "my," never "our" Padrinho or Conselheiro.[108]

We do know that municipal authorities offered little resistance to the settlement of believers initially. Conselheiro's *jagunço* bodyguards did not faze backlanders; indeed, there was a tradition of such protective service to priests and other religious persons in the region.[109] Fazendeiro complaints were mostly limited to accusations that cattle thieves were using Canudos as a sanctuary in which to hide. In fact, however, there were no wanted criminals in Conselheiro's flock, as later charged; the life was pastoral, centered around livestock raising, seasonal planting, and daily religious ministrations. Da Cunha, seeing how the die had been cast in Masseté, in hindsight permitted himself to describe the scene in the dramatic language of *Os sertões*:

> This transient settlement of wandering woodsmen . . . was within a short space of time to be transformed and expanded into the mud-walled Troy of the *jagunços*. It was to become a holy site, surrounded as it was by a protective ring of mountains, where the long arm of the accursed govern-

ment never would reach. Its interesting topography in the eyes of these simple folk made it appear as the first broad step of the stairway to heaven.[110]

What da Cunha overlooked or chose not to acknowledge was the fact that the region's demographic profile had been pivotally altered in recent decades. Ravaged by the worsening impact of regional droughts, tens of thousands of backlanders had fled the arid zone of the Northeast and migrated to the coastal cities; others had wandered in the direction of the *tabuleiro-praia* region and the more southerly plantation zones. Others relocated within the *sertão* itself. For some, then, the decision to relocate to Canudos may have been affected not only by the attractiveness of Conselheiro's religious vision, but also by the desire to migrate for economic reasons.[111]

According to one newspaper report, Queimadas, in Bomfim, declined from 4,504 residents in 1892 to three occupied houses in September 1897. Some five thousand adult males from Itapicurú were reported to have taken up residence in Canudos, most of them "jagunços," as well as four hundred from Capim Grosso, "great numbers" from Pombal, three hundred from Itabaianinha in Sergipe, and a "large number" from Ituiuba in Bahia. Families came from as far away as Feira de Santana in the Recôncavo, outside the capital.[112] Herds of livestock came from the Jeremoabo region, Bom Conselho, and Simão Dias. At the same time, political infighting between rival *vianista* and *gonçalvista* factions grew more intense, engulfing the entire region in charges and counter-charges, extending even beyond Bahian politics into neighboring states.[113] The drain on the labor supply began to be keenly felt.

For the archdiocese in Salvador, the turning point came in May 1895, when the new archbishop of Salvador, Dom Jerónymo Thomé da Silva, encouraged by the governor, Joaquim Manuel Rodrigues de Lima, sent a pastoral delegation to Canudos to bring Conselheiro's flock under church control. Given the tone set by the visitors and the rigidity of their demands, their mission, which was essentially an ultimatum, was predestined to fail. That the church sent the mission at the request of state officials despite otherwise cool if not hostile relations after 1889 was not unusual for the Northeast, where republican-era secularism could never fully take hold as long as religious and political leaders shared common objectives. Heading the delegation was an Italian Capuchin missionary, Father João Evangelista de Monte Marciano, flanked by another Capuchin, Caetano de Leo, newly arrived in Brazil in July 1894 and speaking virtually no Portuguese, along with the curate of Cumbe, old Padre Sabino, Conselheiro's ally.

Lacking sufficient numbers of Brazilian clergy, the archdiocese had turned to Europe for Capuchin friars to perform evangelical work in the interior, especially among Amerindians in mission villages. In the *sertão*, these newcomers encouraged the establishment of weekly *feiras* and helped to develop agriculture, but they tended to approach local customs with rigidity and some disdain. Da Cunha describes how the delegation to Canudos crossed the river and, walking past the first outlying huts, approached the square, which was filled with "near to a thousand men, armed with blunderbusses, shotguns, knives, etc.," Conselheiro having been advised in advance of the visit. That the *jagunços* were armed should not have shocked the clerics (although they did profess to have been so), since for generations backlanders had carried knives and manufactured ammunition from saltpeter and other materials found naturally on the banks of the São Francisco River. Indeed, fifteen years earlier the Lazarites had described Canudos's *sertanejos* as heavily armed; all *vaqueiros* carried knives, and many in the region carried pistols.

As they made their way uneasily to Padre Sabino's house, closed for more than a year since the curate's visits had stopped, on church orders, the callers were most frightened by the sheer size of Conselheiro's entourage. They passed eight coffins being carried by pallbearers to the cemetery, bearing bodies that had not had the benefit of sacramental rites. Conselheiro himself continued to work on repairs to the chapel until the emissaries sought him out. They intoned a salutation of peace, "Praised be Our Lord Jesus Christ"; Conselheiro welcomed them affably and addressed them with the called-for response: "May our blessed Lord be praised forever!"[114]

The visitors noted that Conselheiro appeared pleased by their presence and that he dropped his habitual reserve and stubborn silence, showing them the progress of his work and acting as their personal guide. Frei Evangelista's lack of tact undermined the spirit of cordiality. Approaching the choir loft, he addressed Conselheiro in the form of a warning. He later reported:

> I seized upon the occasion to inform him that my mission was a wholly peaceable one, that I was greatly surprised to find armed men here, and that I could not but disapprove of all these families living here in idleness, lewdness [he offers no evidence for this assertion], and under conditions so wretched that they led to eight or nine deaths a day. Accordingly, by the order and in the name of His Lordship the Archbishop, I proposed to give a holy mission and advise the people to disperse and to return to their homes and daily tasks, both for their own sakes and for the general welfare.

He was shocked to hear, at this point, shouts of loyalty to Conselheiro from the people. Conselheiro replied: "It is to protect myself that I keep these armed men with me; for your Reverence must know that the police attacked me and tried to kill me at the place called Masseté, where the dead were piled up on one side and the other. In the days of the monarchy, I let myself be taken, for I recognized the government; but today I will not, because I do not recognize the Republic." The Italian visitor said to Conselheiro: "Sir, if you are a Catholic, you must remember that the church condemns revolts and, accepting all forms of government, teaches that the constituted authorities rule the peoples in the name of God."[115]

In this way the mission began badly and continued for four days in the same spirit. Conselheiro permitted the guests to offer mass to more than five thousand in the congregation, including men who retained their arms. He stood beside the altar, and when something was said of which he disapproved, he shook his head, in turn provoking vocal protests from the congregation. Note was taken of the "incredible faults of pronunciation" of the kyries chanted by the faithful. The visitors sanctified fifty-five marriages of "couples living in concubinage," performed 102 baptisms, and heard over four hundred confessions,[116] but little compromise was ventured on either side. On the seventh day of the mission, João Abbade, Conselheiro's chief lieutenant, led a mob to the front of the guests' house, where they shouted vivas to Jesus Christ and let the priests know that "when it came to the matter of eternal salvation, the population of Canudos had no need of their ministrations."[117]

Unhappy with the separation of church and state under the 1891 Constitution, members of the Bahian archdiocese were sensitive to the political charge that devout Catholics, especially in remote rural areas, were secret monarchists. The language of the eight-page relatório published by the archdiocese in Salvador under Frei Evangelista's signature, condemning Canudos as a "political-religious sect" and as a source of "resistance and hostility to the constituted government in the country," reveals the hierarchy's position.[118] The document described living conditions in Canudos in some detail, emphasizing the detrimental effect of overcrowding on the general state of public health, the poor sanitation, and the provocative attitudes of Conselheiro's lieutenants with respect to civil and church authority.[119] These points could have been made for any urban settlement in the northeastern backlands, of course, but to the inexperienced visitor Canudos seemed both unique and ominous. Indeed, the choice of Frei Evangelista, a zealous missionary unfamiliar with the psychology of the Brazilian rustic, contributed to the report's aggressive and condemning mien. Yet not even the shocked cleric in his cold hostility claimed what others later falsely charged. He admitted, for example, that Conselheiro was not arrogating any sacerdotal functions.[120] And as a result of the visit Padre Sabino, the seasoned vicar of Cumbe who maintained a simple mud-brick house in Canudos, was permitted to resume his twice-monthly visits to perform baptisms and marriages.[121]

Conselheiro was not visibly affected by the officials' tour in any way. He continued to leave the day-to-day administration of the city to his aides, concentrating his personal attention on the work being done on the shabby Canudos chapel and the large new church. In his writings there is nothing to suggest any kind of mania or unbalanced behavior. He always signed himself "Antônio Vicente Mendes Maciel," not "Santo" or "Bom Jesus" or, for that matter, "Conselheiro."[122] In Canudos, he continued to dress in the same faded and dirty tunic and worn sandals, his long hair streaked with white, bearing a wooden staff and calling passersby "my brethren," and he always ended conversations with the phrase "sanctified be Our Father Jesus Christ." We do not know just how reliable the woodcut of "the fanatic" Antônio Conselheiro that appeared in Porto Alegre's *Gazetinha* is (see Fig. 8),[123] but it does follow contemporary eyewitness descriptions.

Two handwritten books attributed to Conselheiro reveal further his religious orientation. The first, dated 1895 and titled *Preceitos*, is a collection of several hundred commentaries on the New Testament, some copied verbatim from the *Missão abreviada*. Used by missionaries in the Portuguese overseas territories throughout the nineteenth century, the handbook preached the imminent fiery coming of the apocalypse in bloody allusions to death, heaven and hell, the Final Judgment, and Christ's passion.[124] In so doing, it incorporated language close to precepts condemned by the Vatican, including the doctrine of individual salvation, and an exaggerated sense of personal sin.[125]

The second book, dated January 1897, contains many of the same homilies and commentaries but also indicates Conselheiro's refusal to recognize the republic. He refers to the "province" of Bahia, makes negative references to slavery (Princess Isabel, he says, in signing the Golden Law emancipating slaves, was only carrying out instructions from God), and attacks Protestants, Masons, civil marriage, and Jews (they "only believe in the laws of Moses").[126] Transcribed in the midst of the Brazilian army's march on Canudos, this collection of pieties, speeches, and prayers suggests that Conselheiro may have been trying to leave a message for his adversaries.[127] Both books were found in his meager house after his death.

Throughout 1895 and 1896, Conselheiro devoted most of his attention to the construction of his new church, which he designed himself. The wood for the edifice, for which Conselheiro's agents had paid cash in advance to representatives of the city's strongman, Col. João Evangelista Pereira e Mello, was shipped by boat to the Bahian river port of Juazeiro, sixty miles distant from Canudos. But that city's chief magistrate, Dr. Arlindo Leoni—who as judge in Bom Conselho two years earlier had seen Conselheiro's *jagunços* attack the town and been forced temporarily to flee—ordered the wood confiscated, apparently to settle his personal score with the *conselheiristas*. Da Cunha asserts that Conselheiro himself made trouble by threatening, even before the contract was formally broken, to send armed men to Juazeiro to take the wood. Judge Leoni, an ally of Governor Vianna, then sent an urgent telegram asking for troops "to assure the safety of the population and halt the exodus of the population," fearing a rumored *jagunço* assault. Colonel Pereira e Mello joined a second appeal for military intervention. Governor Vianna, who since his inauguration had found one pretext or another not to interfere, was now forced by political pressure to act.[128]

Toward the end of 1896 a contingent of one hundred state police, commanded by a lieutenant, set out to intercept the group from Canudos, which had stopped in Uauá for prayers en route to Juazeiro. This was the first force sent against the settlement itself, coming three years after the confrontation at Masseté; accordingly, it became known as the First Military Expedition.

It was claimed that three thousand men, most of them armed, made up the procession of Canudenses. Actually there were probably about five hundred, and over 150 of them were killed. Eyewitnesses later stated that the flock, which carried rosaries carved from coconut husks, religious banners, and a large wooden cross, was far from bellicose. The police, however, were exhausted after nineteen days of marching and fired without either warning or provocation. The peasants used tree limbs, old rifles, farm implements, knives, iron bars, and cattle prods (*chuços*) to defend themselves. Ten soldiers were killed and sixteen wounded at Uauá, at which juncture the remaining troops retreated to Juazeiro.

The Vianna administration was vilified in the state assembly, where it faced accusations that it had not seriously intended to attack the larger problem of Canudos, but meant only to disperse the *jagunços*. Vianna, cornered in an untenable political position, sought reconciliation with his enemies.[129] The price exacted of him was that he request federal intervention. In an interview published in August 1897 in Rio de Janeiro's *Gazeta de Notícias*, he boasted that he had warned the president of the republic that the "fanatical horde" at Canudos "neither recognized nor obeyed" the laws, and had committed "acts of extortion, beggary, and frequently robbed neighboring properties."[130] Overwhelming consensus, now firmly in the embrace of the *visão do litoral*, set the stage politically for a wholesale massacre, and symbolically for a life-and-death struggle between "civilization" and "barbarism."

# FOUR

# The Conflict

*"La mer s'est élevée avec les pleurs"*

Backland life followed its own pace, one that irritated travelers from the coast, who considered the region lethargic. When calamity struck—as during the cyclical droughts, the effects of which grew ever more severe owing to the increased population density of the region—*sertanejos* rarely acted unless life itself seemed threatened. Push and pull factors were roughly equal among the pressures that led to the startlingly rapid growth of Conselheiro's community. The Canudos phenomenon was unprecedented in the region's history, and it contrasted with later patterns of outmigration from the Northeast to the industrial Center-South by backlanders hoping to improve their living standards.

Seaboard observers could see no logic at all in such apparently spontaneous migration to a desolate location. Most visitors to the backlands in the late nineteenth century found the land stark and unbroken, of strange aspect, largely sterile, fixed in the melancholy of unrelieved horizons. In contrast to outside observers, however, local populations, especially nontechnical societies, develop their perceptual senses to a high degree of acuity, not only seeing detail and subtle coloration differences where outsiders see only monotone, but also learning intimately "every bush, every stone, every convolution of the ground."[1]

The region's physical and climatic harshness dismayed the city-bred *bacharéis*, medical students, and young military officers transported to a land characterized as cauterized by aridity and burning, sterilized air. The outsiders found the local inhabitants unkempt, listless, and disoriented, yet still able to toil at hard labor for ten to twelve hours a day with nothing more to eat than a handful of manioc meal and a palm-sized piece of jerked beef or almost-rancid goat meat. The backlanders' psychological traits also puzzled visitors: on the one hand, the rustics

9. Drawing of Canudos, 1897, from records of the Fourth Military Campaign. Courtesy Fundação Casa Rui Barbosa, Rio de Janeiro.

averted their gaze when addressed, staring at the ground and uttering monosyllabic replies or simply remaining mute; on the other, they exhibited fierce independence, and laughed at authority.

The clumsy, "primitive" folk functioned with astonishing skill and energy when left to their own devices in their own environment.[2] Herders raised cattle and goats under extremely difficult conditions. Not only were more than two thousand houses in Canudos constructed almost overnight, but the *conselheiristas* built water cisterns, a schoolhouse, warehouses, armories, and Conselheiro's ambitious but unfinished new church, Bom Jesus.

The mud-and-wattle thatched huts built close together across the landscape were identical in size and construction not only to houses throughout the backlands of that era, but also to lower-class rural housing a century later. Military artists, however, in a drawing of Canudos's town square and the adjacent vicinity (Fig. 9), rendered these houses as handsome, modern structures, perhaps with tiled roofs and stuccoed exterior walls, and standing on an even surface devoid of stones, rubble, and dirt—in sharp contrast to a photograph of Canudos seen from the south (Fig. 10).

Citizens of Salvador, Recife, Rio de Janeiro, and the rest of Brazil were clearly foreigners in their own country when they came to the backlands. They displayed colonial impatience mixed with disbelief that

10. Photograph of Canudos, 1897, from the south. Photograph by Flávio de Barros. Courtesy Paulo Zanettini.

such statusless men and women could defy the progressive and modern benefits of civilized life. The propensity of urban elites to hold rural culture in disdain exacerbated the inability of visitors to the backlands to view life there with compassion or with any reasonable objectivity. Urban Brazilians were proud of their material and political accomplishments and felt only shame at the dark, primitive world of the hinterland.[3]

We have noted that writers on Canudos not only made frequent reference to the dark pigmentation of most of Conselheiro's followers but also pointed out that many upper-class *sertanejos* were swarthy or dark complexioned. In the late nineteenth century, racial determinism, rooted in the axiom that the "strong ethnic element 'tends to subordinate to its destiny the weaker element with which it comes in contact,'" led, in the Brazilian case, to the widely accepted view that the "rude fellow-countrymen of the north . . . variable, of all shades of color and all the shadings of form and character," represented inevitable casualties of miscegenation.[4] The fact that eyewitnesses to the Canudos conflict shared suspicions and fears about the retrograde if not degenerate nature of the *sertanejo* population undermines what objectivity might have obtained in descriptions of Conselheiro's followers. But to the extent that the settlement's population profile can be pieced together from available sources, the residents of Canudos likely came from much more diverse origins than have thus far been recognized.

Canudos was a fully functioning community that housed a population ranging in age from newborns to men and women too old to work or even to walk. Indeed, its age structure reveals that the migration to Canudos was unusual for the backlands. Typically, male migrants in the *sertão* were fifteen to thirty years of age, and female, twenty to thirty. Canudos, however, attracted whole families, even the elderly, a migration pattern that otherwise prevailed only when circumstances were onerous: in times of severe drought, or during widespread roundups by military press gangs or *capangas*. Yet none of these circumstances held in 1893.

Da Cunha, recounting what he considered the bizarre—even though the descriptions on which he relied were generally clinical rather than exotic—offers a striking picture of the physical and age variation among Canudos's residents. There were the "pious women, rivaling the witches of the Church," and the "old maids" (rural slang for promiscuous women); there were young girls and young women, timid and circumspect. Under the spell of the place, all of the disparate elements from far and wide "were welded into one uniform and homogeneous community, an unconscious brute mass . . . in the manner of a human polyp." Of the women, he wrote that

> Here, finally, were the respectable mothers of families, all kneeling together in prayer. The wrinkled faces of old women, skinny old viragoes on whose lips prayer should have been a sacrilege; the austere countenances of simple-minded matrons; the naive physiognomies of credulous maidens—all mingled in a strange confusion; all ages, all types, all shades of racial coloring.[5]

His choice of descriptive terms typified the immersion of the seaboard intellectual in Proustian metaphor:

> Here and there, at a glance amid this rag heap, one might catch sight of a very beautiful face, standing out impressively from the wretchedness and gloom of the other wrinkled visages, and displaying the lines of that deathless beauty which the Jewish type has immutably preserved down the ages. The face of a madonna on a fury; deep, lovely eyes, black pupils sparkling with a mystic madness . . . all this was a cruel profanation, lost in this vagabond assemblage, from which there exuded at once the foul smell of unclean bodies and the slow drone of benedicites, mournful as responsories.[6]

These words were written about the survivors, after the settlement was destroyed. During Belo Monte's normal existence, however, residents looked little different from any backland inhabitants. Men and women alike appeared wizened because of exposure to the harsh climate and because of their hard lives. Women of twenty-five appeared haglike to visitors, but not because of any fanaticism. Life expectancy in the rural Northeast in the 1890s did not exceed twenty-seven years for either men or women.[7]

Overall, women in Canudos likely outnumbered men two to one during the first two years of the community's existence.[8] One possible reason for this curious fact is that women whose husbands had died or abandoned them may have sought refuge in Canudos; in the backlands, a woman fared very poorly as head of household unless she had unusually strong extended family ties.

Near the end, women constituted an even higher percentage of Canudos's population. Many men deserted Conselheiro in the community's last months, slipping away through still-open *sertão* trails, often leaving their wives and children behind. As contemporaries claimed, moreover, the women in Canudos were more faithful to their leader than the men. This seems puzzling, given Conselheiro's misogyny in his private life. Although females were welcome in the community, he did not deal with them directly, to the extent that he avoided eye contact when possible. Following backland custom, women were segregated from men in the chapel. His aversion seems to have been chronic. Even what we know about Maciel's marriage to a woman described as an aggressive harridan and deserter is not nearly enough to explain his attitude. Given Conselheiro's aversion to women at Canudos, perhaps we can surmise that he rejected his wife years earlier because she failed to conform to his expectations about behavior. After all, across the *sertão* women were judged harshly. A woman married in a civil ceremony but not in church was considered a *puta testemunhada*—a "witnessed" whore in God's eyes. The severe religious strictures imposed in the Maciel household served as the basis for his attitudes toward women when he became a penitent and ascetic.[9] That the devout female residents of Canudos accepted inferior status yet remained staunchly loyal to him reflects the harsh nature of backland piety, which judged them as guilty of sins simply because they were women.

At Canudos, Conselheiro did permit a small number of women acolytes to serve him personally. One very close to him was "Aunt Benta," born in Itapicurú, who previously had made her living as a midwife; in Bom Conselho she had run a unique boarding school for boys from remote locations in the region sent there by their families. Described as a "fat mixed-breed," she was also skillful in business matters. She accumulated real estate, which she sold for a good sum when she left the village to follow Conselheiro to Canudos. There she took care of his austere residence and cooked for him. Her fate is unknown. Another anonymous *beata*, captured in the last days of the fighting (and the person who revealed the location of Conselheiro's grave to the military officials), supposedly slept in a house "with internal access" to Conselheiro's own "holy" room.[10]

A handful of women are known to have been permitted to fight in defense of the city. One, Maria da Guerra de Jesus, had served as a nurse at Cocorobó and in the last days of the battle in Canudos killed a legalist soldier with a sickle.[11] Women performed heavy manual labor, as did children and the elderly, just as in every other part of rural Brazil. Some worked in the fields with the livestock and took care of other agricultural chores; some carried stones from a quarry to the site of the new church, or salt from a quarry in Vargem, five and a half miles away. Asked about the heavy work, a survivor said that if the load was unbearable, Conselheiro "would touch it" and it would become lightened.[12]

Contemporary writers claimed that sexual promiscuity was common in the *sertão*, despite the draconian code of honor that often led to vengeance killings and bitter family feuds. This assertion shocked coastal observers. In any case, Conselheiro imposed a rigorous standard of public morals based on his unease with (and possibly anger against) women. Adolescent girls accused of flirting were punished, and prostitution, common in every Brazilian urban center, was banned.[13] Conselheiro also attempted to prohibit the consumption of *cachaça*, in da Cunha's words the "national hashish." Whether he was successful is not known, but merchants were warned not to sell it.

The population of Canudos comprised not just *caboclos*, but a wide range of groups from all races, admixtures, and social classes.[14] By *sertão* standards, some residents had even been wealthy: one man sold three houses before arriving in the settlement with his family.[15] Simply stated, Canudos embodied a cross-section of the *sertanejo* population. Of eighty-eight entries for Canudos for 1896 in the baptism book of Cumbe's vicar Sabino, brought to the settlement during his visits there, all but one of the children born were listed as *pardos*.[16] Although in northeastern usage of the day, *pardo* was simply a generic term for mestizo, similar data (the Cumbe baptism book specifically has never been cited) have led some observers to claim that Belo Monte was made up mostly of dark-skinned folk, even that Canudos was Brazil's last *quilombo*, or refuge for fugitive slaves. One *fazendeiro*, Antero de Cerqueira Gallo, sarcastically referred to the defenders of Belo Monte as "o povo 13 de Maio," a reference to the date of abolition.[17]

Residents of nearby villages with predominantly aboriginal populations and organized in colonial times by church missions came to Canudos. Many of these were Kiriris, as well as members of their extended *mameluco* families, mixed with others. Some of the Kiriri celebrations, including a mid-August festival in which participants imbibed *jurema* liquor brewed from local berries, smoked tobacco, and drank *cachaça* (all allegedly banned by Conselheiro), were held in Belo Monte. The two last Kiriri chiefs (*pajés*) died in Canudos and, with them, the secret of preparing *jurema* liquor, thus ending the festival.[18]

Many Canudos residents were descendants of African slaves, a somewhat unusual circumstance in the far reaches of the *sertão*, although blacks were a substantial element in the formation of the rural *caboclo*, at least in Ceará and in the Bahian *tabuleiro* zone.[19] In some coastal areas where there were small sugar plantations, as we have seen, many of those who were mesmerized by Conselheiro were pious slaves or ex-slaves; these individuals traveled four leagues or more to hear Conselheiro preach, bringing no food with them and having no idea how they were going to manage.[20] Farther into the backlands, some of the descendants of fugitive slaves who had come to the region earlier in the century, together with slaves who had been emancipated in the years leading up to the formal abolition of slavery in 1888, had settled near the Vasa-Barris River. In the early 1850s, the largest group of runaway slaves and their children lived in a cluster of some thirty houses along the banks of the seasonal Tapiranga River, fugitives from sugar *usinas* in Sergipe and Alagoas. Some had been ironworkers, others woodworkers and mechanics. Conselheiro, who before 1888 in his writings had castigated slavery as an abomination, attracted these and other blacks to his side; they then moved to Canudos when the city was established.[21]

We have no evidence that Conselheiro publicly advocated abolition, but in his writings he referred to slavery as an abomination. He hinted that the empire's long delay in freeing the slaves may have led to the proclamation of the republic as God's punishment. In Canudos, ex-slaves may have lived in housing of their own design. At least one observer who did not simply dismiss the community's buildings as primitive noticed a distinction between the dwellings constructed by *caboclos* and those built by former slaves. A certain alley in Canudos, it was claimed, was called the "street of the Negroes."[22] Another chronicler asserted that black women in Conselheiro's community dressed according to African custom. We are told of the "outlandish topknots" in their hairstyles, in contrast to the "straight, smooth hair" of the *caboclo* women.[23] Newspaper reports from the front occasionally specified that one or another captive was a black; Salvador's *Diário de Notícias* reported, for example, the death in Belo Monte of a woman named Senhorinha, "a highly venerated black," for whom the other women in the community held a long candlelit wake, cut short by bullets.[24]

Those considered mestizos encompassed a diverse number of Brazilian categories describing racial mixes clustered around mulattoes (mainly men and women from black-white pairings) and *caboclos*, based as much on hair color and texture and the contours of the nose and lips as on skin pigmentation.[25] Since racial categories in postimperial Brazil were to a degree as reflective of social status as of anything else, it is misleading to rely too heavily on official descriptions. In parts of the Northeast—especially Paraíba—between 1868 and 1880, all baptized children of color who were not slaves were called *meio-branco*, or "part-white."[26] In the region in and around Canudos, priests tended to identify the race of baptized children according to one of three categories: *branco, cabra*, or *pardo*. In 1889, the baptism registry for Jeremoabo, for example, listed about one-fourth of the infants baptized as "white," another one-tenth as "mixed," and the rest as "dark."[27] In other sources of classification—such as court records—sedentary laborers of high color from the coast would typically be classified as *negros* or *pretos*. Rural backlanders would usually be called mulattoes. Poor, dark-complexioned people would typically be classified as Negro, or *preto*, while backland *vaqueiros* would usually be called mulattoes.

A person of mixed parentage racially but of well-to-do background, perhaps a party to a fortunate marriage, would likely be called either *pardo* or, more generically, *caboclo*. Certain cases required particular social delicacy; some of the orphans rescued from Canudos after its destruction, for example, were taken in by elite coastal families, and their formal documents refer to them as *acaboclados*, or "*caboclo*-like," a term that elevates them above others of the same dark skin color but of lower social status.[28]

To eyewitnesses, Conselheiro's followers were pitiful; at best, they were contradictory, inconstant, and warlike. The poverty and exacting asceticism required of residents in Canudos were taken by outsiders as a justification for withholding respect for the faithful, whose belief, as observers saw it, consisted in little but having followed a raving lunatic. Even most of the "whites" who lived there, many of whom had been small property owners in the *sertão* who sold their assets to join Conselheiro's flock, wore "ragged garments without style" and were living amid "wretchedness and gloom."[29]

The woeful physical condition of the settlement and its inhabitants appalled visitors. Indeed, the northeastern peasant's diet significantly declined in quality over the period from 1870 to 1920; because it was based on two nutritionally complementary rations, beans and manioc, however, calorie for calorie it may have been more healthful than the single carbohydrate staple common in so many other parts of the world. Yet even in relatively good years, the rural diet often fell short in calories, carbohydrates, animal fats, vitamins, thiamine, and protein.

The chroniclers whose descriptions astonished newspaper readers during the long months of the conflict did not expect the region to be so well supplied. Manoel Benício, an honorary army captain born in the Northeast, writing for Rio de Janeiro's *Jornal do Commércio*, noted with wonder that even during the fighting, Canudos's inhabitants kept their pastures clean and searched for strayed goats. The river bank was planted in vegetables, corn, beans, watermelons, squash, cantaloupes, sugar cane, arrowroot, and potatoes. Fighters carried with them packets of *grogotuba*—an energy-giving mixture of manioc flour and *xiló*, a squash—wrapped in corn husks.[30] Occasionally travelers saw banana trees, rarely found in the backlands except at oases in the Ceará-Mirim Valley. Manioc and other foodstuffs were planted in the humid valleys adjacent to the settlement. There was a slaughterhouse, and warehouses were stocked with surplus food. Dried fruits and meat were kept in clay vessels stored in every residence.[31]

A study of the Canudos conflict prepared years later for the Army Chiefs of Staff Military College found that the community supported a regular internal commerce in edibles.[32] In the vicinity of the settlement could be found both horticulture and animal husbandry, with cattle, sheep, and goat raising (though the total number of cows was small). Goat hides provided a good portion of the capital needed to buy provisions from outside, mostly from Bahia's São Francisco River port of Juazeiro to the north until the conflict over lumber precipitated the fateful clash with government troops in 1896. Conselheiro's emissaries dealt directly with Juazeiro's chief merchant, Col. João Evangelista Pereira e Mello. In fact, commerce in goat hides from Canudos's four leather works and three leather trading houses provided some revenue, which helped to pay, ironically, the export taxes levied with increasing frequency by the state of Bahia, ever more dependent on such assessments owing to the republican constitution of 1891. When funds ran low, Conselheiro wrote personal letters to contacts outside and sent emissaries, including José (Zé) Venâncio and the merchant Joaquim Macambira, to ask for donations of cattle.[33]

That Canudos, before the government assault, functioned effectively in spite of its swollen population and the antipathy of local bosses was inexplicably either taken for granted or ignored. The inhabitants of the rural hinterland seemed to outsiders to be stunted and subhuman. We know that backlanders suffered from every malady encountered on the coast, as well as from some illnesses more or less restricted to the interior, such as bubonic plague.[34] The reputation that Canudos had as a "nucleus of maniacs" colored visitors' impressions even further. Some families, although there was no obligation to do so, relinquished their worldly possessions when they arrived, as a voluntary penitential act. Men dressed in dirty striped cotton trousers, rough shirts, and uncured leather sandals. Women's clothing—ill-fitting shirts and blouselike wrappings

often so lacking in material that breasts and upper arms were left exposed—smelled of sweat and rancid oil. Some of the clothing was manufactured in Canudos, of fibers taken from the surrounding fields, but
machine-milled cloth was also available, imported by resident merchants.

The houses contained only sticks of furniture—neither beds nor tables, but only wooden planks or hemp hammocks for sleeping, foot-
stools, hampers made of wood or straw, leather bags or gourds to hold
water. Cooking was done over open fires made of sticks, in utensils
handcrafted from wood and scraps of tin. Consider the undisguised
contempt in this description of a rough-hewn altar in one of the homes
of the faithful: "[It housed] atrociously carved saints and images, an
objectivization of the mestizo religion with its pronounced traces of idol-
atry: proteiform and Africanized St. Anthonys with the gross appearance of fetishes, and Blessed Virgins ugly as Megaeras."[35]

Yet in any of the wretched hamlets throughout the *sertão*, life proceeded on the same scale of deprivation: a legacy of misery afflicted the
Canudos region, with whole towns depopulated by refugees fleeing
hunger.[36] Indeed, Canudos may well have boasted more urban refine-
ments than most of its neighbors: although houses in Conselheiro's city,
as everywhere else, were of mud-and-wattle construction with solid roofs,
most were painted—a rarity for the *sertão*—and many were plastered with
white clay. Three "neighborhoods" were painted mostly in gray, two in
red. Although no houses had doors or windows, and most contained only
two rooms, some were relatively large and boasted several rooms.[37]

There was only one conventional street, Campo Alegre, which divided the city in two, but winding lanes and alleyways led everywhere.
Linking many houses were underground tunnels, which may have functioned as *casamatas*, dual-purpose root cellars used also as barracks and
for storing arms.[38] Canudos also supported commercial establishments,
warehouses, a barracks, armories, and two cemeteries. The churches
faced a central square, with the river off to one side. Many houses had
basements, as did the new church.

In recent years, archeologists who have studied the Canudos site have
indicated that Conselheiro and his lieutenants deserve even greater
praise for their choice of location and for the steps they took to develop
it. Geologically, the holy city was founded exactly at the point of highest
fluvial drainage from the Vasa-Barris. Water was available not only from
the river but also from wells dug into porous rock—a rarity for the
region. The mountainous terrain enhanced the city's defensibility and
facilitated ambushes and surprise attacks by Canudenses. Conselheiro's
sagacious military commanders enticed regular troops into the waterless
and naturally formed labyrinths along the Catarina ridge, then block-
aded the entrance. Thus the *jagunços* drew the government troops onto

the left bank of the Umburanas River, land almost completely lacking potable water. The defenders controlled the other side, known as the "Lagoa de Sangue" (Lake of Blood), which was well irrigated.

The escarpments surrounding Canudos—Cana Brava, Poço de Cima, Cocorobó, Vermelha, Vigário, Angico, and others—functioned as natural walls, overlooking the canyons through which the army had to pass. Within the escarpment wall, moreover, geologists later observed a natural system of horizontal, ladderlike ridges slanted at angles that permitted defenders to control the heights and to fire down on the invaders. The only point of entry for army contingents and their equipment was dominated by high ground in the Serra do Angico, which the *jagunços* commanded. Such practices as singing hymns in full voice while fighting, then launching into filthy invective, unnerved the government corps as the sounds echoed across the valley's walls. The *jagunços* took aim first at officers, easy targets in their popinjay uniforms, and repeatedly fired at close range from positions of ambush. The backlanders frequently dispatched small units to the rear of troop columns to capture food, ammunition, and equipment; thus they maintained Canudos's supplies and at the same time severely hindered resupply efforts for the legalist troops.[39]

Journalists sent to write about the war sensed that Canudos seemed diabolically positioned to resist invasion; moreover, army strategists stubbornly refused to change their tactics in response to environmental conditions. Still, Conselheiro and his advisors probably chose the site because of its capacity to support agriculture. The settlement was in the valley at the widest point of its seasonal river, which reached some hundred meters in breadth during the wet season. Because Canudos lay at the center of one of the hottest regions of the continent, it could not have survived without ample water, even if its inhabitants were used to living amid parched conditions.

In fact the site did provide extraordinary opportunities for defense. Not only did the *conselheiristas* use the scrub for camouflage, but the underbrush actually deflected incoming fire. The truncated vegetation surrounding the valley was exceedingly dense, frequently obscuring bends and dips in the wandering, dirt trails. The *sertanejos*, of course, had little trouble traveling in and out; indeed, Canudos was well connected to neighboring towns. Several trails led in and out of the valley, and until the army sealed off the site in the final days of battle the city was always well supplied with food, cattle, weapons, and anything else it needed. Individual *jagunço* fighters were able to sneak through the ring of troops and escape with relative ease—and many did so when the cause appeared lost. The outsiders were astonished at the dexterity with which local inhabitants traversed their land.

What is remarkable about Canudos is that it functioned smoothly despite its large population. Conselheiro, like a regional *coronel*, presided over a "state within a state," delegating authority to aides at various levels as needed. His armed lieutenants included several men who had committed crimes, or at least had been accused of doing so in a region where the definition of crime was ambiguous: one man's *vaqueiro* was another's *jagunço*. Little wonder that newspaper readers following the almost-daily reports from the front were horrified by the savage images. There was Estevam, "a burly, misshapen Negro with a body tattooed by bullet and dagger wounds"; "Shackle-Foot" Joaquim; "Crooked-Mouth" Raymundo of Itapicurú, a "gallows-bird mountebank with a face twisted in a cruel grimace"; the agile "Kid Ostrich"; Quimquim de Coiqui, a "self-abnegating religionist"; the "quack doctor," "Sturdy Manoel"; the "decrepit imam, Old Macambira"; "Bear's Noodle"; "Peter the Invisible"; and others. That some of the armed *jagunços* were deeply religious only seemed to accentuate their malevolence. The brothers Chiquinho and João da Motta, for example, "[gave] the impression of being a single individual as they [said] the beads of the same rosary with the air of staunch believers." And "Pious Anthony," a "lean and seedy-looking mulatto, emaciated from fasting, . . . half-sacristan, half-soldier, . . . [was] the altar boy"; he acted as a kind of religious policeman, "shrewdly worming his way into the homes and ferreting out every nook of the village." Sharing the same predilection was José Félix, the "Chatterbox," guardian of the churches and Conselheiro's janitor and majordomo, who oversaw the pious women who served Conselheiro and the other leaders.[40]

Conselheiro's chief political deputy was João Abbade, known by the residents of Canudos as the *comandante da rua* (street commander, or mayor) or, according to Frei Evangelista, the "people's chieftain." He commanded the Guarda Católica, Conselheiro's eight-hundred-man full-time militia, and was a close friend of Antônio Vilanova, the most prosperous merchant in Canudos (both lived in houses with tile roofs, a mark of high status). Abbade had grown up in Tucano, on the other side of the Ovó Mountains. He was tall, looked "like a priest," and was very wily. Even his clothing differed from that of the other men, causing him to stand out in a crowd. His parents, of "good family" according to survivors, had come from Pé de Serra. Some believed that Abbade had been born in Ilhéus and fled to the backlands after killing his fiancée, but the rumor was without basis. Another widely believed story was that he perpetrated his first crime on the Tucano-Itapicurú road when he saw a man beating a woman; when the intervention led to murder, he sought refuge in Canudos. Still another version of his background had him apprenticed to two local rifle-toting bandits, João Geraldo and "David." Abbade had led the *jagunço* forces against the Bahian state police at Masseté in 1893. His men obeyed him without question. He was killed during one of the last days of the fighting, when legalist troops entered Canudos to engage in hand-to-hand combat.

According to one source, Abbade had a trusted aide, Pajeú, who, a former private in the Pernambuco provincial militia, had deserted in the region around Baixa Verde after committing several crimes. His birthplace was Pajeú das Flores (Riacho do Navio), presumably the origin of the name by which he was known. In the last days of Canudos he took command of the guerrilla resistance. Although most contemporary accounts cited his death in battle, he may well have escaped. Descriptions refer to Pajeú as Conselheiro's "negro ardiloso" (valiant Negro), using the language of the period. Da Cunha's description of him typifies his masterful, and provocative, images of primitivism:

> A full-blooded cafuso [half Indian, half African], he was endowed with an impulsive temperament which combined the tendencies of the lower races from which he sprang. He was the full-blown type of primitive fighter, fierce, fearless, and naïve, at once simple-minded and evil, brutal and infantile, valiant by instinct, a hero without being aware of the fact—in brief, a fine example of recessive atavism, with the retrograde form of a grim troglodyte, stalking upright here with the same intrepidity with which, ages ago, he had brandished a stone hatchet at the entrance to his cave.[41]

Other lieutenants included Zé Venâncio, wanted for eighteen murders in Volta Grande and possibly a former member of the Volta Grande gang of *cangaceiros* in Lavras Diamantinhas in the early 1890s. Venâncio ordered the destruction of nearby *fazendas* and smaller residences on the outskirts of Canudos so that they could not be used by approaching forces. But the most effective of all the rebel fighters was Pedrão, who survived Canudos and died a half-century later. Born and raised in Várzea de Ema, he joined Conselheiro after the itinerant preacher passed through the village in 1885. In 1893 he married Tiburcia, a girl from a family in Souré that also had joined Conselheiro's minions, and whose brother was killed in Masseté. The vicar of Cumbe officiated at Pedrão and Tiburcia's wedding, which was held in the old Canudos church. Of the couple's seven natural and ten adopted children, one, along with her mother, was wounded in the final round of fighting, but all endured and fled after taking personal leave of Conselheiro. In the early 1930s, Pedrão was recruited, with other *cangaceiros*, by Bahia's interventor, Captain Juracy Magalhães, to combat the bandit Lampião. Pedrão later migrated to the state of Piauí but returned to Várzea de Ema before his death. His funeral in 1958 was attended by hundreds.[42]

One of Conselheiro's aides, Barnabé José de Carvalho, was related by marriage to Pedro Celeste, a major landowner in Bom Conselho. Blond, blue-eyed, and with a heavy-set "Flemish" or "Dutch" countenance, he was the only male among Conselheiro's lieutenants to be listed as "white" in the documentation. Other well-connected residents included the merchants Conselheiro permitted to do business in Canudos, thus assuring the flow of supplies. One of these men, Antônio da Motta, came to a bad end. The most affluent citizen of Canudos before Conselheiro's arrival thanks to his thriving goatskin business, he was invited to remain. After the first military expedition against Canudos in November 1896, however, he was anonymously accused of having leaked information to the state police. Condemned without a trial, he and his oldest sons were shot in broad daylight, allegedly right in front of Antônio Conselheiro.[43] Da Motta's wife and remaining children escaped, taking refuge in the house of another merchant in the city and eventually fleeing through the *sertão*. His inventory was confiscated and his store looted.

Joaquim Macambira and Norberto das Baixas were two more local merchants and planters who had been welcomed to stay in Canudos. Both were *caboclos* with large families. Macambira ran a dry goods store and farmed. Known locally as a peaceful man, he enjoyed reasonable relations with political chieftains throughout the region, including Juazeiro's Colonel Pereira e Mello. Macambira's sons fought with Conselheiro's Guarda Católica, and one was killed attempting to disable an army cannon. Most of the rest of his family died in the final charge, although five children, one gravely wounded, were taken to Salvador and ultimately resettled in the Bahian *sertão*. Army officials gave the Macambira family special treatment because only one member, the merchant's fallen son, had been a combatant. As for Norberto das Baixas (named after his *fazenda*), he had held considerable influence in the region as well as in Bom Conselho, where he owned additional property. Much of his income came from importing wood from Bom Conselho to Canudos and its neighboring hamlets. Norberto fought with the Guarda Católica and fell in battle. Three daughters survived the final offensive. Two were taken away by soldiers, and a third, seven years old, was placed under the protection of a citizen's welfare society, the Comité Patriótico da Bahia, in Salvador, organized by journalist Amaro Lélis Piedade.

The most vigorous merchant in Canudos, Antônio Francisco de Assunção (or Vilanova), enjoyed more authority than anyone in the community except Conselheiro and João Abbade, for not only did he control the local economy, but he consulted frequently with Abbade on political matters as well. His chits substituted for currency in the settlement, and he sat as a kind of justice of the peace. His tile-roof house stood alongside the two churches. Leaving his hometown of Ceará after a drought, he settled in Vilanova (today, Senhor do Bomfim) in Bahia and established a trading business (hence his adopted last name of Vilanova). As early as 1873, a priest in Vilanova advised him to speak with Antônio

Conselheiro about the possibility of supplying the priest's followers; then, when Canudos was established, he moved not only his business but also his extended family to the *sertão*. One family member, his brother Honório, came with his lissome wife, Pimpona, who was known for her elegance in dressing and who therefore must have stood out among the Canudos women in their penitential poverty.

Antônio Francisco was tall, bearded, and always dressed in suit and tie. He quickly took over the lion's share of commerce in Canudos, aided by Abbade, who took steps to favor him over the competition. One merchant, Jesuíno Correio, was expelled; Antônio da Motta was killed. During the fighting Vilanova stockpiled and distributed arms and ammunition in his store and helped arrange for shipments of weapons. Just before the end, he calmly arranged for his family to leave, receiving personal permission from Conselheiro, then near death. He rescued all of his relatives in small groups, burying four boxes of silver in the ground but carrying with him to Ceará, according to Honório, several kilograms of broken gold and some jewelry. When he died, of natural causes, he was considered a rich man.[44]

Men and women who did not join Conselheiro's sect also lived freely in the community. Conselheiro, who at one point in his life had taught children, established schools in Bom Jesus, Bom Conselho, and another in Canudos. The first one did not last long: the teacher who was hired under Conselheiro's direction proved to be an alcoholic and was dismissed. Conselheiro directed the Canudos school himself, importing a teacher named Moreira from Souré who died shortly before the outbreak of war. Conselheiro then hired twenty-two-year-old Maria Francisca de Vasconcelos, also from Souré. She had studied at Salvador's Escola Normal, but when her family forbade her to marry a working-class youth, the couple fled to Souré and then took up residence in Conselheiro's Belo Monte. Soon thereafter, her husband abandoned her.

Boys and girls attended school together daily, a fact that would have shocked traditionalists had it been known outside Canudos (and that, moreover, contradicts Conselheiro's image as someone who abhorred "modern" practices). Each child paid a monthly tuition of 2,000 réis. There were several teachers, one of whom escaped the final fighting and fled to Salvador, where she died in 1944. Fanatics or not, Conselheiro's followers were encouraged to give their children a formal education, a privilege virtually none of them would have had in the hamlets and villages of their birth.

There was at least one physician, whom the *jagunços* called their *curador*. According to one story, this man, Dr. Fortunato Raymundo de Oliveira, had been kidnapped from the army after the battle at Cocorobó. The *conselheiristas*, of course, claimed that he had enlisted voluntarily.[45]

Canudos had a small jail (called the "dustbin" by Conselheiro's militiamen) in which wrongdoers were incarcerated for misdeeds, even though the town was said to be virtually crime free.[46] Some men were imprisoned for refusing to serve in the militia. Inebriation was punishable by jail time also, although *cachaça* was banned in Canudos and not readily available. Until the first military incursion against Canudos, Conselheiro usually cooperated with the local police. When a fleeing murderer, "Black Marcos," appeared in the city, Conselheiro's militia apprehended him and turned him over to the police in Monte Santo, where he was tried and sentenced to prison in Salvador. The same courtesy did not always extend the other way. When men loyal to Conselheiro wandered away from Canudos and were arrested (for loitering, or on suspicion of being wanted for unnamed crimes), they were often pressured or manipulated into making formal statements against other Conselheiro followers, providing an excuse for the police to enter Belo Monte and make further arrests.[47]

Individuals from the region's "better" families spread rumors of *conselheirista* crimes, as if to rationalize the brutality that would be deployed against the "fanatics." A landowning cousin of Baron Jeremoabo's, João Américo Camillo de Souza Velho, claimed in a broadside that he published and distributed himself that immediately after the defeat of the army's third expedition, on March 6, 1897, he was awakened at one in the morning by some of his "spies," local cowboys who told him that Conselheiro's *jagunços* were coming to punish him for supplying the Moreira César expedition. As a result, he claimed, he had been forced to evacuate his entire family, including his son who was ailing with a high fever, and flee on foot through terrain so wild that "only gypsies and fugitives" had ever penetrated it. When the *jagunços* found his family gone, he charged, they reduced his home, with all its furniture and possessions, to ruins.[48]

In his pamphlet, Camillo ferociously attacked one Leovigildo Cardoso Ribeiro—a local *coronel* and possibly, until the military attack, an ally of Antônio Conselheiro—for not defending him. By this time, other landowners in the region, even those not directly involved with Canudos, had convinced themselves that Conselheiro was their mortal enemy. Typical was a letter from Antero de Cerqueira Gallo to Baron Jeremoabo warning, almost certainly without any basis in fact, that Conselheiro had told his men that when the battle was over they would move on to attack Cumbe, Monte Santo, Pombal, Tucano, Souré, and Itapicurú.[49] Backland residents were not the only ones to feel alarm; by March 1896 news about Canudos had spread to every part of urban Brazil, where incredulous readers were prepared to believe the worst.

Yet the fragments of letters sent by citizens of Canudos to family members and associates show us that, in fact, outsiders saw largely what they were predisposed to see. Júlio Procópio Favilla Nunes, the *Gazeta de*

*Notícias* correspondent who collected these letters (the bulk of which, sadly, were subsequently lost), claimed as evident fanaticism what was little more than a simple message from a semiliterate backland resident of nearby São Caetano in 1895: news was circulating, this letter writer commented, that Conselheiro had warned that anyone intending to come to Canudos should do so, for unspecified reasons, before August. Another, José Félix of Belo Monte, writing in a firmer hand and using better grammar, urged his correspondent to come with his family to Canudos as quickly as possible, because "the mark of Christ has already been placed on those Christians who wish to enjoy His company. . . . Do not bring anyone," José Félix added, "who would likely not be acceptable to Sr. Conselheiro." Several residents warned that Conselheiro would not accept followers of doubtful moral character. Some letters were written in the same hand but attributed to diverse writers, suggesting that one person may have written messages for correspondents who did not know how to write, a common occurrence in the region. Others asked that their correspondents bring a needed commodity, such as a jar of vegetable oil. One letter described the Masseté attack, attributing the writer's salvation to the protection of the Virgin Mary.[50]

The most interesting letter was taken from the pocket of Antônio José de Lisboa, a *conselheirista* captured near Monte Santo in late December 1897 and returned to the front, where he was executed. It reads:

> Our Conselheiro said that whoever doesn't leave for here will come to ill, as it is now the time of Salvation. The backlands will protect no one, so you should come here now . . . no one knows what may happen. Afterward you may not [be able to] pass freely. Be advised that the destruction of the Republicans is now beginning to such an extent that in a radius of five leagues, there is not a single house that our Conselheiro has ordered razed that is still standing. Don't take unnecessary risks, as you have done in the past. It isn't just once or twice that I have written to you.[51]

## THE CONFLICT

Is it surprising that trouble would break out in the remote backlands of Bahia? During the ten years preceding the arrival of the man called Antônio Conselheiro there had been strife and calamity—economic despair, a major drought in 1866–68, and electoral disorder in 1868 and 1871. Clan wars tore apart Monte Santo, Itapicurú, and other towns.[52] The early 1890s witnessed sporadic lootings of warehouses, train robberies, and savage beatings of political enemies by hired thugs. Rival factions battled one another in the legislature, in the press, and across the land. The republic brought further insecurity to the Northeast and generated political realignments, which at the local level often spilled over into intimidation and violence. The national climate of anxiety deepened as the decade advanced, and the backlands sank deeper into volatility.

The 1896 decision to intervene in Canudos with massive armed force was made after the relatively minor incident mentioned earlier, when the Juazeiro city magistrate, Dr. Arlindo Leoni, requested troops to check Conselheiro's band, fearing that they would create a civil disturbance after having failed to receive the prepaid lumber for the community's new church. Da Cunha's description of the events that led to the attack on the Canudenses at Uauá is uncharacteristically unclear. We do not know how Conselheiro learned that the lumber would not be delivered, or on what grounds the magistrate claimed that an attack by *conselheiristas* was imminent. Official documents shed little light on the matter. In his summary report a year later to the president of the republic on his reasons for sending troops, Governor Vianna explained that he had been informed by Dr. Leoni "of rumors which were current, and which were more or less well founded, to the effect that the flourishing city in question [Juazeiro] was to be assaulted within a few days by Antônio Conselheiro's followers. He requested my aid in assuring the safety of the population and in halting the exodus of the inhabitants, which had already begun."[53]

What was not said was that the decision to send 104 troops from Bahia's Ninth Infantry Battalion was apparently made *prior* to the alleged flight of population from Juazeiro in anticipation of a supposed attack by the Canudenses. Colonel Pereira e Mello personally telegrammed Governor Vianna (whose family was prominent in the area and considered Pereira e Mello a loyal ally)[54] for military assistance, without offering any explanation for the missing lumber.

Da Cunha himself conceded that news of the approach of the troops did not prevent a population exodus; rather, it hastened it. In his own report to military headquarters, the commander of the Third Military District, General Frederico Solon (who happened to be da Cunha's father-in-law), simply explained that he had been asked by Governor Vianna to send men from his garrison to "combat the fanatics of the Canudos settlement."[55] It is interesting that the soldiers who set out to destroy superstition in the name of progress moved up their departure from Juazeiro to nightfall on October 12 so they would not have to set out on the thirteenth of the month, an unlucky day.

The detachment of soldiers had encountered setbacks in procuring supplies, and they did not know the region across which they planned to march 125 miles from Juazeiro to Canudos. They hired guides from Juazeiro to accompany them. Meanwhile, word of their plans reached Canudos. On the second day of their march, their commanding officer ordered them to travel twenty-five miles over searing desertlike terrain. They stopped at Lagôa de Boi, where a few remnants of water remained. Most of the dwellings and *fazendas* along the trail, however, had been abandoned in anticipation of worsening drought.

Uauá, described as an ugly-looking cluster of ill-made houses and dilapidated shanties, a cross between an Indian camp and a village, lay at the intersection of four roads and was a regional *feira* site on Saturdays. At nightfall, as the soldiers rested, the entire village slipped away without being seen by the sentries, fleeing to the *caatinga* brush. Some ran to Canudos, where they arrived at dawn on the morning of the twentieth, giving the alarm. On the twenty-first, bearing aloft the Banner of the Divine and a great wooden cross, Conselheiro's Guarda Católica appeared on the road, droning the kyrie eleison. About one thousand strong (though later accounts trebled that number), they were armed with old muskets, pikes, scythes, long poles, and implements of the land, and they carried with them saints' portraits, icons, and "withered palms taken from the altars." The multitude "resembled one of those penitential processions which the credulous backwoodsmen used to stage by way of propitiating Heaven when the long summers brought the scourge of the drought."[56]

The forces clashed in a battle that generated more noise than casualties. After four hours, having lost ten of his men (and his two guides) and with sixteen more wounded, the commander ordered a retreat. His troops returned to Juazeiro by forced march, arriving in four days, "their uniforms in shreds, wounded, crippled, exhausted . . . the very picture of defeat."[57] For the government, there could be no turning back now, even though Bahia's governor continued to argue that the backland disturbance was a common annoyance with which his police could cope. The military commander in Bahia was not as confident.

The patriotic impulse among residents of the coast drowned out any arguments that Conselheiro had simply been trying to defend himself. Bahia's Governor Vianna telegrammed Vice-President Manoel Vitorino, the acting president, for help; Vitorino acted without consulting the ailing Prudente. The second expedition—the first one to involve regular army troops—numbered 543 federal and state forces under the command of Major Febrônio de Brito. It included fourteen field officers, three surgeons, and several dozen police troops, as well as two small Krupp cannons: less than a brigade and a little more than a full battalion.[58]

The second expedition failed as miserably as the first. What shocked coastal Brazilians, who were now following the news of the conflict in their daily newspapers, was the way in which the defenders had gained the upper hand. Conselheiro's fighters laid waste to the countryside within a radius of seven miles of Canudos, burning ranches and farm buildings and leaving a circle of charred earth. The government force, the first regular expeditionary force to be sent against Canudos, had been curiously unprepared to carry out its orders. It had departed Monte Santo on January 12, 1897, after spending two weeks in preparation, using the town of Friar Apollonio de Todi (the name almost bigger than the place) as its base of operations. Once they struck out from their camp, they were ambushed by *conselheirista* troops led by João Abbade. After finding themselves hopelessly outflanked by the enemy, the government forces could only fall back, fighting as they retreated. Their humiliation was so complete that the viability of the republic itself seemed precarious. Federal military and civilian authorities suddenly elected to consider Canudos a threat to national order.

Quickly organized against a background of journalistic war cries amid generalized panic, the third military expedition now took shape. This expedition was commanded by the fearsome infantry commander Colonel Antônio Moreira César, who died in the fighting. (One contemporary, the landowner Antero de Cerqueira Gallo, wrote the baron of Jeremoabo that in Tucano it was speculated that the colonel had been shot by his own men, who hated him.)[59] The contingent included three branches of the service and initially had as its nucleus a brigade that was reinforced by three other corps. The 1,300 thoroughly equipped soldiers carried seventy rounds of cannon balls and sixteen million rounds of ammunition. These forces were bolstered further by an artillery battery, four cannon, and a squadron of cavalry. All were transported on treacherously narrow roads over ground pulverized by the unprecedented weight of the moving army.[60]

But both the second and third expeditions failed in the face of guerrilla tactics, with the defenders of Canudos firing from the cover of dense vegetation.[61] Scores of government soldiers deserted, fleeing into the wilderness. Although this epidemic of desertion by men facing combat was long whispered about, it was not until 1990 that documents were finally made available that listed the names of some of the *desaparecidos*, the presumed deserters.[62]

To the Jacobins and other nationalists most anxious to smash Canudos and so prove the army's ascendancy in the life of the nation, Moreira César became the symbolic successor to the last military president, Floriano Peixoto, Brazil's "Iron Marshal," whose reputation derived from his unconditional crusade to suppress dissent. So powerful was Peixoto's ambition that the federalist-minded citizens of Desterro, the capital of Santa Catarina, targeted their hatred at Peixoto's name itself—making it all the more ironic that, following the army's crushing of regionalist insurrection, the city was pompously renamed Florianópolis in tribute to its bloody captor.

Da Cunha's profile of Moreira César is masterful, and it reflects the fact that of all the personages brought to national attention during the

Canudos affair, the leader of the third military expedition, more than anyone else except Conselheiro himself, captured the public's eye (Fig. 11). Even backlanders were star-struck, as the dozens of *cordel* ballads composed during the campaign and remembered for years afterward attest.[63] Moreira César had come to the notice of the military nationalists in 1844 when, as a young captain, he had volunteered to assassinate a journalist who had libeled the honor of the army; for performing this deed he had been transferred to Mato Grosso, only to be recalled after the proclamation of the republic.

Now a hero to his fellow officers, after the navy rebellion in Rio de Janeiro harbor in 1893 he was sent by Floriano Peixoto himself to Santa Catarina, where he received the complete discretionary powers that permitted him to shock public opinion with his ruthlessness. He installed a reign of terror, arresting citizens who obviously had had no role in the federalist uprising, sacking their homes, and ordering the execution of officers, including Marshal Manoel de Almeida Lobo d'Eça, a hero of the Paraguayan War.[64]

Moreira César's appearance contradicted the warrior image he had earned—he was short, frail, flabby, and bow-legged—but it did not prevent public opinion from bestowing on him a hero's reputation. Da Cunha attributes to him other qualities that made him qualified to destroy Canudos: cruelty, tenacity, vindictiveness, patience. He also suffered from epilepsy, to which da Cunha attributed his "weird, uneven temperament."[65] In the anxious, jittery atmosphere that prevailed after the failure of the first two military expeditions against Canudos, it was in Moreira César that the republic put its faith and hopes for a swift end to the backland insurgence.

On February 3, 1897, Colonel Moreira César set out for Bahia heading the force of 1,300 men hastily assembled for him by the General Army Staff. Along the way, the colonel was stricken by an epileptic seizure, but he did not let it interrupt his intent to get to the front with lightning speed and to hurl "a thousand-and-some bayonets against Canudos in double-quick time."[66] This approach simply duplicated in larger scale the reckless overconfidence of the two earlier expeditions, and can be explained only by the fact that Moreira César and his fellow officers were too arrogant to believe that any rural peasant could resist superior military force. The colonel's military engineers made their assessments by sight, not by instrument, and they based their report about water availability, terrain, soil conditions, and the like on cursory briefings of local inhabitants, who were accustomed to describe distance in leagues, a vague unit of distance—all in striking contradiction to the scientific mentality that the positivists had supposedly brought to Brazilian military planning.

Moreira César then decided, precipitously and without heed to the

11. Colonel Moreira César, ca. 1897. Anonymous studio portrait. Courtesy Fundação Casa Rui Barbosa, Rio de Janeiro.

intense heat and parched land, to dispatch his troops to Canudos by forced march. Wagon trains loaded with supplies sank up to their hubs in sand. The men arrived at their first stopping point after an eight-hour walk in desert conditions, only to find that the military engineers could not sink an artesian well because they had brought the wrong equipment. The officers could only order the exhausted soldiers to march fifteen miles farther, dragging their heavy equipment through tangled briars, with arrival after nightfall.

They had entered the danger zone; the officers now slept with their horses' reins fastened to their hands. At dawn, when the men were awakened abruptly to march again, they saw along the road the still-glowing embers of bonfires, remnants of meals of roast turtle and goat, and fresh tracks in the sand. All along the line of march Conselheiro's scouts had kept watch, as was apparent to the soldiers, who must have reacted with rising apprehension. They made their camp at midday, doused by a sudden thunderstorm that soaked their equipment and bathed them in mud. In the midst of the confusion, the camp was startled by the sounds of horsemen riding toward them at full speed. They turned out to be a small group of escorts sent out by a local landowner, but the incident created momentary panic. More supplies arrived, and the next day at sunup the battalions began their rapid march to the next destination. All this activity was contrary to the original plan, which, taking into account the need for rest and proper precautions in safeguarding the army, had specified a marching column some two miles long as the troops entered enemy territory.

Despite these ominous signs, the troops were said to have entered the final portion of their march optimistically. Da Cunha describes the scene:

> Above them was the beautiful blue-arching sky of the backlands with its rainbow tints, shading gently, imperceptibly, from the deep blue of the zenith to the dazzling purple in the East. Besides, had not the enemy left the road clear for them up to now, failing to take advantage of the most favorable stretches to attack them? There was but one thing that worried them: what if they should find this nest of rebels empty when they arrived? This likely disappointment proved an alarming thought: the entire campaign transformed into a long forced march; and then, their inglorious return, without having fired a single cartridge.[67]

Such was not to be. Just as the advance troops reached the Pitombas *fazenda*, the enemy attacked, only to withdraw after a brief and indecisive exchange of fire. Colonel Moreira César examined a rifle that had been left behind and declared it "insignificant," saying to his aides that "these people are unarmed." He ordered the march resumed at a faster pace. The engagement only emboldened the soldiers, who became as excited as their commander about finally reaching Canudos. While the troops rested, still panting from their latest six-hour march, Moreira César, ill from the effects of the seizure, ordered that the troops proceed at quick-step to the Umburanas Hills, within artillery range of Conselheiro's settlement. The sun beat down on the battalions as they reached the top of Mount Favella, overlooking Canudos and its "pile of huts and labyrinth of narrow alleys, some of which came out on the wide square where the churches stood, [giving] the observer . . . the precise impression of having unexpectedly stumbled upon a large city."[68]

Four Krupp steel cannon were arranged in battle formation and commenced firing into Belo Monte. Adobe walls shattered, huts were smashed, fires erupted. The bombarded city lay enveloped in dust and smoke as the bell of the old church rang in alarm. There was no resistance. When the smoke cleared, the incredulous observers watched small groups of men swarm in and out of public places, carrying rifles and disappearing into the brush. Women and children sought refuge behind the walls of the new church. Quiet resumed; at one o'clock hundreds of government soldiers scrambled down the hills on two sides, their bayonets fixed. The soldiers were flanked by artillery that had been mounted at the highest point directly above the river, facing the new church. "This was," da Cunha wrote, "the most rudimentary of battle lines, a simple parallel formation, adapted to those rare cases of battle in the open country where a superiority in the matter of numbers and of bravery renders more complex maneuvers unnecessary."[69]

The result was tragic miscalculation, as had occurred so often in dealing with "lesser" peoples in unfamiliar circumstances. Moreira César disdained more cautious (and complex) tactics; not only did he willfully forget the experience of the previous two expeditions, but he also refused to give the backlanders credit for either sagacity or heroics. The summary of what happened next illustrates why da Cunha's words so shocked his readers, for he made his rustic subjects seem uncannily able if not superhuman:

> With the battalions attacking at once from two sides and bearing down upon a single objective, within a short space of time they would be facing each other and exchanging bullets intended for the jagunço. While the artillery at the beginning might bombard the churches and the center of the town, the scope of its action would gradually be limited as the troops advanced, until finally it would be obliged to fall silent just as the battle reached its decisive phase, from fear of firing upon the troops themselves as they mingled in hand-to-hand combat with the enemy in that labyrinth of huts.[70]

The initial resistance seemed futile: the backlanders fired lead and pebbles from antiquated blunderbusses as the troops crossed the river, bugles sounding. But the battle quickly broke up into individual skirmishes when the soldiers reached the maze of alleys that wound across the town. The clay-brick huts proved sturdy; when blown up by grenades, the mud rubble only slowed the attackers. In the end, the very primitiveness of Canudos's construction aided its defense. The settlement itself became a trap into which the arrogant invaders had been lured. Whole battalions were swallowed up into the mass of huts "as in[to] some dark cave." The defenders ambushed the soldiers, using knives, rifles, scythes, cattle prods, and broken household furniture as weapons. When a backlander was captured and killed, the women who had remained to watch would sob and "cower in the corner." Some soldiers stopped to loot the houses and eat from the bags and clay vessels hanging from the walls and ceiling that were filled with *passoca* (roasted nuts mixed with manioc flour, sugar, and salt), water, sun-dried meats, and fruit. More than once, doing so proved foolhardy: soldiers were ambushed and shot or stabbed in the midst of such stolen repasts.

Sharpshooters fired with precision from the church tower, killing government soldiers almost at will now that the artillery had ceased to safeguard the attacking troops. The bell of the old church started ringing once again. Moreira César, beginning to panic, ordered a cavalry charge into the city, but the winded steeds refused to enter the barrage of rifle fire that raked over the Vasa-Barris River. The attack became increasingly disorganized. "This was not an assault," da Cunha wrote. "It was merely a rash battering of a monstrous barricade, which became all the more formidable every moment as it tumbled in ruins and went up in smoke."[71]

As night fell on the exhausted federal troops, they retreated, filthy and singed, only to be set upon by the enemy. The entire battle line fell back. Men deserted their platoons and jumped into the river, trampling the wounded, beating off one another as they retreated. From the old Canudos church came the haunting strains of the Ave Maria; it was the hour of the Angelus. The fleeing soldiers dragged their cannons after them and improvised a camp in broken ranks. Moreira César lay dying. More than a hundred wounded men huddled in the center of the encampment, untreated and forced to lie in darkness lest they reveal their location.

Before midnight, the surviving officers unanimously voted to retreat. When the feeble Moreira César refused to agree, they ignored him. He died before dawn. The broken battalions fell back with no semblance of military formation. When it was obvious that the republican army was about to retreat, the entire population of Canudos thronged into the square and broke into a "prolonged, shrill, deadly intentioned whistling." The *jagunços*, of course, pursued, picking off soldiers one by one as the ranks disintegrated. Eight hundred men fled, dropping their rifles and equipment and the litters on which they had been carrying the wounded.

Moreira César's body was dumped by the roadside along with all the others.

The body of the man who had attained the status of a larger-than-life national hero in the service of the republic was discovered by *conselheiristas*, who buried him. An eyewitness, Maria Avelina, remarked nearly five decades later that, "dead, Moreira César had the appearance of a dark, little old man."[72] The army continued to flee in disarray; only the artillery, at the rear, maintained any semblance of order and discipline. The new expedition commander, Col. Pedro Nunes Tamarindo, was wounded and asked that his aide shoot him. Finally, the *jagunços* attacked the artillery and captured most of its guns. The third expedition was destroyed; "it had vanished utterly."[73]

News of the rout of the Moreira César expedition shocked and scandalized Brazil. The humiliating defeat collapsed republican self-confidence like a hot-air balloon punctured by an arrow. The news sent mobs into the streets of Brazil's major cities. In the South, angry citizens torched monarchist newspaper offices in a display of violence that made a mockery of the hysteria over the rustic backlanders' defeat of the forces of "civilization." Governors, state legislators, and editorialists clamored for retribution. National mourning was declared, and masses for the dead were celebrated in all churches. University students and other young men of social standing joined volunteer battalions, as did hardened veterans of the naval revolt. The president of the republic declared that if need be he would mobilize members of the federal congress to arms. Civil engineers offered plans to construct a "miraculous railway" over the summit of Mount Itiúba to Monte Santo, to be completed in thirty days, "at the end of which time a shrill chorus of steaming locomotives would burst triumphantly upon the fierce backlands."[74]

In the backlands, however, the death of the celebrated military hero yielded only renewed prestige for Antônio Conselheiro and his followers. As a contemporary *cordel* troubadour put it:

> Moreira César,
> Who killed you?
> It was a bullet from Canudos
> Sent by the Conselheiro![75]

Salvador during this time faced a frenzy of excitement. As the state capital and transportation nexus for the entire mid-Atlantic coast, the city was affected by the conflict from the beginning, and in significant ways. It received daily dozens and sometimes hundreds of soldiers and others destined for the front or returning from it. Casualties and those stricken by disease arrived in special trains, as did small groups of women and children rescued from the settlement of Belo Monte. Supplies, of course, entered through Salvador, including large pieces of artillery unloaded from naval ships in the port.[76]

Merchants profited handsomely from outfitting officers and journalists and from selling supplies to the army as well as fad items of clothing—neckties, canes, and hats, for example—popularized by military heroes. No youth from a prominent family, it was said, ventured out in public without his Moreira César hat, which sold for 18 milréis at the Mateus emporium.[77] More seriously, the influx of troops set off a wave of rowdy behavior that included attacks by drunken soldiers on policemen and streetcars (the *bonds*, named after the method by which they were financed), robberies of stores and street vendors, and attacks on "defenseless women."[78]

As late as March 20, 1897, backland *coronéis* were still reporting to one another that people continued to emigrate *to* Canudos.[79] Such news only fueled the conviction that the backlands were in the grip of crazies, and stiffened military resolve. The fourth offensive took two months to organize, beginning in June 1897. It gathered the resources of the entire Brazilian army, twenty-five line battalions, cavalry, machine guns, Krupp field cannon, and three thousand soldiers from ten Brazilian states and the Federal District, many of them from Piauí, Ceará, Rio Grande do Norte, Paraíba, and Pernambuco. Most were from the cities, but some, especially those from Bahia and Sergipe, were backlanders pressed into uniform (see Fig. 13).

The war minister, Marshal Carlos Machado Bittencourt, gave his commanding officers permission to employ flexible tactics and subdivide the republican forces into autonomous, compact, and mobile fighting units. One, a force of 2,350 men (many of whom were backlanders themselves), under General Cláudio do Amaral Savaget, marched 175 miles from Aracajú to Canudos, carrying two light Krupp cannon. Another well-prepared contingent was the Fifth Corps of Bahian State Police, formed of *sertanejos* recruited from the northeast portion of the state bordering the São Francisco River. Engineering detachments rebuilt the stretches of road that had been damaged or that needed widening. The government forces no longer mocked their adversaries—just the opposite. Tales of the backlanders' tenacity grew into wild stories of hobgoblins, foreign mercenaries, fighters allied with the devil; *jagunços* now were seen as macabre, bloodsucking demons. Tales spread that the *jagunços* had taken Monte Santo, Cumbe, Massacará, even Jeremoabo. The campaign proceeded with extreme caution.

Many but not all of the rumors were exaggeration or sheer fiction. Nevertheless, the defenders did employ brilliant psychological tactics. When the fourth expedition's troops set out in June 1897 for Canudos, three months after the defeat of the third expedition, they saw things along the line of march that curdled the blood. Hanging from the stunted trees were the drooping, rotted corpses of the third expedition; bleached skulls lined the roadside, and the shreds of onetime uniforms fluttered from the tree branches. One of these cadavers was none other than Colonel Tamarindo, Moreira César's hapless successor as leader of the third expedition.

In the first major skirmish between *conselheiristas* and soldiers, the legalist forces were lured into a trap constructed by the crafty Pajeú. With hundreds of the republican soldiers slaughtered by sharpshooters firing from ambush, it looked for a while as if the fourth campaign would fail just as the others had.

The town of Monte Santo, physically striking because of its proximity to the peak that gave it its name but otherwise quite ordinary, was transformed overnight by the arrival of the military command, which used it as its main staging area. Officers commandeered the most passable housing for themselves, summarily evicting the buildings' occupants. Favilla Nunes, the *Gazeta de Notícias* correspondent, communicated his dislike of the locals in an article claiming that only two "paizanos" (the word presumably used to mean fellows hale and well met) lived in the town: one, the circuit judge; the other, the merchant João Caldas, whose shop was served admirably by the conflict, with customers lining up for two hours to buy whatever merchandise and food he had in stock.[80]

## LAST DAYS

The events during the final two Canudos campaigns traumatized the entire region, from the front right to the city of Salvador. Unlike the earlier confrontations, when the *conselheirista* forces generally bided their time and waited to ambush their adversaries, skirmishes now occurred wherever members of the Guarda Católica encountered government troops, possibly because Conselheiro's men were now better armed with captured weapons. The records of the Bahian State Police for 1897 register deaths in places as far from Canudos as Tucano, Ángico, and Cocorobó.[81] Those wounded who could be transported were taken to Salvador, where, by September 1897, all hospital facilities had become overextended (Fig. 12). One hundred thirty beds were set up in the Medical School museum, another hundred in the library, twenty-eight in the surgery theater, and thirty more in the faculty lounge. Most of the last-year medical students went directly to the front; the newer students remained at the school to tend to the wounded as best they could. One-third of the members of the Bahian state militia died in combat or from their wounds. The small pharmacy operated around the clock, although almost all medicines were quickly exhausted.

Amid the widespread sense of alarm, rumors spread alleging that

12. Hematology Ward, Medical Faculty of Bahia, Salvador, 1897. Courtesy Instituto Geográfico e Histórico da Bahia, Salvador.

starving *jagunços* were fleeing Canudos and ambushing individual legalist soldiers. Newspapers published woodcut illustrations made from photographs of some of Conselheiro's closest aides, including Antônio Vilanova, as a form of "wanted" poster.[82] At the same time, the city was buffeted by streams of visiting dignitaries, for whom lavish banquets were prepared as they disembarked en route to Monte Santo or the front. Such attention was disorienting, and in the main depressing, for those with family members residing in the interior or serving in one of the military forces engaged in fighting.[83]

Hundreds of legalist soldiers deserted, but they were quickly replaced by fresh troops.[84] The final assault began in July. Involved in the fourth expedition were more than eight thousand men under three generals and War Minister Bittencourt, who ensconced himself in a house in Monte Santo. One of the commanders, General Savaget, posted fifteen hundred men to the top of Mount Favella, to hold it at all costs.

Almost six thousand men in five brigades, led by the commander of the Second Military District, General Artur Oscar de Andrade Guimarães, departed for Canudos to encircle it and starve the population into submission (Fig. 13). General Oscar was a "red Florianist," the hero of the federal government in the regionalist rebellion in Rio Grande do

13. Army Infantry Battalion, Fourth Military Campaign, in their makeshift tents outside Canudos, 1897. Courtesy Paulo Zanettini.

Sul. The column's field officers included the most successful veterans in the Brazilian army: Carlos Telles, hero of the siege of Bagé during the civil war in Rio Grande do Sul; Olympio da Silveira, commander of artillery; Salvador Pires, commandant of the Fifth Police, a man known for his vicious temperament and success in disciplining *sertanejo* recruits. The army lost a thousand men in the initial assault. This setback, together with the great unpopularity of President Prudente de Morais and the exploitation by his opposition of monarchist fears, only fueled the conviction among government supporters that the uprising must be smashed without mercy. The campaign continued.

From June through the last assault at the beginning of October, the carnage was appalling. In later years, dozens of corpses washed up during rains, some partially mummified in their blue and crimson striped uniforms.[85] Every time it rained heavily, bones and skulls were exposed; crumbling in the air, they were finally crushed to a residue of flint and powder as men and pack animals walked over the ground. Hundreds of defenders and federal troops were killed on each day of fighting, with many more wounded or felled by rampant disease.[86] Reports of the fighting, filed daily by war correspondents, flooded the country. The most absurd rumors spread wildly and were believed. It was said, for instance, that arms were arriving for Conselheiro from Argentina via Minas Gerais, and that foreign soldiers were being sent from the United States and also from Austria to restore the monarchy. Of course, it was true enough that the *sertanejos* were scattering through the backlands, attacking towns and supply trains and so enlarging the scope of the confrontation.[87] Stories of misappropriation of war supplies and treachery multiplied, too, as long as the fighting fared badly.

The battle had raged fiercely, led by the remaining *conselheirista* fighters who, parched and starving, refused to give up. An undetermined number, though, did desert Conselheiro in the last days of battle, fleeing into the brush under cover of darkness, and in many cases leaving their wives and children behind. The backlanders believed that if they were captured they would suffer *degola* (slitting of the throat, a practice employed on Brazil's southern frontier by the *gaúchos* of Rio Grande do Sul) and probably be tortured first. Although arguably quicker than the *cangaceiro* practice of slitting the victim's stomach and letting him die slowly, the *degola* shocked the coastal elites, bringing even more notoriety to the Canudos episode.

The most loyal *conselheiristas*, however, stayed. José Travassos, who walked away from the battle under cover of night to (he said later) "live in the *caatinga*, eat cactus, and sleep wherever God willed," left his family as well as his father, who died later in the fighting.[88] The backland fighters knew that they could not trust the army. Some of the last defenders, though, were lured when the General Staff sent word in September through a captured emissary that those who surrendered would be spared. Disarmed, the men were sent to gather their families and prepare for evacuation from the vanquished settlement, which was about to be set afire. Then, just before the announced "trip," the men were taken, surrounded by soldiers, and hacked to death in front of hundreds of witnesses, including many of their wives and children.[89]

Da Cunha's description of the end of Canudos during the first week of October is terrible and eloquent, accentuating his ambivalence about the survivors: "Canudos did not surrender. The only case of its kind in history, it held out to the last man. Conquered inch by inch, in the literal meaning of the words, it fell on October 5, toward dusk—when its last defenders fell, dying, every man of them. There were only four of them left: an old man, two other full-grown men, and a child, facing a furiously raging army of five thousand soldiers."[90]

Close scrutiny of Figure 14, a photograph taken of the survivors by the professional cameraman Flávio de Barros shortly before their execution by *degola*, reveals da Cunha's description to be inaccurate.[91] Many of the women are young and, although appearing stunned by their capture, neither "wizened" nor "hags." Most appear to be black or *caboclo*, but some are light-skinned, no more *jagunços* than da Cunha him-

14. Survivors of the Fourth Military Campaign, October 1897. Photograph by
Flávio de Barros. Courtesy Paulo Zanettini.

self. In the back of the crowd sit several dozen men, as ethnically varied
as the women and children.

On the morning after the final assault, soldiers smashed, leveled, and
burned all 5,200 houses in the settlement. Troops slit the throats of
prisoners both at the front and at the detention camp at Queimadas,
near Monte Santo. Canudos had to be burned, officers explained, because of the rising smell of putrefying corpses, which, by October 7, had
turned the air rancid. Vultures circled overhead. Dogs that had crawled
away during the fighting now returned seeking their masters, howling
pathetically. Even after the fires died down, packs of hungry canines
prowled the vicinity of the settlement, attacking goats and cows until the
predators were hunted down and shot.[92]

Before Canudos was torched and then dynamited, Conselheiro's body
was exhumed (Fig. 15). On the orders of the chief battle surgeon, Major
Miranda Curió, the head was removed by a knife thrust. It was displayed
on a pike and subsequently taken to the coast, where it was held high at
the front of a military parade for all to see and finally given to Prof.
Raimundo Nina Rodrigues to be examined for congenital abnormalities.
The partially preserved head remained a curiosity on display at the
Medical Faculty until the building burned down at the beginning of the
twentieth century.

It was determined later that Antônio Conselheiro had died on Sep-

15. The exhumed corpse of Antônio Conselheiro, 1897. Courtesy Paulo Zanettini. The head was removed and taken to Salvador, where it was displayed on
a pike at the front of a military parade. It was stored at the Medical Faculty but
later was destroyed in a fire that consumed the building.

tember 22, likely of dysentery, some two weeks before the final storming
of his city. He had been treated with herbs, but no medicine had been
available. Those closest to him refused for nearly a week after his death
to bury him, anticipating—as Conselheiro allegedly had prophesied—
that he would be resurrected after three days in flesh and blood and that
thousands of archangels would fill the sky with flaming arrows. When
the odor became too strong, they reluctantly agreed to inter the corpse.
Conselheiro was nearly seventy, and he had been in failing health; although in the photograph of his remains he does not appear emaciated,
as might have been expected, some of the corpulence may be attributed
to the swelling of tissues that occurs some days after death.[93]

The dead, most of whom were buried in shallow graves or simply
dumped into rocky crevices or ravines on the battlefield, numbered more
than fifteen thousand on both sides, including two hundred army
officers.[94] Many had perished from disease. Men under fire from modern
cannon died "like ants" with each firing. Not all expired immediately, of
course; many agonized for days before dying from their wounds, medical
arrangements being so inadequate and transportation available only
intermittently.[95]

That most of the federal troops and state police forces mobilized to battle the Canudos *jagunços* were unprepared to fight only underscores the republic's vulnerability. The Bahian State Police force in 1894 had only 1,812 men responsible for 120 *municípios*, and the desertion rate was high. Many conscripts were tricked and sometimes forcibly impressed into service. Soldiers in the rank of private collected a miserable monthly wage, barely enough to purchase a pair of shoes. In the midst of the final assault on Canudos, the commanding general requested five thousand additional men, remarking bitterly that of the nearly ten thousand supplied so far, only 2,600 had been found fit for service.[96] Boys were enlisted as young as thirteen. Some became servants; others actually fought. A number of youths of fourteen fell on the battlefield in the conflict.[97] Separated by a chasm of class and status from their officers, the troops were poorly instructed, badly housed, and sometimes not paid, because of either inadequate appropriations or dishonest paymasters. Equipment was in disrepair. Medics were recruited from the pool of enlisted men and given little or no training.[98]

Everyone near the front walked covered with dust in the more than 100-degree heat of the day; there was only barely enough water to drink, and that, a newspaper reporter said, was "the color of coffee with milk and tasting of cattle urine."[99] The wounded were often bedded in the same improvised hospitals with patients carrying contagious disease.[100] Medical supplies were sold to military hospitals for five times the street price. One soldier in thirty-three in 1897 suffered from beriberi, compared to one in 3,800 in the general population.[101] An Alagoinhas physician commissioned by the state Inspectorate of Public Health to survey the Canudos site listed not only an epidemic of malaria, reportedly carried by government troops marching from Pernambuco, but also dysentery and a host of other ailments amounting to a "plague," in part the result of unburied corpses rotting in the heat.[102]

Not surprisingly, assignment to the front was considered a punishment. Captured deserters were sent to Canudos; soldiers arrested and convicted for military infractions were given prison terms that were suspended as long as the soldier fought. Because officers knew that their men might desert if they remained away from their families, the troops were permitted to take along their wives and any other women who joined them on the way.[103] More than two hundred of these women, known as *vivandeiras*, followed the federal troops entering from Sergipe. A few wives, some with small children, accompanied their soldier husbands all the way from the South of Brazil. They slept on the ground, clearing a space in the brush, while their men slept in army tents. One woman, a *gaúcha* named Busa, remained with the troops after her soldier companion was killed and worked as a volunteer hospital aide at the front until she contracted smallpox and died.

Married men were charged for their wives' keep, though the women were generally expected to work as well, some as washerwomen or cooks, others as medical aides at the front. One contingent of families was housed temporarily at Sixth Military Region headquarters in Salvador on the way back from Canudos while their men awaited reassignment. Unaccustomed to such surroundings, some of the women began to behave wildly, yelling, "dancing sambas," and "making lewd advances to soldiers indiscriminately." The offenders were ordered evicted by the commanding officer.[104]

Officers were expected to discipline their men and send them into battle. Official records note commendations given for display of "cold-blooded enthusiasm" in combat.[105] In the Bahian State Police, enlisted men could earn commissions after passing through the lower ranks, but those who did were usually white and literate, meaning that they came from much better social backgrounds than the common soldiers.

Each side eagerly used brutality against the other. Even in times of peace, backland residents feared soldiers of the state militias as much as they feared bandits; in any case, many of the "troops of the line" had been induced to enlist when drunk or had been taken from prison. Many captured defenders, including women, were executed despite a promise uttered publicly by General Artur Oscar near the end of the battle to spare rebels who surrendered. Marciano de Sergipe, one of the last defenders, after capture was bayonetted in his joints, legs, arms, and fingers and had his eyes gouged out.[106]

In the midst of the brutality, one humanitarian act stood out. In August 1897, during the worst of the fighting, a citizens' committee was formed in Salvador to aid injured soldiers. After visiting the front, the members soon turned to helping the survivors as well. The Comité Patriótico, unprecedented in Brazilian history, was in part a response to the intense barrage of press coverage of the Canudos conflict, which reached its fullest extent at the onset of the fourth and last military campaign. Reporting, as we have seen, ran the gamut from satire and ridicule, mostly directed against Conselheiro, to searching questions about the inhumanity being directed toward the *jagunços*. In the face of published reports that survivors were being forced into servitude and prostitution, the Bahian committee went into action.[107]

Collection boxes were placed on major streets. The committee's president, Franz Wagner, was a Protestant, rare for Brazil and rarer for the Northeast. Although only a few of the city's leading families were represented, with names including Barreto Filho, Redomarque, and Dias Lima Sobrinho, other members included newspapermen, the owner of the Salvador music store, and some German and Silesian priests from the Franciscan and Capuchin convents, recruited by Wagner; several local physicians were enlisted to help as well.[108] Outsiders (and working journalists) did most of the organizing work. Smaller committees were established in Queimadas and Alagoinhas to process women and children survivors left there by the retiring troops.

In late August, a delegation carrying medicine traveled by train and then wagon to the staging area in Cansação, to comfort the wounded and bury the dead. A few children from villages en route, orphaned in attacks by Conselheiro's *jagunços*, were taken by committee members back to Salvador, along with the more than one hundred surviving women and children found in Canudos, most of them wounded and found silently weeping. An eyewitness, Frei Pedro Sinzig, noted in his diary that the wretched contingent reminded him of a "slave market."[109]

Sinzig, a Franciscan missionary born in Saxony who had arrived in Salvador in 1893 at the age of seventeen, was named by his convent superiors to the Comité Patriótico, together with a Salesian father, Gabriel Groemer; they were joined by a third priest, a sixty-six-year-old Capuchin named Jeronymo de Montefiore. These men accompanied other committee members in late August 1897, journeying by special train ordered by the governor, to the site near the front. Sinzig's diary, written in German, sheds much light on the mission. Initially, the visitors treated the excursion as a pleasurable outing. Wagner brought along ample stores of mineral water, tea, wine, and *cachaça*, with provisions for varied menus of lunches and dinners. Residents of Queimadas brought fresh milk and treated the visitors handsomely, telling them stories of dubious authenticity about the gullibility and the foolish belief of Conselheiro's followers that the mystic actually worked miracles.

Soon enough, reality began to assert itself, although the diary never wavers from its bland, reportorial style. The committee members saw vultures circling rotting animal carcasses. They spoke with orphaned children. They observed residents shrinking from contact, terrified of contracting smallpox. Women kindled animal excrement in front of their huts as a disinfectant. They watched troops arrive, accompanied by cannon. They saw trains unload the sick and wounded. As Canudos lay under its final siege, hundreds of *jagunço* prisoners were brought to the staging area, many "horribly wounded." Women prisoners suffered noiselessly, muffling their sobs. The committee found abandoned children, one three years old, by the wayside (Fig. 16). Eight hundred more prisoners arrived. Men were bound so "barbarously" that the ropes cut through their flesh. The priests offered sacraments: marriages, baptisms, communions, confessions. When the committee members returned to Salvador by train, they rejoiced in being able to bathe again.[110]

Priests who remained in the vicinity of Belo Monte spent most of their time giving last rites and baptizing the "pagan" wounded. They were

16. Surviving *jaguncinhos* (children) with army officers, Fourth Military Campaign, October 1897. Courtesy Paulo Zanettini.

kept away from the prisoner encampments, but learned of continued "horrible cruelties" practiced against the survivors. Some were shot when they could not keep up with the forced march. A pregnant woman whose labor pains had started was placed in an empty shack by the side of the road and abandoned. Soldiers killed children by smashing their skulls against trees, much as the "fanatics" at Pedra Bonita had done decades earlier. Wounded *conselheiristas* were drawn and quartered or hacked to pieces limb by limb. Their carcasses were doused with oil and burned—the same treatment as was given the surviving dwellings in Canudos. The army systematically eradicated the remaining traces of the holy city as if it had housed the devil incarnate.[111]

The state of Bahia set up a temporary hospital in Alagoinhas to treat the wounded and vaccinate (and revaccinate) local residents and prisoners against malaria. In its first month of operation, the hospital housed forty-seven women and children taken from Canudos and three soldiers. All but twelve died. The next month brought a larger contingent of wounded; those survivors were sent to Salvador to be cared for by the Comité Patriótico. In mid-November, Amaro Lélis Piedade, the *Diário de Notícias* correspondent and mainstay of the citizens' delegation, affirmed that children rescued from Canudos would no longer be taken "to orphanages, factories, or tutors" without all efforts to find living relations being first exhausted.[112]

The committee's reports from the front frequently stressed the human dimension of the conflict. On September 6, 1897, Lélis Piedade reported his conversation with some women prisoners and an eight-year-old boy captured in Belo Monte. The child, who asked for a cigarette, "spoke as freely as a parrot and managed his rifle as handily as any man"; he said that he was no longer a *jaguncinho*, but "a soldier and a republican." Asked about food supplies, the women said that there was still *farinha* in the settlement. Probably seeking to please her captors, one claimed that the women were forced to live in Canudos by their "husbands and lovers," whom Conselheiro had threatened to have skinned alive if they deserted.[113]

Another story was related fifty years later by an eyewitness, Capt. Domingos Jesuíno, da Cunha's guide. A woman with a child at her breast was taken prisoner; in the presence of a newspaper reporter, she asked that the soldiers kill her quickly but that they kill her infant first, "because death would at least bring him peace." When an officer replied that no one wanted to kill either of them, she shook her head: "You killed my father, my mother, my husband, and took my two older sons." She then asked again to be killed without delay, stamping her bare feet on the ground in rage. She was eventually calmed, and taken to Monte Santo.

"I have never seen such a display of fanaticism in my life," wrote Jesuíno.[114]

Day after day, Lélis Piedade's newspaper reports conveyed a sense of anguish and horror. He quoted an ill-trained medic: "Today, September 18, we received 57 cases: 18 wounded, 12 sufferers from beriberi, 2 with cirrhosis, 1 'hidrópico,' 4 victims of tuberculosis, 2 with whooping cough, 1 with advanced syphilis, 1 rheumatic, 7 with hernias, 1 with cardiac arrest, and 8 with various maladies of the eye."[115] He also reported on unsanitary conditions in the miserable hamlets that housed the reporters and military brass; the slaughterhouse in Queimadas, where the vultures picked at the wounded before they could be dressed; places infested with malaria; towns, like Serra Branca, totally abandoned; the groups of pathetic backland women who had followed their men to Canudos only to be widowed and left injured, ill, or destitute.

In the records of the citizens' committee, forty-one of the 146 women and children saved (sixteen over the age of twenty, the rest children, mostly under twelve years old) were described as "white."[116] In several cases, clarifying notations were added gratuitously: "white, blond, and of good family." Even given the wide latitude in racial classification at the end of the nineteenth century—and not discounting that captives of more European appearance were more likely to be spared—the fact that 28 percent of Canudos's survivors were identified as white undermines the prevailing view of Conselheiro's followers as nothing but *caboclo* peasants. They came from all parts of the region, not just from the villages and hamlets of the high *sertão*, but from Feira de Santana in the Recôncavo, Alagoinhas, and from as far away as Fortaleza and Itabaianinha, Sergipe. One man was not a resident of Canudos but had come there on a pilgrimage and been trapped by the fighting.[117]

We do not know, of course, how many more Canudenses escaped or else met ill fate at the hands of soldiers or others in the backlands. Even during the fighting, many soldiers had forcibly taken women and girls as concubines; whole families of children were put to work as barracks cleaners and servants. Da Cunha personally took responsibility for a boy of six or seven years, an orphan, who lived with him at the front in the journalist's tent and then accompanied him to Rio de Janeiro and finally São Paulo.[118]

Other survivors fared less well. The records of several of the girls brought to Salvador by the committee indicate that they had been raped by soldiers, beaten, or "abandoned to the streets." Nineteen were listed as gravely ill or wounded. Some annotations: a *mulata* of fifteen, who had left her parents dead at Canudos, with "land, a house, livestock and benefactors" in Salgado; or a *caboclo*, aged ten, "intelligent and alert, commended in the Canudos school for his vivacity, orphaned, of legitimate birth of parents from Genepapinho." The orphaned children were either placed with relatives, if locatable, or entrusted to the care of volunteer families. Women, upon recovery, were at first restricted to Salvador, where they worked as domestic servants, but after a while they were permitted to return to the interior. To ensure that they would not be impeded on their journey back to the *sertão*, the citizens' committee issued safe-conduct passes—with a photograph of Lélis Piedade so that illiterates, recognizing his likeness, would honor the document.

Amaro Lélis Piedade was a remarkable individual, typical of republican culture in his rhetoric but singular in his capacity and willingness to act and not just talk. A man of very humble origins, his father, Camilo de Lélis Piedade, was an artist and tailor who lived in a small house adjacent to the São João Theater. The youth was an able student and, despite his lack of family connections, sailed through his preparatory work and graduated with a degree in pharmacy from the Medical Faculty in Salvador. Like many of his contemporaries, he never practiced in the field of his training; instead he plunged into journalism, having already become known as a fervent republican and abolitionist. A public man who reveled in debate as well as civic and cultural activity, he not only served as a deputy to the first republican state constituent assembly and a legislator in the subsequent two sessions, but also created the Fine Arts Academy, where he lectured on aesthetics and art history. Until 1886 he worked as editor of the *Diário de Notícias*, whereupon he moved to the rival *Jornal de Notícias*. When he died, never having married, in 1908 from an undisclosed illness, his long obituary mentioned his work with the Comité Patriótico only briefly. A special train was sent to bring his body back to the capital. Of him it was said that "to the poor, to the sick, to invalids, to orphans, to anyone who came to him with tear-filled eyes or hard luck, Lélis Piedade was an 'apostle for good.'"[119]

Northeastern state governments, although chronically impoverished and usually unable to meet expenses without resorting to bond issues and foreign loans, allocated special funds for massive festivities to celebrate the return of the troops after the republican victory. "With your help," wrote Sergipe's governor to the district attorney of Aracajú, who was helping track down monarchists in his state capital during the final military campaign, "[we are prevailing] against the traitorous hands seeking to destroy the democratic institutions of our country."[120] In the euphoria of victory, the human cost of the conflict was forgotten. The four campaigns entered Brazilian history as the Canudos War, its heroes blown up larger than life, its victims reviled as rebels, fanatics, and demons.

# FIVE

# Conselheiro's Vision

*Só Deus é grande* (Only God is great)
ANTÔNIO CONSELHEIRO

Until the ultramontane reforms enacted by the Holy See in the 1860s began to restore ecclesiastical orthodoxy to the Brazilian church, most clergy under the monarchy were "political priests." Owing their preferment to the secular government, often lax in their moral discipline, and tending to be hostile to Rome, they clustered in the more affluent parishes of the wealthier cities. Astonishingly, during the empire only seven hundred secular priests ministered to fourteen million people.[1] Even given the revival of the Brazilian episcopacy and the presence of new reformist seminaries and foreign-born priests in the *sertão* after the mid-1860s, it is remarkable that Antônio Conselheiro and his fellow backland *beatos*, lay missionaries, and self-made holy men did not stray even further from orthodoxy than they did.

Instead, Antônio Conselheiro's homilies and prayer texts reveal a theological vision consistent with the teachings of the nineteenth-century church. In practice, of course, his emphasis on penitence, personal sin, and the imminence of holy judgment deeply disturbed observers who took apocalyptic warnings less literally. Conselheiro's imagination embraced a lucid picture of good and evil, one that departed in emphasis if not in content from more refined urban Catholicism. It was elaborated through a penitential and messianic tone that must have been responsible at least in part for the charismatic appeal his words held for so many of his flock. At least one historian of the Brazilian church suggests that Conselheiro realized that Rome was attempting to reinforce the authority of the Vatican. Although Conselheiro never added the Holy Father to his list of enemies, knowledge of Rome's intent may explain Conselheiro's alliances with local clergy, for backland priests were quite aware that the campaign to restore neo-orthodoxy posed an acute threat to the long-standing local tradition of vicariate autonomy.[2]

Conselheiro's theology was complex, and it enabled listeners to hear selectively. It borrowed from accessible sources, including the *Hours of Mary* and the teachings of Padre Ibiapina, popularized through oral tradition. In its comprehensiveness, Conselheiro's preaching represented, if not an original statement about life and death, then certainly one that was clear and extraordinary. Although we must beware of falling into the same judgmental trap as da Cunha and his contemporaries, it is tempting to find much of Conselheiro's theology rooted in the severity of backland life and in the frustrated experience of a rigid and tormented individual holding his church and fellow men to exalted standards.

Conselheiro never wavered from his commitment to the principle that "só Deus é grande," "only God is great." This tenet hardened him against the human temptation to succumb to the adoration of his flock, who wanted to call him "the Good Jesus," or "Santo Antônio Conselheiro," thus attributing to him characteristics of one who gives his life and willingly suffers for man's sins. His central view of God also permitted him to ignore the condemnation heaped on him by the institutional Catholic church, which he considered morally corrupt and excessively powerful.[3] His habit of preaching in a soft voice, just as Jesus did, lent an air of intimacy to his public appearances; the fact that listeners had to be silent to hear him probably contributed to observers' impressions that he mesmerized his flock, adding to the mystic aspect of his demeanor.[4]

We know from Conselheiro's breviaries and from descriptions of his sermons that his religious vision derived most significantly from Padre José Gonçalves Couto's 993-page *Missão abreviada*, the lengthy collection of reflections and saints' lives widely used by both lay missionaries and regular clergy around the world.[5] First published in Pôrto in 1873, by 1878, the date of Conselheiro's copy, the work was already in its eleventh edition. In the *Missão*, Couto, a missionary who worked primarily in Goa in Portuguese India, hurled threat upon threat of eternal damnation and fiery perdition. Sin, he said, would cause earthquakes, plagues, hunger, and war. Jesus' role was stripped of its biblical dimension and reduced to suffering and death, which were warranted, Couto pronounced, in order to satisfy divine justice in the face of human sinfulness. Majesty overwhelmed compassion in this revelatory tome; saints in their plurality were celebrated for their joyful acceptance of suffering, resignation, conformism, and martyrdom.[6] This emphasis, certainly, was not foreign to the Northeast; indeed, it was quite consistent with its cultural tradition. In all Brazil, the Northeast's religious art always was the bloodiest, portraying the suffering Christ in stark detail, celebrating, as it were, saintly pain and humiliation.

Couto's *Missão* did not, however, provide the exclusive basis for Conselheiro's sermons and teachings. Most of what Conselheiro communicated to his listeners consisted of familiar homilies, emphasizing ethics, morality, the virtues of hard work, and piety. Taken as a whole, his version of popular Catholicism contained a worldview and ways of thought that had little in common with the traditional and less charismatic texts intoned by priests representing the liturgical custom of the late nineteenth-century institutional church.

As we have seen, Conselheiro's two collections of commentaries, prayers, and homilies were found by government troops inside the ruins of his house in Belo Monte. Each book, meticulously copied by hand— probably by Leão de Natuba (Leão da Silva), Conselheiro's personal secretary[7]—on parchment and sturdily bound, bears the mark of a careful editor. Selections, which veer in tone toward Jansenist precepts of individual salvation, incorporate long passages from the *Missão abreviada*, though much of the text comes right out of the Bible. Taken by themselves, the books, which deal with aspects of the liturgy that Conselheiro considered important, seem to be addressed to lettered congregants, not common folk; most likely, he simplified the esoteric language and arguments in his public preaching. In any event, we can reconstruct to some extent Conselheiro's religious outlook from the passages he selected.

The overarching concern of the handbooks is penitential, drawn from the *Hours of Mary*—specifically, the poverty of the Virgin Mary, "Our Lady of Sorrows," at the time of the birth of Jesus; her humiliation before the Temple; her anguish at Simon's prophecy; and her torment upon learning of the demise of innocents and over the martyrdom and death of her son. Only the briefest reference is made—once or twice in the hundreds of pages of text—to charity or forgiveness. The books denounce the forces of evil: the Jews who "vomited injuries against the Savior," the blindness of "false Christians." The Ten Commandments and selected biblical texts are commented on in legalistic language, with frequent references in Latin. A final, specific section comments on the abolition of slavery and attacks the republic, Portugal's "barbarous" expulsion of the Jesuits, civil marriage, and the treatment of the imperial family. "It is obvious," Conselheiro writes, "that the Republic exists under a false principle and therefore lacks any legitimate standing. . . . Who is it who does not know that the dignified Prince Pedro III holds legitimate power constituted by God to govern Brazil?"[8]

Conselheiro was personally compassionate, but his God was absolute, stern, vicarious, and demanding, a remote figure who conferred redemption only through bodily pain and humiliation. To some extent the priest's conception of God was contradictory, combining notions of a holy warrior ready to fight Canudos's enemies with a kindly vision of "O Bom

Jesus." In his life, Maciel/Conselheiro emphasized the harsh and penitential side. He lived on alms and refused all luxuries, even a bed.
One of his followers constructed for him a crude cedarwood oratory, en-
closing an image of Christ. This he carried with him, suspending it from
a tree limb for prayer; when he approached a town, his flock would bear
the oratory aloft overhead, entering the site "to a chorus of litanies."[9]

This behavior and outlook departed significantly from those of his
predecessor, Padre Ibiapina, who avoided dramatic gestures. Ibiapina's
God was just and compassionate, yet exacting in requiring Christians to
follow the true faith. Conselheiro's theology was Christ-centered (Jesus
as the *only* savior) but influenced by the religious tradition of popular
Catholicism in its backland variant—a heritage reliant on the personal
intervention of saints as agents of Christ.[10] Life on earth, Conselheiro
argued constantly, is a test, an arduous passageway to eternal life. Therefore, the world's goods must be cast aside. The institutional Catholic
church must be veritable and legitimate; it is as subject to temptation as
any other institution, even though it was founded by Jesus. True Catholics, he warned, must strive to imitate Christ; only then will they earn
admission to heaven.

Conselheiro borrowed Ibiapina's commitment to the poor and the
afflicted, teaching that God demands a sense of human charity. Thus he
became an apostle of charity, although, unlike Ibiapina, Conselheiro
emphasized physical works—rebuilding chapels and spoiled cemeteries,
for instance; he did not establish shelters for children or houses of charity.
Padre Ibiapina, moreover, tended to work in larger towns and cities
wealthy enough to support charitable institutions. Conselheiro made no
such distinction in his choice of places to visit.

Conselheiro railed against the hosts of the Antichrist, seen everywhere
and especially in the political arena. Occasionally he singled out the
residents of a particular village, either individually or collectively, as
personally marked by evil.[11] He was especially moved by hostility to
Masons, another trait he shared with both Ibiapina and Father Agripino
da Silva Borges, vicar of Itapicurú, who after an initial clash with Conselheiro in his parish made peace with Conselheiro and befriended him,
engaging in private discussions about theology.

In some ways, Conselheiro's ability to focus on specific enemies is
remarkable, because the mystic in all other aspects of his personal life
effectively avoided, through his austere behavior, all but the most transient contacts with society. One consequence of his enforced self-
distancing was that he had little basis on which to know his hated
enemies: "Jews and their imitators, including Masons, republicans, Protestants," and followers of other false sects—all sons of the devil. It is

unlikely that Antônio Mendes Maciel ever met a Jew in his life. Outside of the larger towns and cities in the region there were probably few Masons or Protestants, either.[12] Yet all of these usurpers, he charged, want to liquidate the church and wage war to tyrannize "genuine" Catholics. He appealed for divine understanding. Those who impugn the republic, he once wrote, should implore God to be granted peace.

The identification of the Brazilian republic with Satan or the Antichrist was not unique to Conselheiro's *orações* (prayers). Backland troubadours were known to refer to the "republican dragon" and to invoke the intervention of Saint George to slay it.[13] Two "ABC" chapbooks (brief popular texts, in which the first word of each sentence began with a new letter of the alphabet in sequence) dating from the period and found in Canudos by soldiers made similar references. One called the republic "Brazil's disgrace brought on November 15, 1889, a 'foreign' law bringing oppression to the people." It also called "o Liodoro"—Marshal Deodoro, the hero of the republic—an Antichrist, one who would enslave the "simple people." The ABC's also transmuted the word *eleição* (election) into *a lei cão*, or, as da Cunha noted, "the law of the *hound*."[14]

Conselheiro had other reasons to despise the government. He rebuilt backland churches and cemeteries because public authorities permitted them to lie in ruins. His longtime friend and supporter, Cônego Agripino, lost his assembly seat when the anticlerical republic was promulgated. There was also the matter of the continued willingness of priests to ally themselves with local landowners. Throughout the second half of the nineteenth century it had been customary for backland politicians, especially in more affluent districts, to intervene in the selection of individual priests for parish posts. This made reform difficult and frustrated would-be reformers within the Church. As an outsider neither linked to any faction nor particularly interested in forging political alliances—he personally disdained such worldly activities—Conselheiro threatened this system. His poverty won him credibility among *sertanejos* and embarrassed priests who had opted for a comfortable life as clients of local elites. Willingly or not, he assumed the role of de facto political boss.[15]

How can we understand the dark and somber nature of Conselheiro's religious orientation? One explanation derives from the fact that Antônio Mendes Maciel shared the tendency of backland inhabitants to address issues concretely, without abstraction. His reliance on the polemical *Missão abreviada* illustrates his quest for a simplified, medieval system of signs.[16] This is not to say that his theology, or the theology of the *Missão*, was naive—as contemporaries took for granted. Conselheiro's language may have been metaphorically rudimentary, but it was not unsophisticated. In backland culture, where the vast majority of people were unlettered, Conselheiro's stark imagery was apt and effective. These men and women, after all, were conditioned by their religious faith to question every act as a potential mortal sin. Moreover, they lacked the comfortable presence of authority figures—that is, priests—to define the boundaries between permissible and sinful behavior. In Belo Monte, Conselheiro provided this role, to which his followers reacted with euphoria; the stern discipline that he imposed on them was a small price to pay.

Consider Conselheiro's access to the *Missão*. He did not come across it in any devious or mysterious way. The missal was widely known in Catholic circles in Brazil, though rarely utilized extensively. Conselheiro, more than other preachers and pious Catholics of his day, measured secular events against the absolute standards of his creed. What outsiders did not understand was that he did not intend Canudos to challenge or to overturn the prevailing social order in the region. Rather, he wanted it to be a refuge for those who wished to live in an observant community apart from worldly temptation—thus his instruction to his followers that they leave their possessions behind and withdraw peaceably to the shelter of their "New Jerusalem."

Had their leader been more flexible, he might have been able to negotiate an accommodation with his enemies. He certainly had good role models. Padre Ibiapina, for instance, had established twenty-two "charity houses," secular institutions found throughout the region that, rather than antagonizing local officials by drawing away labor, functioned as rudimentary factories producing cottage-industry textiles for the poor, thus putting indigents to work.[17] Then there was Padre Cícero, whose leniency in permitting his lieutenants to strike political deals made his theocratic community a force in northeastern politics. But Conselheiro was too stiff-necked to follow either lead, even though his initial support of Vianna's partisans suggests that he may, at least for a time, have tried conformity to the regional pattern.

In a discussion of historical Christianity, Aron A. Gurevich queries whether the will to join the collective community might have represented an unconscious attempt to avoid the individual trial looming ominously before each and all on the Day of Judgment.[18] The behavior patterns of the backland faithful—their near-morbid fatalism and their anxious willingness to perform penitential acts in order to achieve divine forgiveness—testify to an almost palpable sense of the imminence of the end of the world. Conselheiro's vision, which he must have transmitted to his disciples, lacked any hint of a protracted future. Beneath the surface of Conselheiro's theology was the tradition of Sebastianist prophecy.[19] By mixing in the popular mind a longing for the return of the fatherly Emperor Pedro II with regional devotion to penitential and apocalyptic references, he modified the Sebastianist tradition to his own ends: the emperor would return, not the saint. In any case, for backland inhabitants, accustomed as they were to unrelieved misery and to a popularized religious faith rooted in dire warnings, hell and damnation were not allegories or abstractions, but the logical extensions of their real assumptions and experiences.

Canudos's faithful drew conviction from collective beliefs and notions. In both cases, the need for personal contact with sacred principles was filled by the saints, who were seen as direct actors in the secular and mundane world. Therein lies another striking lesson of the Canudos episode. In history, messianism occurs among so-called primitive people exactly during periods of forced acculturation, when an archaic or bypassed culture clashes with a more developed civilization. The church, after all, taught that the Second Coming could be expected upon completion of earthly experience. We may speculate that backlanders saw in the abolition of slavery, the departure of the "beloved" Emperor Pedro II, and the incursion of the vilified republican government ever more fully into their lives a hastening of the Judgment Day.

By lending emphasis to the "cycle of sinning, divine punishment, repentance, devotion and petitions for supernatural assistance and for salvation after death," and by blaming human behavior for the alienation of God and the saints, backland Catholicism by its very nature offered a millenarian view of history.[20] Anthropologist Patricia Pessar found in the 1970s that not only was apocalyptic millennial thought incorporated into rural Brazilian *orações*, hallelujahs (*benditos*), and the "stories on a string"—the little pamphlets in verse sold in the street and at markets— but it pervaded everyday discourse.[21] Traditionally, many believed that drought and suffering were harbingers of the end of the world and the dawning of the millennium.[22]

Backland Catholicism contained elements of resentment. Conselheiro himself warned that the rich and powerful would face eternal torment on the Day of Judgment. The fact that the elites, who were expected to protect the poor, embraced the hated republic exactly at a time of hardship and bewildering change likely encouraged "collective acts to express the immorality of the elite and to call for divine punishment."[23] The power of local bosses—landowners like Jeremoabo, and clients—reached a low ebb in the 1890s, before it revived again under the "politics of the governors," instituted soon after the Canudos conflict. Not only did traditional patrons witness their ability to dominate the rural population diminish, but they also found themselves less able to protect and provide help to their own dependents, thanks to the new system, which redistributed power to different players in the political game.[24]

All of this, moreover, was taking place in the last decade of the nine-

teenth century, only a few years before the advent of the millennial year
1900, which raised fears and wonderment around the world. The eschatology of official Brazilian Catholicism, attributing rewards and punishments to the "end of time," seemed distant and abstract; backlanders
who gathered to hear Conselheiro's sermons were more inspired, rather,
by his warnings based on a discourse of fear, oral tradition, and regional
memory. Whereas the institutional church, now stretched thin by impossible demands on its small numbers of priests, had always, in its
willingness to adjust to local social conditions, displayed in the remote
hinterland what Gurevich calls "a certain flexibility in its relations with the
culture of the *simplices*," its theology remained unchanged and appeared
wan and haggard before the captivating majesty of Conselheiro's prophecies and threats.[25] Backlanders, who rarely had contact with the archbishop in the palace overlooking the Bay of All Saints, seemed more
willing than ever to listen to religious men humble enough to come into
their midst, missionaries who preached that the elites were full of sin and
soon to be disciplined by the inferno of Judgment Day.

Da Cunha claimed in *Os sertões* that some of Conselheiro's prophecies
were written down in "numerous small notebooks which were found in
Canudos."[26] There is no evidence that these prophetic sayings were
Conselheiro's, and even if they were there is no evidence that he communicated them to his flock. Other prophecies attributed to Conselheiro
were common to the region: Frei João Evangelista de Monte Marciano,
for example, quoted one, attributed to Conselheiro but in fact common
to the backlands, that a time would come "when it would no longer be
necessary to work, when rivers of milk would run."[27] In vivid, biblical
prose, the prophecies predicted misfortunes for each year leading to the
millennium. Oddly, one millenarian prophecy, named "Jerusalém" and
attributed by da Cunha to Conselheiro, was dated 1890 but, given the
historical events it mentions, was probably written in 1897. It relates
incidents reaching back to 1822, mixing references to Brazil's independence and the Regency with a cholera epidemic in 1854, "many railroad
tracks," allusions to the church-state conflict of the 1870s, and a "great
revolution" in May 1888, presumably abolition. The advent of the republic is described as apocalyptic: people falling on top of one another;
eruptions of plague, death, hunger, and want; and exile of the emperor
by "disgraceful Brazilians." In 1891, nation would be pitted against nation
in war; in 1892, there would be a "great multitude of sinners"; 1893 would
see a "shortage of silver, gold, and copper; instead there will be red-
colored notes manufactured by men's hands, weakening the Treasury."
This last "prediction" is a clumsy reference to the burst bubble of the
speculative *Encilhamento* and the national economic malaise that followed.

For backland landowners and republican politicians, the prophecies attributed to Conselheiro struck a more general alarm, for they were certainly inflammatory, if confused:

> In truth I say unto you, when nation falls out with nation [borrowing from Revelations], Brazil with Brazil, England with England, Prussia with Prussia, then shall Dom Sebastião with all of his army arise from the waves of the sea.
> . . . On that day when he and his army shall rise, then shall he with the edge of the sword free all from the yoke of the Republic.
> The end of this war shall take place in the Holy House of Rome, and blood shall flow even in the great assembly.

It is unlikely, of course, that many *conselheiristas* knew about Prussia or England, or even the Holy House of Rome, whose Holy Father, Leo XIII, in 1897 lay dying. Conselheiro's erudite references, in fact, baffled his listeners; still, we are told that his use of Latin phrases and flowery vocabulary formed part of his mystique. Brazil in the 1890s faced no conflicts with foreign nations, and there is no obvious basis to Conselheiro's prophecy of war. Most of his attacks on the republic centered on its denial of Catholicism: notably, the state's new insistence on civil marriage. Sometimes Conselheiro condemned the republican government for "robbing the people," but the thrust of his criticism was invariably religious, not social.[28]

The lines that da Cunha excerpted and edited, taken out of their original context, do seem ominous:

> In 1896 a thousand flocks shall run from the *praia* to the backlands; and then the backlands will turn into *praia* and the *praia* into backlands;
> In 1897 there will be much pasturage and few trails, and one shepherd and one flock only;
> In 1898 there will be many hats and few heads;
> In 1899 the waters shall turn to blood, and the planet shall appear in the east with the sun's rays, the bough shall find itself on the earth, and the earth shall find itself in heaven.
> There shall be a great rain of stars, and that will be the end of the world.
> In 1901 the lights shall be put out.[29]

Da Cunha took these pronouncements at face value, accepting them as evidence that Conselheiro's teachings were simply an idiosyncratic approach to Catholicism, a faith that the mystic, da Cunha believed, did not thoroughly understand. But Conselheiro's language was doubtless meaningful to the backland rustic. It should be remembered that the word *praia* in Bahia alludes to the *tabuleiro* zone, where rainfall occurs more regularly than in the *sertão*, especially in the early months of the year. In the above lines, then, *praia* referred not to the ocean but to places receiving seasonal rainfall. Conselheiro was simply predicting that it would rain in the *sertão* but turn dry in the usually humid littoral. The reference to the single flock is from the Gospel of Saint Luke, where it is stated that there will be "one flock out of this sheepfold, [which must be] united that there may be one shepherd and one flock only."

This millenarian component of Conselheiro's vision—the imminence of the promised kingdom of God—adds a fiery dimension that seems to contradict the more passive view, which asked simply that the faithful wait and be penitent. To the true Catholic, Conselheiro argued, the worldly church sat over an abyss awaiting the world's end. Secular society was mired in usury, high taxes, avarice, corruption, greed, and adultery. The time had come for flight from this life and its evil ways. Let the faithful give up all transient undertakings and make of their lives a stern purgatory. For the end was surely coming, along with the greatest Judge of all.

◇  ◇  ◇

Visitors were unnerved by the unselfconscious behavior, based on prayer and religious devotion, exhibited by the inhabitants of Belo Monte. The daily prayers of residents included kissing icons and counting rosary beads as they walked in the streets. They sang and chanted "melancholy litanies" constantly, even as their fighters marched into battle. The Uauá attack was accompanied by dirges and loud prayers, which gave the impression of a penitential procession. Government soldiers in their trenches could hear the melancholy choruses of the kyrie eleison, sung low as the *jagunços* gathered the dead for burial. One old *beata*, a survivor of Canudos, recited to a reporter years later at the site of the conflict a prayer that she had sung as a member of the community:

> Father, look at the sad state in which I am put by evil;
> Forgive me, Father, for my acts
> Lest they turn into sins.[30]

Da Cunha's account does, however, bring two special characteristics of the Canudos story into focus, though it does not dwell on either at any length. One is the exceptional quality of light in the region during the long drought season, effected by the extreme dryness of the air and the intense sun. The other concerns Conselheiro's settlement as a backland Jerusalem, his flight to his backland sanctuary as a "hegira." The two points are linked: when the traveler in the Middle East ascends the plateau by day to approach the ancient city of Jerusalem, the light becomes dazzling; a luminous quality of the air bathes the centuries-old limestone walls in pastel hues of pink and yellow and beige.[31] That Conselheiro's vision was derived from orthodox Catholic doctrine, and that he modeled his millenarian community, if only figuratively, on Jerusalem, is consistent with the symbolic centrality of Jerusalem in Christian culture.

Scholars remind us that some of the most significant developments in European religious life confirmed the primacy of the city generally, and also that heresy often originated in towns. Also, although coastal Brazilians in their fear excoriated the backlanders for their uncivilized attitudes, Belo Monte was an urban place, a "holy city," albeit transient and camplike (Fig. 17). In Greek and Latin, the words for citizen—*polis*, *civis*—had given birth to new words describing culture and order: "civil," "civic," "polity," "polite."[32] Belo Monte, then, grew out of the sanctification of light and divine presence; its origins recalled the same aspirations to civic virtue and compassion shared by forward-looking Brazilians in the stately cities of the Center-South. Who knows what quality of life might have evolved had Canudos been permitted to survive and had Conselheiro's insistence on biblical virtue been tempered by time?

## THE LARGER CONTEXT

Many of the backland practices so demeaned by coastal visitors help us to understand the ease with which Conselheiro recruited followers. Backlanders were chronically superstitious, fully believing in the harmful effect of curses. Epidemics of fear and flagellation, a dread of hell and damnation—all embodied, in the phrase of Marc Bloch, a powerful "social fact." The intuitions of the people often were accurate, even if some of their fears were self-fulfilling prophecies. These anxieties were made all the more acute by the shock of the fall of the monarchy, which accompanied a verifiable breakdown in the observed and traditional unity of church and society. To be sure, political change in the interior often brought hard times; backlanders were not the only citizens to worry about the effect of the transition from empire to republic.

What Conselheiro and other backland charismatics achieved by their combination of "magical harmful formulas with purely scholastic circumstantiality and logicality," then, was an effective symbiosis of biblical damnation and teaching about the divine hierarchy.[33] Perhaps unconsciously, backlanders brought to their untutored popular Catholicism just as many external adaptations, "misunderstandings," and syncretisms as their Afro-Brazilian counterparts on the coast who substituted a panoply of Christian saints for African spiritist deities.

Conselheiro and his followers shared a religious worldview considered primitive and blasphemous by elitist outsiders, but that was familiar, even soothing, to the faithful backlander. Indeed, we might best understand Conselheiro's dire warnings as a sort of ritualized and formalized speech,

17. Conselheiro's unfinished Bom Jesus Church before its final destruction by the army. Photograph by Flávio Barros. Courtesy Paulo Zanettini. Some of the men posing are soldiers. Others may be backlanders brought along to serve the troops; they could not have been survivors—no males were left alive.

a code whose utterance, in the oral tradition of earlier Christianity, had the same effect as a deed. The ritual of Conselheiro's blandishments, rather than the warnings themselves, were the basis of community life. Da Cunha believed that the backland faithful, in their willingness to follow Conselheiro, demonstrated a form of epidemic psychosis, much like the demonopaths of Varzenis and the Stundists of southwest Russia, a millenarian sect founded by German Lutheran evangelical pastors among the German settlements of the Ukraine.[34]

We must remember that Belo Monte's residents, depicted by chroniclers as pathetic *caboclo* cult followers who had delivered their souls to their master, encompassed a wide range of racial and social types, including merchants, schoolteachers, ex-slaves, Indians, and hundreds of *jagunços* and other backland characters who made up his militia. All these people, refined and ruffian alike, removed their hats and lowered their weapons in Conselheiro's presence. The rougher men, however, did not join the inner ranks of the religious community, and they deftly sidestepped the ritualized and austere life prescribed for the faithful. Given that the trails to and from Canudos were open and that, far from being sealed, the holy site was freely accessible, it is possible, if not likely, that only part of the total population complied with the full range of Conselheiro's prescribed work and prayer rituals. Yet Conselheiro's utopian dictatorship affected all the inhabitants of his holy city to some degree. Betrayal of his vision was punishable by death—as we have seen in the execution of the merchant Antônio da Motta and his sons. Even the most cynical journalists remarked that, in contrast to all other places in the *sertão*, prostitution did not exist in Belo Monte, nor was drunkenness a public problem, nor was the city jail full of vagrants or petty criminals. In this regard, Canudos was more like a Calvinist Geneva than a Jerusalem or a typical Brazilian urban center.

Conselheiro's unusual sensitivity to the political impact on religious life of the separation of church and state, most notably its suspension of religious orders and assertion of civil authority over registration of births, marriages, and deaths, could only have intensified his ire. The new laws, to which the highest levels of the Brazilian church acquiesced with little opposition, to Conselheiro (and to the *Missão abreviada*) threatened to abolish God's word and to dethrone God himself in favor of atheism.[35] As far as the coastal church hierarchy was concerned, Conselheiro, together with his frequent accusations that the church was infiltrated by enemies of Catholicism and lacked moral fiber, was an irritant and an embarrassment. The irritation he posed only increased as the numbers of his followers swelled.

It has been argued that Antônio Mendes Maciel was burdened by a social context of violence and oppression. Yet backland life in the late nineteenth century differed little from that of other periods in Brazilian history; it does not, in itself, explain Conselheiro's vehemence.[36] Historians and chroniclers, da Cunha among them, have suggested that crises in backland society—political, climatic, or both—contributed to the rise of messianism, religious fanaticism, and lawlessness. Just as the region was grappling with the decline and ultimate abolition of slavery and the weakening bonds of social control due to such modernizations as highways (permitting mobility with fewer hindrances), it witnessed as well not only the establishment of two "hostile" religious communities—Belo Monte in 1893 and Padre Cícero's "Holy City" of Juazeiro, in Ceará, in 1899—but also a surge in banditry to uncommonly high levels. Both Canudos and Padre Cícero's Cariri Valley attracted large numbers of displaced and dispossessed *jagunços*, men inured to violence because of the nature of their society and their livelihood.[37]

At least part of the impetus for Canudos's rise was rooted in state politics. We have seen that in the first state elections in Bahia after the inauguration of the republic, the faction loyal to the baron of Jeremoabo emerged victorious and immediately began to propose legislative steps against Conselheiro. His antirepublicanism, then, reflected the threat of punitive action by the state government. When soldiers attacked his followers at Masseté, Conselheiro preached, at the side of his old friend Padre Sabino, that God had selected Belo Monte to be Jesus' battleground. As he spoke, Conselheiro was said to have held up his copy of the *Missão* to emphasize his point.

## ANALYSIS BY OTHERS

Observers and defenders of the republic justified the settlement's destruction on the basis of a falsehood: that Canudos housed crime and madness. European, and especially French, writers provided the model of civilization and progress, invoking "scientific" diagnoses of social evolution and social degeneration.[38] Criminologists and sociologists of the 1890s linked fears of crime with falling birth rates; in 1892, Max Nordau published his widely translated *Degeneration*, which identified and castigated the extremes of mysticism and crude nationalism.[39] Da Cunha borrowed from the writings of the turn-of-the-century English psychiatrist Henry Maudsley to describe Conselheiro's madness.

In Salvador, Conselheiro's personality was measured and evaluated by leading physicians and academicians. Among them, Raimundo Nina Rodrigues—a professor of legal and forensic medicine at the Bahian Medical Faculty, and himself one of the rare *mulatos* to attain such a high position at that time or later—stands out for the lucidity of his analysis and the forcefulness of his convictions. Moreover, his conclusions reveal the thinking of the elite not only about Conselheiro's mental state but about the backland population as well. Nina Rodrigues examined the physical traits of criminals and, randomly, of the *mulato* population to find symptoms of degeneration that stemmed from racial mixing. It was to him that Conselheiro's skull was presented for study, since he had gained prominence through his theories about the degenerative effects of miscegenation and the links between mental illness and "messianic contagion."[40]

The very title of Nina Rodrigues's article "Epidemic of Insanity at Canudos"—published during the last month of the conflict and therefore while Conselheiro was still alive—is revealing. Conselheiro, he charged, suffered from "chronic delirium" and was given to "progressive psychosis that reflects the sociological conditions" of his environment.[41] The text included several singular assertions: that Conselheiro mistreated his wife; that she had been raped by a policeman in Ipú before leaving him; that he had a violent side to his personality and at one point had wounded his brother-in-law; that his frequent job changes represented instability and a "delirium of persecution." In Nina Rodrigues's narrative, Conselheiro finds a "formula for his delirium" and an expression for his "megalomania" in railing against luxury and pleasure. He disrupts the "peaceful life of the agricultural population" of the backlands, advocating instead "errant living and communism." His arrest leads him to reveal publicly his paranoia; he begins to act like Christ and becomes consumed with his "hallucinatory" vision.

The *jagunço*, Nina Rodrigues wrote, is a "perfect type to be affected," because as a hybrid product of miscegenation he "suffers from the fusion of unequal races." He is not just "any kind of mestizo"; the recipient of "virile qualities from his savage Indian and Negro ancestors," he lives a rudimentary but free life, in contrast to the mestizo on the coast, who is "degenerate and weak." The *jagunço*, in short, is "naturally a monarchist." Canudos's curse, the professor averred, results from the "fetishistic belief of the African deeply rooted in our population."[42] Nina Rodrigues's unshakable belief in biologic determinism permitted him to denigrate the results of miscegenation despite his own origins, and thereby to rationalize elite acceptance of the brutal suppression of the insurgents.[43]

Both Nina Rodrigues and da Cunha epitomized the contradictory nature of the *visão do litoral*. As a passionate disciple of now-discredited French and Italian theories about crime and atavism, Nina Rodrigues was more innovative than da Cunha and other contemporaries in that he acknowledged the impact of sociological factors on the behavior of Conselheiro and his followers. When Conselheiro's severed head was subjected to medical examination, the professor registered surprise at the lack of degeneration, which adherents of the European theories expected.[44] His reaction had been similar when he examined the skull of Lucas de Feira, a fugitive slave who committed many crimes earlier in the nineteenth century. Finding the skull to be entirely normal, Nina Rodrigues praised the slave, saying that in Africa he would have been a great warrior but that, transported to Brazil and forcibly domesticated, he became a criminal for social reasons.[45]

Following in Nina Rodrigues's footsteps, generations of writers on Brazil used Canudos as evidence for their individual interpretations of Brazilian culture. Most used a common point of departure: *Os sertões*. Yet that work is so multifarious, so expansive, that the closer one looks for da Cunha's central message, the more elusive it becomes. In modern terms, da Cunha wrote not only as a traditional historian, offering causal explanation, but also as a historical anthropologist, interpreting social interaction ("thick description") and thus in a sense anticipating Victor Turner's model of social drama by concentrating on symbols and rituals as well as concrete events.[46]

Conservatives, generally, have been content to accept da Cunha's postmortem. Others, mostly on the ideological left, have appropriated the Canudos events to illustrate their analyses of society.[47] Liberation theologians, for example, have recast the episode in the model of a loving community rooted in fraternal solidarity, destroyed by plutocratic *fazendeiro*-exporters and their bourgeois clients.[48] Brazilian Communist party ideologists called Canudos the result of mobilized peasant consciousness, a prime example of class conflict and warfare.[49] Those seeing Conselheiro's sanctuary as a by-product of the Afro-Brazilian legacy, and thus dubbing it Brazil's last refuge for fugitive slaves, offered little concrete evidence from Canudos itself. But in that *quilombos*, traditionally, were relatively self-contained units of economic production, linked to coastal markets but managing to preserve their independence, this comparison seems appropriate. Few, however, have attempted to explain Canudos as a natural if extreme extension of regional conditions.

We know, of course, that Canudos was not unique; it was, rather, one among many expressions of *jagunço* bellicosity in the tradition of Xique-Xique, Andarahi, Cochó, Lenções, Belmonte, Canaveiras, Brejo-Grande—all Bahian towns and hamlets where violence had been provoked—and scores of other localities in Brazil. The difference, Nina Rodrigues noted, was that Canudos was the first conflict rooted in the monarchist convictions of the *sertanejo*, "too primitive in his social evolution" to understand republican law. Conselheiro's crazed delirium of religious mission, the professor concluded, combined all too naturally with the troublemaking instinct of the fanatical *jagunços*.[50]

Few people understood that until the Canudos conflict and all the exaggerated charges that arose from it, the term *jagunço* in the late nineteenth century referred neutrally to rustic backlanders engaged in cattle raising and agriculture, not, as Ronald Daus avers, to a "mixture of cowboys and bandits."[51] Time did not diminish the practice of exaggeration. An analysis published in 1903 compared Conselheiro's behavior to that of Muhammad, arguing that the backlanders, themselves semi-savages, were like desert Arabs, ready at any moment to join a religious leader of "superior energy."[52] Six decades later, a scholar wrote in the staid journal of the Paulista Academy of Letters that Conselheiro's followers were "a band of disgraceful creatures, convinced of their perdition." Their behavior, he continued, represented "obstinate psycho-erotic infantilism, fixed among various provisional instincts of puerile lives."[53] Yet another historian exulted that Conselheiro fought all his life against the church of Rome, thus distorting the record to make Conselheiro a "hero of socialism."[54]

Largely ignored by analysts was the long tradition of violence in the countryside, and the fact that police and militia troops were as feared as outlaws in the small towns of the interior. Many borrowed da Cunha's morbid fascination with what he called the primitive tenacity of the backlanders without accepting his deep respect. The possibility that individual decisions to join Conselheiro may have been systemic, rooted in economic or psychological need, was disregarded. Religious and political meanings in rural societies such as Canudos, however, are both intertwined and reinforcing, yielding a behavior model that for participants is certainly rational.[55]

Da Cunha, Nina Rodrigues, and the other outsiders who have dissected the Canudos events noted that the harsh environment of the backlands shaped behavior and set the stage for conflict between rural backwardness and coastal progress. But in their feverish effort to close the books on the revolt, the intellectuals and journalists disregarded analyses of rural deprivation, replacing them with dismissals of the resistance as a fanatic aberration. Publicists for the republic regularly distanced themselves from the lower classes. In a handbook for foreign travelers to Brazil, it was claimed that the death rates in Brazilian cities and Europe compared favorably, underscoring the fact that "the negro and the lower class mulatto between them account for some 75 percent of mortality in Brazil."[56] Cultural figures who used Canudos as evidence of national racial weakness included novelist Monteiro Lobato, conservative historian Oliveira Vianna, and the critic Paulo Prado.

Others selected the *caboclo* to symbolize the freedom and anarchic individualism of the pastoralist nomad, much as the Indianist vogue among intellectuals of the nineteenth century attributed to native culture characteristics of primitive nobility. Gilberto Freyre later acknowledged that his "lusotropical" interpretation of Brazilian race mixture was strongly influenced by the positive side of da Cunha's view of the backlander.[57] Still others, emphasizing the feudal structure of backland society and the class conflict that underlay Canudos, extolled the *sertanejos* as soldiers against latifundism: in the words of Rui Facó, Conselheiro launched "an unconscious but spontaneous rebellion against the monstrous and secular oppression of semifeudal latifundia."[58] But Canudos was not a spontaneous rebellion: it was a peaceful sanctuary attacked by those seeking its destruction. E. J. Hobsbawm, in stressing the community's millenarian character, probably comes closer to capturing the motivation of the Canudos faithful, though we have no evidence confirming that Conselheiro ever advocated social insurrection.[59]

Conselheiro understood well that the external world was changing, and he warned that unless his precepts were followed disaster would ensue. During particularly severe droughts, backlanders witnessed periods as long as thirty months without rain. By 1900, at least three hundred thousand northeasterners had fled to the Amazon region, driven by drought and despair, drawn by the rubber boom.[60] The arm of coastal government seemed to be reaching inexorably into the interior. The first major nationwide census, in 1872–74, enumerated all citizens and asked questions about their occupations, race, and income. Metricization and the standardization of weights and measures, which threatened the informal mechanisms of the *feira* market system, led to the Quebra Quilo riots in the *agreste* region of four northeastern provinces in 1874–75.[61] To officials, these leaderless revolts signaled sedition. To the rural population, the penetration of government into the backlands meant higher taxes, more controls, and an increased threat of forced military induction.

The monarchy's demise in 1889 and the subsequent promulgation of secular republican laws, especially those requiring civil marriage and registry of deaths, shook backland Catholics, whose simply expressed faith considered Emperor Pedro II a father figure and a kind of earthly saint, despite the renewal of the church in the 1870s and its conflict with the government. Discreetly, Conselheiro never commented on Pedro's Masonic connection (he was a Mason of the thirty-third degree) or on the emperor's passivity during the angry struggle between the imperial government and the church in 1874. Perhaps he considered Pedro a victim of the fact that the world, as it seemed, was being shaken to its foundations. In France, the election of "progressive" Pope Leo XIII led to fears that the "real" pope had been kidnapped and imprisoned by the Masons in the cellar of the Vatican.[62] Conselheiro was quick to repeat and embellish these stories. He bitterly opposed the secular republic for reasons that his backland followers personally understood. Once, allegedly, he explained that the republic's troubles were evidence of God's anger at the forced separation of church and state under the 1891 republican constitution. Monarchists, at least in the case of one extreme *conselheirista*, saw the defeats of Febronio Brito and Moreira César as further evidence of God's plan to test Brazilians by permitting them, upon the monarch's withdrawal, to convert to a higher, spiritual loyalty, a loyalty to "God the only legitimate monarch and his Prince, Dom Pedro III."[63]

As early as 1874–75, poor men and women, alarmed by rumors that the church had been taken over by evildoers, assaulted churches and destroyed books and furnishings in Recife and in Acarapé and Quixeramobim in Ceará.[64] Conselheiro may also have pointed out the high number of foreign priests sent to the backlands, objects of suspicion and distrust for their strange accents and unfamiliar ways. He understood the backland tradition of pilgrimages. *Promessas* made it easier for residents of the region to leave their homes and seek new lives, because such vows were personal and sanctified by their religious weight. The vow provided the only vehicle through which temporal strictures on behavior could be overridden. Backlanders never questioned the power of such penitential acts, although coastal observers took public displays of piety as evidence of religious fanaticism and irrationality.

That parents in both Canudos and the backland towns and hamlets through which Conselheiro passed named him godfather of their newborn infants epitomizes his great influence. Choice of a godfather was one of the few acts of free will left to the poor in the region. By naming Conselheiro (always registered properly under his Christian name, Antônio Vicente Mendes Maciel), the parents dispensed with the custom of designating a landowner or politician or someone else who could be asked to help in time of distress. Yet the selection of Conselheiro as *padrinho* generated ties of fierce loyalty between him and the families who so honored him. Thus we find a rational explanation for the tenacity with which Conselheiro's flock fought for him: they considered him as close to their families as any blood relation.

Residents of the region were inured to hardship and faced life stoically. Good Friday services attracted more worshippers than Easter. More so than on the coast, crucifixes and other religious art carved by backland artisans emphasized suffering. Self-flagellation was another major element in backland religious practice: if God brought suffering, hunger, disease—then one must simply pray harder and sacrifice more.[65] Penitents wore hair shirts and bloodied their knees climbing stone steps to chapels and shrines. All but the strictest flagellant sects were not so much masochistic, however, as manifestations of backland Catholicism's deep-rooted belief that life, a vale of tears, needed to be spent in self-purification. Backland families felt they had little control over life-altering events. Sacrifice symbolized at least a demonstration of control over one's self. Harsh conditions led to martyrlike submission in some but created the strength for martyrdom in others. Self-sacrifice taken to an extreme separated one from one's peers, creating a sense of moral superiority and impecunious nobility for the practitioner.

Conselheiro's settlement was able to survive for nearly four years because during that time political infighting in Bahia had been stalemated, leaving Canudos in peace. Inevitably, however, Canudos's sudden explosion in growth disrupted the precarious balance of the *sertão*'s extremely low population density and corresponding lack of infrastructure. The local elites were the first to feel—or at least respond to—the strain. The traditional system of agriculture and livestock raising in the parched backlands required landowners to exploit large numbers of sedentary manual laborers, both as squatters and as pitiful day laborers. The presence of a docile lower class also anchored the political system of the republic, which depended on control of the rural vote by local *coronéis*. Canudos abruptly challenged both arrangements. Its threat to the republic was certainly exaggerated; but to the extent that it threatened to disrupt the local status quo, regional interests were justified in opposing the community.

From a moribund hamlet of a few families, Canudos grew to five thousand people in 1895, and to at least fifteen thousand, possibly more, by 1896. The depletion of population from the surrounding region, mostly to the south and east, affected merchants and *fazendeiros* in direct proportion to the degree of migration from each *município*. The situation was worsened by the fact that once Canudos grew to the size of a small city, most transactions there were done with scrip rather than currency. This circumstance arose less from Conselheiro's aversion to republican money (he was reputed to have burned some of it once in public as a symbolic gesture) than from a simple shortage of cash.

In other ways, Conselheiro showed flexibility. Hide sales produced only minimal revenues, and the community had no other source of income except when Conselheiro sent his people to work as contract laborers at nearby ranches and *fazendas*. A generation later in Ceará, Padre Cícero also hired out members of his community as laborers, as a pragmatic measure designed to keep neighboring overlords satisfied. Conselheiro, more feared than Cícero and less knowledgeable about the political system, kept his holy city more isolated—and ultimately paid the consequences for his more unyielding militancy.

Isolation, we have seen, was a relative concept. There was always commerce, and even during the final armed conflict sympathizers linked to the Vianna faction of the PRF-Bahia (including a Colonel Leitão in Santa Luzia, about whom little else is known) furnished materials, thus supplementing what Conselheiro's forces looted from military supply trains and from dead and injured soldiers. There must have been still other channels of goods, especially given the political enmities in the state. If the picture of Conselheiro as a crazed fanatic isolated from reality is accurate, his followers' ability to defend themselves against thousands of armed troops and heavy artillery surely defies logic. Cut off and completely surrounded for weeks, Canudos kept up defensive gunfire until the end, with no shortage of functioning weapons or bullets. As might be expected, moreover, the need to supply the long military conflict yielded unprecedented commercial revenues—"immense profits," in the words of one government report—in Salvador and in the larger trading cities in the São Francisco region, especially Juazeiro.[66]

The ability of the settlement to function as well as it did testifies to the organizational adeptness of Conselheiro and his aides. They had no transport except by mule, and no manufactured medicines. On the road and in the trenches, soldiers and *jagunços* alike chewed the roots of shrubs for nourishment. In Monte Santo, the principal staging area for the government forces (and less than a day's march from Canudos), prices soared, to 2½ milréis for a dozen eggs and 4 milréis for a kilo of "old cheese, four to five times prices in the capital." Salaried full-time workers—a tiny elite within the lower-class population—earned only 30 to 55 milréis monthly.[67] In Canudos, twenty cows were slaughtered daily up to the end of the fighting, and the settlement raised large crops of beans and manioc. Even given the people's hunger at the end, Conselheiro's logistical miracle could have occurred only if his city was well connected to the regional economy and to regular sources of trade.

What can be said about the men and women who made Canudos their home? They lived crowded into a city whose river ran only intermittently, and their day-to-day existence must have been arduous in the extreme. They were certainly resourceful: in later decades, when a new community rose on the site of Conselheiro's city, local priests used manioc for the host when celebrating mass.[68] Although the settlement likely reached its saturation peak in early 1897, many residents fled during the final months of battle, and at the very end only a few hundred women and children remained.[69] Whatever the precise size of his flock, Conselheiro exercised an immense influence over it, one that Gilberto Freyre and others have attributed to a deep-seated residue of Sebastianism in the backland population, but that was likely more personalist than Sebastianist in nature.[70]

It is doubtful that Canudos's residents consciously thought King Sebastian would appear in the heavens—even though Conselheiro's appeal seems consistent with our understanding of the strong place of Sebastianism in nineteenth-century Luso-Brazilian Catholicism. Because Sebastianism focused on the mystical state of the soul and the promise of salvation, chroniclers have assumed that it must have been present in Canudos. There is, however, no evidence for the assertion. Interestingly, a study of more than forty thousand names of drought refugees, mostly from Ceará but touching on every part of Brazil's Northeast, found not one Sebastião, although virtually every other religious and biblical name appeared dozens or even hundreds of times.[71]

Rituals—the cult of the saints, festivities, novenas, and prayers—furnished ways to win the good graces of the supernatural world. This was the relationship of *do ut des*: giving in order to receive in kind. Rural culture was reflectively spiritualist, an environment in which saints and other rarefied beings interceded personally to overcome daily problems. In this culture, drought, crop failure, disease, and suffering were typically blamed on divine punishment. Granted, such beliefs legitimate institutions of hierarchy and exploitation, but they also reinforce hope in messianic intervention.[72]

Antônio Conselheiro, in fact, played the paradigmatic role of the renouncer, a public figure who by various means rejects the temporal world.[73] He lets go of his past and invests in the millennium, combatting and overcoming his own pride and vanity in order to abandon the material world with its wealth and injustice.

> He must be totally consistent, and he cannot enjoy any longer the privileges of inconsistency between his words, deeds, living, and being. He must live for his group, leaving aside egoistic interests and creating a vast external space where he can implement the rules he himself invents. He can no longer rely on the laws, decrees, and hierarchies of his original social group. . . . He individualizes himself, thus creating the conditions to make relative and somehow unreal the world from which he came.[74]

By "renouncing" the temporal world, finally, Conselheiro revealed to his fellow men the fragility of their conventions, thereby creating the possibility of a new order. This behavior, so similar to Jesus', characterized Antônio Conselheiro and many of his *beato* predecessors in the backlands.

For the citizens of Canudos, piety filled the empty space that separated the family from the rest of civil society. There was a constant concern with penitence and judgment. After Conselheiro's death, stories began to spread through the *sertão* that he had murdered not only his wife and mother but at least two others as well, and that his wandering, abstemious life was a divine punishment. For others, Conselheiro was simply a saint. He performed pious works, and he usually spoke soothingly and gently to the people who came to hear him, though at times he affected a more fiery stance, causing his followers to tremble.[75] To the backlanders, saints were not abstract but characteristically human, palpable presences in family life. When Conselheiro died, condemned by both church and state, his place in daily backland religious practice was taken by the Holy Trinity, Santo Antônio, the cult of the Guardian Angel, Jesus Maria José, and the Senhor do Bomfim.[76]

The role of the Catholic church leadership in the affair presents a singular irony. Confronted by Conselheiro's orthodox but institutionally unsanctioned piety, the church hierarchy looked to the state to rid it of an impostor priest whose appeal threatened its political power. Canudos occurred at a critical time: not only was the church confronting ultra-montanist pressure from Rome to contain backland "libertinism" and improve the quality of the clergy,[77] but church and state were, as a result of positivist influence on the federal constitution of 1891—and over vehement church protests—newly separated as well. Yet in the end, orthodox Catholics, hostile to the backland preacher's missionary emphasis on redemption and his stern demands for more, not less, observance of Catholic doctrine, turned their backs on a genuine expression of popular spirituality.[78]

Canudos touched political nerves as well. Local elites well remembered how quickly the fabric of authority unraveled when the rampaging Quebra-Quilo mobs threatened to invade major cities.[79] To partisans of the new republican government, the monarchist Conselheiro assumed larger-than-life proportions, even if in reality his personal powers were quite modest. Local conditions were in flux and economically strained, and national institutions (the armed forces, the civilian regime) untested. "In Brazil, where politics and institutions do not inspire confidence," read the headlines introducing a feature story on Canudos in the *Folha de São Paulo* some eighty years after the event, "Antônio Conselheiro attains new elements of meaning."[80] The readiness of commentators to accept Canudos as a threat even as they cloaked their observations in moralizing patriotism helps explain why Canudos, unlike other, equally bloody uprisings, made such an impact.[81]

# Conclusion:
# Canudos as a Millenarian Experience

Canudos did not represent an isolated event in its own national and regional context. Rather, it constituted part of a broad set of related phenomena occurring in virtually every part of Brazil from the colonial period to the mid–twentieth century. In the 1500s, dozens of insurrections broke out among indigenous populations, some of them magico-religious or messianic in nature, such as the Confederação de Tamoios (1563), the Santidade de Jaguaripe (1584, reappearing at least five additional times down through 1892), and the Tupi-Guaraní resistance to the Portuguese from the sixteenth century on, which took the form of migratory flight.[1] The first of Brazil's millennial impulses rooted in Christianity were directed into sporadic dramatizations of Portuguese Sebastianism, which held popular currency in Portugal for centuries and which erupted periodically in diverse parts of the Luso-Brazilian world.[2] Sebastianism was deeply rooted in *sertanejo* folk religion; indeed, it exercised a much stronger influence in the backlands than on the coast.

The second millennial impulse, inspired by Christian as well as spiritualist ideals, contributed to small outbreaks of religiosity accompanied by the appearance of new saints. Short-lived, these movements have occurred up through the present day.[3] In rural areas, they usually are millenarian in nature; in urban settings they vary according to local circumstances. When authorities intervene, or when claims for miraculous cures are not sustained, these movements fade away rapidly. They have occurred most frequently in the Northeast. An exception was the twentieth-century "Fraternal Eclectic Universal Spiritualists" led by army veteran Oceano de Araújo Sá (known also as Yokaanam), which was located in Rio de Janeiro, though its leader was born in northeastern Maceió.[4]

The third tradition, and the most intense, was primarily millenarian although influenced to a lesser degree by Sebastianic and other legends. Followers would assemble to pray (or to live) in expectation of the final Day of Judgment. Their leaders were seen as prophets, saints, and even messiahs, personally leading the faithful to the promised land. Some claimed to be Christ reincarnated, as in the case of the German-born leader of the Anabaptist Mucker uprising in Rio Grande do Sul, which began in the early 1870s.[5] Antônio Conselheiro denied being the Savior but may have unconsciously identified himself with Jesus Christ. Some of these more strictly millenarian movements dispersed peacefully, usually in response to mediating influence by the Catholic church; many, however, ended in bloodshed and massacre.

Given the strength of Sebastianism and the relative ineffectuality of institutional Catholicism within the Portuguese colonial empire, it is likely that dozens or even hundreds of millenarian and messianic movements sprang up and died of their own accord over the centuries.[6] Many were little more than sharply focused attempts to gain salvation, which, after all, is a characteristic of Christianity. Others went beyond the traditional nature of the religion, embracing nationalist or antiforeign motives. For the modern period, we can identify eight Brazilian millenarian movements in addition to Canudos that left a particular mark.

1. *Rodeador.* Between 1817 and 1820 in the Rodeador Mountains in southern Pernambuco, not far from the site of Canudos, backlanders became caught up in a religious crusade to march, without bloodshed, to Jerusalem, free it from its worldly imprisonment, and witness the coming of the Kingdom of God on earth. Their leader was Silvestre José dos Santos, an ex-soldier hailed as a prophet, who, together with four hundred disciples, founded a "City of Earthly Paradise." Skeptics, he proclaimed, would be dazzled by the peaceful return of King Sebastião and his armies.

Authorities suppressed the movement, believing it to be connected to the political separatist action of the same time in Pernambuco; yet remarkably, there was apparently no link. Despite some dissatisfaction with the repressive governor of the time and with the military draft system, the movement evidently had as its major, if not sole, inspiration the millenarian hope of salvation.[7] Notably, considering later (and unproven) claims about Canudos, prisoners captured at Rodeador believed unshakably that once the faithful initiated their march there would be no need to fight; enemies would be converted to their faith, in a latter-day variation on the medieval Children's Crusade.[8] Most of the faithful were massacred when the governor ordered Rodeador attacked on October 25, 1820.

2. *Pedra Bonita.* Also in Pernambuco, in the central *agreste*, Pedra Bonita was the site of a terrible incident in the late 1830s, at the "En-

chanted Kingdom of Vila-Bela." There, between two monoliths one
hundred feet in height, rural folk—led by a self-proclaimed prophet,
João Ferreira—presuming that they had to demonstrate their unequiv-
ocal faith, offered blood sacrifices to effect the return to earth of King
Sebastião.[9] (Ferreira had assumed control when the originator of the
cult, João Santos, his brother-in-law, found that his ardor had cooled.)
The first to be killed in this way was Ferreira's own father. Three days
later, on May 14, 1838, dozens more were sacrificed, including thirty
children, twelve men, eleven women, and fourteen dogs: Ferreira, aided
by subordinates, slit the victims' throats or dashed their heads against the
rocks. It is believed locally that the fanatics were convinced that in addition to salvation, they would achieve the inversion of the worldly order: mulattoes and blacks would be transformed into whites, and the
poor would be granted riches and eternal life.[10] The movement ended
abruptly when the police invaded the sacrificial site; they encountered
no resistance because, as Sebastianists, the believers had been taught that
an attack on them would signal the beginning of the restoration of the
kingdom. Most of the faithful died singing religious songs, and the
movement leaders were imprisoned. João Santos was arrested and killed
while in detention.[11]

3. *Cabanada.*   Unlike most other Brazilian movements with millenarian underpinnings, this crusade in Pernambuco's *agreste*, called by contemporaries the Cabanada, or the War of the Cabanos, in fact started for
expressly political reasons. It was triggered in April 1832 by restorationist rebellions in Recife and Rio de Janeiro. Although the instigators,
mostly Portuguese militiamen, were crushed, the movement spread into
the hinterland, where it soon became transformed into a three-year
guerrilla war. Outside support came from Portuguese merchants in Recife and restorationist politicians in Rio de Janeiro.

The rebels sought to return Pedro I, now in Portugal, to the throne,
for, despite Brazil's declaration of independence in 1822, he had never
renounced his emperorship.[12] Small landowners and some *senhores de
engenho* fought alongside thousands of lower-class men and women
(whites, slave and free blacks, Indians, *cafuzos*, mulattoes), who constituted the majority of the participants in the movement. Most participants, however, dispersed after government forces attacked, leaving the
"Cabano Republic" reduced to an army of five hundred men, chiefly
blacks. In the end, as many as fifteen thousand people died in battle, of
disease, or of hunger; more than a hundred sugar plantations in Pernambuco and forty in Alagoas were destroyed. Sugar production fell by
at least one-quarter, causing deficits that took years to overcome.

The movement took on millenarian proportions when the guerrilla
commander, Vicente Ferreira de Paula, the son of a priest and a former

sergeant who had deserted from the army, used the news of Pedro I's death in September 1834 to warn his followers that they were living in sin; they must, he exhorted, fight to save both the new emperor and their religion from the anti-Portuguese upstarts who were governing independent Brazil, whom he labeled Jacobins.[13] Ferreira de Paula escaped after the main body of rebels capitulated in 1835, and managed to survive with a small band of followers in a wretched colony where the residents subsisted by eating snakes, insects, wild fruits, and lizards. The survivors held out because they feared that if they were captured they would be skinned alive, and that their own leaders would kill them if they did not obey.[14]

4. *Muckers*. "Mucker," a German term meaning a religious hypocrite, was the derisive label applied to members of a messianic sect established in 1868 in Ferrabrás in São Leopoldo, Rio Grande do Sul. The adherents were also referred to as *os santarrões* (sainted ones), in mockery of their extreme devoutness. The sect grew up within a colony of impoverished German agriculturalists on the eastern flank of the Serra who had received small plots of land from the provincial government to plant rye and potatoes. The farmers' destitution was due in part to a lack of capital, which had forced them to abandon their traditional methods of cultivation and to use the native slash-and-burn techniques.

The movement leaders were Anabaptist healers Jacobina Maurer and her husband, João Jorge Maurer. They were monarchists, like Conselheiro. The Maurers claimed that they had been elected by God to lead the faithful to establish a Holy Kingdom on earth. The intrusion of the outside world, most visibly in the form of steamship links between Pôrto Alegre and São Leopoldo and a railroad line completed in 1871, disrupted the region's former isolation; the Muckers even tried to prevent the railroad from operating.

Their followers were almost exclusively illiterate German and German-Brazilian farmers suffering from falling social status and economic hardship. The movement's exclusivity angered its neighbors and led to acts of arson, armed conflict, and eventually the sect's refusal to obey local authorities. On June 28, 1873, the Muckers defeated a force of one hundred police, killing its commander. The army subdued the rebels only after a series of engagements involving artillery. The survivors, rather than being executed, were sentenced to prison terms of up to thirty years; all were pardoned in 1883. They then returned to Ferrabrás, and the old conflict with their neighbors started up again. Skirmishes continued through the 1890s, and in 1896 it was rumored that the sect was regrouping at Nova Petrópolis. By 1898, one year after the fall of Canudos, the remaining Muckers had all been killed, though traces of the movement survived until at least the mid-1950s, when adepts held a "reunion" of families in Taquaraçu in anticipation of the Day of Judgment.[15]

5. *Padre Cícero*.  In the 1850s, a schismatic movement was born in southern Ceará's backland Cariri Valley, the home of the Serenos, a cult demanding penitential scourging of its members. Two decades later, a newly ordained priest, Cícero Romão Baptista, came to the area, immediately before the calamitous droughts of 1877–79. Padre Cícero encouraged the faithful to dig wells, build shelter, and plant crops of manioc. In 1889, Cícero became involved in a religious dispute over the veracity of a supposed miracle that had occurred under his jurisdiction, in which during a mass the host had been divinely transformed into the blood of Christ. The more his backland settlement in the Ceará hamlet of Juazeiro attracted followers, the more church officials found fault with his religious practices, and in 1892 he was suspended from the priesthood by Ceará's bishop. By now firmly entrenched in his adoptive community, he became involved in a lifelong conflict with the church.

Ralph della Cava has aptly demonstrated that by attracting pilgrims to labor-shy regions of Bahia and Ceará, both Conselheiro and Padre Cícero accumulated the equivalent of political power. Work hands, traditionally dominated by the *coronéis*, under the republic represented potential wealth and votes.[16] Unlike Conselheiro, Padre Cícero initially displayed a greater willingness to work with the local archdiocese. Later, however, when Ceará's bishop refused to acknowledge the claimed miracle, he appealed directly to Rome, in addition to seeking support from local *coronéis* and lay leaders for his request to be reinstated as a priest. When their leader was threatened with excommunication, Cícero's followers raised funds through lay Catholic associations to send emissaries to argue their case, in addition to publishing statements in both the religious and secular press and gathering dozens of petitions. Padre Cícero himself traveled to Rome in 1898, though without success. During the priest's lifetime, his messianic movement became institutionalized. "'Miracles' and extreme forms of religiosity were discouraged [at Juazeiro]," René Ribeiro writes; there, "social relationships and the political machinery . . . were almost indistinguishable from those prevailing in general in Brazilian peasant society."[17]

Both Juazeiro and Canudos illustrate the fact that manifestations of popular religion stirred passions and led to conflicts involving violence. We know that *beatos* and other religious figures found it necessary to surround themselves with bodyguards, who were often merely rough-and-tumble men carrying arms. Sometimes, too, the faithful were at fault. Conselheiro's followers invaded Bom Conselho and briefly seized the town hall. At Alagoa de Baixo in Pernambuco, after a sermon by the local priest disparaging the well-known "miracles" of Padre Cícero at

Juazeiro, followers and penitents loyal to Cícero assaulted the church, attempting to beat and expel the prelate on the grounds that he had become an agent of the devil.[18] Right down to the present, backland families throughout Ceará and the entire Northeast—even those well integrated into the regular Catholic church—have hung images and effigies of the "saint" Padre Cícero in their houses, to ward off evil spirits and invoke his protection.

6. *The Contestado.* This monarchist uprising in a remote southern region contested by the states of Paraná and Santa Catarina—hence the area's name, the Contestado—began in 1912 when a *curandeiro* (herbal-medicinal faith healer) and seer, José Maria (born Miguel Lucena Boaventura), gathered three hundred homeless followers and appealed to them to reject the republic. Like Antônio Conselheiro, José Maria, a literate man of about forty who probably deserted from the Paraná State Police, had been an itinerant holy man wandering through the backlands.[19] Erudite to an unusual degree even for a man of his background, José Maria read aloud passages from *The History of Charlemagne* to his followers to encourage monarchist feelings and to remind them of the holy war against the Moors. In preparation for battle, he dressed twenty-four of his soldiers in white robes adorned with green crosses, naming them the *pares de França*, the peers of France, after Charlemagne's imperial guard.[20]

Parallels with Canudos are striking. José Maria preached that the republic was evil and that the monarchy should be restored. He frequently invoked the name of Saint Sebastian. Conselheiro and José Maria both asked the faithful to withdraw from civil society to a holy city, where they would wait for evil to consume the rest of the world. Women played a major role in the Contestado movement, generally joining José Maria's settlement with greater enthusiasm than their husbands. Like Canudos, the holy city was open to all, *patrões* as well as the landless.

When local landowners instigated an attack by police, José Maria was killed; but a successor, José Eusébio Ferreira dos Santos, established a "holy" settlement on lands that he owned. A lay religious organizer, José Eusébio had invited José Maria to participate in the annual Bom Jesus Festival at Perdizes Grandes, a tiny hilltop village. The regional political boss, Francisco de Albuquerque, expelled them, driving the band—by now known as *os fanáticos* (the fanatics)—into Paraná. Citizens on the coast, memories of Canudos still fresh in their minds, began to receive reports of the nascent conflict.

Some officials interpreted the movement of José Maria's band as a disguised effort by Santa Catarina to occupy disputed Paraná territory. The migrants settled near Irani, on hilly land populated by *posseiros* (squatters). Many of these men were armed, the nucleus of José Maria's own *jagunço* fighting force. The new holy city was named Taquaraçu. In March 1914, men, women, and children defended themselves against machine-gun fire by draping themselves in a large green and white flag, convinced of their immunity to the army's weapons. A massacre ensued.[21]

At its height, the Contestado rebellion went further than Canudos. After the Taquaraçu massacre the rebels went on the offensive, attacking and burning nearby *fazendas*. Twenty thousand insurgents took control of 3 percent of the national territory, or 11,000 square miles. In 1915, the Brazilian army used a scorched-earth policy to starve the holy city, which by now had a population of ten thousand, into submission. The rebellion was finally stamped out in 1916.[22]

Economic crisis, regional droughts, the changing market system, and local political infighting all combined deleteriously with dislocations of a spiritual nature both at Canudos and in the Contestado.[23] Sale of public land by state governments and the incursion of the United States–owned Brazil Railway Company forced at least 150,000 squatters off Contestado lands. The sudden acquisition of hundreds of square miles of land by outside investors in 1906 set in motion a series of destabilizing circumstances for the local population: the introduction of twenty-five thousand Polish, Russian, Ukrainian, and German immigrants as agricultural colonists; purchases of additional land by a timber company; and the construction of the largest sawmill in Latin America. All these developments undermined landowner-client relations based on the traditional *agregado* system. Landowners now became labor brokers, transferring their power over the lives of rural people to the labor bosses, who hired workers at low wages for shifts lasting twelve to fourteen hours and prohibited use of company lands to raise cattle or crops. Up to 30 percent of the regional population found access to land restricted or threatened by the economic development that occurred between 1907 and 1912.

7. *Caldeirão/Pau de Colher.*   After Padre Cícero's death in 1934 and the return of parish control to Salesian clergy sent by the church, some of the faithful relocated to Caldeirão, an abandoned *fazenda* in the Bahian municipality of Casa Nova, where *beato* José Lourenço, a former aide to Padre Cícero, led the construction of a "new Juazeiro."[24] An illiterate black cowhand about forty years old in the mid-1930s, Lourenço chose to dress in leather cowboy clothing but otherwise assumed the role of a penitent. Before joining Padre Cícero in Ceará, he had spent his time praying at gravesites and sustained himself by begging for alms.

His peasant followers worked diligently, constructing a smaller version of Juazeiro to await the return to earth of the padre. Work was performed communally. Men, women, and children dressed in black as a sign of their mourning; the men cut their hair short and wore beards, while women wore long dresses and covered their faces with veils.[25] Community workers constructed a system of gathering and distributing water; agriculture and stock raising were developed, and women wove cloth and manufactured clothing. Like Canudos to some extent, but more rigorously collectivist in that it was designed to be self-sufficient, Caldeirão during its existence avoided both civil and ecclesiastical interference. Although recalcitrants within the community were flogged and beaten, few of the faithful deserted.

In May 1937, just as had occurred in the Canudos case, a small contingent of soldiers was sent to disperse the settlement. In the resulting skirmish, five of the eleven uniformed men were killed by the angry mob of José Lourenço followers. The local police chief reacted by requesting an all-out attack to wipe out the "pseudoreligious" movement of "blind fanaticism."[26] Four months later, a force of 150 men from the Ceará police attacked, supported by two military aircraft, which raked the housetops with machine-gun fire and dropped bombs. The agricultural community, acclaimed by one observer as the most successful ever achieved in Ceará to that time, was burned to the ground.[27] Estimates of the number of deaths ranged from seven hundred to a thousand. José Lourenço fled.[28] A second beato, a short white man named Severino, a middle-aged widower with two daughters, took up the leadership of the besieged penitents.

From 1933 to 1935, Severino had roved through the backlands, praying and offering counsel. One of his wanderings took Severino to a fazenda named Pau de Colher, about halfway between Ouricuri and Lagôa do Alegre in the caatinga region, where there was a source of potable water. The local population practiced a folk Catholicism characterized by frequent festivals in honor of popular saints and the presence of faith healers. This life was one of vivid spiritual images, arising from a land that, in the words of Roger Bastide, "yielded, in times of drought, visions of the Last Judgment."[29] Allying with a local resident, one José Senhorinho, whose enthusiasm for the cause (based in part on frequent consultation with the Bible and the Missão abreviada) elevated him to the status of beato, Severino remained committed to the renewal of the Caldeirão community.

During the short rainy season after October, another beato, named Quinzeiro, arrived in the region. His appearance was propitious, for Severino had preached that a "new disciple" would come. Quinzeiro set up his hammock and stayed. Meanwhile, José Lourenço sent word to the faithful to follow him back to Caldeirão. Quinzeiro became the leader of this group, which for the time being remained on the *fazenda*. He and the other *beatos* gave themselves new names: Quinzeiro became "*meu padim* [little father] Cícero"; the others, "São José," "Moisés," "Aaron," and "Mother Santa Cruz." They elaborated religious theories, one of them being that death for nonbelievers was a "communal good, not a heinous crime."[30] They stabbed to death several members who had not obeyed the community's regulations, including one who had tried to enter the place where the women slept to visit his wife. As in Caldeirão, men and women dressed the same, in black. They were not afraid of death, because, again as in Caldeirão, they believed that Padre Cícero would protect them and that, in any case, individual death would bring salvation. Food was distributed daily on a proportional basis, depending on family size.

The Pau de Colher episode ended when José Senhorinho began to use force to recruit new adherents, in preparation for the triumphant return to Caldeirão. When three local men refused to be seduced, his emissaries murdered them. In reaction, a posse of four soldiers and thirty civilians penetrated the *fazenda* on January 10, 1938, killing many of the *beatos* while they slept. By that time Pau de Colher housed fourteen hundred men and somewhat fewer women. The intruders were set upon, and two of the four military men were murdered.[31] The survivors fled. Federal and state authorities then sent three heavily armed police brigades to surround Pau de Colher and destroy it. Unlike Canudos, Pau de Colher fell within twenty-four hours. Four hundred occupants of the settlement died. The news was telegraphed by the commander of the motorized squadron of the Bahian Military Police, Captain Maurino Tavares: "I declare extinct," the message read, "the hideout of the fanatics."[32]

8. *Panelas.* Individuals in the *município* of Panelas in the Pernambucano *agreste* flocked to a messianic movement in the late 1930s, led by a man whose actions suggested that he was feeble-minded. Of course, coastal Brazilians expected that all adherents to unorthodox religious movements must by definition be insane or mentally defective. Yet when a psychiatrist, José Lucena, interviewed and tested members of the sect, his findings "demolished the assumption that they had abnormal personalities or suffered from any active psychosis."[33] In fact, only one case of mental deficiency was found.

The fact that Brazilian society gave birth to so many violent movements over what was a relatively short span of time is remarkable. Moreover, such movements occurred quite widely within the Lusophone world: Portuguese Angola, for example, experienced both traditional and transitional forms of nativistic or messianic mass movements in the nineteenth and twentieth centuries, including the emergence of four Bakongho

prophets. One of them, Simon Kibangu (or Kimbangu), fought for political emancipation; another, Andrew Grenard Matswa, a Catholic by
birth, was martyred in 1939 as "Jesus" Matswa.[34]

In Brazil there were likely dozens or even hundreds of movements that
never developed to the point of threatening the status quo and so required no intervention, or that simply went unrecorded in history. The
millenarian, and particularly the Sebastianist, tradition was very much a
part of Luso-Brazilian life during the colonial period.[35] Millenarian sects
flourished well into the twentieth century, one of the most notable recent
movements being the "Blue Butterfly" cult of the 1960s, studied by René
Ribeiro.[36] Such activity points to a reservoir of alienation in Brazilian life
over time. When this alienation has erupted into collective mobilization,
confrontations have resulted that the seekers of spiritual redemption
have never won.

## CANUDOS AS A MILLENARIAN MOVEMENT

Canudos differed from all other episodes in large as well as small ways.
Antônio Conselheiro preached salvation of the individual soul, not for
his entire community. Although his vision was messianic and millenarian, from the standpoint of its theology and prescriptions for social
behavior it was unthreatening: he never sought to impose his personal
vision on others. Violence was brought to bear against Canudos; it was
not exported from Canudos to the surrounding region, even though
residents of one nearby city, Juazeiro, on the Pernambuco shore of the
São Francisco River, were driven to panic by unsubstantiated rumors
that the conselheiristas would besiege and loot the city in retribution for an
undelivered shipment of lumber.

The conflict at Canudos occurred at a distinctive juncture in Brazilian
history, when a new (and feared) political system had begun to aggravate
long-standing conditions of deprivation.[37] As had occurred in medieval
Europe, Conselheiro's movement affected not only people cut off from
the source of social change—in this case, the world of the coastal elites—
but also elements seeking change not in the rural environment per se,
but in pious behavior. The reforms sought by the ultramontane clerics
for backland Catholic practice were likely as troubling to sertanejos as the
fall of the monarchy, the advent of the railroad, and the penetration of
the republican government.

The closing years of the nineteenth century also witnessed a broadening gulf between the culture of the emerging national elite and that of
rural society. Coastal Brazilians either gentrified religion or, in the influential Masonic lodges and parlors of the secular humanists, ignored it,
while backlands religionists, through means remarkably similar to what

Robert Darnton calls the remote mental universe of the eighteenth-century French village, "presented man as a slave of passion" and filled their heads "with visions of threatening, occult forces . . . miracles, and hagiography."[38] Whereas in Old Regime France popular literature served as an ideological substitute for class consciousness among the masses, in the Brazilian case rural folk religious belief—so different from orthodox Catholicism in its coastal (and ultramontane) form—not only provided a common basis of attraction to holy men like Conselheiro, but also deflected attention "from the real world of toil and exploitation."[39]

To Conselheiro's followers, the state represented "structural, cataclysmic upheaval" in its efforts to extend its power to the remote rural interior.[40] In response, the faithful willingly accepted prescriptions for life that provided comforting structure and direction. At Canudos, residents were assigned work and lived according to a routine that must have brought a sense of security to people with lives traumatized by deprivation and by the vicissitudes of drought, clan disputes, and economic uncertainty.

Backlanders questioned the secularized republican order. Some may have viewed the new requirement for civil registration and census questions about racial origins as threats to restore slavery, abolished by the monarchy a year before it fell.[41] Conselheiro had pulled down and burned notices of new municipal taxes in 1893. Even the election of a president rather than the lifetime investiture of a fatherly monarch raised fears. Many backlanders preferred to seek refuge in Canudos, a communal settlement led by a protective patriarch. In the words of a contemporary backland *cordel* verse,

> Cursed are those
> Who make elections,
> Putting down the law of God
> To raise the law of the devil.
>
> The Antichrist has arrived
> To govern Brazil,
> But in the interior is the Conselheiro
> To free us from him.[42]

Conselheiro's charismatic appeal had many sources. Given the scarcity of priests in the remote backlands of northeastern Brazil in the last quarter of the nineteenth century, itinerant lay preachers were heavily influential. Imperfect like all human beings, they inevitably stamped their own mark on the theology they transmitted to the faithful. They adopted and added to the assumptions present among their flocks, and they contributed new emphases to the stream of popular religious culture.[43] It is understandable that the Canudos conflict has taken on symbolism of dramatic proportions, for Conselheiro did at some point promise his followers salvation—even, under the duress of invasion, the Second Coming in the millennial year 1900. But most of his preachments were not apocalyptic or thaumaturgic: they simply demanded personal morality and hard work in return for spiritual protection from the corrupted secular world. That world, in the *sertão* as elsewhere, was locked in economic crisis, as it had been to a greater or lesser degree for generations. Belo Monte was thus a place where the faithful could lead disciplined lives according to Catholic precepts, removed both from modern infamies and from hunger and want; yet it also seemed an environment of primitivism and audacity.

It is true that the settlers in Canudos represented a motley assortment of impoverished *caboclos*, including former criminals and ex-prostitutes, as outsiders have long been quick to note. Yet Belo Monte remained always under Conselheiro's watchful eye: behavior that he considered immoral was simply not to be tolerated. Canudos drew together not deviants, but men and women alienated from their society who sought redemption by living voluntarily in a controlled and secure penitential environment.

What outsiders chose to see as a rebellion was in fact a collective statement by a unified community demanding the right to live in a place they considered a haven from an unfriendly world. Belo Monte had to be crushed, then, because it upset the stability of the status quo in the *sertão*. It affected two major elements of the rural oligarchical power structure: the pliant labor system and the "herd vote," by which rural bosses captured all the votes under their control and delivered them to republican politicians in exchange for local power. Large-scale migration from all parts of the backlands to Canudos posed a real threat to the system. If the punitive expedition sent to meet Conselheiro at Masseté had not been defeated, there would have been less apparent justification for retaliation; nevertheless, another pretext would have come sooner or later, given the political realities of the day.

Educated Brazilians were terrified by the image of Conselheiro and his followers as renegades and savages; rural folk, after all (and this was true even before the introduction of "scientific" racism), were known to be unsophisticated and prone to disaster.[44] It is noteworthy that Conselheiro has not been remembered as an abolitionist, even by those seeking lessons of social injustice in the Canudos drama. Although Conselheiro inveighed regularly against the evils of slavery, those who feared him distrusted his motives, remembering that he also advocated restoring the monarchy and, if only by implication, the paternalistic (and nonmodern) social order it represented. A visionary and a prophet, he conveyed a message that disrupted commonplace assumptions about social and institutional relationships. The hold he exerted on his followers was evidently related to their insecurity and desperation. His protesting voice allowed enemies to label him an insurrectionist and, therefore, to justify his destruction on grounds of law and order.

Canudos was peaceful and nonviolent. The Canudenses did not proselytize; in this sense, they were heirs to the hapless Rodeador movement of eight decades before. Anthropologist and psychiatrist René Ribeiro notes that testimony from apprehended Rodeador participants revealed the "essential gentleness" of their holy crusade, by which they sought to establish at Jerusalem the Kingdom of God on earth. A political uprising in the same region in 1817 hardly affected these religious folk and their dreamlike concept: prayer and waiting for King Sebastião took precedence over militancy.[45] So, too, in Canudos. The holy city was a refuge, theocratically organized though pragmatically connected to the surrounding environment—an achievement that in itself bespeaks considerable flexibility on the part of Conselheiro and his aides.

Neither his personal mannerisms nor his comportment as a mendicant preacher was particularly unusual for the backlands. His career followed the standard pattern of apostolic missionaries, except that in founding Canudos and drawing followers away from their homes he overstepped the bounds of his welcome in the region by disrupting economic life. His coarse blue robe secured at the waist by a knotted cord was the standard garb not only of *beatos* in the Brazilian hinterlands but of several religious orders throughout Latin America, including the Capuchins, the principal clerical order in the Northeast in the late 1800s.[46]

Conselheiro never claimed to be the Messiah, though he did exercise a powerful spell over his flock.[47] His unshakable personal faith has never been questioned; to those who encountered him he projected a "sense of foreboding . . . pervasive and unappeasable."[48] Conselheiro broke the hold of the traditional system of social control and offered new lives for the faithful, especially in the heady period before the settlement was attacked.

Never a revolutionary movement, Canudos shared only some similarities with other millenarian alternatives to religious (and political) traditions.[49] As individuals, Conselheiro's followers displayed millennial expectations by voluntarily leaving their homes and going to Canudos when their region was in crisis. Although Conselheiro failed to maintain and capitalize on his early alliances with some landowners and backland *coronéis* in the area, his was no idealistic utopia. As Patricia R. Pessar has noted, millenarianists of his stripe were not rejecting hierarchy and the unequal distribution of wealth per se; rather, they condemned the selfish, immoral acts of new (and threatening) kinds of patrons.[50]

Sebastianism may have influenced backland religion, but by the nine-teenth century it was likely expressed mainly at the level of the subcon-scious. The residents of Canudos assuredly were not driven by crazed religious fanaticism. Economic depression, residual effects of crippling drought, increased use of the state police to enforce political demands, and the disappearance of the monarchy and its traditional authority combined to make the structured life promised by Conselheiro seem powerfully desirable.[51]

Canudos's residents behaved rationally. They willfully and coura-geously abandoned their former lives to enter Conselheiro's holy city. They displayed the same characteristics ascribed by Roderick J. Barman to the Quebra-Quilo rioters—an "independent, aggressive group pos-sessing a well-established way of life which they were capable of defend-ing with concerted, effective action and without much regard for the wishes of those usually considered to be the dominant elements in rural society."[52] It is thus insufficient to dismiss Canudos and like movements as responses to *anomie* or as a breaking down of the traditional extended family owing to urbanization, the decline of paternalism, and so forth.[53] Nor was Belo Monte simply a kind of "dumb theater," as outsiders tended to regard it—a pathetic, year-round version of the carnivalesque practice whereby the poor become rich and enact waking dreams of social in-version.[54] Those who elected to live in Conselheiro's austere commune were likely motivated by the acceleration of destabilizing change in the backlands and by the continual hardship in individual lives.

Before Canudos was besieged, its residents were too busy building the settlement and following Conselheiro's austere precepts to be lured by end-of-the-world fantasies. Many residents, of course, did not partici-pate in the religious routines of the community, whereas the truly faith-ful may have followed Conselheiro as a prophet because of the emphasis in rural folk Catholicism on saints and on the possibility of saintly inter-cession in their lives. Conselheiro also served as a kind of regional *co-ronel*, exerting a similar power over his flock.[55] Conselheiro's paternal theology protected his subjects from Leviathan—that is, the new repub-lican government, which they believed to be evil both for mystical rea-sons (the coming millennium, the "kidnapping" of the fatherly Em-peror) and on concrete grounds (the threat to legitimacy and inheritance posed by obligatory civil registry of births, marriages, and deaths).

Deprivation and Conselheiro's spellbinding exhortations on the evil-ness of modern life brought these people together, but they were not "fanatics" until circumstances united them in common defense against armed outside attack. After the carnage began, those who did not flee may well have capitulated to the mood of fiery prophecy described by da Cunha. But they also knew of their likely fate if captured outside the settlement—fears confirmed in the first weeks after Canudos's de struction.

Any mass attachment to a religious cult is generally linked to more than just religious causes. Ironically, what outsiders overlooked was the sheltered but otherwise very normal existence that Conselheiro estab lished for his followers; indeed, for a locality in the stricken *sertão* in the late nineteenth century, the community could even be considered pros perous. Republican Brazil was too insecure and rent by factional warfare to dismiss such pious folk without bloodshed.

According to Roger Bastide, messianism does not hinder the advance ment of peoples but represents an awakening, one that often leads to a conscious awareness of the causes of deprivation. He links it to anti colonial feelings and overt manifestations of nationalism.[56] There is little evidence that this was the case at Canudos, even though Conselheiro did interject a political dimension to his message by ranting against the re public for its ungodly separation of church and state and advocating a return to the imagined security of the empire, under the paternalistic yet noninterfering eye of Emperor Pedro II. The republic's modernizing impetus threatened to bring new influences to the backlands, all of which Conselheiro, as a social reactionary, opposed. Liberation theolo gians and others who have embraced Conselheiro as an early leader of the proletariat against injustice have failed to understand the man's beliefs and fears.

## CATEGORIES OF BELIEF

In the original sense, the millennium relates to the fixed period of a thousand years originating in the Judeo-Christian tradition and men tioned in Revelation 20 as the time when holiness will prevail and Christ will reign on earth; sociologists, however, apply the term figuratively "to any conception of a perfect age to come, or of a perfect land to be made accessible."[57] René Ribeiro, the Recife-based anthropologist trained in psychiatry, divides millenarian experiences in Brazil into five categories, differentiated on the basis of leadership, ideology, and social character. The first two originated in indigenous religion predating Portuguese settlement, each based on belief in the existence of a land without evil. The other three derived from folk Catholicism arising after the eigh teenth century and had greatest influence among peasants.[58]

Analysts have explained that almost all millenarian movements re sult from political and social unrest, deprivation, the arousal of mass anxiety and tension, collective psychopathic disturbances, or as forms of social protest. Ronald Chilcote, for example, argues that Conselheiro's "charismatic fanaticism" was likely the essential element that allowed

Canudos to evolve into a unified community. Ribeiro, however, warns that these conclusions may be too reductionist. He notes, for instance, that Roger Bastide, using a sociostructural approach, found Brazilian messianic movements to be rooted in the extreme stratification of society, marked by geographic and cultural isolation. Yet Bastide overlooks the fact that blacks in Brazil, subject to the same frustrations and difficulties as *caboclos*, have not "resorted" to messianic movements.[59]

Ribeiro accepts the relevance of sociocultural and physical causes but in addition asks that we consider the aesthetic appeal of the idea of a perfect age and the attractiveness of new types of leadership. Many millenarian movements involved physical distancing—to remote places, isolated valleys, mountains, or secret terrains—to permit the faithful to prepare for the imminent coming of the millennium. Ribeiro explains:

> Miracles, visions, dancing and feasting or flagellation and fasting, songs of mythical or esoteric content, hymns, processions and other religious and ritualistic activities, all kindled by fervor and religious exaltation, would take precedence over the previous routine of life. When a people's dominant world view has been one of impending cataclysm, as in the case of the Tupi-Guaraní, or of a certain apocalyptic end along with expectation of the long-announced arrival of a messiah who will usher the faithful into Paradise, is it surprising that many individuals should find their hopes resting on very small pretext, and that they should go to extremes in seeking their fulfillment?[60]

Conselheiro neither spoke frequently about miracles nor claimed miraculous powers. Although backland folklorists have uncovered three miraculous acts attributed to Conselheiro during Canudos's lifetime, no evidence truly links them to him. As miracles, they are very small in scale; most likely, they were simply journalistic adaptations of traditional backland stories, fitted to the Canudos events. All three date from the period of heaviest combat, when journalists were scratching for copy to send to their newspapers. The first story claimed that the leaves of a tree in Chorrochó under which he had been sitting fell upon his departure. The second told of a chronically ill woman from Aratuipe who sent for a piece of Conselheiro's robe; when she received it, she burned it and made a potion of the ashes, which she drank, becoming cured. The third told of a nursing woman whose breasts were dry; she asked Conselheiro to touch them, and they were said to have filled with milk.[61]

Observers who see in popular religious movements signs of antisocial or pathological behavior often fail to realize that the same behavior may seem perfectly reasonable and normal to the practitioners. However disappointing or tragic the outcome of individual millenarian movements in Brazilian history, it is possible to see them as episodes in a long tradition of hope and expectation. This perspective provides an insight into the usual passivity and gentleness of millenarians—until outsiders react to them and move to neutralize or destroy them. In Brazil, institutionalized religion has been popularly perceived to be allied with the interests of the state; until relatively recently, moreover, the Catholic church hierarchy there has left the population largely to its own devices. Is it any wonder, then, that a dissatisfied believer, committed to millennial precepts, might rise up to capture the imagination of others who share his dreams of imminent salvation and emerge as a thaumaturge or charismatic leader?

What of Conselheiro himself and his remarkable appeal to the folk of the backlands? Psychiatrists studying messianic delusion have found a greater occurrence of personal identification with God among Christians than among practitioners of religions lacking deities in human form. Specialists consider the messianic psychotic experience as part of a wider, mystic event, defined by the acute sense on the part of the messianic subject that he has been elected for a task of salvation.[62] Madness invested in mythical delusional systems that inspire great emotional discharge is, according to Roger Bastide, an "island of resistance" to the dominant system.[63] By socializing his new self-assertiveness, the messianic subject projects his previous feelings of emptiness, fear, or anger onto all humanity.[64] Further, the collective symbolism communicated by the charismatic leader helps reinforce the sense of mission and chosenness. The messianic personality, consciously expressing no dependent needs, occupies a position in which everything is given and nothing is to be received.[65] For the messianic leader, the faithful become objects onto whom he projects his needs.

These conditions and preconditions seem to fit both Antônio Conselheiro and his faithful followers at Belo Monte. But a question that finds no easy answer follows: why Antônio Mendes Maciel and not many others? Why did his particular millenarian vision strike a nerve? What moved thousands of backland people to follow him but not heed other contemporaries? Socioeconomic explanations that focus on religious reaction to the stress of cultural conflict and deprivation provide answers; other theories do not.[66] Indeed, a student examining dozens of messianic visionaries throughout history has found that they are most likely to emerge "in times of crises of culture clash."[67]

Unfortunately, we know less about Conselheiro after than before the establishment of his holy city in 1894. Nor do we know to what degree his apocalyptic preachments were concrete, as opposed to simply symbolic. Yet even if he did emphasize prophetic visions as frequently as his enemies would have us believe, such images were not new to Christian convention, or to the backlands.[68]

During the great age of European popular insurgency from the fourteenth to the seventeenth centuries, lower-class groups reacted actively to the deterioration of their living standards, and when they fought for alternative social structures, it was usually at the behest of religious visionaries or charismatics. Traditional millenarian protest movements drew their inspiration from Christian eschatology, "envisioning the replacement of existing society by paradise on Earth."[69] At Canudos, we simply do not know what emphasis Conselheiro gave to the imminence of the apocalypse. As in pre-seventeenth-century Europe, the backland inhabitants tended to accept that society was basically unchangeable, and that alterations in climate to the detriment of the poor or epidemics of disease that ravaged the land were expressions of God's will. As Engels noted, however, even during the Middle Ages a kind of revolutionary underground tradition existed, appealing to apocalyptic scripture and making a conscious social as well as religious appeal to the poor.[70] Whether Conselheiro inherited this tradition (typified by the Fraticelli heretics of fourteenth-century Florence) is not known. Millenarianism is one thing, utopianism another. To assume that the *conselheiristas* were revolutionaries simply because of their religious idiom is dangerous, and in fact typifies the *visão do litoral*.

Millennial movements based on utopian dreams of salvation have, as we have seen, been of frequent occurrence, especially among marginalized groups of Brazil's rural poor whose already precarious lives were further threatened by economic or political change or who, though deeply religious, were cut off from the institutional church.[71] In normal times life was hard enough, but it enjoyed a certain basic security rooted in paternalistic landowner-peasant relations. Crises that shook this foundation encouraged terrified men and women to take risks and follow interpretations of messianic prophecy, especially those that promised to reverse age-old relationships, placing unbelievers in servitude to the faithful.

Studies of the social character of millennial sects emphasize accumulated tensions from social causes as well as from religious anxiety or fear, but the spiritual element, harder to pin down, is usually slighted. In the end, of course, illiterates groping for meaning in the harsh landscape of poverty leave no historical testimony. Lacking the ability to read people's minds, we must therefore rely on what we can decipher about the pressures they felt. Norman Cohn finds that medieval fears of universal disaster reflected a popular sense concerning the unworthiness of the popes, and that millennial movements took shape when near-psychopathic individuals "sense[d] that tension [was] near breaking-point and exploit[ed] the situation as leaders."[72]

Is there a connection between group insecurities and the rise of millenarian movements? After all, history is filled with examples of non-millennial social protests and revolts. The answer must lie in the religious mentality of those seeking the fantasy of a perfect age: in addition to growing social tension and fear of change, an underlying religious element often provokes desperate measures to find salvation. Scholars acknowledge that this element is present in Judaism, Islam, and Christianity. Antônio Saraiva, by extension, argues that messianism flourished in Brazil because of the "profound yet unconscious penetration of Judaism" among the inhabitants of the Luso-Brazilian world, presumably through the preservation of crypto-Judaism in Marrano culture.[73] Certainly this interpretation is dubious, however: except among fringes of the dispersed (and desperate) Jewish population in Central and Eastern Europe, all discussion of the coming of the Messiah remained metaphorical, not a spur to popular movements.

Christianity, especially in the intensely personal form experienced by rural northeastern Brazilians (interpreted as often as not by lay preachers, healers, mystics, and secular enthusiasts), was fertile ground for direct hopes for the millennium. In the historical mainstream, millenarianism remained a powerful force in the Christian church as long as Christians were an unpopular minority threatened with persecution. To medieval Christians—and to many Brazilian backlanders—Jerusalem was not only the place where Christ had lived his life, but also the site of the Kingdom of Heaven, the new home of the faithful after personal redemption. The holy cities of the faithful were pre-Jerusalems, spiritual waiting rooms for the faithful who would be ushered triumphantly into the "land fruitful above all others," to the miraculous realm abounding in both spiritual and material blessings.[74]

Many studies of millenarian movements idealize not only precapitalist conditions but their moral economy as well. The "political/revolutionary" school, exemplified by Eric J. Hobsbawm's 1959 study *Primitive Rebels*, sees millenarianism as a political tool for organizing protests against changes associated with the penetration of capitalism within a primitive, isolated peasantry.[75] Variants of this approach cast the faithful in the role of peasant heroes revolting against feudal exploitation in armed class struggle.[76] In his comparison of Canudos with the Padre Cícero experience, for instance, Ralph della Cava demonstrates how the two movements were rooted both in the social and ecological conditions of the backlands and in national politics—a view supported by Eul-Soo Pang's analysis of the economic and agrarian causes of millenarianism.[77]

Maria Isaura Pereira de Queiroz, in contrast, finds structural weaknesses in the unstable, kinship-based society of the backlands to be the chief cause of messianism.[78] In her view, violence within and among clans exacerbated tensions and ultimately created a feeling of *anomie* in the region, the result of the "built-in social disorganization of this type of rural society."[79]

In still another approach, Todd A. Diacon and Steve J. Stern argue that *anomie* alone does not explain the emergence of millenarian movements, and that disorganization and disorientation are commonly present in times of social change, regardless of whether millennialism ensues.[80] Diacon's study of the Contestado amalgamates several themes; taken together, they lead him to conclude that external pressures associated with the transition to capitalism can in certain situations produce spiritual crises.[81] This argument comes back to Ribeiro's conviction that changes in social, economic, or cultural conditions will favor the rise of messianic movements among people who accept and even seek the possibility of divine intervention and who regard structured communal life as a means to obtaining personal redemption. Prophecy, perhaps because institutional Catholicism left so many unattended amid lives of stress, seems to have flourished on Brazilian soil.

## DEFENSIVE REACTORS

In our century, historians have often depicted rural men and women as reacting parochially and defensively to unfavorable external forces.[82] They tend to agree that people who get caught up in rural conflict have often been provoked by the intrusion of "modernization" into their lives, either in encounters with the destructive impact of the modern capitalist world economy or in less specific clashes of values and authority. Peasant consciousness is typically considered to be "quite limited and predictable."[83] While such assessments are likely valid, in the case of Canudos a new framework is needed to permit us to weigh Conselheiro and his followers on their own terms. Politically, the residents of Canudos were inert; socially, however, they were active initiators, continually engaging their political world and causing significant impact by their collective decision to live apart and to participate in Conselheiro's holy city.[84]

One of the most remarkable aspects of the Canudos episode was that although the residents of the community resisted assault tenaciously, to a degree far beyond what could have been expected, their behavior up until the initial engagement with government troops was both quiescent and passive. George Rudé and others have found for preindustrial populations in Europe as well as African and Asian populations during the nineteenth century a "hatred" of the rich and powerful that seems to have been totally lacking at Canudos.[85] Riots did occur in Brazil's Northeast over changes in regulations governing the weekly markets, but these were brief and discontinuous. Day-to-day behavior indicated no lasting hatred or class conflict. Rather, the rural poor accepted their condition—though, as Canudos showed, their deep, almost mystic fatalism did not prevent them from defending themselves when provoked. Only in a most diffuse sense, then, can it be said that Canudos was influenced by social conflict.

Studies of rural populations have evolved through several stages of interpretation. The first generation of peasant studies debated whether their subjects were revolutionary or conservative, and whether it was the development of capitalism or the demands of the state that pushed rural inhabitants into revolt.[86] In the next generation, historians emphasized the diversity of the peasant experience by means of detailed case studies of individual localities. The third generation synthesizes the findings of the first two. It is now generally acknowledged that rural unrest usually arises from reductions in autonomy, security, or mobility, which lead to deep grievances and perceived opportunities to sabotage the existing system or to flee from it.

In the case of Canudos, the grievances of the faithful apparently produced not aggressiveness but deeper psychological regression. Deep-rooted local customs, including those bearing on race and on the self-image of the poor, undermined rural autonomy and the capacity for collective action.[87] With the sort of charismatic leadership provided by a man like Antônio Conselheiro, however, spiritual revolt could yield messianic hope, resulting in the determination to leave the secular world and find refuge in a disciplined, protected community—such as Canudos. Then again, the very willingness of rural men and women to accept authority and to shrink from confrontation predisposed many—perhaps the most depressed members of the population—to heed Conselheiro's message, to have the courage to follow him, and to accept Belo Monte's austerity.

It is unclear whether rural mores restrained the poor from casting off their docility. To be sure, northeastern *caboclos* lived "far away" from the state in the sense that their behavior was incomprehensible to coastal observers and even to the landowning elite; but they also lived all too "close" in terms of their awareness of the unwritten nuances of regional, factional, and clan rivalries, not to mention the incursion of civil regulations that affected their way of life.[88] The remarkable endurance of those faithful who did not flee Belo Monte but resisted to the end may be explainable by theories about the "density" of popular culture. Social psychologists have also suggested that when belonging to or joining a group demands considerable sacrifice from a member, that person tends to give greater prestige to his or her association with that group.[89] This behavior seems to fit with what we know about Canudos under Conselheiro's leadership. The same determination that outsiders considered merely a primitive effort to block change may in fact have been a form

of coping, or even of assertiveness; in the end, group cohesiveness under
Belo Monte's utopian framework was reinforced by Conselheiro's promise that the faithful, not the outside world, would be redeemed.[90]

How may we measure the extent to which the courageous decision of
thousands of backlanders to pull up roots and follow Conselheiro to his
holy city represented a collective statement of defiance? The popularity
during the 1980s of deconstructionism—first in European and then in
U.S. academic circles, as well as among Brazilian intellectuals—raised
problems with earlier political definitions of behavior, including the
resistance-acquiescence quandary. To deconstructionists and others, as
Colin Gordon states, "The binary division between resistance and non-
resistance is an unreal one. . . . The existence of those who seem not to
rebel is a warren of minute, individual, autonomous tactics and strategies which counter and inflect the visible facts of overall domination, and
whose purposes and calculations, desires and choices resist any simple
division into the political and the apolitical."[91]

Antônio Conselheiro's decision to remove his followers to the relative
safety of a defended holy sanctuary was not in the least insurrectionary,
though it did threaten the status quo. This sense of threat was exacerbated by his manner of dealing with local landowners and with civil and
ecclesiastical authorities. Conselheiro, stubborn and quick-tempered,
was as ready to label his enemies heretical agents of the Antichrist as his
detractors were to call him a crazed fanatic. Perhaps he genuinely believed that the millennium would bring divine intervention. In any case,
he was not a revolutionary, and his community was neither subversive
nor deliberately provocative. The characterization by da Cunha and his
contemporaries of a "rebellion" in the backlands was accurate only in-
sofar as the physical act of abandoning one's former home is rebellious.
From the outset, Conselheiro knew only too well that overt rebellion
would result in immediate military retaliation.

Given that he was not promised protection from local landowners
and others sympathetic to him (as Padre Cícero was), Conselheiro's own
outlook must have changed dramatically during 1895 and 1896. Either
he became more arrogant, convinced of his city's invincibility, or he
believed that the millennial scenario was irreversible and that armed
conflict would only speed the Day of Judgment. Had Conselheiro been
concerned with the day-to-day secular world rather than, as he was, being
entirely consumed by the spiritual dimension, he might have encouraged his followers to emphasize more mundane forms of resistance—
foot-dragging, deception, dissimulation, feigned ignorance, false compliance, sabotage, sit-downs, malicious gossip, and so on—thus avoiding
direct symbolic confrontations with authority or with elite norms. The

tolerance of rural folk culture for malefactors may signal vicarious admiration for those known for noncompliance.[92]

There is also the matter of women's place in Belo Monte, where, at least to a limited extent, traditional social roles were exchanged for new ones. Although they were physically segregated because of Conselheiro's misogyny, at the same time they were more independent than would have been the case outside the settlement. They were assigned tasks as difficult as those given to men, and their daughters were permitted to attend primary school alongside their sons.[93]

Overall, Conselheiro's invitation for backlanders to join him in a utopian settlement seems a halfway point between passivity and open defiance. Here, the dour, psychologically depressed condition of rural backlanders—not only in the nineteenth century, but well into the twentieth as well—probably precluded more overt manifestations of aggressiveness. The normative, raw material of daily experience educates participants in strategies for interpreting who holds power, how that power may be used against one, and what conduct will be tolerated or not. In many parts of the world, passive compliance characterizes the lives of the dispossessed.[94] Occasionally, in the words of James C. Scott, the dispossessed "reject the denigrating characterizations the rich deploy against them."[95] Such open challenges occurred in the high São Francisco *sertão* only rarely, when aggrieved squatters took matters into their own hands and struck out at representatives of individual landowners. Canudos, of course, was an exception to the rule.

It is easier to consider rural backlanders as able to reject the existing social order by embracing Conselheiro's blandishments if one situates their world in the black-and-white universe envisioned by da Cunha rather than in the more complex and less isolated Bahian backlands that in fact existed in the late 1800s. The very notion of *sertão* as desert (the etymological derivation of the Portuguese word) is proven false by the experience of Belo Monte, which became productive and fertile on harsh land within months of its creation. How many more of the pejorative stereotypes describing backland life would have been exploded if Canudos had been allowed to survive?

James C. Scott has reminded us that "[if] it requires no great leap of the imagination to reverse the existing social order, then it should come as no surprise that it can as easily be negated."[96] Conversely, the radicalism of Conselheiro's millenarian and utopian vision may be seen as a negation of the existing pattern of misery and exploitation. What the faithful thought they were going to experience was essentially a particular form of postearthly society—not one that would simply erase the distinctions between rich and poor, where all people would be equal (the typical goal of a millenarian movement), but one in keeping with Conselheiro's dark, unforgiving Catholicism, an inverted society where the rich would become poor and the poor rich.

Millenarianism may, of course, remain dormant for years, but the tradition is usually continuous and deep-seated in popular culture. In medieval France, the millenarian forms were very similar to Conselheiro's. Deprivation need not be present to trigger millenarian impulses, although it was very present in the case of Canudos. Rather, simply the deroutinization of daily life, or political change that causes the "normal categories with which social reality is apprehended no longer [to] apply," may trigger millennial activity. In Brazil, the monarchy's fall—the exile of the patriarchal emperor—and the establishment of the republic with its secular laws hostile to the Catholic church were sufficient cause for resistance. Millennial movements, not limited to the Judeo-Christian universe but present as well in Buddhist and Islamic regions around the world, paradoxically envision radical changes in the distribution of power, status, and ownership, yet at the same time are centered on a leader—a prophet, a king—to set things right. In the case of Canudos, Conselheiro, despite his own frequent disclaimers, was construed by his followers as the prophet, agent, and interpreter of a vaguely defined trinitarian deity composed of the Messiah, Saint Sebastian, and God rolled into one. Conselheiro's utopia also openly maintained the symbolic kingship of the beloved Emperor Pedro II, now exiled. Belo Monte, then, was very much a monarchist redoubt—if not precisely in the political sense in which coastal elites understood monarchism after the *fait accompli* of the 1889 coup.[97]

Both the nature of Conselheiro's ministry in Canudos and the exodus of northeasterners to his holy city doomed his movement to intervention by the state. Prophecy coupled with diatribes against sin played a regular part in backland lay Catholicism, as communicated not only by Conselheiro during the wandering phase of his ministry but also by others influenced by the tone and content of Father Couto's *Missão abreviada*.

There is no evidence in the case of Canudos or any other millenarian movements in Brazil that powerless and subordinate populations accepted their continued domination as inevitable. Symbolic mockery and even physical attacks on hegemonic systems have been common and continuous in that country.[98] What made Canudos's fate different was that Conselheiro, unlike the more politically astute Padre Cícero, was unwilling to use his understanding of the political system to buy immunity for his followers, who in their own way were just as devout and—to outsiders—just as childlike and gullible as the residents of Cícero's Juazeiro. Perhaps he risked (and even invited) armed repression through his obstinate acts because of a gathering psychosis, far more pronounced at the end of his life than even in the early days of Belo Monte. In the final analysis, though, we have only the words of unfriendly outsiders on which to base our judgments and so should refrain from speculation.

Almost everything prophesied by Conselheiro for his flock (not *demanded*, for there is a difference) fit easily within the professed values and hegemony of local backland elites.[99] Belo Monte's residents denied the legitimacy of the existing power structure not by rising against it, but by taking refuge in Conselheiro's holy city, a place both apocalyptic and protective. The grievances of Conselheiro and his devout followers were backward-looking, seeking to restore elements of a world that had been taken away by the hated republican government.

The survival of Conselheiro's settlement from 1893 through 1897 clearly indicates a growing withdrawal from the dominant regional culture by the thousands of backlanders who opted to take up residence there. Whether this withdrawal was based on foolish gullibility or on "mystic evasion," Conselheiro's cult offered "a critique of the existing order and a [potentially explosive] alternative symbolic universe."[100] Canudos nurtured new social links and cultural dissent in the form of a variant—exaggerated but not necessarily heretical—of the dominant Roman Catholic religion.

Belo Monte as a dissident subculture reflected a demand for new economic and social arrangements, for disciplined lives while awaiting the millennium, and for adjusted patron-client relations and independence from the powerful landowners in the region. The powerful in backland society were willing to accept the republic because its political structure promised them increased control through the strengthened system of *coronelismo*. Those who had nothing saw no benefits. Perhaps of all that da Cunha described, it was the Canudenses' strongly independent spirit, carried to deadly lengths at Canudos, that most disturbed the elites, and rightfully so.

The tragic Canudos affair had repercussions far greater than were immediately understood. The impact was probably felt less in the Northeast than elsewhere, although it would be some years before the hamlets and towns from which the faithful had departed regained their former "normality." Yet even though the basic economic activities of the region were resumed, modernizing pressures and population outflow continued, now in the form of migrants leaving the arid interior for the coast or in quest of hoped-for industrial employment in the South. The local political system of *coronel* domination enforced by personal violence and economic pressure, too, persisted well into the twentieth century.[101] The church did little to increase the numbers of priests in the rural interior, and perhaps as a consequence, other charismatic religious figures, notably Ceará's Padre Cícero, continued to exercise spellbinding influence over backland residents still seeking new lives.

Nationally, influential citizens had dreaded that the stubborn independence of the Canudenses would spread to incite regionalist insurrection. This never happened, though skirmishes did take place within a larger theater than that documented by da Cunha. What coastal elites refused to accept was that Conselheiro's words were rhetorical, not summonses to aggression. His followers *withdrew* to Canudos to await the Day of Judgment. They tended to themselves and did not proselytize. Conselheiro's hatred of the republic was real enough, but at least in the early days of his settlement he and his lieutenants managed to ally themselves with local landowners and other members of the backland elite on a purely pragmatic basis.

Anxiety over the republic's vulnerability caused fears to be directed to the international arena as well, an extension of the false assumption that monarchists outside the Northeast were supporting the resistance. Both the Portuguese and the British (seen to be pro-monarchist ever since the 1893 Naval Rebellion, when they stopped unloading their ships in Rio harbor) were rumored to be supplying Conselheiro. Incoming president Campos Salles had to deal with strong apprehension that monarchist restorationism and the government's troubles at Canudos would adversely affect Brazil's credit rating. There was further anxiety over rumored British and Portuguese intervention in the Amazon, which had seen a good deal of foreign commercial investment and whose vast reaches were far from secure under Brazilian military control. It is also possible (though unprovable) that city-based republicans, especially among the radicals and Jacobins, feared that if the new regime did not demonstrate its fitness to govern by maintaining public order, unrest would spread to an urban theater.

Because all but the final military campaign against Canudos failed miserably, it was inevitable that republican sympathizers would exaggerate the nature of the threat. Otherwise, the disgrace suffered by the armed forces would have been all the more stinging. In the states, officials fanned restorationist fears to justify raising the number of militiamen under arms. São Paulo sent troops to Canudos, the only state south of Bahia to do so. Then, too, while the military debacle at Canudos encouraged the growth of state militias, it also strengthened civilian control over the government.

Among the republican Jacobins, the most politicized drew parallels between the French Revolution and post-1889 Brazil. The Vendeé analogy was indeed powerful—for the Jacobins and for their enemies both—if historically inaccurate. The Jacobins believed that if the last campaign had not succeeded when it did, there might well have been bloodshed beyond the Bahian *sertão*. But they failed to achieve meaningful change, perhaps because they shared fundamentally the same traditional values of their political enemies in the elite, despite their cries for more radical change.[102]

Following Canudos's end, observers expressed overwhelming relief, and acceptance of the hypothesis that the backlands and coast were vexingly disparate. Yet this view was in its own way deeply ambiguous. Da Cunha, as a positivist long troubled by the "staining" of national progress by miscegenation, considered his analysis not a defense of the *sertanejo* but an attack on the barbarity of the "civilized" leaders of the land. It would have been too much to expect contemporary Brazilians, badly shaken by the news from the backlands and uncomfortable with the early republic's failure to address the complaints that had brought down the monarchy, not to see Canudos as an evil force and a threat to the modernizing ideology of the late nineteenth century. A handful of participants and eyewitnesses, to be sure, did change their outlook, becoming more sensitive to the plight of the victims—Lélis Piedade, for example, and the Indianists Luis Bueno Horta Barbosa and Cândido Rondon.[103] Most, however, seem to have used the Canudos incident only to corroborate their prejudices.

With the republic in 1889 came tacit acceptance among politically conscious Brazilians of the progressive view of history. This outlook clashed with the stubborn backland conviction that life was cyclical, that worldly things were subordinate to the eternal struggle against sin. Conselheiro, by interjecting messianic and millenarian elements, modified this belief, placing emphasis on the imminence of divine intervention.[104] Yet few in the elite, except da Cunha himself and those rare countrymen who understood rural life, were willing to acknowledge that this position, if antimodern, represented strength and genuine religious faith. The *visão do litoral* could not tolerate such an admission.

The events at Canudos shattered confidence in the national armed forces and their Jacobin allies. They also deeply affected how Brazil as a nation came to see itself and poked holes in the nineteenth-century positivist myth of Progress, though positivism remained influential for years. By 1898, however, few republicans likely believed any longer that the social and psychological distance between urban and rural Brazil—between the coast and the backlands—could be bridged by imposing a modern façade of "civilizing" institutions. Rural fears—openly enunciated in the press long before Canudos, as well as among members of the elite at their local and regional meetings (at the agricultural congresses held in Rio and in Recife in 1878, for example)—were only reinforced by the manner in which journalists presented Canudos: as a "rebellion" of crazed fanatics who, if not belligerent, were a dead weight on civil progress. This allegation, of course, had a strong racial dimension.

Canudos's most lasting impact on Brazil was psychological, largely thanks to Euclydes da Cunha's remarkable prose, which was rich in imagery and emotional effect and immensely authoritative. Over the decades, critics have declared his book a classic, and historians have tended to grant *Os sertões* unchallenged status. As military history, it falls within the old romantic school of Sir Edward Creasy and the Prussian Hans Delbrück—a matter of seeking scapegoats—not in the tradition of John Keegan, where the goal is simply to present a humane study. *Os sertões* (and subsequent treatments of Canudos), to borrow from Keegan on Delbrück-influenced French, German, and Russian military historiography, "bears all the marks of circumscription, over-technicality, bombast, and narrow xenophobia."[105]

Keegan suggests that in Europe, the weight of centuries of brutal military engagements has encouraged military historians to resist taking a more dispassionate approach—this in contrast to the English-speaking countries, where, except for the U.S. Civil War, all major engagements took place on foreign soil.[106] The European narrative tradition of battlefield description, followed by the Brazilian coverage of the military campaigns against Canudos, is set against the unspoken assumption, espoused by Creasy, that successful battles against barbaric enemies save civilization from extinction—or, in da Cunha's case, at least from humiliation. Even if he was ambivalent about the foe—admiring the *sertanejo*'s perseverance despite his threat to the republic—da Cunha's positivism encouraged him to see the military campaigns as crusades against the forces of darkness.

What anthropologists term the "density" of popular culture is a measure of autonomy within a community.[107] Belo Monte's tight, reciprocal communal structure of tasks and psychological rewards was attractive to those courageous enough to act on their hopes or desperate enough to uproot their miserable but predictable lives—attractive, that is, in contrast to the typical life of marginalized backlanders in a region characterized by unchecked economic decline. Timing was fortuitous as well. Canudos might not have attracted the thousands it did without the recent shock of the termination of the monarchy, a significant and frightening event for backlanders who paid only scant attention to politics.

In its national context, Canudos was a trauma that raised far-reaching questions. That the community became a threat was largely circumstantial. Local landowners found themselves vulnerable economically in the wake of the difficult 1890s and the weakened position of the northeastern states under the federalist republican constitution. Regional and national politicians found the passive Canudenses to be perfect scape-goats to blame for imagined monarchist machinations. The transition to the republic was not the bland, consensual process that Brazilian history textbooks portray it to be; rather, it was a tumultuous contest of com-peting goals for the future of the nation. The Jacobins, who initially sought for Brazil the *liberté ancienne* of ancient Greece, soon abandoned these ideals in favor of positivist authoritarianism.[108] The specter of Canudos, in fact, led many to embrace the Jacobins' dark view of the Brazilian people. Yet Canudos was merely a community to which people withdrew to do penance and find personal salvation, not a center for spreading revolt or fomenting subversion.[109]

The Brazilian nation that willfully ignored the plight of its rural pop-ulation and conveniently dismissed the implications of the war against Canudos was essentially antinational and morally bankrupt—as much so as any late nineteenth-century "nation" that adopted an image of mod-ernizing progress shared by only a tiny percentage of the population.[110] Even in the backlands, contemporaries who considered themselves forward-looking mocked the Canudenses and denied their religiousness legitimacy. A *cordel* troubadour, Ugolino Nunes da Costa, composed a verse expressing such an opinion in 1896, while Canudos was flourishing:

> He [Conselheiro] pretends to be pious
> In order to cast illusions;
> He enticed some of the people to come to him;
> Together they act disgracefully.[111]

The historic site of the Belo Monte community lies below a reservoir, constructed in the late 1970s under the auspices of the federal drought-relief agency.[112] The irrigation system created by the project provides only intermittent water to the adjacent town, Nova Canudos, whose ground still turns up bullet shells, skull fragments, and other remnants of the furious armed conflict that led to the first Canudos's destruction. Chronic poverty afflicts the region. Conselheiro's prophecy of water coming to the *sertão* was fulfilled, but his backlanders gained little im-provement in their lives.

# NOTES

## PREFACE

1. "Backlands" will be used in this book as a synonym for *sertão*. (See glossary entry.)

2. See Roderick J. Barman, *Brazil: The Forging of a Nation, 1798–1852* (Stanford: Stanford University Press, 1988), 25–30.

3. Michael A. Mullett, *Popular Culture and Popular Protest in Late Medieval and Early Modern Europe* (London: Croom Helm, 1987), 64.

## INTRODUCTION

1. See Gilberto Freyre, *Order and Progress: Brazil from Monarchy to Republic*, ed. and trans. Rod W. Horton (New York: Alfred A. Knopf, 1970), 164. Western readers, however, did not always come away enlightened about Brazil; instead they tended to see the country through a lens of condescension and racism. See Susan Sontag, "Afterlives: The Case of Machado de Assis," *New Yorker*, May 7, 1990, 102–8; Augusto Tamayo Vargas, "Interpretaciones de América latina," in *América latina en su literatura*, ed. César Fernández Moreno (Mexico City: Siglo Veintiuno Editores, 1977), 457; Maria Tai Wolff, "Estas páginas sem brilhos: o texto-sertão de Euclydes da Cunha," *Revista iberoamericana* 50, no. 126 (January–March 1984): 47–61.

2. Stefan Zweig, *Brazil: Land of the Future* (New York: Viking Press, 1942), 159–60, quoted in Samuel Putnam, "Translator's Introduction" to *Rebellion in the Backlands (Os sertões)*, by Euclydes da Cunha (Chicago: University of Chicago Press, 1944), iii.

3. José Maria Bello, *Inteligência do Brasil: ensaios sobre Machado de Assis, Joaquim Nabuco, Euclides da Cunha e Rui Barbosa*, 3d ed. (São Paulo: Editora Nacional, 1938), 153.

4. See Thomas E. Skidmore, "Racial Ideas and Social Policy in Brazil, 1870–

1940," in *The Idea of Race in Latin America, 1870–1940*, ed. Richard Graham (Austin: University of Texas Press, 1990), 11.

5. Josué de Castro, *Death in the Northeast* (New York: Random House, 1966), 23.

6. Bello, *Inteligência do Brasil*, 178.

7. João Cruz Costa, *Pequena história da república* (São Paulo: Editora Brasiliense, 1968), 72. Writing two generations later, Cruz Costa indicates that he agreed with da Cunha's assessment.

8. Joseph L. Love, "Latin America and Romania, 1860–1950," in *Guiding the Invisible Hand: Economic Liberalism and the State in Latin American History*, ed. Joseph L. Love and Nils Jacobsen (New York: Praeger, 1988), 10–12.

9. Other nineteenth-century Latin American intellectuals also debated the struggle, as they saw it, between civilization and barbarism—for example, the Argentine Domingo Faustino Sarmiento, in *Civilización y barbarie: vida de Juan Facundo Quiroga* (Buenos Aires, 1845); and the Peruvian novelist Clorinda Matto de Turner, in his *Aves sin nido* (1889; reprinted Cuzco: Universidad Nacional del Cuzco, 1948). See E. Bradford Burns, "The Destruction of a Folk Past: Euclides da Cunha and Cataclysmic Cultural Clash," *Review of Latin American Studies* 3, no. 1 (1990): 29–30.

10. Euclydes da Cunha, *Rebellion in the Backlands*, 78, 85.

11. Burns, "Destruction of a Folk Past," 27.

12. Marshall Berman finds this trait to be characteristic of underdeveloped societies, calling it the "Faustian split"; see *All That Is Solid Melts into Air: The Experience of Modernity* (New York: Simon & Schuster, 1982), 43, cited by Burns, "Destruction of a Folk Past," 27.

13. For a view of fears of rural revolt in earlier days, see Yves-Marie Bercé, "Rural Unrest," in *Our Forgotten Past*, ed. Jerome Blum (London: Thames & Hudson, 1982), 133–56.

14. Charles A. Hale, "Political and Social Ideas in Latin America, 1870–1930," in *The Cambridge History of Latin America*, vol. 4: *Ca. 1870 to 1930* (Cambridge: Cambridge University Press, 1986), 402.

15. I am indebted to Charles A. Hale for this observation. Da Cunha explained his bedrock simile in the 1905 edition of *Os sertões* (*Rebellion in the Backlands*, 481), in which he writes: "I did encounter in the backlands (sertanejo) type an ethnic subcategory already formed and one which, as a result of historical conditions, had been freed of the exigencies of a borrowed civilization such as would have hindered its definitive evolution. This is equivalent to saying that in that indefinable compound—the Brazilian—I came upon something that was stable, a point of resistance reminiscent of the integrating molecule in the initial stage of crystallizations. And it was natural enough that, once having admitted the bold and inspiring conjecture that we are destined to national unity, I should have seen in those sturdy caboclos the hardy nucleus of our future, the bedrock of our race."

16. Justo Sierra, "México social y político: apuntes para un libro" (1889), in *Obras*, 9:128–31, citing Le Bon's article published in 1888 in the *Revue scientifique*; Justo Sierra, *The Political Evolution of the Mexican People*, trans. Charles Ramsdell (Austin: University of Texas Press, 1969), 368, quoted by Alan Knight,

"Racism, Revolution, and Indigenismo: Mexico, 1910–1940," in *The Idea of Race in Latin America, 1870–1940*, ed. Richard Graham (Austin: University of Texas Press, 1990), 78. See also Hale, "Political and Social Ideas," 404.

17. See, for example, the short-story writer Elias José's "O Salvador," in *Um pássaro em pânico* (São Paulo: Editora Ática, 1977); and Malcolm Silverman, "Alienation and the Fiction of Brazil's Elias José," in *Los Ensayistas: Brazil in the Eighties*, ed. Carmen Chaves McClendon and M. Elizabeth Ginway, nos. 28–29 (Athens: University of Georgia Press, 1990), 199–216. The Canudenses are depicted as heroes in José Antonio Sola's *Canudos: uma utopia no sertão* (São Paulo: Editora Contexto, 1989).

18. R. B. Cunningham Graham, *A Brazilian Mystic: Being the Life and Miracles of Antonio Conselheiro* (London: William Heinemann, 1920).

19. Mario Vargas Llosa, *A guerra do fim do mundo* (Rio de Janeiro: Francisco Alves, 1982); published in English as *The War of the End of the World*, trans. Helen R. Lane (New York: Farrar, Straus & Giroux, 1984). See also the hostile response by Edmundo Moniz, "Canudos: o suicídio literário de Vargas Llosa," *Encontros com a civilização brasileira* 29 (1982): 7–20; Edmundo Moniz, *A guerra social de Canudos* (Rio de Janeiro: Civilização Brasileira, 1978); and Alfred MacAdam, "Euclides da Cunha y Mario Vargas Llosa: meditaciones intertextuales," *Revista iberoamericana* 50, no. 126 (January–March 1984): 157–64.

20. See Eric Van Young, "To See Someone Not Seeing: Historical Studies of Peasants and Politics in Mexico," *Mexican Studies/Estudios mexicanos* 6, no. 1 (Winter 1990): 133–59.

21. See J. P. Favilla Nunes, "Population, territoire, électorat," in *Le Brésil en 1889 avec une carte de l'empire en chromolithographie*, ed. Frederico José de Santa-Anna Nery (Paris: Librairie Charles Delagrave, 1889).

22. My decision to use this translation was based on the necessity to quote from da Cunha extensively, and if I were to use the original Portuguese-language edition for my study, I would have to retranslate; Putnam's masterful prose is preferable.

23. Euclydes da Cunha, *Os sertões: edição didática*, ed. Alfredo Bosi (São Paulo: Editora Cultrix, 1985).

24. See Yonina Talmon, "Millenarianism," in *International Encyclopedia of the Social Sciences*, ed. David L. Sills (New York: Macmillan/Free Press, 1979), 10: 349–60.

25. See Mullett, *Popular Culture and Popular Protest*, 131, 135, 147.

26. See Alfred Cobban, *A History of Modern France*. Vol. 3: *1871–1962* (Harmondsworth, Middlesex: Penguin Books, 1965), 39.

## CHAPTER 1

1. Steven C. Topik, "Brazil's Bourgeois Revolution?" (ms., 1990), 1. For an informed assessment of the republic's origins, see José Murilo de Carvalho, *A formação das almas: o imaginário da república no Brasil* (São Paulo: Companhia das Letras, 1990). On the characterization of common folk as "beastlike," see José

Murilo de Carvalho, *Os bestializados: o Rio de Janeiro e a república que não foi*, 3d ed. (São Paulo: Companhia das Letras, 1989); the phrase was Aristides Lobo's.

2. Alberto Torres, *A organização nacional*, 297, quoted in Carvalho, *Formação das almas*, 33.

3. See, for example, Décio Saes, *A formação do estado burgûes no Brasil (1888–1891)* (Rio de Janeiro: Paz e Terra, 1985).

4. For a provocative overview of Brazil's nineteenth-century economic history, see Nathaniel H. Leff, *Underdevelopment and Development in Brazil*, 2 vols. (London: Allen & Unwin, 1982).

5. Rui Facó, "A guerra camponesa de Canudos," *Revista Brasiliense* (São Paulo) 1 (November–December 1958): 131–32.

6. Some suggest that the roots of Brazil's pre–World War I identity crisis and the crumbling of the previously entrenched moral foundation of Western society may be traced to accelerating events during the last decades of the nineteenth century. See, for example, Eric J. Hobsbawm, *The Age of Empire, 1875– 1914* (New York: Random House, 1987), 10–11.

7. See Hale, "Political and Social Ideas," 368–69, 382.

8. See Burns, "Destruction of a Folk Past," 18–19.

9. Boris Fausto, "Brazil: Social and Political Structure, 1889–1930," in *The Cambridge History of Latin America*, vol. 5: *Ca. 1870 to 1930*, ed. Leslie Bethell (Cambridge: Cambridge University Press, 1986), 791.

10. Victor Nunes Leal, *Coronelismo: The Municipality and Representative Government in Brazil*, trans. June Henfrey (Cambridge: Cambridge University Press, 1977), 76–77.

11. Richard Graham, *Patronage and Politics in Nineteenth-Century Brazil* (Stanford: Stanford University Press, 1990), 269–70.

12. See Hobsbawm, *Age of Empire*, 22. On the role of the United States as model for Brazil's republic, see José Maria dos Santos, *A política geral do Brasil* (São Paulo: J. Magalhães, 1930), 208; Francisco de Assis Barbosa, *JK: uma revisão na política brasileira* (Rio de Janeiro: José Olympio Editora, 1960), 103 and passim; Eduardo Silva, *Idéias políticas de Quintino Bocaiúva*, vol. 1 (Brasília and Rio de Janeiro: Senado Federal and Fundação Casa Rui Barbosa, 1986), 25–26, 292–310.

13. Emília Viotti da Costa, "Brazil: The Age of Reform, 1870–1889," in *The Cambridge History of Latin America*, vol. 5: *Ca. 1870 to 1930*, ed. Leslie Bethell (Cambridge: Cambridge University Press, 1986), 747.

14. See Richard Graham, *Patronage and Politics*, 263, 272.

15. Costa, "Brazil," 750; Freyre, *Order and Progress*, 13.

16. Freyre, *Order and Progress*, 13–14.

17. See the comments on the etymology of the word by Warren Dean in his "The Frontier in Brazil," paper read at the Woodrow Wilson International Center for Scholars, Washington, D.C., June 23, 1990, referring to Pero Lopes de Souza, *Diário de navegação* (Rio de Janeiro, 1867).

18. See, for example, Colin Henfrey, "Peasant Brazil: Agrarian History, Struggle and Change in the Paraguaçu Valley, Bahia," *Bulletin of Latin American Research* 8, no. 1 (1989): 1–24.

19. If Brazil's Northeast had any peasants at all, they were the landless squatters and tenants on the coastal plantations. Poor backlanders had fewer ties to the land and enjoyed (if the word is not too ironic) the freedom to migrate in the face of drought or hunger. Sometimes *caboclo* was used to designate rural

*sertanejos*, but the term holds pejorative racial connotations and is therefore inaccurate, since not all backlanders were mulattoes. In some parts of the region, the term *matuto* was common, but in other places *matuto* held its original meaning, that of a landless Portuguese peasant immigrant. Perhaps the closest parallel comes in comparison with the São Paulo term *caipira*, denoting a rural person living on the land, lacking education or social poise, clumsy in public, timid; see Carlos Rodrigues Brandão, *Os caipiras de São Paulo* (São Paulo: Editora Brasiliense, 1983). See also Agrippino Grieco, *Evolução da prosa brasileira* (Rio de Janeiro: Editora Ariel, 1933), 281–86; Zweig, *Brazil*, 159–60; Bezerra de Freitas, *História da literatura brasileira* (Porto Alegre: Editora Globo, 1939), 251–52; Eduardo Portella, *Literatura e realidade nacional*, 2d ed. (Rio de Janeiro: Tempos Brasileiros, 1971), 36–37; Nicolau Sevcenko, *Literatura como missão: tensões sociais e criação cultural na Primeira República* (São Paulo: Editora Brasiliense, 1983), esp. chap. 4.

20. This zone of influence was defined by Silvio Romero in *A Notícia* (Aracajú), January 28, 1897, 4.

21. Recent historiography on the French Revolution offers a case in point; see, for example, Alan B. Spitzer, "In the Beginning Was the Word: The French Revolution," *Journal of Interdisciplinary History* 19, no. 4 (Spring 1989): 621–33.

22. This approach is described by James C. Scott in his article "Resistance Without Protest and Without Organization: Peasant Opposition to the Islamic *Zakat* and the Christian Tithe," *Comparative Studies in Society and History* 29, no. 1 (July 1987): 417–20; and by Patricia A. Pessar, "Unmasking the Politics of Religion: The Case of Brazilian Millenarianism," *Journal of Latin American Lore* 7, no. 2 (Winter 1981): 255–78. See also Pessar's "When Prophecy Prevails: A Study of Millenarianism in Brazil" (Ph.D. diss., University of Chicago, 1976) and "Revolution, Salvation, Extermination: The Future of Millenarianism in Brazil," in *Predicting Sociocultural Change*, ed. Susan Abbott and John van Willigen (Athens: University of Georgia Press, 1980), 95–114. The effort to emphasize culture as a meaningful part of social relations and to try to understand the personal motivations of backlanders acknowledges the work of Clifford J. Geertz; see Bradd Shore, "An Introduction to the Work of Clifford Geertz," *Soundings* 71, no. 1 (Spring 1988): 15–27. The concept of "social location" is discussed by David Hunt in "The Measure of Popular Culture," *Comparative Studies in Society and History* 31, no. 2 (April 1989): 367–68. Sandra Lauderdale Graham follows this approach in her interesting *House and Street: The Domestic World of Servants and Masters in Nineteenth-Century Rio de Janeiro* (Cambridge: Cambridge University Press, 1988).

23. See Putnam, "Translator's Introduction," iii. In 1984, Canudos was the focus of a novel by the prominent Peruvian novelist, Mario Vargas Llosa, translated into English as *The War of the End of the World*. An earlier novel along the same lines appeared in France in 1953, by Lucien Marchal (*The Sage of Canudos*, trans. Charles Duff [New York: E. P. Dutton, 1954]). The term *caboclo* comes from the Tupi language: *kari* (white) + *boka* (descended from) (courtesy of Eduardo Silva).

24. Burns, "Destruction of a Folk Past," 30. Burns cites historian Pedro Calmón, probably the most influential Brazilian scholar of the pre-1960 generation, for his characterization of Canudos as "a religious conflict generated by

backlands barbarism" (História da civilização brasileira, 4th ed. [São Paulo: Editora Nacional, 1940], 345).

25. Olímpio de Souza Andrade, "'Os sertões' numa frase de Nabuco," Planalto 1, no. 14 (December 1, 1941), cited by Putnam, "Translator's Introduction," iii; Roberto Akira Goto, "Os sertões e a imaginação de um leitor deste final de século," Revista do Instituto de Estudos Brasileiros 31 (1990): 113–28. Another reason for lagging research on Canudos has been the long-standing belief that documentation was lost or destroyed. For example, the Luiz Vianna archive was damaged beyond repair during a flood of the Paraguaçú River while stored in the house of Dr. Aristides Milton in Cachoeira; see Luiz Viana Filho to Ataliba Nogueira, Salvador, December 13, 1974, cited in Nogueira, Antônio Conselheiro e Canudos: revisão histórica, 2d ed. (São Paulo: Editora Nacional, 1978), x. See also Walnice Nogueira Galvão, "Uma ausência," in Os pobres na literatura brasileira, ed. Roberto Schwartz (São Paulo: Editora Brasiliense, 1983), 53.

26. Sylvio Rabello, Euclides da Cunha, 2d ed. (Rio de Janeiro: Civilização Brasileira, 1966), 7–8; Putnam, "Translator's Introduction," xi. A comparison of the facial features of Euclydes and his two brothers may be made by observing a studio photograph of the three, ca. 1900, in Joel Bicalho Tostes, "Cronologia de Euclides da Cunha," Revista do Livro 4 (September 1959): 8.

27. See Jornal de Alá (Salvador), 2, no. 3 (March 1940): 31–35; Dante Moreira Leite, O caráter nacional brasileiro, 4th ed. (São Paulo: Editora Pionera, 1983), 222–30; Putnam, "Translator's Introduction," x–xvii.

28. The influences on da Cunha with regard to racial questions are examined in Adelino Brandão, Euclides da Cunha e a questão racial no Brasil (Rio de Janeiro: Editora Presença, 1990). For a detailed analysis of the European racial thinkers known to da Cunha, see George L. Mosse, Toward the Final Solution (New York: Howard Fertig, 1978), esp. pt. 1.

29. See, for example, Ernest Hambloch, His Majesty the President: A Study of Constitutional Brazil (London: Methuen, 1935), 37.

30. Euclydes da Cunha, on page 616 of the third (1905) edition of Os sertões (Rebellion in the Backlands, 481), offers an author's note in which he explains his use of "bedrock" to refer to his view that the backlander is the end result of Brazil's generalized miscegenation. For a broader view of attitudes toward race in the late nineteenth and early twentieth centuries, see Thomas E. Skidmore, Black and White: Race and Nationality in Brazilian Thought (New York: Oxford University Press, 1974).

31. See Walnice Nogueira Galvão, Gatos de outro saco: ensaios críticos (São Paulo: Editora Brasiliense, 1981), esp. "Os sertões para estrangeiros," 62–84.

32. Putnam, "Translator's Introduction," xiii.

33. "Euclides da Cunha," in Dictionary of Brazilian Literature, ed. Irwin Stern (Westport, Conn.: Greenwood Press, 1989), 102–3.

34. The publisher, Laemmert, issued subsequent new editions in 1914, 1923 (two), 1925, 1926, 1927, 1929, 1933, 1936, 1938, 1940, 1942, 1944, 1945, 1946 (two), 1950, and, the twenty-second, in 1952. Thereafter several publishers brought out competing versions.

35. Putnam, "Translator's Introduction," xviii; Alfredo Bosi, "Euclides da

Cunha: vida e obras," introduction to *Os sertões: edição didática* (São Paulo: Editora Cultrix, 1985), 9–12. Dirce de Assis Cavalcanti, in *O pai* (Rio de Janeiro: Casa-Maria Editorial, 1990), offers an autobiographical account of being the daughter of the man who shot Euclydes. The details of da Cunha's personal life are summarized succinctly by Walnice Nogueira Galvão in "*Os sertões* para estrangeiros," in *Gatos de outro saco*, 62–70. Richard M. Morse compares da Cunha's use of antithesis to Thucydides's histories: see "Erecting a Boomstone," paper presented at the Conference on the Rise of the New Latin American Narrative, 1950–1975, Woodrow Wilson International Center for Scholars, Washington, D.C., October 18–20, 1979, 31–33 (courtesy of Dain Borges). For da Cunha's career, see J. Galante de Sousa, "Algumas fontes para o estudo de Euclides da Cunha," *Revista do Livro* (Rio de Janeiro), September 1959, 183–220; and J. Galante de Sousa, *Exposição comemorativa do centenário do nascimento de Euclides da Cunha, 1866–1966* (Rio de Janeiro: Biblioteca Nacional, 1966).

36. *O rei dos jagunços*, cited in Galvão, *Gatos de outro saco*, 77.

37. José Maria Bello, *A History of Modern Brazil, 1889–1964*, trans. James L. Taylor (Stanford: Stanford University Press, 1966), 151.

38. Roberto Ventura, "'A nossa Vendéia': Canudos, o mito da Revolução Francesa e a formação de identidade cultural no Brasil (1897–1902)," *Revista do Instituto de Estudos Brasileiros* 31 (1990): 130.

39. Richard M. Morse, "Brazil's Urban Development: Colony and Empire," in *From Colony to Nation: Essays on the Independence of Brazil*, ed. A. J. R. Russell-Wood (Baltimore: Johns Hopkins University Press, 1975), 180–81.

40. In the backlands of Minas Gerais and Bahia, the term *jagunço* was used more often than *cangaceiro*, whereas through the rest of the Northeast, from Sergipe to Ceará, the opposite was the case; see José Calasans, "Os jagunços de Canudos," *Caravelle* (Toulouse), no. 154 (1970); and Galvão, *Gatos de outro saco*, 74–75.

41. Putnam tells us that da Cunha thought of using "Our Vendée" instead of "Os sertões" as his title; see *Rebellion in the Backlands*, 162n.179; also, v. There is an irony in da Cunha's choice of the illustration, as Simon Schama observes, for to some the Vendée conjures up the savagery and inhumanity of its peasant rebels, but to others it is a reminder of the equally savage acts of retribution and massacre committed by the republican side; see Schama's *Citizens: A Chronicle of the French Revolution* (New York: Alfred A. Knopf, 1989), 692–93.

42. Galvão, *Gatos de outro saco*, 73.

43. Richard Graham, *Patronage and Politics*, 56, points out that this attitude is consistent with a hierarchical view of society.

44. José Murilo de Carvalho, paper presented to Brazilian Studies Committee, Conference on Latin American History, American Historical Association, San Francisco, December 30, 1989; summary, by Steven Topik, in *Hispanic American Historical Review* 70, no. 3 (August 1990): 536–37.

45. See Maria de Lourdes Mônaco Janotti, *Os subversivos da república* (São Paulo: Editora Brasiliense, 1986).

46. Maria Aparecida Rezende Mota, "A guerra de Canudos na produção do Instituto Histórico e Geográfico Brasileiro," Núcleo do Sertão Archive, Salvador, 1979, Typescript; Bello, *History of Modern Brazil*, 154–55.

47. Galvão, *Gatos de outro saco*, 72–73.

48. See Janotti, *Subversivos da república*, 265.

49. This was wishful conjecture. The mythology of Brazil's peaceful history notwithstanding, authorities always waged war against rebellious or "uncivilized" populations. Consider, for example, the expeditions against the runaway slave "republic" of Palmares in the 1690s. The Inconfidência Bahiana of 1798, also known as the Revolt of the Tailors, saw literate mulatto (part-Caucasian, part-African) freedmen conspire to import the French Revolution to Brazil in order to end both slavery and the monopoly of whites on government jobs and other privileges.

50. Alfred de Carvalho, "A imprensa baiana de 1811 a 1899," *Revista do Instituto Histórico e Geográfico da Bahia* 6, no. 6 (1905): 21–22, cited by Walnice Nogueira Galvão, *No calor da hora: a guerra de Canudos nos jornais, 4ª expedição* (São Paulo: Editora Ática, 1974), 15.

51. "Manifesto de Antônio Conselheiro," in *A Notícia* (Rio de Janeiro), n.d., cited in Galvão, *No calor da hora*, 43–44.

52. *Diário de Notícias*, September 22, 1897, 1.

53. For example, the Monumento Department Store ran the following advertisement: "The Canet Cannon, which is expected to arrive soon, with its 10 centimeter bore and caliber in excess of 32, will not cause the astonishment that will be created by the varied assortment of inexpensive shoes available at O Monumento" (July 23, 1897; see Galvão, *No calor da hora*, 49–53).

54. Eduardo's older brothers included Antônio, a leading slaveholder planter-entrepreneur and imperial-era politician linked to São Paulo's commercial success, and Martinho, Jr., an outspoken republican. See Darrell E. Levi, *The Prados of São Paulo, Brazil: An Elite Family and Social Change, 1840–1930* (Athens: University of Georgia Press, 1987).

55. Quoted in ibid., 172.

56. See the journalist Carlos de Laet's angry response, cited in Ataliba Nogueira, "Centenário de Carlos de Laet," *Revista da Academia Brasileira de Letras* 74 (1984): 73, cited in Nogueira, *Antônio Conselheiro e Canudos*, 21.

57. For the conventional view, see Major R. A. Cunha Mattos to Col. Souza Menezes, Cumbe, March 5, 1897, Núcleo do Sertão Archive, Salvador.

58. Bello, *History of Modern Brazil*, 153.

59. Quoted in Levi, *Prados of São Paulo*, 172–73.

60. Delso Renault, *A vida brasileira no final do século XIX* (Rio de Janeiro: José Olympio Editora, 1987), 178.

61. Carlos de Laet, as cited in Nogueira, "Centenário de Carlos de Laet."

62. Levi, *Prados of São Paulo*, 174, 245n.62. See *O Estado de São Paulo*, March 1–20, 1897. Prado's last major monarchist statement, *Salvemos o Brasil*, was published in Rio de Janeiro in 1899 under the pen name "Graccho." See also June E. Hahner, *Civilian-Military Relations in Brazil, 1889–1898* (Columbia: University of South Carolina Press, 1969), 175.

63. Carlos de Laet, as cited in Nogueira, "Centenario de Carlos de Laet," 246.

64. Da Cunha, *Rebellion in the Backlands*, 279/*Os sertões*, 249.

65. Raimundo Nina Rodrigues, *As collectividades anormaes* (1897; reprinted Rio de Janeiro: Civilização Brasileira, 1939), 70. David Pace examines the broad

nineteenth-century search for a systematic science of human nature, which motivated Nina Rodrigues and his contemporary analysts of Canudos; see Pace, *Claude Lévi-Strauss: The Bearer of Ashes* (London: Routledge & Kegan Paul, 1983), 79. See also Charles Rosenberg, "The Bitter Fruit: Heredity, Disease, and Social Thought," in *No Other Gods: On Science and American Social Thought* (Baltimore: Johns Hopkins University Press, 1976), 25–53; and Mariza Corrêa, "As ilusões da liberdade: a escola Nina Rodrigues e a antropologia no Brasil" (Ph.D. diss., Universidade de São Paulo, 1982). Nina Rodrigues's career and writings are discussed also by Brandão, *Euclides da Cunha*.

66. "Wolsey" [César Zama], *Libello republicano: acompanhado dos commentários sobre a campanha de Canudos*. Salvador: *Diário da Bahia*, 1899.

67. The speech was scheduled to have been made to the Senate on November 6, 1897; it was published years later in *Obras completas de Rui Barbosa* (Rio de Janeiro: Ministério da Educação e Saúde, 1987), 24:183–87.

68. Interview with Francisco de Assis Barbosa, Rio de Janeiro, Fundação Casa Rui Barbosa, June 16, 1985.

69. Euclydes da Cunha, *Canudos e inéditos (diário de uma expedição)* (Rio de Janeiro: José Olympio Editora, 1939), 41.

70. The best study of this event and its context is Kenneth R. Maxwell's *Conflicts and Conspiracies: Brazil and Portugal, 1750–1808* (Cambridge: Cambridge University Press, 1973). "Savage" Brazilindians, it should be noted, fared no better. On May 3, 1808, Dom João VI declared war on the Botocudo Indians in Minas province and sent military forces against Espírito Santo, Pôrto Seguro, Bahia, and São Paulo. In 1817, a republican revolt in Pernambuco was led by priests and Masons, most graduates of the seminary at Olinda; it was crushed by naval bombardment and by the invasion of troops from loyalist Bahia. Bloody revolts occurred in Pará in 1831, in Pernambuco (the restorationist War of the Cabanos) in 1832–35, in Minas in 1833, in Mato Grosso and Maranhão in 1834, in Rio Grande do Sul in 1835–45, and in Pernambuco again (the Insurreição Praieira) in 1848–49. See José Carlos Ferreira, "Princípios jacobinos, sedição de 1798 na Bahia," *Revista do Instituto Geográfico e Histórico da Bahia*, no. 267 (1900): 371–411. See also Leslie Bethell and José Murilo de Carvalho, "Brazil from Independence to the Middle of the Nineteenth Century," in *The Cambridge History of Latin America*, ed. Leslie Bethell (Cambridge: Cambridge University Press, 1986), 3:679–746; Emília Viotti da Costa, *The Brazilian Empire: Myths and Histories* (Chicago: University of Chicago Press, 1986); Peter Flynn, *Brazil: A Political Analysis* (London: Ernest Benn, 1978), 11. On Pernambuco, see Edison Carneiro, *A insurreição praieira, 1848–1849* (Rio de Janeiro: Civilização Brasileira, 1960).

71. Abguar Bastos, *A visão histórico-sociológica de Euclides da Cunha* (São Paulo: Editora Nacional, 1986), 7–8.

72. For *candomblé*'s influence in urban households during the 1890s, see the novel by Xavier Marques, *O feiticeiro* (1897; reprinted São Paulo and Brasília: Editora GRD and Instituto Nacional do Livro, 1975); Dain Borges, "El reverso fatal de los acontecimientos: dos momentos de la degeneración en la literatura brasileña," in *Humanismo e hispanidad: ensayos en homenaje a Juan Marichal*, ed. Birute Ciplijauskaite and Christopher Mauer (forthcoming) (courtesy of Dain Borges).

73. See Riolando Azzi, "Elementos para a história do catolicismo popular," *Revista Eclesiástica Brasileira* (Petrópolis) 36, no. 141 (March 1976): 95–130.

74. See Alexandre H. Otten, S.V.D., "'Só Deus é grande': a mensagem religiosa de Antônio Conselheiro," 2 vols. (Ph.D. diss., Pontifica Universitas Gregoriana, Rome, 1987), anexo, 6.

75. *Falla do Presidente da Provincia da Bahia . . . 1887* (Salvador, 1887).

76. The French Catholic church was motivated in the late eighteenth century to launch evangelical preaching missions in both Paris and the provinces for precisely the same reason; see Schama, *Citizens*, 169.

77. Cobban, *History of Modern France*, 39.

78. The movement to neo-orthodox centralization, ultramontanism, literally means "beyond the mountains," that is, to transfer power from the secular states of northern Europe—England, France, and Germany—back to Rome; see *New Catholic Encyclopedia* (New York: McGraw Hill, 1967), 10:967, 14:380. Ironically, the ultramontanist doctrine, in holding the state, considered a profane institution, subordinate to the church, permitted the Brazilian church hierarchy to accept the separation of church and state in 1891, since doctrinally it was no longer essential that the church fight in the political arena.

79. Courtesy of Renato Ferraz. See Ralph della Cava, *Miracle at Joaseiro* (New York: Columbia University Press, 1970), 20–22.

80. *New Catholic Encyclopedia* 10:968.

81. Luiz Gomes Palacin, S.J., in Luiz Gomes Palacin and Francisco José de Oliveira, *História da diocese de Paulo Afonso* (Goiania: Diocese de Paulo Afonso, 1988), n.p. (courtesy of Janaína Amado).

82. See Steven Topik, *The Political Economy of the Brazilian State, 1889–1930* (Austin: University of Texas Press, 1987), 12.

83. Ralph della Cava, "Brazilian Messianism and National Institutions: A Reappraisal of Canudos and Joaseiro," *Hispanic American Historical Review* 48, no. 3 (August 1968): 405. *Beatos* and *beatas* were not simply pious lay persons; their status had to be conferred by a priest (courtesy Ralph della Cava).

84. Luiz Gomes Palacin, in Palacin and Oliveira, *História da diocese de Paulo Afonso*.

85. Burns, "Destruction of a Folk Past," 19.

86. Da Cunha, *Rebellion in the Backlands*, 148, cited in ibid., 22.

87. Consuelo Novais Sampaio, "Da transição política da república ao movimento de Canudos," paper presented at the seminar "A República e o Movimento de Canudos," Museu Eugenio Teixeira, Salvador, October 17, 1989.

88. See telegram from editors of the newspapers *Correio de Notícias, Jornal de Notícias, Diário da Bahia, Gazeta de Notícias, Pantheon, Diário de Notícias,* and *Cidade do Salvador* to their counterparts in Rio de Janeiro, March 14, 1897, cited in Aristides A. Milton, "A campanha de Canudos: memória lida no Instituto Histórico e Geográfico Brasileiro," *Revista trimensal do Instituto* (Rio de Janeiro) 63, pt. 2 (1902): 33–35 (printed text of a presentation to the Instituto de História e Geografia, Rio de Janeiro, October 17, 1897).

89. *Falla com que abriu no dia 1º de maio de 1889 da Assembleia Legislativa Provincial da Bahia o Exmo. Desembargador Aurélio Ferreira Espinheira, 1º Vice-Presidente da Província* (Salvador: Diário da Bahia, 1889), 60.

90. See ibid., 98, blaming the necessity of importing foreign workers "due to the law of May 13th"; and Secretaria da Agricultura, Viação e Obras Públicas, *Relatório apresentado ao Dr. Gov. do Estado da Bahia pelo Engenheiro Civil José Antônio Costa* (Bahia: Typ. *Correio de Notícias*, 1897), 31. In the end, unlike subsidized colonization programs in the South, which brought up to two hundred thousand settlers from Europe each year, very few immigrants came and stayed in Bahia or in other northern states.

91. Sampaio, "Da transição política," 7. See Robert M. Levine, *A velha usina: Pernambuco na federação brasileira, 1889–1937* (Rio de Janeiro: Paz e Terra, 1980), app. C, 267.

92. *Falla com que abriu no dia 1º de maio de 1889*, 60–64.

93. The following were prohibited from voting: women, males under the age of twenty-one, beggars, men who could not sign their names, members of cloistered religious orders, and foot soldiers.

94. See Eduardo Prado, *A ilusão americana* (1892; reprinted São Paulo: IBRASA, 1980).

95. See Joseph L. Love, *São Paulo in the Brazilian Federation, 1889–1937* (Stanford: Stanford University Press, 1980), esp. 104–79.

96. Topik, *Political Economy*, 32–36.

97. Francisco Marques de Góes Calmon, *Vida econômico-financeira da Bahia: elementos para a história de 1808 a 1899* (reprinted Salvador: Imprensa Oficial, 1982), 134. For an excellent treatment of exchange rates and economic policy in the old republic, see Winston Fritsch, *External Constraints on Economic Policy, 1889–1930* (Pittsburgh: University of Pittsburgh Press, 1988). See also Topik, "Brazil's Bourgeois Revolution?" 3.

98. Eul-Soo Pang, "Banditry and Messianism in Brazil, 1870–1940: An Agrarian Crisis Hypothesis," *Proceedings of the Pacific Coast Council on Latin American Studies* 8 (1981–82): 1–24.

99. See Nertan Macedo, *Memorial de Vila Nova* (Rio de Janeiro: Typ. *O Cruzeiro*, 1964), 117; Pang, "Banditry and Messianism," 15.

100. See Angelina Nobre Rolim Garcez, "Aspetos econômicos do episódio de Canudos" (Master's thesis, Universidade Federal da Bahia, 1977), esp. 5–12; Pang, "Banditry and Messianism," 4.

101. Campos Salles to Prudente de Morais, São Paulo, April 2, 1897, Prudente de Morais Papers, cited by Hahner, *Civilian-Military Relations*, 171.

102. *A República* (Rio de Janeiro), February 20, 21, 22, 1897.

103. See Janotti, *Subversivos da república*, 154–55.

104. Cited by Hahner, *Civilian-Military Relations*, 168–69.

105. This account draws on Hahner's comprehensive study, *Civilian-Military Relations*.

106. See della Cava, *Miracle at Joaseiro*, 9–31.

107. General Commandante em Chefe Arthur Oscar de Andrade Guimarães, Ordem do dia 102, Canudos, October 6, 1897, in Museu da Polícia Militar, São Paulo.

108. *O Jacobino*, October 13, 1897, 2.

109. Bello, *History of Modern Brazil*, 156. See also Prudente de Morais to Rui Barbosa, Rio de Janeiro, November 13, 1897, thanking Barbosa for his "services

to the cause of legality" after Major Bittencourt's death; Casa Rui Barbosa Archive.

110. Raymundo Faoro, *Os donos do poder: formação do patronato político brasileiro* (Porto Alegre: Editora Globo, 1977), 2:561.

111. Rui Barbosa, speech, Salvador, July 7, 1897, in *O Comércio de São Paulo*, July 9, 1897, 1.

112. The most influential were Rodolpho Theophilo's *A secca de 1919* (Rio de Janeiro: Editora Imperial, 1922) and José Américo de Almeida's *A Parahyba e seus problemas*, 2d ed. (Porto Alegre: Editora Globo, 1937). For an overview of the literature on the drought as a regional issue, see Roger L. Cunniff, "The Great Drought: Northeast Brazil, 1877–1880" (Ph.D. diss., University of Texas, Austin, 1970); Robert M. Levine, *Pernambuco in the Brazilian Federation, 1889–1937* (Stanford: Stanford University Press, 1978).

113. See Charles Ballard, "Drought and Economic Distress: South Africa in the 1800s," *Journal of Interdisciplinary History* 17, no. 2 (August 1986): esp. 359–360.

114. Gerald Michael Greenfield, "Images of a Region: The Brazilian Northeast and the Great Drought in the Nineteenth Century," paper presented at the 46th International Congress of Americanists, Amsterdam, July 4–8, 1988, 1–3; Evaldo Cabral de Melo, *O norte agrário e o império, 1871–1889* (Rio de Janeiro: Editora Nova Fronteira, 1984), 13, cited in ibid., n. 2.

115. Greenfield, "Images," 3–4. See also the same author's "Migrant Behavior and Elite Attitudes: Brazil's Great Drought, 1877–89," *The Americas* 43, no. 1 (July 1986): 69–85; and Melo, *O norte agrário*.

116. Brazilian authors in favor of the monarchy such as Manoel de Oliveira Lima contributed to this interpretation, arguing that the "democratic" monarchy under Pedro II had entered after 1850 a "golden age" (Lima, *América latina e América inglesa: a evolução brasileira comparada com a hispano-americana e com a anglo-americana* (Rio de Janeiro: Livraria Garnier, 1914), as did the North American missionaries D. P. Kidder and J. C. Fletcher in their *Brazil and the Brazilians, Portrayed in Historical and Descriptive Sketches* (Philadelphia: Childs & Peterson, 1857).

117. Hamilton de Mattos Monteiro, "Violência no Nordeste rural: 1850–1889" (Ph.D. diss, Universidade de São Paulo, 1978), 8–9, 38, 41–43, 67, 69 (later published as *Crise agrária e luta de classes: o Nordeste brasileiro entre 1850 e 1889* [Brasília: Editora Horizonte, 1980]).

118. The unusually high level of violence during the campaign was noted in the study by Francisco Marques de Góes Calmon, commissioned for the commemorative edition of the hundredth anniversary of the founding of the *Diário oficial da Bahia*; see his *Vida econômico-financeira da Bahia*, 120–21.

119. See Linda Lewin, "The Oligarchical Limitations of Social Banditry in Brazil: The Case of the 'Good' Thief Antônio Silvino," *Past & Present* 27, no. 82 (February 1979): 116–36; Hamilton de Mattos Monteiro, "Violência no Nordeste rural," 70–73.

120. José Honório Rodrigues, *The Brazilians: Their Character and Aspirations*, trans. Ralph Dimmick (Austin: University of Texas Press, 1980), 12; see also Janaína Amado, *Conflito social no Brasil: a revolta dos "Mucker"* (São Paulo: Duas Cidades, 1978).

121. See Clóvis Moura, *Rebeliões da senzala: quilombos insurreições guerrilhas* (Rio de Janeiro: Editora Conquista, 1972), 190.

122. Jason W. Clay, "The Articulation of Non-capitalist Agricultural Production Systems with Capitalist Exchange Systems: The Case of Garanhuns, Brazil, 1845–1977" (Ph.D. diss., Cornell University, 1979), 31.

123. Quoted by Rodrigues, *The Brazilians*, 24.

124. Satyro de Oliveira Dias (Diretor Geral), *Relatório sobre a instrucção pública no estado da Bahia* (Salvador: Typ. *Diário da Bahia*, 1894), 5, suppl.

125. *Relatório do Inspector do Thesouro . . . ao Dr. Governador do Estado em 12 de maio de 1896* (Salvador: Typ. *Correio de Notícias*, 1896), 4–20.

126. Richard Graham, *Patronage and Politics*, 177.

127. Jeffrey D. Needell, *A Tropical Belle Epoque: Elite Culture and Society in Turn-of-the-Century Rio de Janeiro* (Cambridge: Cambridge University Press, 1987), 218.

128. Frei Vicente do Salvador, *História do Brasil, 1500–1627*, cited by Lyle N. McAlister, *Spain and Portugal in the New World, 1492–1700* (Minneapolis: University of Minnesota Press, 1984), 271.

129. Barman, *Brazil*, 35.

130. Ibid., 49. See also Maria Beatriz Nizza da Silva's *Análise de estratificação social: o Rio de Janeiro de 1808 a 1821* (São Paulo: Faculdade de Filosofia, Letras e Ciências Humanas, Universidade de São Paulo, 1975) and *Cultura e sociedade no Rio de Janeiro, 1808–1821* (São Paulo: Editora Nacional, 1977).

131. Barman, *Brazil*, 164–65.

132. See Levine, *Pernambuco*.

133. Lauderdale Graham, *House and Street*, 64.

134. See A. J. R. Russell-Wood, "Prestige, Power, and Piety in Colonial Brazil: The Third Orders of Salvador," *Hispanic American Historical Review* 69, no. 1 (February 1989): 60–89.

135. John Lynch, "The Catholic Church in Latin America, 1830–1930," in *The Cambridge History of Latin America*, vol. 4: *Ca. 1870 to 1930* (Cambridge: Cambridge University Press, 1986), 552.

136. On nineteenth-century Latin American photography, see Robert M. Levine, *Images of History: Nineteenth and Early Twentieth Century Latin American Photographs as Documents* (Durham, N.C.: Duke University Press, 1989).

137. De Barros's studio was located at Rua da Misericórdia, N° 3. See Paulo Zanettini, "Memórias do fim do mundo," *Revista Horizonte Geográfico* (São Paulo) 1, no. 3 (September–October 1988): 28–38. A second photographer who accompanied the battle, a Spaniard named Juan Gutierrez, became the first war photographer in Latin America to be killed in action.

138. Katia de Queirós Mattoso, *Família e sociedade na Bahia do século XIX* (São Paulo: Editora Corrupio, 1988), 139. See also Eul-Soo Pang, *In Pursuit of Honor and Power: Noblemen of the Southern Cross in Nineteenth-Century Brazil* (Tuscaloosa: University of Alabama Press, 1988).

139. Linda Lewin, *Politics and Parentela in Paraíba* (Princeton: Princeton University Press, 1987), 186.

140. Vilfredo Pareto, *The Rise and Fall of Elites: An Appreciation of Theoretical Sociology* (Totowa, N.J.: Bedminster Press, 1968); Gaetano Mosca, *The Ruling*

*Class* (New York: McGraw-Hill, 1939). See also Edward C. Hansen and Timothy C. Parrish, "Elites vs. the State," in *Elites: Ethnographic Issues,* ed. George E. Marcus (Albuquerque: University of New Mexico Press, 1983), 270.

141. See Lewin, *Politics and Parentela,* 180–81.

142. Katia de Queirós Mattoso (*Família e sociedade,* 140–42) shows that 35 percent of the total became adoptive *fluminenses.*

143. Pang, *In Pursuit of Honor and Power*; Joseph L. Love, Review of Pang, in *Hispanic American Historical Review* 69, no. 3 (August 1989): 609.

144. Lewin, *Politics and Parentela,* 21; Faoro, *Os donos do poder* 2:568.

145. As late as the nineteenth century, whales migrated northward from Antarctica into Bahian waters, making whale hunting a major activity from May through November; see Nevin O. Winter, *Brazil and Her People of To-Day* (Boston: L. C. Page, 1910), 28.

146. Stuart B. Schwartz, *Sugar Plantations in the Formation of Brazilian Society: Bahia, 1550–1835* (Cambridge: Cambridge University Press, 1985), 75; A. J. R. Russell-Wood, *The Black Man in Slavery and Freedom in Colonial Brazil* (New York: St. Martin's Press, 1982), 27; C. R. Boxer, *The Golden Age of Brazil, 1695–1750* (Berkeley and Los Angeles: University of California Press, 1962), 126–27.

147. Estado da Bahia, *Brazil: o estado da Bahia. Notícias para o emigrante* (Salvador: Empreza Editora, 1897), 3.

148. For an account of how the city of Salvador has only recently begun to preserve memories of urban Afro-Brazilian culture, see "De povo para povo," *Isto é senhor,* September 12, 1990, 53–54.

149. Charles Wagley, *Introduction to Brazil* (New York: Columbia University Press, 1963), 221–22.

150. After the 1920s, Bahian politicians cleverly took advantage of the panoply of gods, becoming sponsors (*ogan*) of one or more cults to court support from urban voters.

151. Gilberto Freyre seemed to consider this a positive characteristic, although he was always publicly ambivalent if privately identified with Afro-Brazilian culture and its "soft, feminine" side; see his rarely cited essay, "Acontece que são Baianos," in *Problemas brasileiros de antropologia,* 2d ed. (Rio de Janeiro: José Olympio Editora, 1959), esp. 270–71.

152. Hakon Mielche, *From Santos to Bahia* (London: William Hodge, 1948), 314.

153. Antonio Sérgio Alfredo Guimarães, "Estrutura e formação das classes sociais na Bahia," *Novos estudos CEBRAP* 18 (September 1987): 68. The term *branco de dinheiro* actually came from Cabo Verde; see Deirdre Meintel, *Race, Culture, and Portuguese Colonialism in Cabo Verde* (Syracuse, N.Y.: Maxwell School of Citizenship and Public Affairs, 1984), 160.

154. Winter, *Brazil and Her People,* 33.

155. Arnold Wildberger, *Os presidentes da província da Bahia, 1824–1889* (Salvador: Typ. Beneditina, 1979), 739; Meintel, *Race, Culture, and Portuguese Colonialism,* 122.

156. João José Reis, "Slave Resistance in Brazil: Bahia, 1807–1835," *Luso-Brazilian Review* 25, no. 1 (Summer 1988): 111–15.

157. Ibid., 128–29, citing Souza Martins, president of the province of Bahia,

to Brazilian Minister of Justice, February 14, 1835, in *Correspondência presidential,* vol. 682, fol. 10–10v, Estado da Bahia, Arquivo Público, Salvador.

158. For example, the census omitted thirty-two parishes throughout the empire, 10,993 Indians in Maranhão, and 4,059 residents of Rio de Janeiro province; see J. P. Favilla Nunes, "Population, territoire, électorat," in *Le Brésil en 1889 avec une carte de l'empire en chromolithographie,* ed. Frederico José de Santa-Anna Nery (Paris: Librairie Charles Delagrave, 1889) (a handbook produced for the Paris Universal Exposition), 191–92. Salvador's population in 1897 was estimated at 200,000; see Mário Augusto da Silva Santos, "Sobrevivência e tensões sociais: Salvador (1890–1930)" (Ph.D. diss., Universidade de São Paulo, 1982), 27.

159. Only three thousand foreign agricultural workers recruited by the government entered Bahia in the 1890s, most of them Spanish or Portuguese who then abandoned their agricultural homesteads and migrated to the capital; see Santos, "Sobrevivências e tensões sociais," 28.

160. Calmon, *Vida econômico-financeira,* 136–38.

161. For a study of rainfall shortages in the *sertão* and the historical impact, see Garibaldi de Mello Carvalho, "Esboço de análise ecológica," in *Estudos nordestinos* (São Paulo) 1 (1961): 49–61.

162. See Francisco Foot Hardman, *Trem fantasma: a modernidade na selva* (São Paulo: Companhia das Letras, 1988), 67–68.

163. See Eul-Soo Pang, *Bahia in the First Brazilian Republic: Coronelismo and Oligarchies, 1889–1934* (Gainesville: University Presses of Florida, 1979), 62.

164. Lauderdale Graham, *House and Street,* 73.

165. Mark D. Szuchman, *Order: Family and Community in Buenos Aires, 1810–1860* (Stanford: Stanford University Press, 1988), 27–28.

166. Ibid., 27. Szuchman's observations for Argentina hold true for Brazil as well.

167. Lewin, *Politics and Parentela,* 10.

168. See Luiz Henrique Dias Tavares, "Duas reformas de educação na Bahia, 1895–1925," Centro Regional de Pesquisas Educacionais da Bahia, Salvador, 1968; Hildegardes Vianna, "Breve notícia sobre acontecimentos na Bahia no início do século XX," Universidade Federal da Bahia, Centro de Estudos Baianos, Salvador, 1983.

169. See Edgard Carone, *A república velha,* vol. 1: *Instituições e classes sociais (1889–1930),* 4th ed. (São Paulo: DIFEL, 1970).

170. For Bahia's role in the federation, see Pang, *Bahia in the First Brazilian Republic;* cf. Levine, *Pernambuco.* For the later period, see Angela Maria de Castro Gomes et al., *Regionalismo e centralização política: partidos e constituinte nos anos 30* (Rio de Janeiro: Editora Nova Fronteira, 1980), esp. pt. 4.

171. For a revealing analysis of railroads and the nineteenth-century Brazilian idea of progress, focusing not on the Northeast but on the penetration of the jungle, see Hardman, *Trem fantasma.* For the Northeast, see Ademar Benévolo, *Introdução à história ferroviária do Brasil (estudo social, político e histórico)* (Recife: Edições Folha da Manhã, 1953).

172. Peter Lasslett makes the same comment for English historians' acceptance of certain features of Marxist historical sociology without making any

"conspicuous effort to understand"; see *The World We Have Lost: England Before the Industrial Age* (New York: Scribner, 1965), 240.

173. Tom Wolfe, "Stalking the Billion-footed Beast," *Harper's*, November 1989, 55.

174. In Brazil this view was expressed as early as 1871 by Sergipe-born Sílvio Romero (1851–1914), who studied themes as diverse as animal magnetism, evolution, literature, and the songs and poems of rural northeasterners and whose characteristic personal mood throughout the period was one of depression. Romero's writing clearly anticipated da Cunha's fears that Brazil's cultural, social, and racial gap between its coastal and hinterland populations imperiled the nation's future. Decades later, the emergence of northeastern regionalist literature continued this preoccupation. Unlike the Paulistas, who emphasized the more exotic Indian heritage, José Lins do Rêgo and contemporary writers dwelled on what they considered to be the anthropological liabilities of *caboclo* and *mulato* race mixture. See Flora Süssekind, *Tal Brasil, qual romance? Uma ideologia estética e sua história: o naturalismo* (Rio de Janeiro: Editora Achiamé, 1984); Dain Borges, "Progress and Degeneration in Brazilian Social Thought of the 1930s," paper presented at the Latin American Studies Association 15th International Congress, Miami, December 5, 1989.

175. Perhaps the best of many works interpreting da Cunha's literary style and significance is Sevcenko, *Literatura como missão*. See also Gilberto Freyre, *Perfil de Euclides e outros perfis* (Rio de Janeiro: José Olympio Editora, 1944). Da Cunha's letters to fellow writers and to academicians are collected in F. Venâncio Filho, *Euclydes da Cunha e seus amigos* (São Paulo: Editora Nacional, 1938).

176. Euclydes da Cunha to José Veríssimo, Lorena, December 3, 1902; and to Francisco Escobar, November 27, 1903; reprinted in F. V. Filho, *Euclydes da Cunha e seus amigos*, 79–80, 113; cited in Needell, *Tropical Belle Epoque*, 221.

177. Sources consulted for this section include the records of the Brazilian army stored at the 6th Military Region headquarters in Salvador; the archives of the Bahian State Police; records of the Cúria of the Catholic church in Salvador; Antônio Conselheiro's own homilies and sermons, the manuscripts of which are stored in the Arquivo Público in Salvador; and material collected at the Centro de Estudos Brasileiros' Núcleo do Sertão Archive, Salvador.

178. As evidence that the *Missão abreviada* was widely circulated, it should be noted that already in 1876 the missal, published in Pôrto and used across the Lusophone world, had gone through five editions. See Padre Manoel José Gonçalves Couto, *Missão abreviada para despertar os descuidados, converter os peccadores e sustentar o fructo das missões*, 1st ed. (Pôrto: Sebastião José Pereira, 1873).

179. Da Cunha, *Rebellion in the Backlands*, 72ff./*Os sertões*, 87ff.

180. Ibid., 94–95/101.

181. The term *caboclo* has varied meanings in Brazil. In the most general social sense, a *caboclo* is the Brazilian approximation of the Spanish-American *mestizo* or, simply, a lower-class peasant. Some maintain that the *caboclo* is essentially a northern type; others contend that the *caboclo* is a phenomenon of the South. The word also has racial connotations: viz., a person of mixed Indian and Caucasian ancestry. Usually, in the case of the backlands, a Negroid admixture

is included as well. See James B. Watson, "Way Station of Modernization: The Brazilian Caboclo," in *Brazil: Papers Presented in the Institute for Brazilian Studies, Vanderbilt University*, ed. James B. Watson et al. (Nashville: Vanderbilt University Press, 1953), 9.

182. Statement of Antonio Marques da Silva, Itapicurú, March 19, 1965, in "Jagunços" file, Núcleo do Sertão Archive, Salvador.

183. See, for example, Regimento Policial da Bahia, *Livro de registro de ordens do dia*, Arquivo Geral do Quartel dos Aflitos, Salvador, 3º Corpo do Regimento Policial da Bahia, 4ª Companhia, 1889–1904.

184. Ronald H. Chilcote, "Protest and Resistance in Brazil and Portuguese Africa: A Synthesis and Classification," in *Protest and Resistance in Angola and Brazil: Comparative Studies* (Berkeley and Los Angeles: University of California Press, 1972), 244–45.

## CHAPTER 2

1. Manoel Jesuíno Ferreira, *A província da Bahia. Apontamentos* (Rio de Janeiro: Typ. Nacional, 1875), 5–7.

2. Durval Vieira de Aguiar, *Descrições práticas da província da Bahia* (1882; reprinted Rio de Janeiro: Editora Cátedra, 1979), 58.

3. On the missions, see Manuel Correia de Andrade, *The Land and People of Northeast Brazil*, trans. Dennis V. Johnson (Albuquerque: University of New Mexico Press, 1980), 141.

4. John Hemming, "Indians and the Frontier in Colonial Brazil," in *The Cambridge History of Latin America*, ed. Leslie Bethell (Cambridge: Cambridge University Press, 1986), 2:515. Hemming notes (519) that many—sometimes half—of the Indians forcibly transported to new sites died during the trek.

5. The first Bahian mission, at Monte Calvário (today, Carmo, a district of the city of Salvador), founded in 1549, was also the first Jesuit mission in Latin America; see Serafim Leite, S.J., *História da Companhia de Jesus no Brasil*, vol. 5: *Da Bahia ao Nordeste: estabelecimentos e assuntos locais* (Rio de Janeiro: Instituto Nacional do Livro, 1945).

6. See Marco A. M. Martins and Marcos L. L. Messider, "Notas sobre a história e a organização política tuxá," Núcleo do Sertão Archive, Salvador, October 1988, Typescript; Thalez de Azevedo, *Italianos na Bahia e outros temas* (Salvador: Empresa Gráfica da Bahia, 1989); Pietro Vittorino Regni, *Os Capuchinos na Bahia* (Porto Alegre: Escola Superior de Teologia São Lourenço de Brindes, 1988).

7. Serafim Leite, *História da Companhia de Jesus no Brasil*, 286.

8. On the Capuchins, see Maria Hilda Baqueiro Paraíso, "Os Capuchinhos e os Índios na sul da Bahia: uma análise preliminar de sua atuação," *Revista do Museu Paulista*, n.s., 31 (1986); Regni, *Os Capuchinos*; Thalez de Azevedo, *Italianos na Bahia*, 37.

9. Courtesy Renato Ferraz. On the missions, see the Franciscan priest Martin of Nantes's *Relation succincte et sincère* . . . (Quimper, ca. 1707; reprinted Salvador, 1952).

10. There were other large landowning families as well, including the

Guedes de Brito clan, which controlled more than 160 square leagues from the Morro do Chapéu to the Rio das Velhas. See Andrade, *Land and People of Northeast Brazil*, 142.

11. These lands, ceded to the Indian villages, were considered legally sacrosanct until 1879, when the director of the Brazilian Indian Service, the viscount of Sergimirim (nephew of the baron of Jeremoabo), nullified the Indian claims. Land was affected in the region of Jeremoabo, Itapicurú, and Pombal. See Carlos Ott, *Vestígios de cultura indígena no sertão da Bahia* (Salvador: Secretaria de Educação e Saúde, 1945).

12. For the history of the ecclesiastical administration of the modern diocese of Paulo Afonso, which includes the former site of Canudos and most of the districts from which Conselheiro's followers came, see Palacin and Oliveira, *História da diocese de Paulo Afonso*. The early history of the region is also treated by da Cunha in *Rebellion in the Backlands*, 79–198.

13. The early history of the district is described in Renato Ferraz, Manuel Antonio dos Santos Neto, and José Carlos da Costa Pinheiro, *Cartilha histórica de Canudos* (Canudos and Salvador: Prefeitura Municipal de Canudos and Universidade do Estado da Bahia, 1991), 15–18.

14. For a case study of the Tuxá mission run by French Capuchins in Missão de Rodas, see Martins and Messider, "Notas."

15. Ferraz, Neto, and Pinheiro, *Cartilha histórica*, 19–27.

16. See Paraíso, "Os Capuchinhos e os Índios na sul da Bahia."

17. Joan Ellen Meznar, "Deference and Dependence: The World of Small Farmers in a Northeastern Brazilian Community, 1850–1900" (Ph.D. diss., University of Texas, Austin, 1986), 111–23. In Paraíba, small plots cost as little as the equivalent of U.S. $50 in the late nineteenth century. *Foreiros* (rent-paying tenants) were sometimes affluent, and when they wanted to could afford to buy land outright. A good overview of the late colonial land tenure system is provided by Stuart B. Schwartz, "Elite Politics and the Growth of a Peasantry in Late Colonial Brazil," in *From Colony to Nation: Essays on the Independence of Brazil*, ed. A. J. R. Russell-Wood (Baltimore: Johns Hopkins University Press, 1975), 133–54.

18. Jeremy Krikler, "Agrarian Struggle and the South African War," *Social History* 14, no. 2 (May 1989): 153–55. A classic overview of European, and especially French, rural life is Marc Bloch's *French Rural History: An Essay on Its Basic Characteristics*, trans. Janet Sondheimer (Berkeley and Los Angeles: University of California Press, 1966).

19. Bom Conselho fell under his control in January 1882; see "Tranquilidade pública," *Relatório com que o Exm.º Sr. Conselheiro do Estado João Lustosa da Cunha Paranaguá passou no dia 5 de janeiro a administração da província . . . ao Dr. João Reis Souza Dantas* (Salvador: Typ. *Diário da Bahia*, 1882), 6.

20. See *Relatório apresentado a Assemblea Legislativa da Bahia pelo Excellentíssimo Senhor Barão de São Lourenço, presidente da mesma província em 6 de março de 1870* (Salvador: Typ. *Jornal da Bahia*, 1870), 6, 12, 19; and *Relatório com que o Dr. José Eduardo Freire de Carvalho passou a administração da Província ao Exm.º Sr. Com. Antonio Cândido da Cruz Machado em 22 de outubro de 1873* (Salvador: Typ. *Correio da Bahia*, 1873), 16; *Falla com que o Exm.º Sr. Conselheiro Theodoro Machado Freire*

*Pereira da Silva abrio (sic.) a 1ª sessão da 26ª legislatura da Assemblea Geral Provincial no dia 3 de abril de 1886* (Salvador: Typ. *Gazeta da Bahia,* 1886), 9.

21. *Falla dirigida à Assemblea Provincial da Bahia pelo 1°vice-presidente Dezembargador João José de Almeida Couto no 1º março 1873* (Salvador: Typ. *Diário da Bahia,* 1873), anexo; *Relatório com que o Exmº Sr. Presidente Dr. Luiz Antônio da Silva Nunes abriu a Assemblea Legislativa Provincial da Bahia no dia 1º de maio de 1876* (Salvador: Typ. *Jornal da Bahia,* 1876), 43.

22. *Relatório com que o Excellentísimo Senhor Conselheiro Barão de São Lourenço passou a administração da provincia ao primeiro vice-presidente o Exmº Sr. Dezembargador João José de Almeida Couto em 20 de maio de 1870* (Salvador: Typ. *Diário da Bahia,* 1870), 16.

23. Victor Turner, *The Ritual Process: Structure and Anti-Structure* (Ithaca: Cornell University Press, 1969), 18; Helena Lepovitz and Dana Tiffany, "The European *Avant-Garde* as a *Fin-de-Siècle* Abbey of Misrule," *Journal of Unconventional History* 1, no. 2 (Winter 1990): 22–23.

24. For São Paulo's experience, which was similar to that of the Northeast with respect to the treatment of the native population, see John M. Monteiro, "From Indian to Slave: Forced Native Labour and Colonial Society in São Paulo During the Seventeenth Century," *Slavery and Abolition* 9, no. 2 (September 1988): 105. See also Nádia Farage, "As muralhas dos sertões: os povos indígenas do Rio Branco e a colonização" (Master's thesis, Universidade Estadual de Campinas, São Paulo, 1986); Stuart B. Schwartz, "Indian Labor and New World Plantations: European Demands and Indian Responses in Northeastern Brazil," *American Historical Review* 87 (1978): 43–79.

25. See *Falla com que abriu no dia 1º de maio de 1880 . . . da Assemblea Legislativa Provincial da Bahia. . . .* (Salvador: Typ. *Diário da Bahia,* 1880), 64–65; *Falla . . . no dia 1º de maio de 1889* (Salvador: Typ. *Diário da Bahia,* 1889), 140; José Calasans, "Antônio Conselheiro e a escravidão," Núcleo do Sertão Archive, Salvador, n.d., Typescript.

26. What little is known about Mulock, who may or may not have returned to England after 1861, is described in Gilberto Ferrez and Weston J. Naef, *Pioneer Photographers of Brazil, 1840–1920* (New York: Center for Inter-American Relations, 1976), 56.

27. Writers sometimes use the term *agreste* for this region, but its characteristics are very different from the true *agreste* of Pernambuco and the states further north. See J. P. Cole, *Latin America: An Economic and Social Geography* (New York: Plenum Press, 1965), 360; Josué de Castro, *Death in the Northeast* (New York: Random House, 1966), 36–37.

28. Morse, "Brazil's Urban Development," 166. For a bleak description of the region during the early nineteenth century, see Auguste de Saint-Hilaire, *Voyage dans les provinces de Saint-Paul et de Sainte-Catherine* (Paris, 1851), vol. 1.

29. Da Cunha, *Rebellion in the Backlands,* 13–15/*Os sertões,* 40–41.

30. Ibid., 16/42. Da Cunha cites the work of Cornell University professor Charles Frederick Hartt, director of the Morgan Expedition (1870–71), for his geologic references.

31. Ott, *Vestígios de cultura indígena,* 60–62.

32. See A. Carneiro Leão, *A sociedade rural: seus problemas e sua educação* (Rio de Janeiro: José Olympio Editora, 1937); Dácio de Lyra Rabello, *O Nordeste* (Recife: Editora Farol, 1932).

33. *Relatório apresentado a Assemblea Legislativa da Bahia . . . em 6 de março de 1870*, 15, 54.

34. Padre Heitor Araújo, *Vinte anos no sertão* (Salvador: Imprensa Gráfica, 1953), 55.

35. Públio Dias, *Condições hygiênicas e sociais do trabalhador dos engenhos de Pernambuco* (Recife: N.p., 1937), 14–17.

36. José Rodrigues de Carvalho, "A cultura do algodeiro no estado da Parahyba: o problema da pequena lavoura," *Annaes Algodoeira* 2 (1916): 318, cited by Lewin, *Politics and Parentela*, 77.

37. Compare with the description of Mexico's Sierra Gorda, an underpopulated region with similarly harsh terrain that in 1847–1850 became the staging area for peasant rebellion; see Leticia Reina, "The Sierra Gorda Peasant Rebellion, 1847–50," in *Riot, Rebellion, and Revolution: Rural Social Conflict in Mexico*, ed. Friedrich Katz (Princeton: Princeton University Press, 1988), 269–94.

38. Francisco Vicente Vianna, *Memoir of the State of Bahia*, trans. Guilerme Pereira Rebello (Salvador: Typ. *Diário da Bahia*, 1893), 507–24.

39. Census data for Bahia in 1872 are summarized in Brazil, Directoria Geral de Estatística, "Resumo histórico dos inquéritos censitários realizados no Brazil," in *Recenseamento do Brazil realizado em 1 setembro de 1920*, vol. 1: *Introdução* (Rio de Janeiro: D.G.E., 1922), 272–73.

40. Aguiar, *Descrições práticas*, 76.

41. See José Alípio Goulart, *Brasil do boi e do couro* (Rio de Janeiro: Edições GRD, 1964–65); João Camilo de Oliveira Torres, *Estratificação social no Brasil* (São Paulo: DIFEL, 1965).

42. Vianna, *Memoir of the State of Bahia*, 507–91, passim.

43. Aguiar, *Descrições práticas*, 84.

44. Cf. Mullett, *Popular Culture and Popular Protest*, 28.

45. See David Crew, "Why Can't a Peasant Be More Like a Worker? Social Historians and German Peasants," *Journal of Social History* 22, no. 3 (Spring 1989): 531.

46. Yves-Marie Bercé, *History of Peasant Revolts: The Social Origin of Rebellion in Early Modern France*, trans. Amanda Whitmore (Cambridge: Polity Press, 1990), 20.

47. See Roberto da Matta, "A propósito de micro-cenas e macro-dramas: notas sobre a questão do espaço e do poder no Brasil," in *Situaciones*, ed. Guillermo O'Donnell, Working Paper no. 121 (Notre Dame, Ind.: Helen Kellogg Institute for International Studies, May 1989), 9.

48. Cf. Clifford Geertz, "Suq: The Bazaar Economy in Sefrou," in *Meaning and Order in Moroccan Society: Three Essays in Cultural Analysis*, ed. C. Geertz, H. Geertz, and L. Rosen (Cambridge: Cambridge University Press, 1979), esp. 142–47.

49. For a comparison, see Mark Girouard, *The English Town: A History of Urban Life* (New Haven: Yale University Press, 1990).

50. Geertz, "Suq," 232–33. See also G. Dalton, "Aboriginal Economies in

Stateless Societies," in *Exchange Systems in Prehistory*, ed. Timothy K. Earle and Jonathan Ericson (New York: Academic Press, 1977), 191–92; M. Spence, *Market Signalling* (Cambridge, Mass.: Harvard University Press, 1974).

51. See Eduardo Hoornaert, *Verdadeira e falsa religião no Nordeste* (Salvador: Editora Benedina, 1972).

52. Patricia R. Pessar, "Three Moments in Brazilian Millenarianism: The Interrelationship Between Politics and Religion," *Luso-Brazilian Review* 28, no. 1 (Summer 1991): 95–116 (Special issue on millenarianism and messianism, ed. Robert M. Levine).

53. See Hilário Franco Júnior, "A outra face dos santos: os milagres punitivos na *Legenda áurea*," in *Sociedade Brasileira de Pesquisa Histórica, Anais da VIII Reunião* (São Paulo: SBPH, 1989), 155–60. See also W. Richardson, "The Golden Legend," *Princeton Theological Review* 1 (1908): 267–81.

54. Topik, *Political Economy of the Brazilian State*, 12.

55. June E. Hahner, *Poverty and Politics: The Urban Poor in Brazil, 1870–1920* (Albuquerque: University of New Mexico Press, 1986), 51–52, citing Minas Gerais, *Relatório apresentado à legislação provincial . . . na sessão ordinaria de 1876*, 52; Pernambuco, *Falla com que o exmº. Sr. João Pedro Carvalho de Moraes . . . 1876* (Recife: M. Figueiroa de F., 1876), 26; Minutes of Enlistment, Junta of Moritiba, Bahia, October 2, 1875; Letter, President of Bahia to Minister of Justice, Salvador, September 1, 1875, Estado da Bahia, Arquivo Público, Salvador.

56. For a discussion of the impact of railroad construction and economic penetration on rural life in Mexico, see Friedrich Katz, "Rural Rebellions After 1810," in *Riot, Rebellion, and Revolution: Rural Social Conflict in Mexico*, ed. F. Katz (Princeton: Princeton University Press, 1988), esp. 532–33.

57. See Thalez de Azevedo, *Italianos na Bahia*, 17–27.

58. Otten, "'Só Deus é grande,'" 1:300. See also Hardman, *Trem fantasma*, esp. 182–83.

59. See Roderick J. Barman, "The Brazilian Peasantry Reexamined: The Implications of the Quebra-Quilo Revolt, 1874–1875," *Hispanic American Historical Review* 57, no. 3 (August 1977): 401–24; and Hamilton de Mattos Monteiro, "Violência no Nordeste rural," chap. 6, esp. 149.

60. Geertz, "Suq," 172.

61. See, for example, Hélio Silva and Maria Cecília Ribas Carneiro, *Os presidentes: Prudente de Morais. O poder civil, 1894–1898* (São Paulo: Grupo de Comunicação Três, 1983), 87.

62. The relationship was almost exactly the same as the French peasant's relationship with state and nobility in the period prior to the Revolution. The use of sinecures to build networks of loyalty was a British device under the Hanovers. See Schama, *Citizens*, 67–71.

63. See Hamilton de Mattos Monteiro, "Violência no Nordeste rural," 38–39; and *relatórios* of provincial presidents, 1870–89.

64. On the question of the relationship between polity and economy in São Paulo, see the interesting exchange of views by Joseph L. Love, Verena Stolcke, and Maurício A. Font in the "Commentary and Debate" section of the *Latin American Research Review* 24, no. 3 (1989): 127–58.

65. Carone, *Instituições e classes sociais*, 275; Lewin, *Politics and Parentela*, 23.

See also Boris Fausto's review of Lewin, *Politics and Parentela*, in *Social History* 14, no. 1 (January 1989): 127.

66. In the Northeast, political organization reflected interconnected status groups, not any distinct social or semifeudal class; see Boris Fausto, Review of Lewin, *Politics and Parentela*, 128.

67. E. B. Reesink, *The Peasant in the Sertão: A Short Exploration of His Past and Present* (Leiden: Institute of Cultural and Social Studies, Leiden University, 1981), 36–37.

68. Ibid., 38; Andrade, *Land and People of Northeast Brazil*, 158.

69. See *Relatório com que o Exm.º Sr. Conselheiro do Estado João Lustosa da Cunha Paranaguá passou no dia 5 de janeiro* . . . , 101.

70. See José Euzébio Fernandes Bezerra, *Retalhos do meu sertão* (Rio de Janeiro: Gráfica Leão do Mar, 1978), 35–36.

71. Ronald H. Chilcote, *Power and the Ruling Classes in Northeast Brazil: Juazeiro and Petrolina in Transition* (Cambridge: Cambridge University Press, 1990), 8, citing Victor Nunes Leal, *Coronelismo, enxada e voto: o município e o regime representativo no Brasil* (Rio de Janeiro: Livraria Forense, 1949), 20.

72. Joseph L. Love, "Commentary" on Henry H. Keith, "The Nonviolent Tradition in Brazilian History: A Myth in Need of Explosion?" in *Conflict and Continuity in Brazilian Society*, ed. Henry H. Keith and S. F. Edwards (Columbia: University of South Carolina Press, 1969), 241–47.

73. Eul-Soo Pang, "*Coronelismo* in Northeast Brazil," in *The Caciques: Oligarchical Politics and the System of Caciquismo in the Luso-Hispanic World*, ed. Robert Kern (Albuquerque: University of New Mexico Press, 1973), 65–88; and Eul-Soo Pang and Ron L. Seckinger, "The Mandarins of Imperial Brazil," *Comparative Studies in Society and History* 14 (March 1972): 215–44.

74. Maria Isaura Pereira de Queiroz, *O messianismo no Brasil e no mundo* (São Paulo: Alfa-Omega, 1977), 313–15.

75. Pang, *Bahia in the First Brazilian Republic*, 12–14.

76. Reesink, *Peasant in the Sertão*, 48.

77. Maria Sylvia de Carvalho Franco, *Homens livres na ordem escravocrata*, 3d ed. (São Paulo: Editora Kairós, 1983), 28.

78. Pereira de Queiroz, *Messianismo*, 317.

79. It has been argued that *cachaça* may have served as a substitute for potable water, always in sparse supply; see Alfredo de Castro Silveiro, *Pequeno dicionário de assuntos pouco vulgares, curiosidades e excentricidades da língua portuguêsa*, 3d ed. (Rio de Janeiro: Livraria São José, 1960).

80. Padre Heitor Araújo, *Vinte anos no sertão*, 34–35.

81. Ibid., 51. Rumo, admittedly, had a reputation, along with Gilbués in Piauí, for being one of the worst frontier towns in the region.

82. Aguiar, *Descrições práticas*, 58–59.

83. *Relatório* from the Secretary of Police, April 2, 1896, sent to Dr. J. M. R. Lima, Governor, 4; in the Instituto Geográfico e Histórico, Salvador.

84. This arrangement lasted until the 1920s, when a rebellious group of *coronéis*, allying out of common interest, defied the state government and in effect fragmented Bahia into a "number of states within a state"; see Fausto, "Brazil: Social and Political Structure," 793.

85. This was strikingly similar to the Argentine experience in the early part of the nineteenth century; see Szuchman, *Order*, 34–71, 187–229.

86. Juan E. Orine Stemmer, "Freight Rates in the Trade Between Europe and South America, 1840–1914," *Journal of Latin American Studies* 21, no. 1 (February 1989): 56–57.

87. Moura, *Rebeliões da senzala*, 218.

88. Torcuato S. Di Tella, "The Dangerous Classes in Early Nineteenth Century Mexico," *Journal of Latin American Studies* 5, no. 1 (May 1973): 79–82.

89. Di Tella, "Dangerous Classes," 81.

90. Belisário Pena, *Saneamento do Brasil* (Rio de Janeiro: N.p., 1918), 30–31; Gregório Bezerra, *Memórias. Primeira parte: 1900–1945*, 2d ed. (Rio de Janeiro: Civilização Brasileira, 1979), 7–180.

91. Mauro Mota, *Paisagem das secas* (Recife: MEC/Instituto Joaquim Nabuco, 1958), 49–52, 13; Thomas W. Merrick and Douglas H. Graham, *Population and Economic Development in Brazil: 1800 to the Present* (Baltimore: Johns Hopkins University Press, 1979), 38–39, 150.

92. "Cidade da Escada," *Diário de Pernambuco*, January 18, 1874; Sociedade Auxiliadora da Agricultura de Pernambuco, *Trabalhos do Congresso Agrícola*, cited by Peter L. Eisenberg, *The Sugar Industry in Pernambuco, 1840–1910: Modernization Without Change* (Berkeley and Los Angeles: University of California Press, 1974), 196–97.

93. Joaquim Correia de Araújo, *Mensagem apresentado ao Congresso Legislativo do estado [de Pernambuco] em 1898* (Recife: Imprensa do Estado, 1898).

94. See Richard Slatta, *Gauchos and the Vanishing Frontier* (Lincoln: University of Nebraska Press, 1983).

95. See Eric B. Ross, "The Evolution of the Amazon Peasantry," *Journal of Latin American Studies* 10, no. 2 (November 1978): 193–218, esp. 194–95.

96. Michael W. Flinn, *The European Demographic System, 1500–1820* (Baltimore: Johns Hopkins University Press, 1981), 55.

97. John D. Wirth, *Minas Gerais in the Brazilian Federation, 1889–1937* (Stanford: Stanford University Press, 1977), 36–37.

98. Antonio Piccarolo, *L'emigrazione italiana nello state di S. Paolo* (São Paulo: N.p., 1911), 60–62.

99. Oddly, the lack of a developed network of market towns in Alagoas is frequently given not only as the reason for the failure of localized revolt to spread south but also as the Achilles' heel of the ill-fated Peasant Leagues a century later; see Barman, "Brazilian Peasantry Reexamined," 417–19.

100. Ralph della Cava, *Miracle at Joaseiro* (New York: Columbia University Press, 1970), 85. Della Cava's is the most thorough study of Padre Cícero and his movement to date.

101. See Shepard Forman and Joyce F. Riegelhaupt, "Market Place and Marketing System: Towards a Theory of Peasant Economic Integration," *Cooperative Studies in Society and History* 12, no. 2 (April 1970): 188–212.

102. See Billy Jaynes Chandler, *The Feitosas and the Sertão dos Inhamuns: The History of a Family and a Community in Northeast Brazil, 1700–1930* (Gainesville: University Presses of Florida, 1972).

103. Courtesy of Peter Beattie.

. *Livros de entradas de navios*, 1837–39, Arquivo Municipal, Salvador, cour-
..sy of Thalez de Azevedo. See his *Italianos na Bahia*, 13–50.

105. Donald Warren, Jr., "The Healing Art and the Urban Setting, 1880–
1930," ms., courtesy of author, 42. The Brazilian Spiritist Federation was established in 1884; linked closely to the French movement founded by Alain Kardec
(1804–69), it was immensely popular in Brazil in the 1850s and was carried
forward by the "Brazilian Kardec," the Ceará-born Adolfo Bezerra de Menezes.
See Eugene B. Brody, *The Lost Ones* (New York: International Universities Press,
1973), 351–462; Frances O'Gorman, *Aluanda: A Look at Afro-Brazilian Cults* (Rio
de Janeiro: Francisco Alves, 1977); Pedro McGregor, *The Moon and Two Mountains: The Myths, Ritual, and Magic of Brazilian Spiritism* (London: Souvenir Press,
1966), 86–119.

106. Ann Q. Tiller, "The Brazilian Cult as a Healing Alternative," 9 (ms.,
courtesy of the author).

107. See Shepard Forman, *The Brazilian Peasantry* (New York: Columbia University Press, 1975), 215–18; I. M. Lewis, *Ecstatic Religion* (Harmondsworth,
Middlesex: Penguin Books, 1971).

108. Da Cunha, *Rebellion in the Backlands*, 159–60/*Os sertões*, 152–53.

109. Interview with Dr. Thalez de Azevedo, Salvador, June 1988. See also
Carole A. Myscofski, *When Men Walk Dry: Portuguese Messianism in Brazil* (Atlanta:
Scholar's Press, 1988), 188.

110. E. Cardoso, "Diambismo ou maconhismo, vício assassino," *Boletim da
Secretaria de Agricultura, Indústria e Commércio*, July–December 1948, 436–43.

111. Judith Devlin, *The Superstitious Mind: French Peasants and the Supernatural
in the Nineteenth Century* (New Haven: Yale University Press, 1987), 59.

112. Ibid., 64; see also Thomas Kselman, *Miracles and Prophecies in Nineteenth-
Century France* (New Brunswick, N.J.: Rutgers University Press, 1983).

113. Devlin, *Superstitious Mind*, 70–71.

114. Limeira Tejo, *Brejos e carrascaes do Nordeste: documentário* (São Paulo:
Scopus, 1937), 55; *Veja e leia* (São Paulo), April 15, 1970, 84. See also Levine,
*Pernambuco in the Brazilian Federation*, chap. 3.

115. José Murilo de Carvalho makes a parallel point in his treatment of the
antivaccination riots in Rio de Janeiro in 1904; see *Os bestializados*; also Todd A.
Diacon, "Down and Out in Rio de Janeiro," *Latin American Research Review* 25,
no. 1 (1990): 246.

116. The Brazilian term for fantastic cures, whereby seriously ill people unexpectedly become completely well, is *milagre do sertão*, a "backland miracle"; see
Warren, "The Healing Art," 3.

117. Margareth Oliveira Carvalho, Márcia da Silva Pedreira, and Ana A.
Calmón de Oliveira, "Um farol de esperanças," Núcleo do Sertão Archive, Salvador, November 1982, Typescript. Members of the sect also had to abstain
from sexual relations for prescribed periods of time, and could not treat their
wounds with medicine.

118. Caio Prado Júnior, cited in Forman, *Brazilian Peasantry*, 30.

119. Gustavo Barroso [João do Norte], "Populações do Nordeste," *Revista da
Sociedade de Geografia do Rio de Janeiro*, 1926–27, 48–49. Luiz Vianna Filho

provides a similar analysis in his 1946 monograph *O negro na Bahia* (Rio de Janeiro: José Olympio Editora, [1946]), esp. chap. 3.

120. Alfonso Trujillo Ferrari, *Potengi-Encruzilhada no vale do São Francisco* (São Paulo: N.p., 1961), 174.

121. Ivaldo Falconi, "Um quilombo esquecido," *Correio das Artes* (João Pessoa) (1949), cited by Moura, *Rebeliões da senzala*, 220. The black inhabitants of this town were described as living in "primitive" conditions, segregated from the rest of the population as if they were "intruders."

122. Gregório Bezerra, *Memórias*, 7–180.

123. Forman, *Brazilian Peasantry*, 17; Tejo, *Brejos e carrascaes*, 47, 136–38.

124. By scrupulously observing expected canons of deferential behavior, the subject "may find that he is free to insinuate all kinds of disregard by carefully modifying intonation, pronunciation, pacing, and so forth" (Erving Goffman, "The Nature of Deference and Demeanor," *American Anthropologist* 58 [June 1956]: 478); James C. Scott, *The Moral Economy of the Peasant: Rebellion and Subsistence in Southeast Asia* (New Haven: Yale University Press, 1976), 232.

125. Devlin, *Superstitious Mind*, 215.

126. Ibid., 230; David T. Haberly, *Three Sad Races: Racial Identity and National Consciousness in Brazilian Literature* (Cambridge: Cambridge University Press, 1983), 161–73.

127. Orlando Parahym, *O problema alimentar no sertão* (Recife: Imprensa Oficial, 1940), 50–103; Ministério da Saúde, Comissão Nacional de Alimentação, *Inquérito sobre hábitos e recursos alimentares* (Rio de Janeiro: Ministério da Saúde, 1959), 32.

128. This taboo was limited to certain backland locations. Da Cunha mentions eating *gerimun*, an edible gourd, with milk in *Os sertões*, 101. No logical explanations have been offered for the taboo on cow's milk.

129. Gregório Bezerra, *Memórias*, 53–56. See also Clóvis Caldeira, *Mutirão: formas de ajuda mútua no meio rural* (São Paulo: N.p., 1956). More recent studies have suggested that the *mutirão* was not as widespread as was earlier believed; courtesy of José Carlos Sebe Bom Meihy, Salvador, December 10, 1989.

130. See, by comparison, Theodore Zeldin, *France, 1848–1945*, vol. 1: *Ambition, Love, and Politics* (Oxford: Oxford University Press, 1978), 135.

131. Francisco José de Oliveira Vianna, *Populações meridionaes do Brasil*, 4th ed. (São Paulo: Editora Nacional, 1938), 75–76.

132. Bernard Siegel, "Social Structure and Economic Change in Brazil," in *Economic Growth: Brazil, India, China*, ed. Simon Kuznets et al. (Durham, N.C.: Duke University Press, 1955), 399.

133. Milton, "A campanha de Canudos." Milton later became a police official and then a deputy to the federal Constituent Assembly.

134. Manoel Ambrósio, *Antônio Dó: o bandoleiro das Barrancas* (Januária, Minas Gerais: Prefeitura Municipal/Lion's Club, 1976).

135. Da Cunha, *Rebellion in the Backlands*, 160/*Os sertões*, 153.

136. Ibid., 405/340.

137. Ibid., 85/96.

138. See *Relatório do Delegado de Polícia de Jeremoabo de 20 de janeiro de 1871*,

submitted to Presidente da Província, Estado da Bahia, Arquivo Público, Salvador.

139. Gregório Bezerra, *Memórias*, 50–52.

140. See Clifford Geertz, *Agricultural Involution* (Berkeley and Los Angeles: University of California Press, 1974).

141. Manoel Rodrigues de Melo, *Patriarcas e carreiros: influência do coronel e do carro de boi na sociedade rural do Nordeste*, 2d ed. (Rio de Janeiro: Irm. Pongetti Editora, 1954), 23; Chilcote, *Power and the Ruling Classes in Northeast Brazil*, 10.

142. Da Cunha, *Rebellion in the Backlands*, 136/*Os sertões*, 134.

143. Ibid., 144/141.

## CHAPTER 3

1. The 1830 date is based on birth records found in Ceará in the mid-1980s; most earlier accounts list 1828 as his year of birth; courtesy Ismar de Oliveira Araújo Filho, Centro de Estudos Euclydes da Cunha, Salvador.

2. João Brígido, "A família de Antônio Conselheiro," *Almanak literária estatística do Rio Grande do Sul, 1898* (Porto Alegre) 10 (1897): 113–17; "Lutas de família: Maciéis e Araújos," *Publicações diversas* (Fortaleza: Typ. Universal, 1899), 95–107; *Jornal do Brasil* (Rio de Janeiro), February 22, 1897 (article transcribed from *O República* [Fortaleza], February 22, 1897). See also Manoel Benício, *O rei dos jagunços: chrônica histórica e de costumes sertanejos sobre os acontecimentos de Canudos* (Rio de Janeiro: Typ. *Jornal do Commércio*, 1899).

3. Ataliba Nogueira (*Antônio Conselheiro e Canudos*, 41) calls him "tall," based on the comments of Frei João Evangelista de Monte Marciano, but evidence suggests that he was no more than five feet six inches.

4. Interview with José Calasans, Salvador, December 10, 1989.

5. Luiz Fernando Pinto, a practicing psychiatrist and professor of neuropsychiatry at the Federal University of Bahia Medical School, has briefly looked into Conselheiro's psychological characteristics; see his paper "Aspectos psicanalíticos da personalidade carismática de Antônio Conselheiro" (Salvador, 1989, Typescript).

6. Abelardo F. Montenegro, *Antônio Conselheiro* (Fortaleza: N.p., 1954), 11; José Calasans, "Canudos não Euclidiano," in *Canudos: subsídios para a sua reavaliação histórica*, ed. José Augusto Vaz Sampaio Neto et al. (Rio de Janeiro: Fundação Casa Rui Barbosa, 1986), 13.

7. Da Cunha, *Rebellion in the Backlands*, 121–23/*Os sertões*, 122–24.

8. Da Cunha cites the memoirs of a contemporary chronicler, Manoel Ximenes, in ibid., 123n.119/124n.1 (note unnumbered). See also Luiz Luna and Nelson Barbalho, *Coronel Dono do Mundo: síntese histórica do coronelismo no Brasil* (Rio de Janeiro: Editora Cátedra, 1983), 234–36.

9. See Colonel João Brígido dos Santos, "Crimes célebres do Ceará, os Araújos e Maciéis," *A República* (Fortaleza), 1889, cited in Alfredo Ferreira Rodrigues, *Almanack literário e estatístico do Rio Grande do Sul para 1898* (Rio Grande: Carlos Pinto, 1899).

10. Commentators writing after the Canudos conflict claimed that the Maciéis "in great part . . . suffered from mental alienation [illness]" (Frei Pedro

Sinzig, O.F.M., *Reminiscências d'um frade*, 2d ed. [Petrópolis: Typ. das Vozes, 1925]).

11. Ricardo Guilherme, "Antônio Conselheiro antes de Canudos," in *O Conselheiro e Canudos* (Fortaleza: Imprensa Universitária da Universidade Federal do Ceará, 1986), 27.

12. See João Brígido, *Ceará (homens e fatos)* (Rio de Janeiro: Gráfica Record Editora, 1969), 43. The article was published in June 1893, before news of the Masseté incident reached the public. Calasans notes that it devoted more attention to Vicente Mendes Maciel than to his son, Antônio.

13. Milton, "A campanha de Canudos," 11.

14. There is no written evidence to prove this assertion, although years later a man calling himself "Antônio Conselheiro Neto" appeared, claiming that Conselheiro was his grandfather; interview with José Calasans, Salvador, December 10, 1989.

15. Pinto, "Aspectos psicanalíticos da personalidade carismática de Antônio Conselheiro," 5.

16. Nogueira, *Antônio Conselheiro e Canudos*, 4–5; Guilherme, "Antônio Conselheiro," 27; Abelardo F. Montenegro, *Fanáticos e cangaceiros* (Fortaleza: Henriqueta Galvão, 1973), 112.

17. Benício, *O rei dos jagunços*, 27.

18. Nogueira, *Antônio Conselheiro e Canudos*, 194; interview with José Calasans, Salvador, December 10, 1989. Many church-owned facilities were in disrepair because of a jurisdictional conflict over fiscal responsibility between the church and the provincial governments at the end of the empire.

19. Otten, "'Só Deus é grande,'" anexo, 12; correspondence between Padre João José Barbosa and Vigário Capitular Msgr. Carlos d'Amour (a French Capuchin), Cúria Archive, Salvador.

20. Statement, D. Claudemira Bezerra, ca. 1950, in Pasta C, Correspondence file of José Calasans, Núcleo do Sertão Archive, Salvador; Statement, "Dona Isabel," taped interview with José Carlos Costa Pinheiro, Centro de Estudos Euclydes da Cunha, Salvador, 1987.

21. Deposition of Marcos Dantas de Menezes, the oldest resident of Crisópolis, ca. 1965, in Núcleo do Sertão Archive, Salvador.

22. Da Cunha, *Rebellion in the Backlands*, 129/*Os sertões*, 126–27.

23. Guilherme, "Antônio Conselheiro," 29. Sabino was well known for his numerous progeny. Conselheiro's willingness to overlook this lapse was virtually the only exception he ever permitted to his strict personal moral code.

24. The words are by Dona Evangelina, taken prisoner during the Fourth Military Expedition; see Manoel Funchal Garcia, *Do litoral ao sertão* (Rio de Janeiro: Biblioteca do Exército, 1965), 172.

25. Myscofski, *When Men Walk Dry*, 118–19; R. Azzi, "Ermitães e irmãos: uma forma de vida religiosa no Brasil antigo," *Convergência* 9, no. 94 (July–August 1976): 370–83; 9, no. 95 (September 1976): 430–41; José Ferreira Carrato, *As Minas Gerais e os primórdios do Caraça* (São Paulo: Editora Nacional, 1963); Eduardo Hoornaert, *História da igreja no Brasil*, 2 vols. (Petrópolis: Editora Vozes, 1977). The first *ermitão* was Antônio Caminha, who founded a shrine in Rio de Janeiro in 1671; the first wandering *ermitão* was Francisco Mendonça Mar,

said to have undergone conversion after hearing Antônio Vieira preach and whose wanderings centered in the São Francisco region, the same as Conselheiro's.

26. Della Cava, "Brazilian Messianism and National Institutions," 405.

27. See Celso Mariz, *Ibiapina, um apóstolo do Nordeste* (João Pessoa: N.p., 1942); José de Figueiredo Filho, "Casa de Caridade de Crato," *A Província* (Crato) 3 (1955): 14–25; Georgette Desrochers and Eduardo Hoornaert, eds., *Ibiapina e a igreja dos pobres* (São Paulo: Editora Paulinas, 1984); J. Comblin, ed., *Instruções espirituais do P[adr]e Ibiapina* (São Paulo: N.p., 1984); della Cava, "Brazilian Messianism and National Institutions," 404–5; Meznar, "Deference and Dependence," 210–11.

28. Otten, "'Só Deus é grande,'" 1:314–19.

29. Vigário Firmino Estrella, S. Gonçalo da Itiúba, to Archbishop Manoel dos Santos Pereira, Salvador, February 24, 1891, Cúria Archive, Salvador.

30. The main difference between the two was that da Silva owned the cemetery and came to be accused of charging high fees to allow burial in a "holy site"; courtesy of Ismar de Oliveira Araújo Filho, Centro de Estudos Euclydes da Cunha, Salvador.

31. Della Cava, "Brazilian Messianism and National Institutions," 409–15. Padre Cícero always spoke as a Catholic priest, even though he had been defrocked; see his letter to D. Joaquim José Vieira, Bishop of Ceará, September 1, 1898, cited in Irineu Pinheiro, *Efemérides do Cariri* (Fortaleza: Imprensa Universitária do Ceará, 1963), n.p.

32. Della Cava, "Brazilian Messianism and National Institutions," 405.

33. Ibid., 406–7.

34. Antônio Joaquim Pereira de Azevedo, Abrantes, to Chief of Police, Salvador, March 14, 1876, Estado da Bahia, Arquivo Público, Salvador.

35. Deposition, D. Claudemira Bizerra [*sic*], ca. 1950, in Pasta C, Correspondence file of José Calasans, Núcleo do Sertão Archive, Salvador. According to local legend, when Conselheiro heard of the vicar's opposition, he said that the town would survive only as long as the Pregas did. When the last member of the family died, the Itapicurú River flooded, and at least for a short time Conselheiro's prophesy came true. See also Padre Vicente Ferreira dos Passos, *vigário encomendado*, Nova Souré, to Presidência da Polícia, Salvador, January 2, 1882, in the Gabinete Arquiepiscopal, Salvador.

36. Putnam, in da Cunha, *Rebellion in the Backlands*, 132n.130; da Cunha, *Rebellion in the Backlands*, 156/*Os sertões*, 150.

37. Da Cunha, *Rebellion in the Backlands*, 133–34/*Os sertões*, 132.

38. Nogueira, *Antônio Conselheiro e Canudos*, 6; see also Hélio Silva and Maria Cecília Ribas Carneiro, *O poder civil* (Rio de Janeiro: Editora Três, 1975), 58–60.

39. Testimony of Bacharel Genes Fontes, in a letter to *A República* (Rio de Janeiro), 1897, cited in José Calasans, "Notícias de Antônio Conselheiro," Núcleo do Sertão Archive, Salvador, n.d., Typescript, 4–5; courtesy of Dr. Calasans. We do not know, however, whether he actually offered prophesy, as the legend asserts.

40. Da Cunha, *Rebellion in the Backlands*, 131–32/*Os sertões*, 130.

41. Ibid., 133/131.

42. See José Calasans, "Antônio Conselheiro, construtor de igrejas e cemitérios," *Cultura* (Rio de Janeiro) 5, no. 16 (1973): 75.

43. Da Cunha, *Rebellion in the Backlands*, 144/*Os sertões*, 141.

44. See *Relatório da commissão especial nomeada para recolher as creanças sertanejas, feitas prisioneiras em Canudos* (Salvador, 1898) (or a briefer version, *Rel. do comitê patriótico constituído na Cidade do Salvador*, published in *Comércio* [São Paulo], 1897).

45. Cited by Macedo, *Memorial de Vila Nova*, 70.

46. Da Cunha, *Rebellion in the Backlands*, 144/*Os sertões*, 141.

47. See Nogueira, *Antônio Conselheiro e Canudos*, 38–40.

48. Estância, however, was the hometown of Sílvio Romero, the "father of Brazilian folklore," then a journalist using the name Bacharel Sílvio Vasconcelos da Silveira Romero, his birth name. Writing in *A Tribuna do Povo*, Romero was the first to refer to Maciel in print as Antônio Conselheiro. It is my guess that he had a hand in *O Rabudo* as well. See José Calasans, "Aparecimento e prisão de um messias," *Revista da Academia de Letras do Bahia* 35 (1988): 54n.2. The newspaper's masthead featured a woodcut of a long-tailed monkey, although the *rabudo*, in Bahia, was a name for a large water rat, and it also was used to describe the (long-tailed) devil. The newspaper referred to itself as a "periódico critico, chistoso, anecdótico, e noticioso."

49. *O Rabudo*, no. 7 (November 22, 1874): 2–3.

50. For example, Reginaldo Alves de Mello to Baron of Jeremoabo, Missão, Bahia, October 6, 1894, Jeremoabo Papers, Fazenda Camuciatá, Itapicurú, Bahia.

51. Paraphrased from an article in *Diário da Bahia* (Salvador), June 27, 1876.

52. Correspondence between Padre João José Barbosa (vicar of N. S. do Apora), Padre João Alves da Silva Paranhos (vicar of N. S. do Livramento do Barracão), Padre Emílio de Santana Pinto (vicar of Divino Espírito Santo de Abrantes); and correspondence between Msgr. Luís d'Armour, vicar in Salvador, and the provincial chief of police, Dr. João Bernardo de Magalhães; all in the Gabinete Arquiepiscopal, Correspondência das Repartições Públicas, Salvador, XVI, 1874–77.

53. Another supporter was the vicar of N. S. da Piedade do Lagarto, Sergipe, João Baptista de Carvalho Daltro, in January 1886; see Daltro to Archbishop D. Luís Antônio dos Santos, Salvador, in Gabinete Arquiepiscopal, Salvador, cited by Calasans, "Canudos não Euclidiano," 6–7.

54. The baron of Jeremoabo was once informed that a priest in Pombal, Msgr. José Bonifácio, had died in an influenza epidemic, leaving his seven children orphaned. See Antônio Roza da Costa, Pombal, to Baron of Jeremoabo, March 21, 1897, in Núcleo do Sertão Archive, Salvador.

55. Dozens of letters to the archbishop from priests assigned to backland parishes are stored in the Cúria Metropolitana Archive, Gabinete Arquiepiscopal, Salvador; see, for example, a letter from Leopoldo Antônio de Gois, Serrinha, to Archbishop Manoel dos Santos Pereira, January 20, 1882.

56. Letter to Archbishop Msgr. Manoel dos Santos Pereira, June 4, 1883, Cúria Metropolitana Archive, Gabinete Arquiepiscopal, Salvador.

57. For an example of the regard in which Father Fiorentini was held in the

church, see Padre João de Sena to the Cúria, Matta de São João, April 14, 1884, Cúria Archive, Salvador.

58. Padre Júlio Fiorentini to Archbishop, Inhambupe, September 21, 1886, Cúria Metropolitana Archive, Gabinete Arquiepiscopal, Salvador.

59. Fiorentini to Cônego Miranda, September 21, 1886, Cúria Metropolitana Archive, Gabinete Arquiepiscopal, Salvador.

60. Letter, ca. 1886, Cúria Metropolitana Archive, Gabinete Arquiepiscopal, Salvador. Some supporters of Conselheiro considered Fiorentini their most dangerous enemy and worked to have him removed from the parish to which he had been assigned. See, for example, Padre Ramos to Archbishop, Inhambupe, September 10, 1887, Cúria Metropolitana Archive.

61. Padre Júlio Fiorentini to Archbishop, Inhambupe, September 9, 1886, Cúria Metropolitana Archive, Gabinete Arquiepiscopal, Salvador; see also Otten, "'Só Deus é grande,'" anexo, 49.

62. Eul-Soo Pang found the sale contract for the Engenho Central do Bom Jardim in the Santo Amaro *cartório*; see also Pang, *O Engenho Central do Bom Jardim na economia baiana: alguns aspectos de sua história, 1875–1891* (Rio de Janeiro: Arquivo Nacional/Instituto Histórico e Geográfico Brasileiro, 1979), 56–57.

63. José Calasans, who has spent years studying Conselheiro's life, summarizes the arrest episode in his "Aparecimento e prisão de um messias."

64. Boaventura da Silva Caldas to Cícero Dantas Martins, Itapicurú, ca. early 1876, Jeremoabo Papers, Fazenda Camuciatá, Itapicurú, Bahia.

65. See *Livro de Baptismos*, 1874–94, Cúria Metropolitana Archive, Gabinete Arquiepiscopal, Salvador.

66. Sinzig, *Reminiscências d'um frade*, excerpted in *Revista Vozes* 69, no. 5 (June–July 1975): 384. For the colonial period, see Schwartz, *Sugar Plantations in the Formation of Brazilian Society*, esp. chap. 14, 379–412. See also Stephen Gudeman and Stuart B. Schwartz, "Cleansing Original Sin: Godparenthood and the Baptism of Slaves in Eighteenth-Century Bahia," in *Kinship Ideology and Practice in Latin America*, ed. Raymond T. Smith (Chapel Hill: University of North Carolina Press, 1984), 35–58.

67. Letter cited in Calasans, "Aparecimento e prisão de um messias," 57.

68. See Calasans, "Canudos não Euclidiano," 5.

69. Extradition letter, J. B. Magalhães, Secretaria de Polícia da Província da Bahia, 2ª seção, Nº 2182, June 5, 1876, to Sr. Chefe de Polícia de Ceará; see Garcia, *Do litoral ao sertão*, 184.

70. See *Diário da Bahia*, June 27 and July 7, 1876; *Correio da Bahia*, July 8, 1876; *Jornal da Bahia*, July 8, 1876; *Diário de Notícias* (Salvador), July 6 and July 7, 1876. A summary of these descriptions appeared in the *Folhinha Laemmert* in Rio de Janeiro later in that year, the first notice of Antônio Maciel in the imperial capital.

71. See Fortunée Levy, "Crentes e bandidos," *Anais do Museu Histórico Nacional* 8 (1947): 41. Another secondary source (Macedo, *Memorial de Vila Nova*, 113) states that Maciel was arrested for nonpayment of debts.

72. Levy, "Crentes e bandidos," 41–42. The record offers no explanation of the fate of Paulo José da Rosa, although presumably he was taken only to Salvador, not shipped to Fortaleza with Conselheiro.

73. See Roger L. Cunniff, "The Birth of the Drought Industry: Imperial and Provincial Responses to the Great Drought in Northeast Brazil, 1877–1880," *Revista de Ciências Sociais* (Fortaleza) 6, nos. 1–2 (1975): 65–82; Gerald Michael Greenfield, "Recife y la gran sequía," in *Cultura urbana latinoamericana,* ed. Richard Morse and Jorge Enrique Hardoy (Buenos Aires: CLASCO, 1985), 203–26.

74. Francisco Carvalho de Passos, Subdelegado em exercício, José Egas de Carvalho, Juis de Pas [*sic*], and Vigário João Dias de Andrade, "Recenseamento, 1 de dezembro de 1863," sent to Sr. Presidente, Bahia; "Recenseamento Geral da Bahia em 1872," Núcleo do Sertão Archive, Salvador, n.d., Typescript.

75. Nogueira, *Antônio Conselheiro e Canudos,* 8.

76. See Sílvio Romero, *O vampiro do Vaza-Barris: intermezzo jornalista em resposta ao vigário Olympio Campos. Complemento ao opúsculo "A verdade sobre o caso de Sergipe"* (Rio de Janeiro: Impressora, 1895). (The "vampire of Vaza-Barris" was Olympio Campos, not Conselheiro.) See also Romero's *Estudos sobre a poesia popular no Brasil* (Rio de Janeiro, 1888; reprinted Petrópolis: Editora Vozes, 1977), 41; also, Calasans, "Canudos não Euclidiano," 4.

77. Benício, *O rei dos jagunços,* 163. This book appeared three years before *Os sertões,* and likely served as a model for da Cunha.

78. Aguiar, *Descrições práticas,* 76. Calasans ("Canudos não Euclidiano," 7–8) avers that da Cunha read Aguiar's book and used part of it without citing it as a source. See also Paulo Ormindo de Azevedo, "Um 'sacro monte' no sertão bahiano" (Paper presented at the Congresso do Barroco Brasileiro, Ouro Preto, September 1981), Núcleo do Sertão Archive, Salvador.

79. Letters to *A República* (Rio de Janeiro), cited without dates by Calasans, "Canudos não Euclidiano," 11.

80. Letters to *A Notícia* (Aracajú), January 28–29, 1897.

81. José Américo, Rosário, to Baron of Jeremoabo, February 28, 1894, Jeremoabo Papers, Fazenda Camuciatá, Itapicurú, Bahia.

82. See J. C. Pinto Dantas Júnior, "O barão de Geremoabo (Dr. Cícero Dantas Martins), 1838–1938," Address to the Instituto Geográfico e Histórico da Bahia, June 27, 1938 (Salvador: Imprensa Oficial do Estado, 1939), 9–22; Pang, *In Pursuit of Honor and Power,* 202. Dantas Martins preferred to use either his imperial title of nobility (barão de Jeremoabo) or the title conferred on him by his law degree (Bacharel Dantas Martins). If he had not been a nobleman, he would probably have been known as a *coronel.* Jeremoabo was a prolific correspondent, sometimes writing fifteen letters a day.

83. Pang, *Bahia in the First Brazilian Republic,* 56–59. For a detailed analysis of the political economy of the rural Northeast in the late nineteenth and early twentieth centuries, see Lewin, *Politics and Parentela.*

84. Montenegro, *Antônio Conselheiro,* 44; della Cava, "Brazilian Messianism and National Institutions," 413n.37.

85. Pro- and anti-Vianna factions hated one another intensely. One anti-Vianna *coronel* called the governor an "assassin" (Alfredo Leão, Rio de Janeiro, to Baron of Jeremoabo, April 16, 1897, Núcleo do Sertão Archive, Salvador). See also Montenegro, *Antônio Conselheiro,* 44; Comunidade de Base (Monte

Santo, Bahia), "Canudos: a sua história e de seu fundador" (Salvador: EMQ Gráfica e Editora, July 1984), 9.

86. Speech, Deputy Antônio Bahia, n.d., published in Bahia, Câmara dos Deputados, *Sessões do anno de 1894* (Salvador: Typ. *Correio de Notícias*, 1894), 104. Deputy Bahia was a public school teacher and a member of the dissident Partido Republicano Constitucionalista, an offshoot of the Partido Republicano Federalista. He was elected from the city of Salvador.

87. Speech, Deputy Manoel Ubaldino do Nascimento Assis, n.d., in ibid., 105–6. See also *Jornal de Notícias*, March 29, 1893; *Diário de Notícias*, October 10, 1892 (both published in Salvador). Ubaldino de Assis was the founder of the Partido Republicano Constitucionalista and remained a major figure in the state legislature until 1909, when he was elected to the federal Chamber of Deputies and moved his residence to Rio de Janeiro.

88. Speech, Deputy Antônio Bahia, in Bahia, Câmara dos Deputados, *Sessões do anno de 1894*, 107. The deputy claimed that the Indians were armed with "arco, flecha, e bésta," the latter a slingshot-type device (see Antônio de Moraes Silva, *Diccionário da língua portugueza* [Lisbon: Typ. Lacerdina, 1813], 1:279).

89. Speech, Deputy José Justino, Bahia, Câmara dos Deputados, *Sessões do anno de 1894*, p. 110. Deputy Justino represented the third *circunscripção* (centered in Senhor do Bonfim) and served in the state Senate until 1908.

90. Comment by Deputy Hermelino Leão, Bahia, Câmara dos Deputados, *Sessões do anno de 1894*, 110. Deputy Leão represented Macaúbas (Rio de Contas). In 1910, he played a major role in Barbosa's presidential campaign. See *Diário Oficial: edição especial do centenário* (Salvador: Typ. *Diário Oficial*, 1923), 24–27.

91. See Bacharel Francisco Borges de Barros, *Diccionário geográphico e histórico da Bahia* (Salvador: Imprensa Oficial do Estado, 1923), 20.

92. "Interview do governador do Estado da Bahia Dr. Luiz Viana e o representante da *Gazeta de Notícias* do Rio de Janeiro" (Feira de Santana: Typ. *O Popular*, 1897) (Pamphlet).

93. Circumstances in the national government conspired against Conselheiro as well. President Prudente de Morais returned to office after his long illness only days after news of the defeat of the third expedition and the death of its commander, Colonel Moreira César, was received. This circumstance led to violent antimonarchist outbreaks and fueled demands for total victory and no mercy. See Hahner, *Civilian-Military Relations in Brazil*, 170–77; also Pereira de Queiroz, *O messianismo*, 203–19; Pang, *Bahia in the First Brazilian Republic*, 59–60; Baron of Jeremoabo (Cícero Dantas Martins), "Antônio Conselheiro," *Jornal de Notícias* (Salvador), March 4–5, 1897.

94. Luiz, Archibishop of Bahia, to Conselheiro João Capistrano Bandeira de Mello, Salvador, June 11, 1887, in Cúria Metropolitana Archive, Gabinete Arquiepiscopal, Salvador; and response, June 15, 1887.

95. The 1891 Marriage Act was also widely misunderstood; its apparent ban on marriage between first cousins, for example, had to be clarified. Courtesy of Linda Lewin. See also Paulo Zanettini, "Canudos, uma história incompleta," *Jornal da Tarde* (São Paulo), October 6, 1988, 21; Otten, "'Só Deus é grande,'" 1:443.

96. Da Cunha, *Rebellion in the Backlands,* 141–42/*Os sertões,* 139.

97. See Bahia's Constitution of July 2, 1891 (Article 125), on tax revenues.

98. Pang, *Bahia in the First Brazilian Republic,* 58; della Cava, "Brazilian Messianism and National Institutions," 412–23. See also Antônio F. Moniz de Aragão, *A Bahia e os seus governadores na República* (Salvador: N.p., 1923); and Montenegro, *Antônio Conselheiro,* 44.

99. Da Cunha, *Rebellion in the Backlands,* 142/*Os sertões,* 139.

100. Manoel Jesuíno Ferreira, *A província da Bahia. Apontamentos* (Rio de Janeiro: Typ. Nacional, 1875), 36, 64, 119.

101. See Benigno Dantas to Baron of Jeremoabo, Salvador, October 5, 1896, Jeremoabo Papers, Fazenda Camuciatá, Itapicurú, Bahia.

102. Durval Vieira de Aguiar, Letter to *Jornal de Notícias* (Salvador), June 13, 1893.

103. Maximiano José Ribeiro, Letter to *Jornal de Notícias* (Salvador), June 16, 1893.

104. See José Calasans, "O *Diário de Notícias* e a Campanha de Canudos," *Universitas* (Salvador) 18 (September–December 1977): 89–96.

105. At least one chronicler claims that the rude mud and straw shacks that covered the hilly slopes of the Favella *morro* were the origin of the name *favela* for the shanties constructed by migrants from the Northeast who flocked to Rio de Janeiro and other southern cities after the turn of the century. Namely, when the government was slow to pay the pensions of soldiers returned from Canudos, a large group camped out on a hill overlooking the War Ministry until their demands were met; they christened their shantytown *favela,* and from that point, all shantytowns in the federal capital became known by the name. See Fortunée Levy, "Crentes e bandidos," 42.

106. See José Calasans, *O ciclo folclórico do Bom Jesus Conselheiro* (Salvador: Tipografia Benedetina, 1950).

107. Communication from the Vicar of Itú, 1898, Cúria Metropolitana Archive, Gabinete Arquiepiscopal, Salvador.

108. See Candace Slater, *Trail of Miracles: Stories from a Pilgrimage in Northeast Brazil* (Berkeley and Los Angeles: University of California Press, 1986), esp. 2–5. Her monograph addresses the Juazeiro of Padre Cícero, but many similarities existed between the two communities.

109. See, for example, Ulysses Lins de Albuquerque, *Um sertanejo e o sertão: Moxotó Bravo e Três Ribeiras* (Belo Horizonte: Editora Itatiaia, 1989), 32; courtesy of Dr. René Ribeiro.

110. Da Cunha, *Rebellion in the Backlands,* 143/*Os sertões,* 140.

111. There would be a drought again in 1898, continuing the historical cycle. For a discussion of the impact of drought on regional geography, see Cole, *Latin America,* 360–61.

112. *O Estado de São Paulo,* September 14, 1897, cited by Ilana Blaj and Cândida Pereira da Cunha, "A urbanização em Canudos como decorrência da necessidade de defesa," in *Anais do VII simpósio nacional dos professores universitários de história,* vol. 1 (São Paulo: Typ. *Revista de História,* 1984), 497.

113. For example, there was a major conflict over the role of Vicar Olympio

Campos, federal deputy for Sergipe and boss of the portion of the Vasa-Barris basin that lay in Sergipian territory; see Romero, *O vampiro do Vaza-Barris*.

114. Putnam (*Rebellion in the Backlands*, 164–65) notes that da Cunha's account follows closely the report submitted by Friar Monte Marciano and published in Salvador by the Curia; see *Relatório apresentado pelo Revd. Frei João Evangelista de Monte Marciano ao arcebispado da Bahia sobre Antônio Conselheiro e seu sequito no arraial dos Canudos* (Salvador: Typ. *Correio de Notícias*, 1895).

115. Da Cunha, *Rebellion in the Backlands*, 166–67/*Os sertões*, 157.

116. *Relatório apresentado pelo Revd. Frei João Evangelista*, 7.

117. Ibid., 5.

118. Ibid., 7.

119. See also Gregório de S. Mariano, "Os Capuchinhos na Bahia," *Congresso de História da Bahia*, vol. 1: *Anais* (Bahia: CHB, 1950), 273–83.

120. *Relatório apresentado pelo Revd. Frei João Evangelista*, 4.

121. Da Cunha, *Canudos e inéditos*, 79.

122. Calasans, "Canudos não Euclidiano," 17.

123. Many lithographs reproduced in newspapers during the late nineteenth century were taken from photographs, but there is no evidence that this was the case here. For the role played by photography in late nineteenth-century Brazil, see Levine, *Images of History*.

124. See Couto, *Missão abreviada*, esp. 198–99, 399, 468; also Pessar, "Unmasking the Politics of Religion," 261.

125. Both books may have been written by Leão de Natuba (or Leão da Silva), who served as Conselheiro's scribe and personal secretary; see Calasans, "Canudos não Euclidiano," 18, referring to *Apontamentos dos preceitos da Divina Lei de Nosso Senhor Jesus Cristo, para a salvação dos homens*, 1895, original copy in Núcleo do Sertão Archive, Salvador; also 76. The two books are likely authentic; had they been forged, they presumably would have contained material deemed more volatile. Each is a standard prayer book, common to its era, although painstakingly copied by hand on parchment paper.

126. Antônio Vicente Mendes Maciel, *Prédicas e discursos de Antônio Conselheiro*, pars. 542, 607–8, 619, 656–67. The handwritten book was obtained by João de Sousa Pondé, a young medical officer and a member of the group sent to exhume Conselheiro's corpse, then given to his friend, Afrânio Peixoto, who gave it in turn to da Cunha. The latter's survivors in 1973 presented it to José Carlos de Ataliba Nogueira.

127. Transcribed and reprinted in Nogueira, *Antônio Conselheiro e Canudos*, 55–181; see also Calasans, "Canudos não Euclidiano," 18–19.

128. Telegram, Gov. Luiz Vianna to President of the Republic, October 1897, citing Dr. Leoni's telegram and explaining that since his own state police garrison was depleted in strength, he had asked the commanding general of the Brazilian army district to send one hundred regular troops; see da Cunha, *Rebellion in the Backlands*, 179. Explanatory notes about Leoni, Pereira e Mello, and General Solon are provided by Samuel Putnam in the translator's footnotes to *Rebellion*. See also "Campanha de Canudos," cited by Nogueira, *Antônio Conselheiro e Canudos*, 16–17.

129. Della Cava, "Brazilian Messianism and National Institutions," 414, citing Montenegro, *Antônio Conselheiro*, 48–49; see also Benigno Dantas to Baron of Jeremoabo, Salvador, October 5, 1896, Jeremoabo Papers, Fazenda Camuciatá, Itapicurú, Bahia.

130. Governor Luiz Vianna, Statement in *Gazeta de Notícias* (Rio de Janeiro), August 7, 1897, 1.

## CHAPTER 4

1. Yi-Fu Tuan, *Topophilia: A Study of Environmental Perceptions, Attitudes, and Values* (Englewood Cliffs, N.J.: Prentice-Hall, 1974), 77–79; he is quoting Elizabeth M. Thomas, *The Harmless People* (New York: Knopf, 1965), 13.

2. For a general application of the concept, see Barry Lopez, *Arctic Dreams: Imagination and Desire in a Northern Landscape* (New York: Bantam Books, 1986), 248–49.

3. In contrast, Europeans during this time tended to be cynical about their governments and about the costs of modernization; see Basil Willey, *The Eighteenth Century Background* (London: Penguin Books, 1965), 19–21, cited by Tuan, *Topophilia*, 44.

4. Da Cunha, *Rebellion in the Backlands*, 87/*Os sertões*, 97–98. See also Raimundo Nina Rodrigues, *As raças humanas: a responsibilidade penal no Brasil* (1894; reprinted Salvador: Livraria Progresso, 1957); Deolindo Amorim, *Sertão de meu tempo* (Rio de Janeiro: N.p., 1978), 6–7. For an overview of attitudes toward race in Brazil, see David H. P. Maybury-Lewis, Introduction to the second paperback edition of Gilberto Freyre's *The Masters and the Slaves* (Berkeley and Los Angeles: University of California Press, 1986).

5. Da Cunha, *Rebellion in the Backlands*, 149, 156/*Os sertões*, 144–150.

6. Ibid., 157/150.

7. Armin Ludwig, *Brazil: A Handbook of Historical Statistics* (Boston: G. K. Hall, 1985), Table III-3.

8. See Salomão de Souza Dantas, *Aspectos e contrastes: ligeiro estudo sobre o estado da Bahia* (Rio de Janeiro: Typ. *Revista dos Tribunaes*, 1922), 146.

9. Courtesy of Cândido da Costa e Silva, Salvador, December 9, 1989.

10. Reported by Lélis Piedade, *Jornal de Notícias* (Salvador), October 19, 1897.

11. José Aras, *Sangue de irmãos* (Salvador: Museu de Bendegó, [1953]), 159–60.

12. Testimony of Maria Guilhermina de Jesus, born in Canudos and a wounded survivor, in Odorico Tavares, *Bahia: imagens da terra e do povo* (Rio de Janeiro: José Olympio Editora, 1951), 272–74.

13. See Roberto Lyra, *Euclides da Cunha: criminologista* (Rio de Janeiro: Typ. *O Globo*, 1936), 11.

14. See Ivo Vannuchi, "Tipos étnicos e sociais de *Os sertões*," in *Enciclopédia de estudos euclidianos*, ed. Adelino Brandão (Jundiaí: Gráfica Editora Jundiaí, 1982), 1:147–60.

15. Jacinto Ferreira da Silva to Rumão S. dos Santos, Canudos, ca. May

1896, reproduced in J. P. Favilla Nunes, *Guerra de Canudos: narrativa histórica*, Fascículo Nº 3 (Rio de Janeiro: Typ. Moraes, 1898), 34.

16. Baptism logbook, Cumbe Church, ca. 1887; photocopies courtesy of Renato Ferraz, Centro de Estudos Euclydes da Cunha, Universidade Estadual da Bahia, Salvador.

17. See Antero de Cerqueira Gallo to Baron of Jeremoabo, Tucano, March 19, 1897; and José Américo to Baron of Jeremoabo, Rosário, February 28, 1894; both in Jeremoabo Papers, Fazenda Camuciatá, Itapicurú, Bahia. João J. Reis notes that the Bahian elite, highly sensitive to the question of racial origins, "believed itself" white and constantly feared a "black avalanche" over its heads; see his "A elite baiana face os movimentos sociais, Bahia: 1824–1840," *Revista de História* (São Paulo) 54 (1976): esp. 375.

18. Maria de Lourdes Bandeira, "Os Kiriris de Mirandela," *Estudos Baianos* (Salvador) 6 (1972): 82–83. During the festival the participants danced to a *taquari*, a long flute.

19. Billy Jaynes Chandler, "The Role of Negroes in the Ethnic Formation of Ceará: The Need for a Reappraisal," *Revista de Ciências Sociais* 4, no. 1 (1973): 31–43. The author notes that in the Brazilian Northeast it is unpopular to acknowledge the presence of blacks in the *sertão*'s racial mix. Yet persons of "recognizable Negroid stock," either total or partial, constituted nearly half the population of Ceará in 1872. At the other end of the historiographical spectrum, it has become fashionable to emphasize the presence of ex-slaves at Canudos, referring to Canudos as the "last *quilombo*," or slave refuge. There is no evidence that this assessment is accurate either.

20. The observer was an Italian employee of the Estrada de Ferro Salvador-Timbó, quoted in Salvador's *Diário de Notícias*, September 3, 1897. See also Baron of Jeremoabo, Letter to *Jornal de Notícias*, March 5, 1897, remarking on the postabolition "servile element" making up Conselheiro's audiences; and Antero de Cerqueira Gallo, Tucano, to Baron of Jeremoabo, March 19, 1897, alleging that the majority of Conselheiro's followers were ex-slaves; both in Jeremoabo Papers, Fazenda Camuciatá, Itapicurú, Bahia.

21. At least one chronicler claimed that some of the runaway slaves had been gun repairmen and that they were used in Canudos to maintain the weaponry; see Aras, *Sangue de irmãos*, 5–6. José Calasans notes that ex-slaves desired houses "with windows and a rear door," which Conselheiro provided for them; interview, Salvador, December 10, 1989.

22. José Calasans, "Antônio Conselheiro e a escravidão," Núcleo do Sertão Archive, Salvador, 1959, Typescript, 4.

23. Da Cunha, *Rebellion in the Backlands*, 157/*Os sertões*, 150–51. On the last years of slavery, see Eduardo Silva, "Por uma nova perspectiva das relações escravistas," in *Sociedade Brasileira de Pesquisa Histórica, Anais da Vª Reunião* (São Paulo: SBPH, 1985), 141–47.

24. *Diário de Notícias*, September 16, 1897. Lélis Piedade, the *Diário* correspondent, used the term *horda negra* to identify the dead woman's background.

25. See Haberly, *Three Sad Races*, 3.

26. One was either a white (*branco*), a *meio-branco*, or an *escravo* (slave); courtesy of Linda Lewin.

27. *Cabra* was used for "dark"; Baptism registry, Jeremoabo, 1889, Cúria Archive, Salvador. Registries from different parishes dating from 1867 through 1906 show roughly the same distribution.

28. Interestingly, outsiders described Conselheiro as *acaboclado*—a rarely used variation on the term *caboclo* employed to convey a softer, less pointed reference to a person's mixed racial status—and da Cunha at one point called Conselheiro a "white gnostic"; see Garcia, *Do litoral ao sertão*, 171.

29. The baron of Jeremoabo himself commented on the presence of former property owners in Canudos. When white residents of Canudos were enumerated on official documents, additional comments were often added, that they were "of good families," for example, or that their children were of legitimate birth.

30. Benício, *O rei dos jagunços*, 171, 405. Over the course of his reporting from Belo Monte, Benício angered Florianists in Rio de Janeiro by averring that the war had nothing to do with monarchism; he was fired from the *Jornal do Commércio* after a unanimous protest letter from the Military Club was presented to the newspaper.

31. Montenegro, *Antônio Conselheiro*, 33, cited by Nogueira, *Antônio Conselheiro e Canudos*, 200.

32. Calmon, *Vida econômico-financeira da Bahia*, esp. 115–20; Escola de Comando do Estado Maior do Exército, *Guerras insurrecionais do Brasil (Canudos e Contestado)* (Rio de Janeiro: SMG Imprensa do Exército, 1966), 9, 15, 25. Overall, however, revenues from hides never amounted to more than 5 percent of Bahia's export income.

33. See Amaro Lélis Piedade, *Histórico e relatório do Comitê Patriótico da Bahia* (Salvador: Typ. Reis, 1901), xi.

34. See Jaime Reis, "Hunger in the Northeast: Some Historical Aspects," in *The Logic of Poverty: The Case of the Brazilian Northeast*, ed. Simon Mitchell (London: Routledge & Kegan Paul, 1981), 41–57; also Reis, "The Abolition of Slavery and Its Aftermath in Pernambuco (1880–1920)" (Ph.D. diss., St. Anthony's College, Oxford University, 1974). For data on army recruits in the late 1920s, see Cel. Arthur Lobo da Silva, "A antropologia do exército brasileiro," *Archivos do Museu Nacional* 30 (1928): 9–300.

35. Da Cunha, *Rebellion in the Backlands*, 145/*Os sertões*, 141. A less subjective description is offered by Dantas Barreto, *Destruição de Canudos*, 4th ed. (Recife: *Jornal do Recife*, 1912), 11–12, originally titled *Última expedição à Canudos*.

36. See *O Rio São Francisco e a Chapada Diamantina* (Salvador, 1938), 34, cited by Rui Facó, *Cangaceiros e fanáticos: gênese e lutas* (Rio de Janeiro: Civilização Brasileira, 1963), 92.

37. See the eyewitness description of housing written by Alvim Martins Horcades, a medical student at Canudos who remained until the last day of the conflict, *Descrição de uma viagem a Canudos* (Salvador: Litotipografia Tourinho, 1899), 177.

38. The presence of so many of these structures linked by tunnels led one military officer, Col. Carlos Silva Teles of the Fourth Brigade, to speculate in 1897 that the settlement at Canudos in fact had fewer inhabitants than the twenty-five thousand frequently cited. Moreover, he suggested, there may have been as few as six hundred actual *jagunço* fighters, but their numbers were ex-

aggerated because of their seeming omnipotence and ability to conduct successful guerrilla warfare. See Regina Bortolo, "Projecto Canudos," *A Tarde* (São Paulo), April 26, 1988, sec. 2, 1.

39. Zanettini, "Canudos, uma história incompleta," 21. The author, an archeologist, carried out extensive surveying and other reconstruction work at Canudos in the mid-1980s; see Bortolo, "Projecto Canudos," 1.

40. The above descriptions are taken from *Rebellion in the Backlands*, 158–59. Subsequent characterizations (below) are based on eyewitness reports collected by Honório Vilanova, cited by Macedo, *Memorial de Vila Nova*; Aras, *Sangue de irmãos*; *Relatório apresentado pelo Revd. Frei João Evangelista*; Benício, *O rei dos jagunços*; José Calasans, *Quase biografias de jagunços (o séquito de Antônio Conselheiro)* (Salvador: Universidade Federal da Bahia, 1986); and Dantas Barreto, *Destruição de Canudos*.

41. Da Cunha, *Rebellion in the Backlands*, 220–21/*Os sertões*, 202.

42. In the 1950s he was interviewed by José Calasans. Pedrão was the only person holding a leadership role in Canudos who commented on his experience, although by the time he was approached he was elderly, and his statements did not add much. Calasans interview, December 10, 1989.

43. Marcelino Pereira de Miranda to Baron of Jeremoabo, Tucano, Bahia, September 27, 1896, Jeremoabo Papers, Fazenda Camuciatá, Itapicurú, Bahia.

44. Honório Vilanova asserted later that after the battle his brother returned to the site and exhumed the rest of the buried metal; interview with José Calasans, Salvador, December 10, 1989.

45. A variation on the origin of Conselheiro's physician holds that a French doctor, immigrating to Bahia in 1897 and learning that medical personnel were needed at the front, left his wife in Salvador and traveled to the interior, where he was captured by *conselheiristas*. Later he escaped, fled on foot until he reached a train station, and returned to Salvador. Arriving at his house at night, he found his wife with another man; she claimed that she had heard he had died and therefore had remarried. Distraught, the physician left Salvador for Rio Grande do Sul. Interview with José Calasans, Salvador, December 10, 1989.

46. Da Cunha mocks the fact that offenders were jailed for "the slight offense of a few homicides" and also for not appearing at prayers (*Rebellion in the Backlands*, 151). There is no evidence to substantiate either claim.

47. Consider, for example, the case of the "Negro Badulque," arrested as a spy for Conselheiro in Cumbe in January 1895. Badulque's testimony led to the arrest and imprisonment of all of the male members of the Alves da Silva family in July 1897. In retribution, Badulque was later murdered. Backland justice prevailed inside and outside of Canudos. See Calasans, *Quase biografias de jagunços*, 81–84.

48. See his curious personal statement, *Breve resposta dada a artigos e telegrammas insertos en jornaes deste estado pelo "El-Supremo do Harém" dos jagunços Ten. Cel. Leovegildo Cardoso, metamorphoseado na pessoa do famigerado Elpídio filho do scelerado Norberto, ex-commandante em chefe das forças de Antônio Conselheiro em operações no arraial dos Canudos* (Serrinha, Bahia, privately printed January 1, 1898), Núcleo do Sertão Archive, Salvador, 5.

49. Antero de Cerqueira Gallo to Baron of Jeremoabo, Tucano, January 23, 1897, Jeremoabo Papers, Fazenda Camuciatá, Itapicurú, Bahia. The letter men-

tions the names of specific *fazendeiro* targets, including Jeremoabo's relative Col. José Américo.

50. José Mendis [*sic*] dos Reis, São Caetano, Bahia, to [?], April 17, 1895; José Felix to Sr. Romão Soares, Belo Monte (Canudos), May 15, 1896; Manuel Senhorinho Pereira to Leão Maximiano de Mattos, n.d.; all cited by Nunes, *Guerra de Canudos*, 31–32. Nearly all these letters refer to previous correspondence and to having received an earlier letter, suggesting that mail service functioned in and out of Canudos.

51. Antônio José de Lisboa to Sr. Venceslau Dutra (?), December 23, 1896, cited by Favilla Nunes, *Guerra de Canudos*, 35. Candace Slater and Milton Azevedo of the University of California, Berkeley, helped me translate the original, which was written in broken colloquial Portuguese.

52. Eul-Soo Pang, "Agrarian Change in the Northeast," in *Modern Brazil: Elites and Masses in Historical Perspective*, ed. Michael L. Conniff and Frank D. McCann (Lincoln: University of Nebraska Press, 1989), 134–35, citing Azarias Sobreira, *O patriarca de Juazeiro* (Juazeiro: Editora Vozes, 1969), 14, 19.

53. Governor Luiz Vianna, Salvador, to President Prudente de Morais, October 1897, cited by da Cunha, *Rebellion in the Backlands*, 179/*Os sertões*, 167–68.

54. See Chilcote, *Power and the Ruling Classes in Northeast Brazil*, 4.

55. Report from General Frederico Solon, Third Military District, Salvador, cited in da Cunha, *Rebellion in the Backlands*, 181/*Os sertões*, 168–69.

56. Da Cunha, *Rebellion in the Backlands*, 185/*Os sertões*, 172.

57. Ibid., 188/174.

58. Ibid., 188–89/174; Bello, *History of Modern Brazil*, 150.

59. Antero de Cerqueira Gallo, Tucano, to Baron of Jeremoabo, March 19, 1897, Jeremoabo Papers, Fazenda Camuciatá, Itapicurú, Bahia.

60. Edward L. Dreyer, a specialist in military history at the University of Miami, notes that sixteen million rounds would have weighed 650 tons and therefore required at least 650 wagons to carry the load to the front. With a normal basic load of three hundred rounds per man, only 450,000 rounds would have been needed. Cannon usually were supplied with seventy rounds each.

61. See Benigno Dantas, Salvador, to Baron of Jeremoabo, July 7, 1897, Jeremoabo Papers, Fazenda Camuciatá, Itapicurú, Bahia.

62. "Campanha de Canudos," list of names of soldiers presumed dead on the battlefield or unaccounted for (*desaparecidos*), Arquivo Histórico do Senado Federal, Brasília, cited in Ilara Viotti, "Segredo a toa," *Isto é senhor*, no. 1079 (May 23, 1990): 42.

63. Original songs were written as well. One, a march, started: "Senhô Moreira César, Vamo pra Canudo, Mata Consèlheiro . . ." (handwritten music score in Núcleo do Sertão Archive, Salvador).

64. See José Calasans, "Os últimos dias de Moreira César," Caderno C, Núcleo do Sertão Archive, Salvador. After one mass execution, Moreira César laconically dispatched a telegram to Prudente de Morais: "Romualdo, Caldeira, Freitas, and others have been shot according to your orders"—a patently untrue statement. In fact, some officers were shot for "crimes" they had committed on instructions from the commander in chief. Prudente was allegedly furious at Moreira César, and never promoted him to general despite his fame and popularity.

65. Da Cunha, *Rebellion in the Backlands*, 230/*Os sertões*, 209. Note that in what follows, short unattributed quotations are from this work as well.

66. Ibid., 235/214–15.

67. Ibid., 251/225.

68. Ibid., 255/228.

69. Ibid., 258/230.

70. Ibid., 259/230–31.

71. Ibid., 265/235.

72. Maria Avelina, "Depoimentos dos sobreviventes," *O Cruzeiro* (Rio de Janeiro), August 19, 1947, 17.

73. For the official account of the retreat, see the report by Major Rafael Augusto da Cunha Mattos to Cel. Souza Menezes, Cumbe, March 5, 1897, Arquivo Geral do Quartel dos Aflitos, Salvador.

74. Da Cunha, *Rebellion in the Backlands*, 284.

75. Quoted by José Calasans, *No Tempo de Antônio Conselheiro* (Salvador: Universidade Federal da Bahia, 1959), 61.

76. Galvão, *No calor da hora*, 50.

77. Ibid., 34.

78. Milton, "A Campanha de Canudos," 96.

79. Antônio Ferreira de Brito, Pombal, to Baron of Jeremoabo, March 20, 1897, Núcleo do Sertão Archive, Salvador.

80. *Gazeta de Notícias* (Rio de Janeiro), August 21, 1897, 1.

81. Polícia Militar da Bahia, 3º Corpo do Regimento Policial da Bahia, 4ª Companhia, *Livro de assentamento de praças*, ms., ca. 1897, Arquivo Geral do Quartel dos Aflitos, Salvador.

82. *Gazeta de Notícias* (Rio de Janeiro), September 1, 1897, 1.

83. See, for example, dispatch from Salvador dated September 5, 1897, in *Correio de Notícias* (Rio de Janeiro), September 10; clipping file, Núcleo do Sertão Archive, Salvador.

84. See Polícia Militar da Bahia, *Livro de registro de ordens do dia, 1889–1904*, ms., n.d., Arquivo Geral do Quartel dos Aflitos, Salvador.

85. Nataniel Dantas, "De Canudos resta apenas a memória," *Cultura* (Brasília) 11, no. 39 (January–March 1982): 38; testimony by José Travassos, "Depoimentos dos sobreviventes," *O Cruzeiro* (Rio de Janeiro), August 19, 1947, 17.

86. Data on casualties from the four military expeditions against Canudos are summarized in José Augusto Vaz Sampaio Neto et al., *Canudos: subsídios para a sua reavaliação histórica* (Rio de Janeiro: Fundação Casa Rui Barbosa, 1986), 24–75. As was noted earlier, documents that came to light only in 1990 indicate that some of the casualties on the government side were listed as *desaparecidos*, meaning that they either deserted or went over to the side of the *conselheiristas*.

87. *La Nación* (Buenos Aires), July 30, 1897; *A República* (Rio de Janeiro), February 20, 1897, 1; February 22, 1897, 1.

88. José Travassos, "Depoimentos dos sobreviventes," *O Cruzeiro* (Rio de Janeiro), August 19, 1947, 17.

89. Statement, "Dona Isabel," Núcleo de História Oral, interview with José Carlos Costa Pimenta, 1987, Centro de Estudos Euclydes da Cunha, Universidade Estadual da Bahia, Salvador. Dona Isabel's mother, grandmother, and

two daughters (one of whom died along the way at Alagoinhas) were among the women taken to Salvador by the Comité Patriótico da Bahia.

90. Da Cunha, *Rebellion in the Backlands*, 475/*Os sertões*, 392.

91. Twelve of Flávio de Barros's photographs taken at Canudos are stored in the archive of the Museu da República in Rio de Janeiro; together with several dozen others taken by war correspondents, they may be seen in the author's videotaped documentary *Canudos Revisited* (1990), produced and distributed by the Center for Latin America, University of Wisconsin, Milwaukee.

92. Paulo Zanettini, Report to Centro de Estudos Euclydes da Cunha, São Paulo, ca. 1987, in Centro Archive, Universidade Estadual da Bahia, Salvador. See also *A Notícia* (Aracajú), December 16, 1897, 1.

93. As late as 1950, one family mounted a vigil on a hill near the site of Belo Monte, believing that Conselheiro would be resurrected at the halfway point of the next millennium; see José Carlos da Costa Pinheiro, "As interferências divinas na obra de Conselheiro," 1988, Centro de Estudos Euclydes da Cunha, Universidade Estadual da Bahia, Salvador, 7.

94. The apparent helplessness of army officers against the untrained *jagunços* shocked civilians and led to a loss of prestige for the military. See, for example, Coronel Pessoa, Ilhéus, to Baron of Jeremoabo, August 31, 1897, Núcleo do Sertão Archive, Salvador: "Isn't there a single general capable of dealing with this question of *beatas*?"

95. "Relatório apresentado a Inspectoria Geral de Hygiene do Estado da Bahia, pelo Dr. Américo Barreira, Médico commissiado," January 30, 1898, Núcleo do Sertão Archive, Salvador, 175.

96. Neto et al., *Canudos*, 69; Pang, *Bahia in the First Brazilian Republic*, 58n.31; Sampaio, "Da transição política da república ao movimento de Canudos," 7.

97. Sinzig, *Reminiscências d'um frade*, excerpted in *Revista Vozes* (Petrópolis) 69, no. 5 (June–July 1975): 384.

98. Correa Bittencourt, "Saúde pública," in *Década republicana*, 2d ed. (Brasília: Editora Universidade de Brasília, 1986), 228.

99. Dispatch published in *Jornal do Commércio* (Rio de Janeiro), August 8, 1897, 3.

100. See "Apontamento de detalhes" files, 3º Districto Militar, Quartel General, Salvador, 1897. Career records of staff medical officers are stored at the Polícia Militar da Bahia, Gabinete do Comando, Corpo 376, Salvador.

101. Bittencourt, " Saúde pública," 234.

102. "Relatório apresentado a Inspectoria Geral de Hygiene pelo Dr. Américo Barreira," 171–76.

103. Officially, orders from General Artur Oscar forbade women from traveling to the front; see *Gazeta de Notícias* (Rio de Janeiro), August 21, 1897, 1.

104. 3º Districto Militar, Quartel General, Salvador, 100: art. 25 (November 22, 1897); 68, art. 23.

105. Polícia Militar da Bahia, Gabinete do Comando, Corpo 376, June 29, 1897, Virgílio Perreira de Almeida file.

106. Testimony of Honório Vilanova, brother of Antônio Vilanova, cited by Calasans, *Quase biografias de jagunços*, 90.

107. See the December 22, 1897, editorial in *O Comércio de São Paulo*, "Diviserunt vestimenta mea," reproduced in Galvão, *No calor da hora*, 103–5.

108. See dispatch published in *O Comércio de São Paulo*, December 22–24, 1897, reproduced in Galvão, *No calor da hora*, 496–510.

109. Sinzig, *Reminiscências d'um frade*, 195.

110. Sinzig, "Diário inédito d'um frade," 61–78.

111. General Artur Oscar ordered a woman's throat slit because she refused to say a *viva* to the republic, according to witnesses. See "Franciscanos em Canudos, 1897," *Revista Vozes* 69, no. 5 (June–July 1975): 394–98.

112. Amaro Lélis Piedade, "Declaração" in name of Comitê Patriótico, Salvador, November 17, 1897, Núcleo do Sertão Archive, Salvador.

113. *Jornal de Notícias*, Salvador, September 6, 1897.

114. Reported by F. Benavides, who in his youth was a schoolteacher in the backlands, in a chronicle written when he was seventy-five years of age; courtesy of José Calasans.

115. *Jornal de Notícias*, Salvador, September 18, 1897.

116. Often additional information was added to the file card: "white, blond, and of good family" was the usual. Of the 146 cases, only one such supplementary notation was added to the file of a nonwhite survivor.

117. Américo Barreto Filho, Carlos F. K. Wagner, and Dias Lima Sobrinho, *Relatório da commissão especial nomeada para recolher as creanças sertanejas feitas prisioneiras em Canudos* (Salvador: Comité Patriótico da Bahia, 1898), xix–xxxi.

118. Da Cunha turned the boy over to the director of the São Paulo Escola Normal, Gabriel Prestes, who raised him. He was given the name Ludgero Prestes. He earned a diploma in elementary education and became a teacher in the city of São Paulo. See José Calasans, "O jaguncinho de E. da Cunha," *Revista de Cultura da Bahia* 7 (1972): 75–78.

119. Obituary, *Jornal de Notícias*, February 3, 1908, 1.

120. Governor of Sergipe to Advogado José Monteiro, Promotor Público, Aracajú, July 3, 1897, Arquivo Público do Estado de Sergipe, Aracajú.

CHAPTER 5

1. Lynch, "Catholic Church in Latin America," 536. For a description of the "Romanization" of the Brazilian church, see Ralph della Cava, *Miracle at Joaseiro* (New York: Columbia University Press, 1970), 20–26.

2. See Azzi, "Elementos para a história do catolicismo popular"; José Luis Fiorim, "O discurso de Antônio Conselheiro," *Religião e sociedade* 5 (1980): 95–129.

3. See Eduardo Hoornaert, *Formação do Catolicismo brasileiro, 1500–1800* (Petrópolis: Editora Vozes, 1974), chap. 2.

4. See Otten, "'Só Deus é grande,'" 1:135.

5. See Couto, *Missão abreviada*. A few in the church still consider the *Missão abreviada* a major work and a "practical guide to Christian life" (in the words of Joaquim Cabral, "Missão abreviada da pobreza de uma teologia" [Ph.D. diss., Pontifica Universitas Lateranense, Rome, 1986], 17).

6. Otten, "'Só Deus é grande,'" 1:269–84, based in turn on Conselheiro's

handwritten prayer books at the Núcleo do Sertão Archive, Salvador, 325. See also J. C. Maraschin, ed., *Quem é Jesus Cristo no Brasil* (São Paulo: N.p., 1974), 55–94; H. Lepargneur, *Antropologia do sofrimento* (Aparecida do Norte, São Paulo: N.p., 1985).

7. See Calasans, "Canudos não Euclidiano," 18, referring to *Apontamentos dos preceitos da Divina Lei de Nosso Senhor Jesus Cristo, para a salvação dos homens*, 1895, original copy in Núcleo do Sertão Archive, Salvador; also 76.

8. Antônio Conselheiro, *Tempestades*, paragraph 568, Núcleo do Sertão Archive, Salvador.

9. Da Cunha, *Rebellion in the Backlands*, 129/*Os sertões*, 129.

10. Otten, "'Só Deus é grande,'" 1:269–84.

11. See Jacinto Ferreira da Silva, Canudos, to Rumão S. dos Santos, ca. May 1896, copied by Favilla Nunes, *Guerra de Canudos*, 34.

12. In the nineteenth century, Brazil's few Jews, most of whom were non-practicing, lived in the cities of the Center-South, although a handful of Sephardic Jews had settled in the Amazon. While no Jews are known to have lived in the towns and cities of the *sertão*, there were "turcos," a label given indiscriminately to Syrio-Lebanese, who earned their living as merchants and sometimes peddlers.

13. See Décio Freitas, "Canudos: uma tragédia de hoje," Introduction to *Canudos: desenhos* by Alves Dias, Núcleo do Sertão Archive, Salvador, n.d., Typescript (published version Olinda, Pernambuco: Recife Graf Editora, 1981).

14. Da Cunha, *Rebellion in the Backlands*, 162–64/*Os sertões*, 155. Da Cunha claimed that the ABC's were copied from Conselheiro's sermons, but this is not proven.

15. Otten, "'Só Deus é grande,'" 2:7–8, 30; Maria Isaura Pereira de Queiroz, *O campesinato Brasileiro: ensaios sobre civilização e grupos rústicos no Brasil*, 2d ed. (Petrópolis: Editora Vozes, 1973), 91.

16. An interesting analysis of the medieval Scandinavian worldview—one that had much in common with Conselheiro's—can be found in Aron Alkovlevich Gurevich, *Medieval Popular Culture: Problems of Belief and Perception*, trans. János Bak and Paul A. Hollingsworth (Cambridge: Cambridge University Press, 1988); see also Peter Burke's preface to the same volume, vii–viii.

17. Ralph della Cava, Presentation to the American Historical Association, New York, December 29, 1966.

18. See Gurevich, *Medieval Popular Culture*, 90.

19. José Aras, an eyewitness who visited Canudos briefly, claimed that Conselheiro referred to the "infant King Sebastião," but there is no further evidence for this, and much of what Aras wrote later was embellished; see his *Sangue de irmãos*, 11; also Otten, "'Só Deus é grande,'" 1:343.

20. Pessar, "Three Moments in Brazilian Millenarianism," 101–2.

21. Ibid.; see also Candace Slater, *Stories on a String: The Brazilian "Literatura de Cordel"* (Berkeley and Los Angeles: University of California Press, 1982), esp. chaps. 1–3.

22. See Patricia R. Pessar, "Millenarian Movements in Rural Brazil: Prophecy and Protest," *Religion* 12 (1982): 187–213. Pessar notes that the *benditos* themselves may have promoted millenarian beliefs.

23. Pessar, "Three Moments in Brazilian Millenarianism," 112.

24. For the impact of the republic on traditional rural bosses, see Amaury de Souza, "The *Cangaço* and the Politics of Violence in Northeast Brazil," in *Protest and Resistance in Angola and Brazil: Comparative Studies*, ed. Ronald H. Chilcote (Berkeley and Los Angeles: University of California Press, 1972), 122–23.

25. Gurevich, *Medieval Popular Culture*, 223.

26. None has survived save for the two long handwritten texts described above; see da Cunha, *Rebellion in the Backlands*, 135n.133/*Os sertões*, 133n.

27. *Cidade de São Salvador*, May 6, 1897, from Frei João Evangelista's 1895 *Relatório*.

28. Virtually the only person who charged that Conselheiro condemned the "economic system" for robbing the people was the local writer and newspaperman Manoel Benício, the source of the famous "Tia Benta" story about Conselheiro's defense of an old woman who could not pay the licensing fee to sit at a local market and sell her simple wares (*O rei dos jagunços*, 162).

29. The handwritten text of the prophecy, dated Belo Monte, January 24, 1890, indicates that the lights would be put out in 1901, but later published versions of the prophecy substitute the year 1900. The handwritten text attributes the prophecy to the Prophet Jeremiah. See da Cunha, *Caderneta de campo*, ed. Olímpio de Sousa Andrade (São Paulo: Editora Cultrix; Brasília: Instituto Nacional do Livro, 1975), 73–75; *Os sertões*, 133.

30. Rubens Rodrigues dos Santos, "Revelações sobre Antônio Conselheiro," *O Estado de São Paulo*, June 10, 1955.

31. During the third, fourth, and fifth centuries, Eastern Orthodox church theologians emphasized light (φός) as a symbol of divinity and the supernatural in human experience. The German theologian Rudolf Otto also devoted considerable attention to the nature of light and illumination as an aspect of the mystical element in the religious experience; see his *The Idea of the Holy*, 2d ed. (London: Oxford University Press, 1950).

32. Mullett, *Popular Culture and Popular Protest*, 13–15.

33. Gurevich, *Medieval Popular Culture*, 214–15.

34. Da Cunha, *Rebellion in the Backlands*, 161, translator's note 176, citing James Hastings, ed., *Encyclopedia of Religion and Ethics* (New York: Scribner, 1925), 11:342–43.

35. See Couto, *Missão abreviada*, 329. The *Missão*, like Conselheiro, blamed Jews and atheists for the attacks on Catholicism and the church.

36. Otten, "'Só Deus é grande,'" 1:289, citing Hamilton de Mattos Monteiro, *Crise agrária e luta de classes*, esp. 157.

37. Billy Jaynes Chandler, *The Bandit King: Lampião of Brazil* (College Station, Tex.: Texas A & M Press, 1978), 16–17.

38. Borges, "Progress and Degeneration in Brazilian Social Thought," 3.

39. Ibid., citing Max Nordau, *Degeneration* (1895; reprinted New York: Howard Fertig, 1968); and John A. Davis, *Conflict and Control: Law and Order in Nineteenth-Century Italy* (Atlantic Highlands, N.J.: Humanities Press International, 1988).

40. See Raimundo Nina Rodrigues, "Métissage, dégénérescence et crime," *Archives d'anthropologie criminelle* (Paris) 14 (1899): 477–516; Borges, "Progress

and Degeneration in Brazilian Social Thought," 3–6; Mariza Corrêa, "As ilusões da liberdade: a escola Nina Rodrigues e a antropologia no Brasil" (Ph.D. diss., Universidade de São Paulo, 1982). According to José Augusto Cabral Barreto, by linking a propensity for insanity not only to mestizos but also to members of the lower classes, he went even further than the then-accepted racialist theories of Lasègue and Falret; see Barreto's "Nina Rodrigues e a 'loucura epidêmica de Canudos,'" *Planejamento* (Salvador) 7, nos. 3–4 (July–December 1979): 275–87.

41. Raimundo Nina Rodrigues, "A loucura epidêmica de Canudos," *Revista Brazileira* (Salvador) 2 (October 1897): 141. For details of Conselheiro's early life, Nina Rodrigues did rely on João Brigido's accounts to some degree.

42. See Raimundo Nina Rodrigues, "O animismo fetichista dos negros bahianos," *Revista Brazileira* 1 (April 15–September 4, 1896).

43. A handful of other *mulatos* achieved positions of some prestige in nineteenth-century Bahian society, although they rarely attained the same social status as the descendants of the colonial landowning class. Photographic portraits of distinguished Baianos in the state geographical and historical association suggest that perhaps two in ten members of the elite were visibly *mulato*. Nevertheless, they were never fully accepted, either socially or in terms of recognition of their work. Some portraits of nineteenth-century Bahian *mulato* members of the elite are reproduced in Sofia Olszewski Filha, *A fotografia e o negro na cidade do Salvador, 1840–1914* (Salvador: Fundação Cultural do Estado da Bahia, 1989), 94–95. Nina Rodrigues's writings, for example, were not acknowledged until 1939 at the initiative of sociologist Afrânio Peixoto. Da Cunha's concluding sentence in *Os sertões*, where he laments that Brazil lacked a Maudsley, is ironic, since Nina Rodrigues had been following the same line of analysis in Salvador since 1897 (*Rebellion in the Backlands*, 476/*Os sertões*, 393).

44. He read, for example, the *Annales médico-psychologiques* (Paris), the *Archives d'anthropologie criminelle* (Paris), and the *Archivo de psiciatria, scienze penali ed antropologia criminale* (Turin). For a more modern treatment of the subject, see Artur Ramos, *Loucura e crime* (Porto Alegre: Editora Globo, 1937), esp. 78–122.

45. See Raimundo Nina Rodrigues, *As collectividades anormaes* (Rio de Janeiro: Civilização Brasileira, 1939), esp. 16. Among the Europeans who influenced him in his notions about links between crime and racial types were Lasègue, Falret, Sighele, Rossi, Le Bon, and Charcot.

46. See Arthur Mitzman's review of Peter Burke's *The Historical Anthropology of Early Modern Italy* (Cambridge: Cambridge University Press, 1987), in *Journal of Social History* 22, no. 3 (Spring 1989): 563–66.

47. See Alcir Lenharo, *Sacralização da política* (Campinas: Editora Papirus/ Editora da Unicamp, 1986), cited by Dain Borges, "Progress and Degeneration in Brazilian Social Thought," 15.

48. Jorge Pereira Lima, José Germano Maia, João Alves de Oliveira, and João da Silva, *Antônio Conselheiro e a tragédia de Canudos* (São Paulo: CEHILA, 1986).

49. See J. Craig Jenkins, "Why Do Peasants Rebel? Structural and Historical Theories of Modern Peasant Rebellions," *American Journal of Sociology* 88, no. 3 (1983): 487–514.

50. Nina Rodrigues, *As collectividades anormaes*, 69–77. Nina Rodrigues omit

ted any consideration of political aspects in *jagunço* lawlessness; in reality, most of the incidents he cited were instigated or led by local *coronéis*.

51. Ronald Daus, *O ciclo épico dos cangaceiros na poesia popular do Nordeste*, trans. Rachel Teixeira Valença (Rio de Janeiro: Fundação Casa Rui Barbosa, 1982), 93, referring specifically to *Os sertões*.

52. José de Campos Novaes, "*Os sertões*," *Revista do Centro de Ciências, Letras e Artes* (Campinas) 2, no. 2 (1903): 45–55.

53. Octacílio de Carvalho Lopes, "*Os sertões*: diagnose e denúncia," *Revista da Academia Paulista de Letras* 24 (June 1967): 26–28.

54. Edgar Rodrigues, *Socialismo e sindicalismo*, 53.

55. See Pessar, "Unmasking the Politics of Religion," 256. For a theoretical discussion of why peasants rebel or follow new patterns of behavior, see the editorial foreword to articles by James C. Scott and others in *Comparative Studies in Society and History* 29, no. 1 (July 1987): esp. 415–16.

56. See David Brookshaw, *Race and Color in Brazilian Literature* (Metuchen, N.J.: Scarecrow Press, 1986), 52.

57. Author's interview with Gilberto Freyre, Recife, July 24, 1986. See the anarchist novel by Fábio Luz, *Na província* (Rio de Janeiro: N.p., 1902). See also "Um pensador de raça," *Veja e Leia* (São Paulo), July 29, 1987, 84–85.

58. Facó, *Cangaceiros e fanáticos*, 833; see also Edgar Rodrigues, *Socialismo e sindicalismo*, 54–55.

59. Ralph della Cava makes this assertion in *Miracle at Joaseiro*, 77, though the main emphasis of his research on backland religious movements has shown that the faithful were "part and parcel of a national social order" and not, as Pereira de Queiroz and others have maintained, independent because rooted in the geographical isolation of the *sertão*. See Pereira de Queiroz, *O campesinato brasileiro*, 321.

60. Rodolfo Teófilo, *História da sêca do Ceará (1877/1880)*, cited by Facó, *Cangaceiros e fanáticos*, 30.

61. See Barman, "The Brazilian Peasantry Reexamined"; Armando Souto Maior, *Quebra-Quilos: lutas sociais no outono do império* (Recife: Instituto Joaquim Nabuco de Pesquisas Sociais, 1978).

62. On *De Rerum Novarum* and the new attitudes of the Catholic Church on republicanism and social change, see Harvey Goldberg, *The Life of Jean Jaurès* (Madison: University of Wisconsin Press, 1968), 66–69; David Shapiro, "The *Ralliement* in the Politics of the 1890's," in *The Right in France, 1890–1919*, St. Antony's Papers, no. 13 (London: Chatto & Windus, 1962), 13–19, 48.

63. Letter from E. P. de Almeida, cited by da Cunha, *Caderneta de campo*, 72–73. See also Otten, "'Só Deus é grande,'" 1:346.

64. Eusébio de Souza, *História militar do Ceará* (Fortaleza: N.p., 1950), 293. Rui Facó notes that similar attacks occurred in Minas Gerais after the proclamation of the republic, acts he links to popular disillusionment at the change in government; see his *Cangaceiros e fanáticos*, 77–124.

65. See José Rafael de Menezes, *Sociologia do Nordeste* (Recife: Editora ASA, 1985), 27–29. For a broader view of the psychological characteristics of rural Catholicism, see Maria Isaura Pereira de Queiroz, "Tambaú, cidade dos mila-

gres," *Cultura, sociedade rural, sociedade urbana: ensaios* (São Paulo: Universidade de São Paulo, 1978), 135–43.

66. Calmon, *Vida econômico-financeira da Bahia*, 120.

67. Salaries are discussed in Lélis Piedade's dispatch published September 18, 1897, in the *Jornal de Notícias* (Salvador); also Garcez, "Aspectos econômicos," 24. On arms shipments, see Tristão de Alencar Araripe, *Expedições militares contra Canudos* (Rio de Janeiro: Impt. do Exército, 1960); "Franciscanos em Canudos, 1897," 387; Favilla Nunes's dispatch, *Gazeta de Notícias* (Rio de Janeiro), August 29, 1897, 1.

68. Miriam Molina, "Canudos: o apocalipse de Antônio Conselheiro," *Manchete*, November 25, 1989, 46.

69. About fourteen hundred graves were exhumed by soldiers as part of their census of houses and occupants after Canudos was captured.

70. For a review of Sebastianism, see J. Lúcio de Azevedo, *A evolução do Sebastianismo*, 2d ed. (Lisbon: Livraria Clássica, 1947).

71. Gilberto Freyre, *Atualidade de Euclydes da Cunha: conferência lida no Salão de Conferências da Biblioteca do Ministério das Relações Exteriores do Brasil, no dia 29 de outubro de 1940*, 2d ed. (Rio de Janeiro: CEB, 1943), 21; Vamireh Chacon, *O humanismo brasileiro* (São Paulo: Secretaria da Cultura, 1980), 139; René Ribeiro, "Brazilian Messianic Movements," in *Millennial Dreams in Action: Studies in Revolutionary Religious Movements*, ed. Sylvia L. Thrupp (New York: Schocken Books, 1970), 58–59. The study of the names of drought *retirantes* is being undertaken by Roger Cunniff, who provided the insight.

72. Pessar, "Unmasking the Politics of Religion," 257; Warren, "A terapia espírita no Rio de Janeiro por volta de 1900." *Religião e sociedade* 11, no. 3 (December 1984): 56–83; Consuelo Pondé de Sena, *Introdução ao estudo de uma comunidade do agreste bahiano: Itapicurú, 1830/1892* (Salvador: Universidade Federal da Bahia, 1979), 142, 153–61; Pereira de Queiroz, *O campesinato brasileiro*, 72. Fredrick B. Pike (*The Politics of the Miraculous in Peru* [Lincoln: University of Nebraska Press, 1986]) speaks of a surge of personal (as opposed to institutional) spiritualism in Latin America from the late nineteenth century to the 1940s, a spiritualism rooted in the belief that spiritual power rests in all individuals. To some extent, this has always been a part of folk Catholicism in Brazil.

73. Roberto Da Matta defines the term in the civic sphere, but extends it to Conselheiro and his investment in the millennium; see *Carnivals, Rogues, and Heroes: An Interpretation of the Brazilian Dilemma* (Notre Dame, Ind.: University of Notre Dame Press, 1991), 210–11.

74. Ibid., 212.

75. Desembargador Polybio Mendes da Silva, Itapicurú, interview with Consuelo Pondé de Sena, cited in her *Introdução ao estudo de uma comunidade*, 156. As a child, he was handed to Conselheiro and kissed his hands; his family in turn offered wood from their *fazenda* to construct Conselheiro's new church at Vila Rica (today Crisópolis).

76. On "rustic Catholicism" in Brazil, see Pereira de Queiroz, *O campesinato brasileiro*, 72–99.

77. For an overview of episcopal reform in Bahia, dating from 1883, see Otten, "'Só Deus é grande,'" anexo, 3–4.

78. A decade later, a similar thing happened when the national church hierarchy rejected opportunities to influence rising labor union militancy, opting instead to ally itself with the government and the retrogressive industrialist elite. For a social history of the Brazilian labor movement, see Margareth Rago, *Do cabaré ao lar: a utopia da cidade disciplinar, 1890–1930* (Rio de Janeiro: Paz e Terra, 1985).

79. Barman, "The Brazilian Peasantry Reexamined," 401.

80. "Cacaso" [Antônio Carlos de Brito], "O pesadelo no país de Canudos," *Folha de São Paulo*, July 5, 1987, 58. See also Nancy P. S. Naro, "Rio Studies Rio: Ongoing Research on the First Republic in Rio de Janeiro," *The Americas* 2 (1987): 429–40; Décio Saes, *A formação do estado burguês no Brasil (1888–1891)* (Rio de Janeiro: Paz e Terra, 1985).

81. See Bello, *History of Modern Brazil*, 224.


CONCLUSION

1. See Chilcote, "Protest and Resistance," 244–47.

2. See the *cordel* poet João Melquíades Ferreira da Silva, *A guerra de Canudos*, and J. Sara, *Meu folclore* (1956), cited in *Literatura popular em verso-estudos* (Rio de Janeiro: Fundação Casa Rui Barbosa, 1973), 1:112–15; Pereira de Queiroz, *Messianismo*, 200–201. On Sebastianism, see Ribeiro, "Brazilian Messianic Movements," 58, 66; and *Grande enciclopédia portuguesa e brasileira* (Lisbon: Editora Enciclopédia, 1945), 28:19.

3. Examples include the "Saint-of-the-Palm-Trees" movement in Pernambuco in 1951, the "Blue Butterfly" movement of Campina Grande, Paraíba, in the late 1970s, and the "telepathic" Christian Jesuit Legion of Cícero José Farias in Recife, with branches in Juazeiro, Ceará, and Arcoverde, Pernambuco, also in the 1970s. See Ribeiro, "Brazilian Messianic Movements," 68–69; Josildeth Gomes Consorte and Lísias Nogueira Negrão, *O messianismo no Brasil contemporâneo* (São Paulo: FFLCH/USP-CER, 1973).

4. Lísias Nogueira Negrão, "Um movimento messiânico urbano: messianismo e mudança social no Brasil," in Consorte and Negrão, *Messianismo no Brasil contemporâneo*, 21–30.

5. On the Muckers, see Amado, *Conflito social no Brasil*; Duglas Teixeira Monteiro, *Os errantes do novo século* (São Paulo: Duas Cidades, 1978); Maurício Vinhas de Queiroz, *Messianismo e conflito social* (Rio de Janeiro: Civilização Brasileira, 1966), esp. 271–74; and Eduardo Marques Peixoto, "Questão Maurer, os Mukers," *Revista do Instituto Histórico e Geográfico Brasileiro* 68, pt. 2 (1907): 393–505. One of the earliest (and best) accounts was written in 1878 and published twenty-two years later, in Germany, by a Jesuit, Ambrósio Schupp: *Die Mucker* (Paderborn: Bonifacius Druckerei, 1900); the Brazilian edition was published in 1911 in Porto Alegre by Livraria Selbach.

6. For Brazil, see Patricia Ann Aufderheide, "Order and Violence: Social Deviance and Social Control in Brazil, 1780–1840" (Ph.D. diss., University of Minnesota, 1976). This occurred in Spanish America as well. On the 1717 Chiapas uprising, see Nancy M. Farriss, *Maya Society Under Colonial Rule: The Col-*

*lective Enterprise of Survival* (Princeton: Princeton University Press, 1984); Victoria Reifler Bricker, *The Indian Christ, the Indian King* (Austin: University of Texas Press, 1981); Nelson Reed, *The Caste War of Yucatán* (Stanford: Stanford University Press, 1964); Steve J. Stern, *Peru's Indian Peoples and the Challenge of Spanish Conquest* (Madison: University of Wisconsin Press, 1982).

7. Ribeiro, "Brazilian Messianic Movements," 65–66; Chilcote, "Protest and Resistance," 255.

8. Ribeiro, "Brazilian Messianic Movements," 66, citing a manuscript in the Seção de Documentos, Arquivo Nacional, Rio de Janeiro, "Devassa acerca dos acontecimentos da Serra do Rodeador," *Governadores de Pernambuco. Correspondência com o Ministério do Reino*, 4–144, 180–87, 234–69.

9. See F. A. Pereira da Costa, "Folk-lore pernambucano," *Revista do Instituto Histórico e Geográfico Brasileiro* 70, pt. 2 (1907): 35–44.

10. Antônio Ático de Souza Leite, "Memória sôbre a Pedra Bonita ou Reino Encantado na camarca de Vila Vela [*sic*]," *Revista do Instituto Arqueológico e Geográfico de Pernambuco* 60 (December 1903): 217–48; T. A. Araripe Júnior, *O Reino Encantado, chronica sebastianista* (Rio de Janeiro: Typ. Gazeta de Notícias, 1878).

11. Nina Rodrigues, *As collectividades anormaes*, 135–39.

12. See Décio Freitas, *Cabanos: os guerrilheiros do imperador*, 2d ed. (Rio de Janeiro: Editora Graal, 1978).

13. Bethell and Carvalho, "Brazil from Independence to the Middle of the Nineteenth Century," 694–95.

14. Eventually the remnants of the group disbanded. Very little research has been done on the Cabanada and other early nineteenth-century movements. See Chilcote, "Protest and Resistance," 248–56; Nina Rodrigues, *As collectividades anormaes*.

15. The survival of the Mucker movement is described in Chilcote, "Protest and Resistance," 259; see also Noel Nascimento, "Contestado, guerra camponesa do Brasil," *Revista Brasiliense* 50 (November–December 1963): 86–88; Maria Isaura Pereira de Queiroz, *La 'guerre sainte' au Brésil: le mouvement messianique du Contestado*, Boletim 187 (São Paulo: Faculdade de Filosofia, Ciências e Letras da Universidade de São Paulo, 1957); Lawrence Hallewell, "Muckers," in *Historical Dictionary of Brazil*, 2d ed., ed. Robert M. Levine and Lawrence Hallewell (Metuchen, N.J.: Scarecrow Press, forthcoming). The best account of the Mucker movement is Janaína Amado's *Conflito social no Brasil*; see also Joseph L. Love, *Rio Grande do Sul and Brazilian Regionalism, 1882–1930* (Stanford: Stanford University Press, 1971), 18–19; Leopoldo Petry, *O episódio do Ferrabraz (os Mucker)*, 2d ed. (São Leopoldo, Rio Grande do Sul: N.p., 1966).

16. Della Cava, *Miracle at Joaseiro*, 76–78.

17. Ribeiro, "Brazilian Messianic Movements," 67; Abelardo F. Montenegro, *História do fanatismo religioso no Ceará* (Fortaleza: Batista Fontenele, 1959).

18. Albuquerque, *Um sertanejo e o sertão*, 32; courtesy of René Ribeiro.

19. He may have taken the name José Maria for its similarity with Monge (Monk) João Maria, a healer famous in the region two decades earlier; see Todd Alan Diacon, "Capitalists and Fanatics: Brazil's Contestado Rebellion, 1912–

1916" (Ph.D. diss., University of Wisconsin, 1987), 1–2. Also see Diacon's master's thesis, "The Contestado Movement and the Caste War of Yucatán: Secular and Religious Responses to Crisis Situations" (University of Wisconsin, 1983); and Paulo Ramos Derengoski, *O desmoronamento do mundo jagunço* (Florianópolis: Fundação Catarense de Cultura, 1986); Bernard J. Siegel, "The Contestado Rebellion, 1912–16: A Case Study in Brazilian Messianism and Regional Dynamics," *Journal of Anthropological Research* 33 (1977): 202–13.

20. José Maria had mistranslated the word for peer into "pair," hence his twelve pairs of guards, or twenty-four soldiers. See Pereira de Queiroz, *Messianismo*, 277; Diacon, "Capitalists and Fanatics," 13.

21. See Vinhas de Queiroz, *Messianismo e conflito social*, 83–86; Demerval Peixoto, *Campanha do Contestado: episódios e impressões* (Rio de Janeiro: N.p., 1916); *A Folha do Comércio* (Florianópolis), September 28, October 2, 30, 1912; *A Notícia* (Lages, Santa Catarina), September 28, November 9, 1912; Governador de Santa Catarina, *Mensagem do Governador Vidal Ramos, 1913* (Florianópolis: Imprensa do Estado, 1913), 18–22, cited by Diacon, "Capitalists and Fanatics," 6–9; see also 15–16.

22. See Marco Antônio da Silva Mello and Arno Vogel, "Monarquia contra república: a ideologia da terra e o paradigma do milênio na 'guerra santa' do Contestado," *Estudos Históricos* 2, no. 4 (1989): 190–213.

23. See Noel Nascimento, "Canudos, Contestado e fanatismo religioso," *Revista Brasiliense* 44 (November–December 1961): 62–67.

24. Account based on Raymundo Duarte, "Notas preliminares do estudo do movimento messiânico de Pau de Colher," Universidade Federal da Bahia, Salvador, 1969, Typescript; and the same author's "Um movimento messiânico no interior da Bahia," *Revista de Antropologia* 11, nos. 1–2 (1963): 45–51; Facó, *Cangaceiros e fanáticos*; Ewerton D. Cortez, "A tragédia do Caldeirão: uma página de sociologia do Nordeste," *A Ordem* (Natal), May 5, 1937, 2; Tarcísio Holanda, "A chacina do Caldeirão," *Jornal do Brasil*, February 1, 1981, 1–2; Mota, "Pedra Bonita e Caldeirão"; Padre Geraldo Oliveira Lima, ed., Special issue of *Cordel número 21* (Crateus, Ceará) (December 1979).

25. The information was obtained from photographs in Djacir Menezes, *O outro Nordeste* (Rio de Janeiro: José Olympio Editora, 1937).

26. Cortez, "A tragédia do Caldeirão," 2; see also *A Ordem*, May 14, 1937, 4, on the "barbarous murder of five soldiers" by three hundred "fanatic followers of the *beato*."

27. *Boletim da Federação das Associações Rurais do Estado do Ceará* (Fortaleza) 9 (March 1955): 6. Also Padre Geraldo Oliveira Lima, Special issue of *Cordel número 21*, the cover of which reproduces a hand-drawn illustration, done in childlike hand, of an airplane dropping bombs on a peaceful rural community. See also Duarte, "Movimento messiânico," 6, citing Clóvis Caldeira, *Mutirão*, 116.

28. In 1938 or 1939 he returned to Caldeirão and tried again to start a settlement, but the Salesian priests who had taken up residence turned him away. Unsuccessful in a court action to regain his land, he did receive a small award that permitted him to purchase a small property in Novo Exu, known as União, where he tried again to reestablish the community. He died in 1946 of bubonic plague. See "Beato José Lourenço," *O Povo* (Fortaleza), May 10, 1981, 2.

29. Roger Bastide, *Brasil: terra de contrastes* (São Paulo: DIFEL, 1959), 80.

30. Duarte, "Movimento messiânico," 19.

31. See Opato Gueiros, *Cangaceiros e fanáticos* (Recife: N.p., 1942), 17; Duarte, "Movimento messiânico," 35.

32. Telegram, Captain Maurino Tavares, Comandante do Esquadrão Motorizado to Coronel-Comandante da Polícia Militar da Bahia, January 19, 1938, published in *A Tarde* (Salvador), February 2, 1938.

33. Ribeiro, "Brazilian Messianic Movements," 68, citing José Lucena, "Uma pequena epidemia mental em Pernambuco: os fanáticos do município de Panelas," *Neurobiologia* 3 (1940): 41–91.

34. See Georges Balandier, *Sociologie actuelle de l'Afrique noire* (Paris: Presses Universitaires de France, 1955), chap. 2; Chilcote, "Protest and Resistance," 297.

35. The subject is addressed in *Luso-Brazilian Review* 28, no. 1 (Summer 1991) (special issue edited by Robert M. Levine).

36. René Ribeiro, "Brazilian Messianism," *Luso-Brazilian Review* 28, no. 2 (forthcoming).

37. See Talmon, "Millenarianism," esp. 354.

38. Robert Darnton, *The Kiss of Lamourette: Reflections in Cultural History* (New York: W. W. Norton, 1990), 239–40.

39. Ibid., 240, commenting on and citing Mandrou's *De la culture populaire aux 17e et 18e siècles* (Paris, 1964).

40. See the French anthropologist Pierre Clastres's *Society Against the State* (New York: Zone Books, 1987), 202, cited by Burns, "Destruction of a Folk Past," 31.

41. Burns, "Destruction of a Folk Past," 20.

42. Calasans, *No tempo de Antônio Conselheiro*, 76.

43. Cf. Mullett, *Popular Culture and Popular Protest*, chap. 4, on John Hus (ca. 1373–1415), San Bernardino of Siena (1380–1444), and Girolamo Savonarola (1452–1498). Two of these men were burned for heresy, and the other, San Bernardino, was accused of it.

44. Aron Gurevich reminds us that even trained specialists use terms such as "naive," "primitive," and "crude" when referring to popular religion or any faith seen as superstitious; see his foreword to *Medieval Popular Culture*, xiv–xv.

45. Ribeiro, "Brazilian Messianic Movements," 65–66.

46. Nineteenth-century Augustinian monks in Cuba, for example, dressed in exactly the same clothing as Conselheiro; see John G. F. Wurdemann, *Notes on Cuba* (Boston: James Munroe, 1844), 22–23. Vargas Llosa's opening description of Conselheiro is quite evocative: "The man was tall and so thin he seemed to be always in profile. He was dark-skinned and rawboned, and his eyes burned with perpetual fire. He wore shepherd's sandals and the dark purple tunic draped over his body called to mind the cassocks of those missionaries who every so often visited the villages of the backlands, baptizing hordes of children and marrying men and women who were cohabiting" (*War of the End of the World*, 3).

47. See Henri Desroche, *The Sociology of Hope*, trans. Carol Martin-Sperry (London: Routledge & Kegan Paul, 1979), 88. José Calasans argues that Conselheiro's messianic phase came about only with his death: in life he never sought it; see his "O ciclo folclórico do Bom Jesus Conselheiro," Núcleo do Sertão Archive, Salvador, 1950, Typescript, 23.

48. The description was written about John Calvin, but it fits Conselheiro perfectly; see John Gross, Review of William J. Bouwsma's *John Calvin: A Sixteenth Century Portrait* (Oxford: Oxford University Press, 1987), *New York Times*, December 8, 1987, 29.

49. Examples include the Eight Trigrams Uprising of 1813 in China and the White Lotus sects that followed; see Susan Naquin, *Millenarian Rebellion in China* (New Haven: Yale University Press, 1976), 269–70.

50. Pessar, "Unmasking the Politics of Religion," 265.

51. See Pike, *Politics of the Miraculous*, 19.

52. Barman, "Brazilian Peasantry Reexamined," 404.

53. See, for example, Pereira de Queiroz, *O campesinato brasileiro*, 42–45, 59–63; and her "Messiahs in Brazil," *Past & Present*, no. 31 (July 1965): 62–86. Todd Alan Diacon evaluates the Pereira de Queiroz view in "Capitalists and Fanatics," 381–84.

54. This theme is treated by Roberto Da Matta in *Carnivals, Rogues, and Heroes*.

55. See Duglas Teixeira Monteiro, "Um confronto entre Juazeiro, Canudos e Contestado," in *História geral da civilização brasileira*, ed. Boris Fausto, vol. 3: *O Brasil republicano*, pt. 2: *Sociedade e instituições (1889–1930)* (São Paulo: DIFEL, 1977), 42–45.

56. Roger Bastide, "Messianism and Social and Economic Development," in *Social Change: The Colonial Situation*, ed. Immanuel Wallerstein (New York: John Wiley, 1966), cited by Chilcote, "Protest and Resistance," 302.

57. Sylvia L. Thrupp, Introduction to *Millennial Dreams in Action*, 12.

58. See Ribeiro, "Brazilian Messianic Movements," 55–69; Thrupp, Introduction to *Millennial Dreams in Action*, 15–17. Maria Isaura Pereira de Queiroz offers her own formula in "Classifications des messianismes brésiliens," *Archives de sociologie des religions* (Paris), no. 5 (January–June 1958): 111–20.

59. Ribeiro, "Brazilian Messianic Movements," 64, citing Roger Bastide, *Les religions africaines au Brésil* (Paris: Presses Universitaires de France, 1960); Wilson D. Wallis, "Socio-cultural Sources of Messiahs," in *Religion, Society, and the Individual*, ed. J. Milton Younger (New York: Macmillan, 1957), 578–86; Bernard Barber, "Acculturation and Messianic Movements," in *Reader in Comparative Religion*, ed. William A. Lessa and Evon Vogt (Evansville, Ill.: Row Peterson, 1958), 474–78.

60. Ribeiro, "Brazilian Messianic Movements," 64–65.

61. *A Notícia* (Salvador), December 11, 1896; *Jornal de Notícias* (Salvador), April 20, 1897.

62. See Leon Perez, "The Messianic Idea and Messianic Delusion," *Mental Health and Society* 5, nos. 5–6 (1978): 266–74, comparing Jewish, Christian, and Moslem subjects in Jerusalem; and George E. Atwood, "On the Origins and Dynamics of Messianic Salvation Fantasies," *International Review of Psycho-Analysis* (London) 5, no. 1 (1978): 85–96.

63. Roger Bastide, *Sociologia de las enfermidades mentales* (Mexico City: Siglo Veintiuno Editores, 1964), n.p., quoted by Leon Perez, "Messianic Idea and Messianic Delusion," 272.

64. P. Horton, "The Mystic Experience," *Journal of the American Psychoanalytic Association* 22 (1974): 364–79.

65. Atwood, "On the Origins and Dynamics of Messianic Salvation Fantasies," 92. As a consequence, since there is nothing to be lost, the subject is protected from a repetition of the traumatic experiences that may have led to the messianic delusion in the first place.

66. This issue is summarized by Joseph A. Dowling, "Millennialism and Psychology," *Quarterly Journal of Childhood and Psychohistory* 5, no. 1 (Summer 1977): 121–40, esp. 125.

67. John Weir Perry, "The Messianic Hero," *Journal of Analytical Psychology* 17, no. 2 (July 1972): 184–200.

68. Hundreds of mendicant preachers and secular priests spoke in apocalyptic language during each century of the medieval period. See Bernd Moeller, "Religious Life in Germany on the Eve of the Reformation," in *Pre-Reformation Germany*, ed. Gerald Strauss (London: Macmillan, 1972), 13–42.

69. Mullett, *Popular Culture and Popular Protest*, 1–2.

70. Ibid., citing Karl Marx and Friedrich Engels, *On Religion* (Moscow: Progress Publications, 1972), 33, 74.

71. The definition is from Thrupp, Introduction to *Millennial Dreams in Action*, 11, citing Norman Cohn, "Medieval Millenarianism: Its Bearing on the Comparative Study of Millenarian Movements," in ibid., 31–43. See also Pessar, "Unmasking the Politics of Religion," 255–78.

72. Thrupp, citing Norman Cohn, *The Pursuit of the Millennium: Revolutionary Millenarians and Mystical Anarchists of the Middle Ages*, rev. ed. (New York: Oxford University Press, 1970), chap. 6.

73. Antônio Saraiva, *O discurso engenhoso* (São Paulo: Editora Perspectiva, 1980), 110–11.

74. Cohn, "Medieval Millenarianism," 33.

75. Eric J. Hobsbawm, *Primitive Rebels: Studies in Archaic Forms of Social Movement in the Nineteenth and Twentieth Centuries* (New York: W. W. Norton, 1959), 106; Diacon, "Capitalists and Fanatics," 379. Hobsbawm's thesis on "social banditry," which parallels his work on primitive rebels, is criticized by Anton Blok, "The Peasant and the Brigand: Social Banditry Reconsidered," *Comparative Studies in Society and History* 14, no. 4 (September 1972): 494–503; Hobsbawm's response follows, ibid., 503–6.

76. See, for example, Francisco Mangabeira, "A realidade social de Canudos e do antigo sertão," in *João Mangabeira: república e socialismo no Brasil* (Rio de Janeiro: Paz e Terra, 1979), 49–58; Moniz, *Guerra social de Canudos*; Facó, *Cangaceiros e fanáticos*, esp. chap. 2; and Facó, "A guerra camponesa de Canudos," 128–51, 162–83. Few of these studies are based on primary sources.

77. See della Cava, *Miracle at Joaseiro*; also Pang, "Banditry and Messianism in Brazil," which complements della Cava's analysis. Billy Jaynes Chandler's biography of the bandit Lampião identified backland poverty, the periodic droughts, the flawed system of law and justice, and the breakdown of the traditional order after the fall of the monarchy in 1889 as the principal causes for *cangaceirismo*; see his *Bandit King*, 13–15.

78. The movements she focuses on are Canudos, the Contestado, and Padre Cícero's; see Pereira de Queiroz, *Messianismo*, 330–31; "Messiahs in Brazil"; *Reforme et révolution dans les sociétés traditionelles: histoire et ethnologie des mouvements messianiques* (Paris: Anthropos, 1968); Duglas Teixeira Monteiro, "Confronto

entre Juazeiro, Canudos e Contestado." Also see Maria Cristina da Matta Machado, "Aspectos do fenômeno do cangaço no Nordeste brasileiro," *Revista de História* 93 (1973): 139–75.

79. Pereira de Queiroz, "Messiahs in Brazil," 84; Diacon, "Capitalists and Fanatics," 382.

80. Diacon, "Capitalists and Fanatics," 383–84, citing Steve Stern, "On the Social Origins of Millennial Movements: A Review and Proposal," 1974, Typescript, 5.

81. Diacon, "Capitalists and Fanatics," 380–81.

82. Steve J. Stern, "New Approaches to the Study of Peasant Rebellion and Consciousness: Implications of the Andean Experience," in *Resistance, Rebellion, and Consciousness in the Andean Peasant World, Eighteenth to Twentieth Centuries*, ed. Steve Stern (Madison: University of Wisconsin Press, 1987), 5.

83. Ibid.

84. Cf. ibid., 9. See also Florencia E. Mallon, *The Defense of Community in Peru's Central Highlands: Peasant Struggle and Capitalist Transition, 1860–1940* (Princeton: Princeton University Press, 1983); Cohn, *Pursuit of the Millennium.*

85. George Rudé, *The Crowd in History: A Study of Popular Dissent in France and England* (London: Lawrence & Wishart, 1981), 61–64; Juan R. I. Cole, "Of Crowds and Empires: Afro-Asian Riots and European Expansion, 1857–1882," *Comparative Studies in Society and History* 31, no. 1 (January 1989): 131–32.

86. Ian Roxborough, Review of John Tutino's *From Insurrection to Revolution in Mexico*, in *Social History* 13, no. 3 (October 1988): 373–74.

87. See Hunt, "Measure of Popular Culture," 363.

88. See Eugen Weber, *Peasants into Frenchmen: The Modernization of Rural France, 1870–1914* (Stanford: Stanford University Press, 1976); Hunt, "Measure of Popular Culture," 368, esp. n. 3.

89. See Hunt, "Measure of Popular Culture," 368.

90. In practice, of course, the collective behavior of the residents of Belo Monte settled into abject servility. Cf. Theodor Shanin, *The Awkward Class: Political Sociology of Peasantry in a Developing Society: Russia, 1910–1925* (Oxford: Oxford University Press, 1972); and Robert Brenner, "Agrarian Class Structure and Economic Development in Pre-industrial Europe," *Past and Present*, no. 70 (1976): 75, cited by Hunt, "Measure of Popular Culture," 371n.12.

91. Colin Gordon, commenting on Michel Foucault, *Power/Knowledge*, cited by James C. Scott, *Weapons of the Weak: Everyday Forms of Peasant Resistance* (New Haven: Yale University Press, 1985), vii–viii.

92. Scott, *Weapons of the Weak*, 29, 41, 304.

93. Ibid., 33n.11. The argument is that women can exercise power when they do not openly challenge the formal order. See Susan Carol Rogers, "Female Forms of Power and the Myth of Male Dominance," *American Ethnologist* 2, no. 4 (November 1975): 727–56.

94. Antonio Gramsci names this process of ideological intimidation *hegemony*, claiming that the ruling class dominates not only the means of physical production but also the means of symbolic production; see his *Selections from the*

*Prison Notebooks,* ed. and trans. Quintin Hoare and Geoffrey Nowell Smith (London: Lawrence & Wishart, 1971). Engels, observing the English rural population, claimed that rural folk were, if anything, more removed from the institutional circuits of symbolic power than their urban counterparts; see his *The Condition of the Working Class in England* (Moscow: Progress Publishers, 1973), 162–63, cited by Scott, *Weapons of the Weak,* 321; see also 315–16.

95. Scott, *Weapons of the Weak,* 304.

96. Ibid., 332. I have borrowed from Scott's compelling analysis of peasant experience in Southeast Asia to discuss the Brazilian case.

97. Ibid., 333.

98. See Slater, *Stories on a String*; Sebastião Nunes Batista, *Poética popular do Nordeste* (Rio de Janeiro: Fundação Casa Rui Barbosa, 1982); *Inácio da Catingueira e Luís Gama, dois poetas negros contra o racismo dos mestiços* (Rio de Janeiro: Fundação Casa Rui Barbosa, 1982).

99. Cf. Scott, *Weapons of the Weak,* 336, who argues the same for the Islamic community of Sedaka in Malaysia. See also Eric Hobsbawm, "Peasants and Politics," *Journal of Peasant Studies* 1, no. 1 (October 1973): 12.

100. Scott, *Moral Economy of the Peasant,* 231.

101. See Edgard Carone, *A república velha,* vol. 1: *Instituições e classes sociais*; and vol. 2: *Evolução política* (São Paulo: Difusão Européia do Livro, 1971).

102. See Suely Robles Reis de Queiroz, *Os radicais da república. Jacobinismo: ideologia e ação* (São Paulo: Editora Brasiliense, 1986), 266.

103. See José Mauro Gagliard, *O Indígena e a República* (São Paulo: Editora Hucitec, 1989), 120–39.

104. See Otten, "'Só Deus é grande,'" 1:255–56.

105. John Keegan, *The Face of Battle: A Study of Agincourt, Waterloo, and the Somme* (London: Jonathan Cape, 1976), 54–55.

106. Keegan notes that in the case of the United States, the only military figure to attain truly cult status was Gen. Robert E. Lee—"the paladin of its only component community ever to suffer military catastrophe" (ibid., 54). In a way, da Cunha's portrait of Conselheiro made him into a kind of cult devil-figure, larger than life, as sinister and malevolent as a Brazilian Rasputin.

107. See Hunt, "Measure of Popular Culture," 368.

108. José Murilo de Carvalho, "The Old Republic," Paper presented to the Brazilian Studies Committee of the Conference on Latin American History, San Francisco, December 30, 1989.

109. See the summary comments by Gerald Michael Greenfield in the *Hispanic American Historical Review* 70, no. 3 (August 1990): 524–25.

110. Steve J. Stern, Introduction to Part 3 of *Resistance, Rebellion, and Consciousness,* 218. Mexico under the Porfiriato offers a case parallel to Brazil.

111. Copied down by Diógenes Figueiredo and submitted, upon the scribe's death at age 101, by Sebastião Nunes Batista to the Núcleo do Sertão Archive, Salvador, November 7, 1978. In Portuguese: "Fingiu-se de religioso / Para poder iludir / Fez parte do povo vir / com ele se desgraçou."

112. See Cristina Barbosa, "Canudos, uma história incompleta," *Jornal da Tarde* (São Paulo), October 6, 1988, 21.

# BIBLIOGRAPHY

The following bibliography has been divided into two sections: sources in English and sources in Portuguese and other languages. The listings are as complete as possible. In some cases, when I worked from photocopies, microforms, or newspaper or journal clippings in files maintained by archives (such as the Núcleo do Sertão in Salvador), no indication of page numbers could be found.

I have followed the standard alphabetizing procedure for each language. In Portuguese, I have used the last element of compound names unless conventional usage differs. Initial definite articles (*o, a, os, as*) have been disregarded in alphabetizing titles.

## SELECTED WORKS IN ENGLISH

Andrade, Manuel Correia de. *The Land and People of Northeast Brazil*. Translated by Dennis V. Johnson. Albuquerque: University of New Mexico Press, 1980.

Atwood, George E. "On the Origins and Dynamics of Messianic Salvation Fantasies." *International Review of Psycho-Analysis* (London) 5, no. 1 (1978): 85–96.

Aufderheide, Patricia Ann. "Order and Violence: Social Deviance and Social Control in Brazil, 1780–1840." Ph.D. diss., University of Minnesota, 1976.

Ballard, Charles. "Drought and Economic Distress: South Africa in the 1800s." *Journal of Interdisciplinary History* 17, no. 2 (August 1986): 359–78.

Barber, Bernard. "Acculturation and Messianic Movements." In *Reader in Comparative Religion*, edited by William A. Lessa and Evon Vogt, 474–78. Evansville, Ill.: Row Peterson, 1958.

Barman, Roderick J. *Brazil: The Forging of a Nation, 1798–1852*. Stanford: Stanford University Press, 1988.

———. "The Brazilian Peasantry Reexamined: The Implications of the Quebra-Quilo Revolt, 1874–1875." *Hispanic American Historical Review* 57, no. 3 (August 1977): 401–24.

*303*

Bastide, Roger. "Messianism and Social and Economic Development." In *Social Change: The Colonial Situation*, edited by Immanuel Wallerstein, 467–77. New York: John Wiley, 1966.

Bello, José Maria. *A History of Modern Brazil, 1889–1964*. Translated by James L. Taylor. Stanford: Stanford University Press, 1966.

Bercé, Yves-Marie. *History of Peasant Revolts: The Social Origin of Rebellion in Early Modern France*. Translated by Amanda Whitmore. Cambridge: Polity Press, 1990.

———. "Rural Unrest." In *Our Forgotten Past*, edited by Jerome Blum, 133–56. London: Thames & Hudson, 1982.

Berman, Marshall. *All That Is Solid Melts into Air: The Experience of Modernity*. New York: Simon & Schuster, 1982.

Bethell, Leslie, and José Murilo de Carvalho. "Brazil from Independence to the Middle of the Nineteenth Century." In *The Cambridge History of Latin America*, edited by Leslie Bethell, 3:679–746. Cambridge: Cambridge University Press, 1986.

Bloch, Marc. *French Rural History: An Essay on Its Basic Characteristics*. Translated by Janet Sondheimer. Berkeley and Los Angeles: University of California Press, 1966.

Blok, Anton. "The Peasant and the Brigand: Social Banditry Reconsidered." *Comparative Studies in Society and History* 14, no. 4 (September 1972): 494–503.

Borges, Dain. "Progress and Degeneration in Brazilian Social Thought of the 1930s." Paper presented at the Latin American Studies Association 15th International Congress, Miami, December 5, 1989.

Boxer, C. R. *The Golden Age of Brazil, 1695–1750*. Berkeley and Los Angeles: University of California Press, 1962.

Bricker, Victoria Reifler. *The Indian Christ, the Indian King*. Austin: University of Texas Press, 1981.

Brody, Eugene B. *The Lost Ones*. New York: International Universities Press, 1973.

Brookshaw, David. *Race and Color in Brazilian Literature*. Metuchen, N.J.: Scarecrow Press, 1986.

Burns, E. Bradford. "The Destruction of a Folk Past: Euclides da Cunha and Cataclysmic Cultural Clash." *Review of Latin American Studies* 3, no. 1 (1990): 17–36.

Carvalho, José Murilo de. "The Old Republic." Paper presented to Brazilian Studies Committee, Conference on Latin American History, American Historical Association, San Francisco, December 30, 1989; summary, by Steven Topik, in *Hispanic American Historical Review* 70, no. 3 (August 1990): 536–37.

Castro, Josué de. *Death in the Northeast*. New York: Random House, 1966.

Chandler, Billy Jaynes. *The Bandit King: Lampião of Brazil*. College Station, Tex.: Texas A & M Press, 1978.

———. *The Feitosas and the Sertão dos Inhamuns: The History of a Family and a Community in Northeast Brazil, 1700–1930*. Gainesville: University Presses of Florida, 1972.

———. "The Role of Negroes in the Ethnic Formation of Ceará: The Need for a Reappraisal." *Revista de Ciências Sociais* 4, no. 1 (1973): 31–43.

Chilcote, Ronald H. *Power and the Ruling Classes in Northeast Brazil: Juazeiro and Petrolina in Transition*. Cambridge: Cambridge University Press, 1990.

———. "Protest and Resistance in Brazil and Portuguese Africa: A Synthesis and Classification." In *Protest and Resistance in Angola and Brazil: Comparative Studies*, edited by Ronald H. Chilcote, 243–304. Berkeley and Los Angeles: University of California Press, 1972.

Clastres, Pierre. *Society Against the State*. New York: Zone Books, 1987.

Clay, Jason W. "The Articulation of Non-capitalist Agricultural Production Systems with Capitalist Exchange Systems: The Case of Garanhuns, Brazil, 1845–1977." Ph.D. diss., Cornell University, 1979.

Cobban, Alfred. *A History of Modern France*. Vol. 3: *1871–1962*. Harmondsworth, Middlesex: Penguin Books, 1965.

Cohn, Norman. "Medieval Millenarianism: Its Bearing on the Comparative Study of Millenarian Movements." In *Millennial Dreams in Action: Studies in Revolutionary Religious Movements*, edited by Sylvia L. Thrupp, 31–43. New York: Schocken Books, 1970.

———. *The Pursuit of the Millennium: Revolutionary Millenarians and Mystical Anarchists of the Middle Ages*. Rev. ed. New York: Oxford University Press, 1970.

Cole, J. P. *Latin America: An Economic and Social Geography*. New York: Plenum Press, 1965.

Costa, Emília Viotti da. "Brazil: The Age of Reform, 1870–1889." In *The Cambridge History of Latin America*, edited by Leslie Bethell, 5:725–77. Cambridge: Cambridge University Press, 1986.

———. *The Brazilian Empire: Myths and Histories*. Chicago: University of Chicago Press, 1986.

Crew, David. "Why Can't a Peasant Be More Like a Worker? Social Historians and German Peasants." *Journal of Social History* 22, no. 3 (Spring 1989): 531–40.

Cunniff, Roger L. "The Birth of the Drought Industry: Imperial and Provincial Responses to the Great Drought in Northeast Brazil, 1877–1880." *Revista de Ciências Sociais* (Fortaleza) 6, nos. 1–2 (1975): 65–82.

———. "The Great Drought: Northeast Brazil, 1877–1880." Ph.D. diss., University of Texas, Austin, 1970.

da Cunha, Euclydes. *Rebellion in the Backlands*. Tr. and with introduction by Samuel Putnam. Chicago: University of Chicago Press, 1944.

Da Matta, Roberto. *Carnivals, Rogues, and Heroes: An Interpretation of the Brazilian Dilemma*. Notre Dame, Ind.: University of Notre Dame Press, 1991.

Darnton, Robert. *The Kiss of Lamourette: Reflections in Cultural History*. New York: W. W. Norton, 1990.

Davis, John A. *Conflict and Control: Law and Order in Nineteenth-Century Italy*. Atlantic Highlands, N.J.: Humanities Press International, 1988.

della Cava, Ralph. "Brazilian Messianism and National Institutions: A Reappraisal of Canudos and Joaseiro." *Hispanic American Historical Review* 48, no. 3 (August 1968): 402–20.

———. *Miracle at Joaseiro*. New York: Columbia University Press, 1970.

Desroche, Henri. *The Sociology of Hope*. Translated by Carol Martin-Sperry. London: Routledge & Kegan Paul, 1979.

Devlin, Judith. *The Superstitious Mind: French Peasants and the Supernatural in the Nineteenth Century.* New Haven: Yale University Press, 1987.

Diacon, Todd Alan. "Capitalists and Fanatics: Brazil's Contestado Rebellion, 1912–1916." Ph.D. diss., University of Wisconsin, 1987.

———. "Down and Out in Rio de Janeiro." *Latin American Research Review* 25, no. 1 (1990): 243–52.

Di Tella, Torcuato S. "The Dangerous Classes in Early Nineteenth Century Mexico." *Journal of Latin American Studies* 5, no. 1 (May 1973): 79–82.

Dowling, Joseph A. "Millennialism and Psychology." *Quarterly Journal of Childhood and Psychohistory* 5, no. 1 (Summer 1977): 121–40.

Eisenberg, Peter L. *The Sugar Industry in Pernambuco, 1840–1910: Modernization Without Change.* Berkeley and Los Angeles: University of California Press, 1974.

Farriss, Nancy M. *Maya Society Under Colonial Rule: The Collective Enterprise of Survival.* Princeton: Princeton University Press, 1984.

Fausto, Boris. "Brazil: Social and Political Structure, 1889–1930." In *The Cambridge History of Latin America,* edited by Leslie Bethell, 5:779–830. Cambridge: Cambridge University Press, 1986.

Ferrez, Gilberto, and Weston J. Naef. *Pioneer Photographers of Brazil, 1840–1920.* New York: Center for Inter-American Relations, 1976.

Flinn, Michael W. *The European Demographic System, 1500–1820.* Baltimore: Johns Hopkins University Press, 1981.

Flynn, Peter. *Brazil: A Political Analysis.* London: Ernest Benn, 1978.

Forman, Shepard. *The Brazilian Peasantry.* New York: Columbia University Press, 1975.

Forman, Shepard, and Joyce F. Riegelhaupt. "Market Place and Marketing System: Towards a Theory of Peasant Economic Integration." *Comparative Studies in Society and History* 12, no. 2 (April 1970): 188–212.

Freyre, Gilberto. *The Masters and the Slaves.* Berkeley and Los Angeles: University of California Press, 1986.

———. *Order and Progress: Brazil from Monarchy to Republic.* Edited and translated by Rod W. Horton. New York: Alfred A. Knopf, 1970.

Fritsch, Winston. *External Constraints on Economic Policy, 1889–1930.* Pittsburgh: University of Pittsburgh Press, 1988.

Geertz, Clifford. *Agricultural Involution.* Berkeley and Los Angeles: University of California Press, 1974.

———. "Suq: The Bazaar Economy in Sefrou." In *Meaning and Order in Moroccan Society: Three Essays in Cultural Analysis,* edited by C. Geertz, H. Geertz, and L. Rosen, 123–313. Cambridge: Cambridge University Press, 1979.

Girouard, Mark. *The English Town: A History of Urban Life.* New Haven: Yale University Press, 1990.

Goldberg, Harvey. *The Life of Jean Jaurès.* Madison: University of Wisconsin Press, 1968.

Graham, R. B. Cunningham. *A Brazilian Mystic: Being the Life and Miracles of Antonio Conselheiro.* London: William Heinemann, 1920.

Graham, Richard. *Patronage and Politics in Nineteenth-Century Brazil.* Stanford: Stanford University Press, 1990.

Gramsci, Antonio. *Selections from the Prison Notebooks.* Edited and translated by Quintin Hoare and Geoffrey Nowell Smith. London: Lawrence & Wishart, 1971.

Greenfield, Gerald Michael. "Images of a Region: The Brazilian Northeast and the Great Drought in the Nineteenth Century." Paper presented at the 46th International Congress of Americanists, Amsterdam, July 4–8, 1988.

———. "Migrant Behavior and Elite Attitudes: Brazil's Great Drought, 1877–89." *The Americas* 43, no. 1 (July 1986): 69–85.

Gudeman, Stephen, and Stuart B. Schwartz. "Cleansing Original Sin: Godparenthood and the Baptism of Slaves in Eighteenth-Century Bahia." In *Kinship Ideology and Practice in Latin America,* edited by Raymond T. Smith, 35–58. Chapel Hill: University of North Carolina Press, 1984.

Gurevich, Aron Alkovlevich. *Medieval Popular Culture: Problems of Belief and Perception.* Translated by János Bak and Paul A. Hollingsworth. Cambridge: Cambridge University Press, 1988.

Haberly, David T. *Three Sad Races: Racial Identity and National Consciousness in Brazilian Literature.* Cambridge: Cambridge University Press, 1983.

Hahner, June E. *Civilian-Military Relations in Brazil, 1889–1898.* Columbia: University of South Carolina Press, 1969.

———. *Poverty and Politics: The Urban Poor in Brazil, 1870–1920.* Albuquerque: University of New Mexico Press, 1986.

Hale, Charles A. "Political and Social Ideas in Latin America, 1870–1930." In *The Cambridge History of Latin America,* edited by Leslie Bethell, 4:367–442. Cambridge: Cambridge University Press, 1986.

Hambloch, Ernest. *His Majesty the President: A Study of Constitutional Brazil.* London: Methuen, 1935.

Hansen, Edward C., and Timothy C. Parrish. "Elites vs. the State." In *Elites: Ethnographic Issues,* edited by George E. Marcus, 257–78. Albuquerque: University of New Mexico Press, 1983.

Hemming, John. "Indians and the Frontier in Colonial Brazil." In *The Cambridge History of Latin America,* edited by Leslie Bethell, 2:501–46. Cambridge: Cambridge University Press, 1986.

Henfrey, Colin. "Peasant Brazil: Agrarian History, Struggle and Change in the Paraguaçu Valley, Bahia." *Bulletin of Latin American Research* 8, no. 1 (1989): 1–24.

Hobsbawm, Eric J. *The Age of Empire, 1875–1914.* New York: Random House, 1987.

———. "Peasants and Politics." *Journal of Peasant Studies* 1, no. 1 (October 1973): 3–23.

———. *Primitive Rebels: Studies in Archaic Forms of Social Movement in the Nineteenth and Twentieth Centuries.* New York: W. W. Norton, 1959.

Horton, P. "The Mystic Experience." *Journal of the American Psychoanalytic Association* 22 (1974): 364–79.

Hunt, David. "The Measure of Popular Culture." *Comparative Studies in Society and History* 31, no. 2 (April 1989): 367–68.

Jenkins, J. Craig. "Why Do Peasants Rebel? Structural and Historical Theories of Modern Peasant Rebellions." *American Journal of Sociology* 88, no. 3 (1983): 487–514.

Katz, Friedrich. "Rural Rebellions After 1810." In *Riot, Rebellion, and Revolution: Rural Social Conflict in Mexico*, edited by F. Katz, 65–94. Princeton: Princeton University Press, 1988.

Keegan, John. *The Face of Battle: A Study of Agincourt, Waterloo, and the Somme.* London: Jonathan Cape, 1976.

Kidder, D. P., and J. C. Fletcher. *Brazil and the Brazilians, Portrayed in Historical and Descriptive Sketches.* Philadelphia: Childs & Peterson, 1857.

Knight, Alan. "Racism, Revolution, and Indigenismo: Mexico, 1910–1940." In *The Idea of Race in Latin America, 1870–1940*, edited by Richard Graham, 71–114. Austin: University of Texas Press, 1990.

Krikler, Jeremy. "Agrarian Struggle and the South African War." *Social History* 14, no. 2 (May 1989): 153–55.

Kselman, Thomas. *Miracles and Prophecies in Nineteenth-Century France.* New Brunswick, N.J.: Rutgers University Press, 1983.

Lasslett, Peter. *The World We Have Lost: England Before the Industrial Age.* New York: Scribner, 1965.

Lauderdale Graham, Sandra. *House and Street: The Domestic World of Servants and Masters in Nineteenth-Century Rio de Janeiro.* Cambridge: Cambridge University Press, 1988.

Leff, Nathaniel H. *Underdevelopment and Development in Brazil.* 2 vols. London: Allen & Unwin, 1982.

Lepovitz, Helena, and Dana Tiffany. "The European *Avant-Garde* as a *Fin-de-Siècle* Abbey of Misrule." *Journal of Unconventional History* 1, no. 2 (Winter 1990): 22–23.

Levi, Darrell E. *The Prados of São Paulo, Brazil: An Elite Family and Social Change, 1840–1930.* Athens: University of Georgia Press, 1987.

Levine, Robert M. *Images of History: Nineteenth and Early Twentieth Century Latin American Photographs as Documents.* Durham, N.C.: Duke University Press, 1989.

———. *Pernambuco in the Brazilian Federation, 1889–1937.* Stanford: Stanford University Press, 1978.

Lewin, Linda. "The Oligarchical Limitations of Social Banditry in Brazil: The Case of the 'Good' Thief Antônio Silvino." *Past & Present*, no. 82 (February 1979): 116–36.

———. *Politics and Parentela in Paraíba.* Princeton: Princeton University Press, 1987.

Lewis, I. M. *Ecstatic Religion.* Harmondsworth, Middlesex: Penguin Books, 1971.

Lopez, Barry. *Arctic Dreams: Imagination and Desire in a Northern Landscape.* New York: Bantam Books, 1986.

Love, Joseph L. "Latin America and Romania, 1860–1950." In *Guiding the Invisible Hand: Economic Liberalism and the State in Latin American History*, edited by Joseph L. Love and Nils Jacobsen, 1–27. New York: Praeger, 1988.

———. *Rio Grande do Sul and Brazilian Regionalism, 1882–1930.* Stanford: Stanford University Press, 1971.

———. *São Paulo in the Brazilian Federation, 1889–1937.* Stanford: Stanford University Press, 1980.

Lynch, John. "The Catholic Church in Latin America, 1830–1930." In *The Cambridge History of Latin America,* edited by Leslie Bethell, 4:527–95. Cambridge: Cambridge University Press, 1986.

McAlister, Lyle N. *Spain and Portugal in the New World, 1492–1700.* Minneapolis: University of Minnesota Press, 1984.

McGregor, Pedro. *The Moon and Two Mountains: The Myths, Ritual, and Magic of Brazilian Spiritism.* London: Souvenir Press, 1966.

Mallon, Florencia E. *The Defense of Community in Peru's Central Highlands: Peasant Struggle and Capitalist Transition, 1860–1940.* Princeton: Princeton University Press, 1983.

Marchal, Lucien. *The Sage of Canudos.* Translated by Charles Duff. New York: E. P. Dutton, 1954.

Maxwell, Kenneth R. *Conflicts and Conspiracies: Brazil and Portugal, 1750–1808.* Cambridge: Cambridge University Press, 1973.

Meintel, Deirdre. *Race, Culture, and Portuguese Colonialism in Cabo Verde.* Syracuse, N.Y.: Maxwell School of Citizenship and Public Affairs, Syracuse University, 1984.

Merrick, Thomas W., and Douglas H. Graham. *Population and Economic Development in Brazil: 1800 to the Present.* Baltimore: Johns Hopkins University Press, 1979.

Meznar, Joan Ellen. "Deference and Dependence: The World of Small Farmers in a Northeastern Brazilian Community, 1850–1900." Ph.D. diss., University of Texas, Austin, 1986.

Mielche, Hakon. *From Santos to Bahia.* London: William Hodge, 1948.

Moeller, Bernd. "Religious Life in Germany on the Eve of the Reformation." In *Pre-Reformation Germany,* edited by Gerald Strauss, 13–42. London: Macmillan, 1972.

Monteiro, John M. "From Indian to Slave: Forced Native Labour and Colonial Society in São Paulo During the Seventeenth Century." *Slavery and Abolition* 9, no. 2 (September 1988): 105–27.

Morse, Richard M. "Brazil's Urban Development: Colony and Empire." In *From Colony to Nation: Essays on the Independence of Brazil,* edited by A. J. R. Russell-Wood, 155–84. Baltimore: Johns Hopkins University Press, 1975.

Mosca, Gaetano. *The Ruling Class.* New York: McGraw-Hill, 1939.

Mosse, George L. *Toward the Final Solution.* New York: Howard Fertig, 1978.

Mullett, Michael A. *Popular Culture and Popular Protest in Late Medieval and Early Modern Europe.* London: Croom Helm, 1987.

Myscofski, Carole A. *When Men Walk Dry: Portuguese Messianism in Brazil.* Atlanta: Scholar's Press, 1988.

Naquin, Susan. *Millenarian Rebellion in China.* New Haven: Yale University Press, 1976.

Naro, Nancy P. S. "Rio Studies Rio: Ongoing Research on the First Republic in Rio de Janeiro." *The Americas* 2 (1987): 429–40.

Needell, Jeffrey D. *A Tropical Belle Epoque: Elite Culture and Society in Turn-of-the-Century Rio de Janeiro.* Cambridge: Cambridge University Press, 1987.

Nunes Leal, Victor. *Coronelismo: The Municipality and Representative Government in Brazil.* Translated by June Henfrey. Cambridge: Cambridge University Press, 1977.

O'Gorman, Frances. *Aluanda: A Look at Afro-Brazilian Cults.* Rio de Janeiro: Francisco Alves, 1977.

Otto, Rudolf. *The Idea of the Holy.* 2d ed. London: Oxford University Press, 1950.

Pace, David. *Claude Lévi-Strauss: The Bearer of Ashes.* London: Routledge & Kegan Paul, 1983.

Pang, Eul-Soo. "Agrarian Change in the Northeast." In *Modern Brazil: Elites and Masses in Historical Perspective,* edited by Michael L. Conniff and Frank D. McCann, 123–39. Lincoln: University of Nebraska Press, 1989.

———. *Bahia in the First Brazilian Republic: Coronelismo and Oligarchies, 1889–1934.* Gainesville: University Presses of Florida, 1979.

———. "Banditry and Messianism in Brazil, 1870–1940: An Agrarian Crisis Hypothesis." *Proceedings of the Pacific Coast Council on Latin American Studies* 8 (1981–82): 1–24.

———. "*Coronelismo* in Northeast Brazil." In *The Caciques: Oligarchical Politics and the System of Caciquismo in the Luso-Hispanic World,* edited by Robert Kern, 65–88. Albuquerque: University of New Mexico Press, 1973.

———. *In Pursuit of Honor and Power: Noblemen of the Southern Cross in Nineteenth-Century Brazil.* Tuscaloosa: University of Alabama Press, 1988.

Pang, Eul-Soo, and Ron L. Seckinger. "The Mandarins of Imperial Brazil." *Comparative Studies in Society and History* 14 (March 1972): 215–44.

Pareto, Vilfredo. *The Rise and Fall of Elites: An Appreciation of Theoretical Sociology.* Totowa, N.J.: Bedminster Press, 1968.

Perez, Leon. "The Messianic Idea and Messianic Delusion." *Mental Health and Society* 5, nos. 5–6 (1978): 266–74.

Perry, John Weir. "The Messianic Hero." *Journal of Analytical Psychology* 17, no. 2 (July 1972): 184–200.

Pessar, Patricia R. "Millenarian Movements in Rural Brazil: Prophecy and Protest." *Religion* 12 (1982): 187–213.

———. "Revolution, Salvation, Extermination: The Future of Millenarianism in Brazil." In *Predicting Sociocultural Change,* edited by Susan Abbott and John van Willigen, 95–114. Athens: University of Georgia Press, 1980.

———. "Three Moments in Brazilian Millenarianism: The Interrelationship Between Politics and Religion." *Luso-Brazilian Review* 28, no. 1 (Summer 1991): 95–116 (Special issue on millenarianism and messianism, edited by Robert M. Levine).

———. "Unmasking the Politics of Religion: The Case of Brazilian Millenarianism." *Journal of Latin American Lore* 7, no. 2 (Winter 1981): 255–78.

———. "When Prophecy Prevails: A Study of Millenarianism in Brazil." Ph.D. diss., University of Chicago, 1976.

Pike, Fredrick B. *The Politics of the Miraculous in Peru.* Lincoln: University of Nebraska Press, 1986.

Putnam, Samuel. Introduction to *Rebellion in the Backlands (Os sertões),* by Euclydes da Cunha. Chicago: University of Chicago Press, 1944.

Queiroz, Maria Isaura Pereira de. "Messiahs in Brazil." *Past & Present,* no. 31 (July 1965): 62–86.

Reed, Nelson. *The Caste War of Yucatán.* Stanford: Stanford University Press, 1964.

Reesink, E. B. *The Peasant in the Sertão: A Short Exploration of His Past and Present.* Leiden: Institute of Cultural and Social Studies, Leiden University, 1981.

Reina, Leticia. "The Sierra Gorda Peasant Rebellion, 1847–50." In *Riot, Rebellion, and Revolution: Rural Social Conflict in Mexico,* edited by Friedrich Katz, 269–94. Princeton: Princeton University Press, 1988.

Reis, Jaime. "The Abolition of Slavery and Its Aftermath in Pernambuco (1880–1920)." Ph.D. diss., St. Anthony's College, Oxford University, 1974.

———. "Hunger in the Northeast: Some Historical Aspects." In *The Logic of Poverty: The Case of the Brazilian Northeast,* edited by Simon Mitchell, 41–57. London: Routledge & Kegan Paul, 1981.

Reis, João José. "Slave Resistance in Brazil: Bahia, 1807–1835." *Luso-Brazilian Review* 25, no. 1 (Summer 1988): 111–15.

Ribeiro, René. "Brazilian Messianic Movements." In *Millennial Dreams in Action: Studies in Revolutionary Religious Movements,* edited by Sylvia L. Thrupp, 55–69. New York: Schocken Books, 1970.

———. "Brazilian Messianism." *Luso-Brazilian Review* 28, no. 2 (Forthcoming).

Richardson, W. "The Golden Legend." *Princeton Theological Review* 1 (1908): 267–81.

Rodrigues, José Honório. *The Brazilians: Their Character and Aspirations.* Translated by Ralph Dimmick. Austin: University of Texas Press, 1980.

Rogers, Susan Carol. "Female Forms of Power and the Myth of Male Dominance." *American Ethnologist* 2, no. 4 (November 1975): 727–56.

Rosenberg, Charles E. "The Bitter Fruit: Heredity, Disease, and Social Thought." In *No Other Gods: On Science and American Social Thought,* 25–53. Baltimore: Johns Hopkins University Press, 1976.

Ross, Eric B. "The Evolution of the Amazon Peasantry." *Journal of Latin American Studies* 10, no. 2 (November 1978): 193–218.

Russell-Wood, A. J. R. *The Black Man in Slavery and Freedom in Colonial Brazil.* New York: St. Martin's Press, 1982.

———. "Prestige, Power, and Piety in Colonial Brazil: The Third Orders of Salvador." *Hispanic American Historical Review* 69, no. 1 (February 1989): 60–89.

Schama, Simon. *Citizens: A Chronicle of the French Revolution.* New York: Alfred A. Knopf, 1989.

Schwartz, Stuart B. "Elite Politics and the Growth of a Peasantry in Late Colonial Brazil." In *From Colony to Nation: Essays on the Independence of Brazil,* edited by A. J. R. Russell-Wood, 133–54. Baltimore: Johns Hopkins University Press, 1975.

————. "Indian Labor and New World Plantations: European Demands and Indian Responses in Northeastern Brazil." *American Historical Review* 87 (1978): 43–79.

————. *Sugar Plantations in the Formation of Brazilian Society: Bahia, 1550–1835.* Cambridge: Cambridge University Press, 1985.

Scott, James C. *The Moral Economy of the Peasant: Rebellion and Subsistence in Southeast Asia.* New Haven: Yale University Press, 1976.

————. "Resistance Without Protest and Without Organization: Peasant Opposition to the Islamic *Zakat* and the Christian Tithe." *Comparative Studies in Society and History* 29, no. 1 (July 1987): 417–20.

————. *Weapons of the Weak: Everyday Forms of Peasant Resistance.* New Haven: Yale University Press, 1985.

Shanin, Theodor. *The Awkward Class: Political Sociology of Peasantry in a Developing Society: Russia, 1910–1925.* Oxford: Oxford University Press, 1972.

Shapiro, David. "The *Ralliement* in the Politics of the 1890's." In *The Right in France, 1890–1919*, edited by David Shapiro, 13–48, St. Antony's Papers, no. 13. London: Chatto & Windus, 1962.

Shore, Bradd. "An Introduction to the Work of Clifford Geertz." *Soundings* 71, no. 1 (Spring 1988): 15–27.

Siegel, Bernard J. "The Contestado Rebellion, 1912–16: A Case Study in Brazilian Messianism and Regional Dynamics." *Journal of Anthropological Research* 33 (1977): 202–13.

————. "Social Structure and Economic Change in Brazil." In *Economic Growth: Brazil, India, China*, edited by Simon Kuznets, Wilbert E. Moore, and Joseph J. Spengler, 388–411. Durham, N.C.: Duke University Press, 1955.

Sierra, Justo. *The Political Evolution of the Mexican People.* Translated by Charles Ramsdell. Austin: University of Texas Press, 1969.

Silverman, Malcolm. "Alienation and the Fiction of Brazil's Elias José." In *Los Ensayistas: Brazil in the Eighties*, edited by Carmen Chaves McClendon and M. Elizabeth Ginway, nos. 28–29, 199–216. Athens: University of Georgia Press, 1990.

Skidmore, Thomas E. *Black and White: Race and Nationality in Brazilian Thought.* New York: Oxford University Press, 1974.

————. "Racial Ideas and Social Policy in Brazil, 1870–1940." In *The Idea of Race in Latin America, 1870–1940*, edited by Richard Graham, 7–36. Austin: University of Texas Press, 1990.

Slater, Candace. *Stories on a String: The Brazilian "Literatura de Cordel."* Berkeley and Los Angeles: University of California Press, 1982.

————. *Trail of Miracles: Stories from a Pilgrimage in Northeast Brazil.* Berkeley and Los Angeles: University of California Press, 1986.

Slatta, Richard. *Gauchos and the Vanishing Frontier.* Lincoln: University of Nebraska Press, 1983.

Sontag, Susan. "Afterlives: The Case of Machado de Assis." *New Yorker*, May 7, 1990, 102–8.

Souza, Amaury de. "The *Cangaço* and the Politics of Violence in Northeast Brazil." In *Protest and Resistance in Angola and Brazil: Comparative Studies*, edited by Ronald H. Chilcote, 109–31. Berkeley and Los Angeles: University of California Press, 1972.

Spence, M. *Market Signalling.* Cambridge, Mass.: Harvard University Press, 1974.

Stemmer, Juan E. Orine. "Freight Rates in the Trade Between Europe and South America, 1840–1914." *Journal of Latin American Studies* 21, no. 1 (February 1989): 56–57.

Stern, Steve J. *Peru's Indian Peoples and the Challenge of Spanish Conquest.* Madison: University of Wisconsin Press, 1982.

———, ed. *Resistance, Rebellion, and Consciousness in the Andean Peasant World, Eighteenth to Twentieth Centuries.* Madison: University of Wisconsin Press, 1987.

Szuchman, Mark D. *Order: Family and Community in Buenos Aires, 1810–1860.* Stanford: Stanford University Press, 1988.

Talmon, Yonina. "Millenarianism." In *International Encyclopedia of the Social Sciences,* edited by David L. Sills, 10:349–60. New York: Macmillan/Free Press, 1979.

Thrupp, Sylvia L., ed. *Millennial Dreams in Action: A Report on the Conference Discussion.* New York: Schocken Books, 1970.

Topik, Steven. *The Political Economy of the Brazilian State, 1889–1930.* Austin: University of Texas Press, 1987.

Tuan, Yi-Fu. *Topophilia: A Study of Environmental Perceptions, Attitudes, and Values.* Englewood Cliffs, N.J.: Prentice-Hall, 1974.

Turner, Victor. *The Ritual Process: Structure and Anti-Structure.* Ithaca: Cornell University Press, 1969.

Vargas Llosa, Mario. *The War of the End of the World.* Translated by Helen R. Lane. New York: Farrar, Straus & Giroux, 1984.

Vianna, Francisco Vicente. *Memoir of the State of Bahia.* Translated by Guilerme Pereira Rebello. Salvador: Typ. *Diário da Bahia,* 1893.

Wagley, Charles. *Introduction to Brazil.* New York: Columbia University Press, 1963.

Wallis, Wilson D. "Socio-cultural Sources of Messiahs." In *Religion, Society, and the Individual,* edited by J. Milton Younger, 578–86. New York: Macmillan, 1957.

Watson, James B. "Way Station of Modernization: The Brazilian Caboclo." In *Brazil: Papers Presented in the Institute for Brazilian Studies, Vanderbilt University,* edited by James B. Watson et al. Nashville: Vanderbilt University Press, 1953.

Weber, Eugen. *Peasants into Frenchmen: The Modernization of Rural France, 1870–1914.* Stanford: Stanford University Press, 1976.

Willey, Basil. *The Eighteenth Century Background.* London: Penguin Books, 1965.

Winter, Nevin O. *Brazil and Her People of To-Day.* Boston: L. C. Page, 1910.

Wirth, John D. *Minas Gerais in the Brazilian Federation, 1889–1937.* Stanford: Stanford University Press, 1977.

Wurdemann, John G. F. *Notes on Cuba.* Boston: James Munroe, 1844.

Young, Eric Van. "To See Someone Not Seeing: Historical Studies of Peasants and Politics in Mexico." *Mexican Studies/Estudios mexicanos* 6, no. 1 (Winter 1990): 133–59.

Zeldin, Theodore. *France, 1848–1945.* Vol. 1: *Ambition, Love, and Politics.* Oxford: Oxford University Press, 1978.

Zweig, Stefan. *Brazil: Land of the Future.* New York: Viking Press, 1942.

SELECTED WORKS IN PORTUGUESE AND OTHER LANGUAGES

Aguiar, Durval Vieira de. *Descrições práticas da província da Bahia.* 1882; reprinted Rio de Janeiro: Editora Cátedra, 1979.

Albuquerque, Ulysses Lins de. *Um sertanejo e o sertão: Moxotó Bravo e Três Ribeiras.* Belo Horizonte: Editora Itatiaia, 1989.

Almeida, José Américo de. *A Parahyba e seus problemas.* 2d ed. Porto Alegre: Editora Globo, 1937.

Amado, Janaína. *Conflito social no Brasil: a revolta dos 'Mucker.'* São Paulo: Duas Cidades, 1978.

Ambrósio, Manoel. *Antônio Dó: o bandoleiro das Barrancas.* Januária, Minas Gerais: Prefeitura Municipal/Lion's Club, 1976.

Amorim, Deolindo. *Sertão de meu tempo.* Rio de Janeiro: N.p., 1978.

Aragão, Antônio F. Moniz de. *A Bahia e os seus governadores na República.* Salvador: N.p., 1923.

Araripe, Tristão de Alencar. *Expedições militares contra Canudos.* Rio de Janeiro: Impt. do Exército, 1960.

Araripe Júnior, T. A. *O Reino Encantado, chronica sebastianista.* Rio de Janeiro: Typ. *Gazeta de Notícias,* 1878.

Aras, José. *Sangue de irmãos.* Salvador: Museu de Bendegó, [1953].

Araújo, Joaquim Correia de. *Mensagem apresentado ao Congresso Legislativo do estado [de Pernambuco] em 1898.* Recife: Imprensa do Estado, 1898.

Araújo, Padre Heitor. *Vinte anos no Sertão.* Salvador: Imprensa Gráfica, 1953.

Avelina, Maria. "Depoimentos does sobreviventes." *O Cruzeiro* (Rio de Janeiro), August 19, 1947, 17.

Azevedo, J. Lúcio de. *A evolução do Sebastianismo.* 2d ed. Lisbon: Livraria Clássica, 1947.

Azevedo, Thalez de. *Italianos na Bahia e outros temas.* Salvador: Empresa Gráfica da Bahia, 1989.

Azzi, Riolando. "Elementos para a história do catolicismo popular." *Revista Eclesiástica Brasileira* (Petrópolis) 36, no. 141 (March 1976): 95–130.

———. "Ermitães e irmãos: uma forma de vida religiosa no Brasil antigo." *Convergência* 9, no. 94 (July–August 1976): 370–83; 9, no. 95 (September 1976): 430–41.

Bacon, Henry. *A epopéia brasileira: uma introdução a "Os sertões."* Rio de Janeiro: Edições Antares, 1983.

Bahia, Estado da. *Brazil: o estado da Bahia. Notícias para o emigrante.* Salvador: Empreza Editora, 1897.

Balandier, Georges. *Sociologie actuelle de l'Afrique noire.* Paris: Presses Universitaires de France, 1955.

Bandeira, Maria de Lourdes. "Os Kiriris de Mirandela." *Estudos Baianos* (Salvador) 6 (1972).

Barbosa, Cristina. "Canudos, uma história incompleta." *Jornal da Tarde* (São Paulo), October 6, 1988, 21–22.

Barbosa, Francisco de Assis. *JK: uma revisão na política brasileira.* Rio de Janeiro: José Olympio Editora, 1960.

Barbosa, Rui. *Obras completas*. Vol. 24. Rio de Janeiro: Ministério da Educação e Saúde, 1987.

Barreto, Dantas. *Destruição de Canudos*. 4th ed. Recife: *Jornal do Recife*, 1912.

Barreto, José Augusto Cabral. "Nina Rodrigues e a 'loucura epidêmica de Canudos.'" *Planejamento* (Salvador) 7, nos. 3–4 (July–December 1979): 275–87.

Barros, Bacharel Francisco Borges de. *Diccionário geográphico e histórico da Bahia*. Salvador: Imprensa Oficial do Estado, 1923.

Barroso, Gustavo [João do Norte]. "Populações do Nordeste." *Revista da Sociedade de Geografia do Rio de Janeiro* (1926–27): 48–50, 66–67.

Bastide, Roger. *Brasil: terra de contrastes*. São Paulo: DIFEL, 1959.

————. *Les religions africaines au Brésil*. Paris: Presses Universitaires de France, 1960.

————. *Sociologia de las enfermidades mentales*. Mexico City: Siglo Veintiuno Editores, 1964.

Bastos, Abguar. *A visão histórico-sociológica de Euclides da Cunha*. São Paulo: Editora Nacional, 1986.

Batista, Sebastião Nunes. *Poética popular do Nordeste*. Rio de Janeiro: Fundação Casa Rui Barbosa, 1982.

Bello, José Maria. *Inteligência do Brasil: ensaios sobre Machado de Assis, Joaquim Nabuco, Euclides da Cunha e Rui Barbosa*. 3d ed. São Paulo: Editora Nacional, 1938.

Benévolo, Ademar. *Introdução à história ferroviária do Brasil (estudo social, político e histórico)*. Recife: Edições Folha da Manhã, 1953.

Benício, Manoel. *O rei dos jagunços: chrónica histórica e de costumes sertanejos sobre os acontecimentos de Canudos*. Rio de Janeiro: Typ. *Jornal do Commércio*, 1899.

Bezerra, Gregório. *Memórias. Primeira parte: 1900–1945*. 2d ed. Rio de Janeiro: Civilização Brasileira, 1979.

Bezerra, José Euzébio Fernandes. *Retalhos do meu sertão*. Rio de Janeiro: Gráfica Leão do Mar, 1978.

Bittencourt, Correa. "Saúde pública." In *Década republicana*, 2:189–308. 2d ed. Brasília: Editora Universidade de Brasília, 1986.

Blaj, Ilana, and Cândida Pereira da Cunha. "A urbanização em Canudos como decorrência da necessidade de defesa." In *Anais do VII simpósio nacional dos professores universitários de história*, vol. 1. São Paulo: Typ. *Revista de História*, 1984.

Borges, Dain. "El reverso fatal de los acontecimientos: dos momentos de la degeneración en la literatura brasileña." In *Humanismo e hispanidad: ensayos en homenaje a Juan Marichal*, edited by Birute Ciplijauskaite and Christopher Mauer. Forthcoming.

Bortolo, Regina. "Projecto Canudos." *A Tarde* (São Paulo), April 26, 1988, sec. 2, 1.

Bosi, Alfredo. "Euclides da Cunha: vida e obras." Introduction to *Os sertões: edição didática*. São Paulo: Editora Cultrix, 1985.

Brandão, Adelino. *Euclides da Cunha e a questão racial no Brasil*. Rio de Janeiro: Editora Presença, 1990.

Brazil. Directoria Geral de Estatística. "Resumo histórico dos inquéritos censitários realizados no Brazil." In *Recenseamento do Brazil realizado em 1 setembro de 1920*, vol. 1: *Introdução*. Rio de Janeiro: D.G.E., 1922.

Brígido, João. *Ceará (homens e fatos)*. Rio de Janeiro: Gráfica Record Editora, 1969.

————. "A família de Antônio Conselheiro." *Almanak literária estatística do Rio Grande do Sul, 1898* (Porto Alegre) 10 (1897): 113–17.

Cabral, Joaquim. "Missão abreviada da pobreza de uma teologia." Ph.D. diss., Pontifica Universitas Lateranense, Rome, 1986.

Calasans, José. "Antônio Conselheiro, construtor de igrejas e cemitérios." *Cultura* (Rio de Janeiro) 5, no. 16 (April–June 1973): 69–81.

————. "Aparecimento e prisão de um messias." *Revista da Academia de Letras da Bahia* 35 (1988): 53–63.

————. "Canudos não Euclidiano." In *Canudos: subsídios para a sua reavaliação histórica*, ed. José Augusto Vaz Sampaio Neto, Magaly de Barros Maia Serrão, Maria Lúcia Horta Ludolf de Mello, and Vanda Maria Bravo Ururahy. Rio de Janeiro: Fundação Casa Rui Barbosa, 1986.

————. *O ciclo folclórico do Bom Jesus Conselheiro*. Salvador: Tipografia Benedetina, 1950.

————. "O jaguncinho de E. da Cunha." *Revista de Cultura da Bahia* 7 (1972): 75–78.

————. *No tempo de Antônio Conselheiro*. Salvador: Universidade Federal da Bahia, 1959.

————. *Quase biografias de jagunços (o séquito de Antônio Conselheiro)*. Salvador: Universidade Federal da Bahia, 1986.

Caldeira, Clóvis. *Mutirão: formas de ajuda mútua no meio rural*. São Paulo: N.p, 1956.

Calmon, Francisco Marques de Góes. *Vida econômico-financeira da Bahia: elementos para a história de 1808 a 1899*. Reprinted Salvador: Imprensa Oficial do Estado, 1982.

Calmón, Pedro. *História da civilização brasileira*. 4th ed. São Paulo: Editora Nacional, 1940.

Cardoso, E. "Diambismo ou maconhismo, vício assassino." *Boletim da Secretaria de Agricultura, Indústria e Commércio* (July–December 1948): 436–43.

Carneiro, Edison. *A insurreição praieira, 1848–1849*. Rio de Janeiro: Civilização Brasileira, 1960.

Carone, Edgard. *A república velha*. Vol. 1: *Instituições e classes sociais*. Vol. 2: *Evolução política*. São Paulo: Difusão Européia do Livro, 1970–1971.

Carrato, José Ferreira. *As Minas Gerais e os primórdios do Caraça*. São Paulo: Editora Nacional, 1963.

Carvalho, Alfred de. "A imprensa baiana de 1811 a 1899." *Revista do Instituto Histórico e Geográfico da Bahia* 6, no. 6 (1905): 21–22.

Carvalho, Garibaldi de Mello. "Esboço de análise ecológica." In *Estudos nordestinos* (São Paulo) 1 (1961): 49–61.

Carvalho, José Murilo de. *Os bestializados: o Rio de Janeiro e a república que não foi*. 3d ed. São Paulo: Companhia das Letras, 1989.

————. *A formação das almas: o imaginário da república no Brasil*. São Paulo: Companhia das Letras, 1990.

Carvalho, José Rodrigues de. "A cultura do algodeiro no estado da Parahyba: o problema da pequena lavoura." *Annaes algodoeira* 2 (1916).

Chacon, Vamireh. *O humanismo brasileiro*. São Paulo: Secretaria da Cultura, 1980.

Comblin, J., ed. *Instruções espirituais do P[adr]e Ibiapina*. São Paulo: N.p., 1984.

Consorte, Josildeth Gomes, and Lísias Nogueira Negrão. *O messianismo no Brasil contemporâneo*. São Paulo: FFLCH/USP-CER, 1973.

Corrêa, Mariza. "As ilusões da liberdade: a escola Nina Rodrigues e a antropologia no Brasil." Ph.D. diss., Universidade de São Paulo, 1982.

Cortez, Ewerton D. "A tragédia do Caldeirão: uma página de sociologia do Nordeste." *A Ordem* (Natal), May 5, 1937, 2.

Costa, João Cruz. *Pequena história da república*. São Paulo: Editora Brasiliense, 1968.

Couto, Manoel José Gonçalves. *Missão abreviada para despertar os descuidados, converter os peccadores e sustentar o fructo das missões*. 1st ed. Pôrto: Sebastião José Pereira, 1873.

da Costa, F. A. Pereira. "Folk-lore pernambucano." *Revista do Instituto Histórico e Geográfico Brasileiro* 70, pt. 2 (1907): 1–641.

da Cunha, Euclydes. *Caderneta de campo*. Edited by Olímpio de Sousa Andrade. São Paulo: Editora Cultrix; Brasília: Instituto Nacional do Livro, 1975.

———. *Canudos e inéditos (diário de uma expedição)*. Rio de Janeiro: José Olympio Editora, 1939.

———. *Os sertões: edição didática*. Edited by Alfredo Bosi. São Paulo: Editora Cultrix, 1985.

Da Matta, Roberto. "A propósito de micro-cenas e macro-dramas: notas sobre a questão do espaço e do poder no Brasil." In *Situaciones*, edited by Guillermo O'Donnell. Working Paper no. 121. Notre Dame, Ind.: Helen Kellogg Institute for International Studies, May 1989.

Dantas, Nataniel. "De Canudos resta apenas a memória." *Cultura* (Brasília) 11, no. 39 (January–March 1982): 36–41.

Dantas, Salomão de Souza. *Aspectos e contrastes: ligeiro estudo sobre o estado da Bahia*. Rio de Janeiro: Typ. *Revista dos Tribunaes*, 1922.

Dantas Júnior, J. C. Pinto. "O barão de Geremoabo (Dr. Cícero Dantas Martins), 1838–1938." Salvador: Imprensa Oficial do Estado, 1939.

Daus, Ronald. *O ciclo épico dos cangaceiros na poesia popular do Nordeste*. Translated by Rachel Teixeira Valença. Rio de Janeiro: Fundação Casa Rui Barbosa, 1982.

Derengoski, Paulo Ramos. *O desmoronamento do mundo jagunço*. Florianópolis: Fundação Catarense de Cultura, 1986.

Desrochers, Georgette, and Eduardo Hoornaert, eds. *Ibiapina e a igreja dos pobres*. São Paulo: Editora Paulinas, 1984.

Dias, Públio. *Condições higiênicas e sociais do trabalhador dos engenhos de Pernambuco*. Recife: N.p., 1937.

Dias, Satyro de Oliveira. *Relatório sobre a instrucção pública no estado da Bahia*. Salvador: Typ. *Diário da Bahia*, 1894.

dos Santos, Rubens Rodrigues. "Revelações sobre Antônio Conselheiro." *O Estado de São Paulo*, June 10, 1955.

Duarte, Raymundo. "Um movimento messiânico no interior da Bahia." *Revista de Antropologia* 11, nos. 1–2 (1963): 45–51.

Escola de Comando do Estado Maior do Exército. *Guerras insurrecionais do Brasil (Canudos e Contestado)*. Rio de Janeiro: SMG Imprensa do Exército, 1966.

Facó, Rui. *Cangaceiros e fanáticos: gênese e lutas*. Rio de Janeiro: Civilização Brasileira, 1963.

————. "A guerra camponesa de Canudos." *Revista Brasiliense* (São Paulo) 1 (November–December 1958): 20–21, 128–183.

Falconi, Ivaldo. "Um quilombo esquecido." *Correio das Artes* (João Pessoa) (1949).

*Falla com que abriu no dia 1º de maio de 1889 da Assembleia Legislativa Provincial da Bahia o Exmo. Desembargador Aurélio Ferreira Espinheira, 1º Vice-Presidente da Província*. Salvador: Typ. *Diário da Bahia*, 1889.

Faoro, Raymundo. *Os donos do poder: formação do patronato político brasileiro*. 2 vols. Porto Alegre: Editora Globo, 1977.

Farage, Nádia. "As muralhas dos Sertões: os povos indígenas do Rio Branco e a colonização." Master's thesis, Universidade Estadual de Campinas, São Paulo, 1986.

Favilla Nunes, J. P. *Guerra de Canudos: narrativa histórica*. Rio de Janeiro: Typ. Moraes, 1898.

————. "Population, territoire, électorat." In *Le Brésil en 1889 avec une carte de l'empire en chromolithographie*, edited by Frederico José de Santa-Anna Nery, 189–203. Paris: Librairie Charles Delagrave, 1889.

Ferrari, Alfonso Trujillo. *Potengi-Encruzilhada no vale do São Francisco*. São Paulo: N.p., 1961.

Ferraz, Renato, Manuel Antonio dos Santos Neto, and José Carlos da Costa Pinheiro. *Cartilha histórica de Canudos*. Canudos and Salvador: Prefeitura Municipal de Canudos and Universidade do Estado da Bahia, 1991.

Ferreira, José Carlos. "Princípios jacobinos, sedição de 1798 na Bahia." *Revista do Instituto Geográfico e Histórico da Bahia*, no. 267 (1900): 371–411.

Ferreira, Manoel Jesuíno. *A província da Bahia. Apontamentos*. Rio de Janeiro: Typ. Nacional, 1875.

Filha, Sofia Olszewski. *A fotografia e o negro na cidade do Salvador, 1840–1914*. Salvador: Fundação Cultural do Estado da Bahia, 1989.

Filho, F. Venâncio. *Euclydes da Cunha e seus amigos*. São Paulo: Editora Nacional, 1938.

Filho, José de Figueiredo. "Casa de Caridade de Crato." *A Província* (Crato) 3 (1955): 14–25.

Filho, Luiz Vianna. *O negro na Bahia*. Rio de Janeiro: José Olympio Editora, [1946].

Fiorim, José Luis. "O discurso de Antônio Conselheiro." *Religião e Sociedade* 5 (1980): 95–129.

"Franciscanos em Canudos, 1897." *Revista Vozes* 69, no. 5 (June–July 1975).

Franco, Maria Sylvia de Carvalho. *Homens livres na ordem escravocrata*. 3d ed. São Paulo: Editora Kairós, 1983.

Franco Júnior, Hilário. "A outra face dos santos: os milagres punitivos na *Legenda áurea*." In *Sociedade Brasileira de Pesquisa Histórica, Anais da VIII Reunião*, 155–60. São Paulo: SBPH, 1989.

Freitas, Bezerra de. *História da literatura brasileira*. Porto Alegre: Editora Globo, 1939.

Freitas, Décio. *Cabanos: os guerrilheiros do imperador*. 2d ed. Rio de Janeiro: Editora Graal, 1978.

———. "Canudos: uma tragédia de hoje." Introduction to *Canudos: desenhos*, by Alves Dias. Olinda, Pernambuco: Recife Graf Editora, 1981.

Freyre, Gilberto. "Acontece que são Baianos." In *Problemas brasileiros de antropologia*. 2d ed. Rio de Janeiro: José Olympio Editora, 1959.

———. *Atualidade de Euclydes da Cunha: conferência lida no Salão de Conferências da Biblioteca do Ministério das Relações Exteriores do Brasil, no dia 29 de outubro de 1940*. 2d ed. Rio de Janeiro: CEB, 1943.

———. *Perfil de Euclides e outros perfis*. Rio de Janeiro: José Olympio Editora, 1944.

Gagliard, José Mauro. *O indígena e a república*. São Paulo: Editora Hucitec, 1989.

Galvão, Walnice Nogueira. *Gatos de outro saco: ensaios críticos*. São Paulo: Editora Brasiliense, 1981.

———. *No calor da hora: a guerra de Canudos nos jornais, 4ª expedição*. São Paulo: Editora Ática, 1974.

———. "Uma ausência." In *Os pobres na literatura brasileira*, edited by Roberto Schwartz, 51–53. São Paulo: Editora Brasiliense, 1983.

Garcez, Angelina Nobre Rolim. "Aspectos econômicos do episódio de Canudos." Master's thesis, Universidade Federal da Bahia, 1977.

Garcia, Manoel Funchal. *Do litoral ao sertão*. Rio de Janeiro: Biblioteca do Exército, 1965.

Gomes, Angela Maria de Castro, Rodrigo Bellingrodt Marques Coelho, Dulce Chaves Pandolfi, Maria Helena de Magalhães Castro, Helena Maria Bousquet Bomeny, and Lúcia Lahmeyer Lobo. *Regionalismo e centralização política: partidos e constituinte nos anos 30*. Rio de Janeiro: Editora Nova Fronteira, 1980.

Goto, Roberto Akira. "*Os sertões* e a imaginação de um leitor deste final de século." *Revista do Instituto de Estudos Brasileiros* 31 (1990): 113–28.

Goulart, José Alípio. *Brasil do boi e do couro*. Rio de Janeiro: Edições GRD, 1964–65.

Greenfield, Gerald Michael. "Recife y la gran sequía." In *Cultura urbana latinoamericana*, edited by Richard Morse and Jorge Enrique Hardoy, 203–26. Buenos Aires: CLASCO, 1985.

Grieco, Agrippino. *Evolução da prosa brasileira*. Rio de Janeiro: Editora Ariel, 1933.

Gueiros, Opato. *Cangaceiros e fanáticos*. Recife: N.p., 1942.

Guilherme, Ricardo. "Antônio Conselheiro antes de Canudos." In *O Conselheiro e Canudos*. Fortaleza: Imprensa Universitária da Universidade Federal do Ceará, 1986.

Guimarães, Antonio Sérgio Alfredo. "Estrutura e formação das classes sociais na Bahia." *Novos Estudos CEBRAP*, no. 18 (September 1987): 61–90.

Hardman, Francisco Foot. *Trem fantasma: a modernidade na selva*. São Paulo: Companhia das Letras, 1988.

Hoornaert, Eduardo. *Formação do Catolicismo brasileiro, 1500–1800*. Petrópolis: Editora Vozes, 1974.

————. *História da igreja no Brasil.* 2 vols. Petrópolis: Editora Vozes, 1977.

————. *Verdadeira e falsa religião no Nordeste.* Salvador: Editora Benedina, 1972.

Horcades, Alvim Martins. *Descrição de uma viagem a Canudos.* Salvador: Litotipografia Tourinho, 1899.

Janotti, Maria de Lourdes Mônaco. *Os subversivos da república.* São Paulo: Editora Brasiliense, 1986.

José, Elias. *Um pássaro em pânico.* São Paulo: Editora Ática, 1977.

Leão, A. Carneiro. *A sociedade rural: seus problemas e sua educação.* Rio de Janeiro: José Olympio Editora, 1937.

Leite, Antônio Ático de Souza. "Memória sôbre a Pedra Bonita ou Reino Encantado na camarca de Vila Vela [sic]." *Revista do Instituto Arqueológico e Geográfico de Pernambuco* 60 (December 1903): 217–48.

Leite, Dante Moreira. *O caráter nacional brasileiro.* 4th ed. São Paulo: Editora Pionera, 1983.

Leite, Serafim, S.J. *História da Companhia de Jesus no Brasil.* Vol. 5: *Da Bahia ao Nordeste: estabelecimentos e assuntos locais.* Rio de Janeiro: Instituto Nacional do Livro, 1945.

Lenharo, Alcir. *Sacralização da política.* Campinas: Editora Papirus/Editora da Unicamp, 1986.

Levy, Fortunée. "Crentes e bandidos." *Anais do Museu Histórico Nacional* 8 (1947): 31–71.

Lima, Jorge Pereira, José Germano Maia, João Alves de Oliveira, and João da Silva. *Antônio Conselheiro e a tragédia de Canudos.* São Paulo: CEHILA, 1986.

Lima, Manoel de Oliveira. *América latina e América inglesa: a evolução brasileira comparada com a hispano-americana e com a anglo-americana.* Rio de Janeiro: Garnier, 1914.

Lima, Padre Geraldo Oliveira, ed. Special issue of *Cordel número 21* (Crateus, Ceará), December 1979.

*Literatura popular em verso-estudos* 1. Rio de Janeiro: Fundação Casa Rui Barbosa, 1973.

Lobo da Silva, Cel. Arthur. "A antropologia do exército brasileiro." *Archivos do Museu Nacional* 30 (1928): 9–300.

Lopes, Octacílio de Carvalho. *Os sertões*: diagnose e denúncia." *Revista da Academia Paulista de Letras* 24 (June 1967): 26–28.

Lucena, José. "Uma pequena epidemia mental em Pernambuco: os fanáticos do município de Panelas." *Neurobiologia* 3 (1940): 41–91.

Luna, Luiz, and Nelson Barbalho. *Coronel Dono do Mundo: síntese histórica do coronelismo no Brasil.* Rio de Janeiro: Editora Cátedra, 1983.

Luz, Fábio. *Na província.* Rio de Janeiro: N.p., 1902.

Lyra, Roberto. *Euclides da Cunha: criminologista.* Rio de Janeiro: Typ. O Globo, 1936.

MacAdam, Alfred. "Euclides da Cunha y Mario Vargas Llosa: meditaciones intertextuales." *Revista Iberoamericana* 50, no. 126 (January–March 1984): 157–64.

Macedo, Nertan. *Memorial de Vila Nova.* Rio de Janeiro: Typ. O Cruzeiro, 1964.

Machado, Maria Cristina da Matta. "Aspectos do fenômeno do cangaço no Nordeste brasileiro." *Revista de História* 93 (1973): 139–75.

Maior, Armando Souto. *Quebra-Quilos: lutas sociais no outono do império*. Recife: Instituto Joaquim Nabuco de Pesquisas Sociais, 1978.

Mangabeira, Francisco. "A realidade social de Canudos e do antigo sertão." In *João Mangabeira: república e socialismo no Brasil*, 49–58. Rio de Janeiro: Paz e Terra, 1979.

Maraschin, J. C., ed. *Quem é Jesus Cristo no Brasil*. São Paulo: N.p., 1974.

Mariano, Gregório de S. "Os Capuchinhos na Bahia." In *Congresso de História da Bahia*, vol. 1: *Anais*, 273–83. Bahia: CHB, 1950.

Mariz, Celso. *Ibiapina, um apóstolo do Nordeste*. João Pessoa: N.p., 1942.

Marques, Xavier. *O feiticeiro*. 1897; reprinted São Paulo and Brasília: Editora GRD and Instituto Nacional do Livro, 1975.

Martins, Marco A. M., and Marcos L. L. Messider. "Notas sobre a história e a organização política tuxá." Salvador, Núcleo do Sertão, October 1988. Typescript.

Mattoso, Katia de Queirós. *Família e sociedade na Bahia do século XIX*. São Paulo: Editora Corrupio, 1988.

Mello, Marco Antônio da Silva, and Arno Vogel. "Monarquia contra república: a ideologia da terra e o paradigma do milênio na 'guerra santa' do Contestado." *Estudos Históricos* 2, no. 4 (1989): 190–213.

Melo, Evaldo Cabral de. *O norte agrário e o império, 1871–1889*. Rio de Janeiro: Editora Nova Fronteira, 1984.

Melo, Manoel Rodrigues de. *Patriarcas e carreiros: influência do coronel e do carro de boi na sociedade rural do Nordeste*. 2d ed. Rio de Janeiro: Irmãos Pongetti Editora, 1954.

Mendonça, Carlos Sussekind de. *Sílvio Romero: sua formação intelectual, 1851–1880*. São Paulo: Editora Nacional, 1938.

Menezes, Djacir. *O outro Nordeste*. Rio de Janeiro: José Olympio Editora, 1937.

Menezes, José Rafael de. *Sociologia do Nordeste*. Recife: Editora ASA, 1985.

Milton, Aristides. "A campanha de Canudos: memória lida no Instituto Histórico e Geográfico Brasileiro, 17 de outubro 1897." *Revista trimensal do Instituto* (Rio de Janeiro) 63, pt. 2 (1902): 33–35.

Ministério da Saúde. Comissão Nacional de Alimentação. *Inquérito sobre hábitos e recursos alimentares*. Rio de Janeiro: Ministério da Saúde, 1959.

Molina, Miriam. "Canudos: o apocalipse de Antônio Conselheiro." *Manchete*, November 25, 1989, 46.

Moniz, Edmundo. "Canudos: o suicídio literário de Vargas Llosa." *Encontros com a civilização brasileira* 29 (1982): 7–20.

———. *A guerra social de Canudos*. Rio de Janeiro: Civilização Brasileira, 1978.

Monteiro, Duglas Teixeira. *Os errantes do novo século*. São Paulo: Duas Cidades, 1978.

———. "Um confronto entre Juazeiro, Canudos e Contestado." In *História geral da civilização brasileira*, edited by Boris Fausto, vol. 3: *O Brasil republicano*, pt. 2: *Sociedade e instituições (1889–1930)*, 42–45. São Paulo: DIFEL, 1977.

Monteiro, Hamilton de Mattos. *Crise agrária e luta de classes: o Nordeste brasileiro entre 1850 e 1889*. Brasília: Editora Horizonte, 1980.

————. "Violência no Nordeste rural: 1850–1889." Ph.D. diss., Universidade de São Paulo, 1978.

Montenegro, Abelardo F. *Antônio Conselheiro*. Fortaleza: N.p., 1954.

————. *Fanáticos e cangaceiros*. Fortaleza: Henriqueta Galvão, 1973.

————. *História do fanatismo religioso no Ceará*. Fortaleza: Batista Fontenele, 1959.

Mota, Mauro. *Paisagem das secas*. Recife: Ministério da Educação e Cultura/ Instituto Joaquim Nabuco, 1958.

Moura, Clóvis. *Rebeliões da senzala: quilombos insurreições guerrilhas*. Rio de Janeiro: Editora Conquista, 1972.

Nascimento, Noel. "Canudos, Contestado e fanatismo religioso." *Revista Brasiliense* 44 (November–December 1961): 62–67.

Neto, José Augusto Vaz Sampaio, Magaly de Barros Maia Serrão, Maria Lúcia Horta Ludolf de Mello, and Vanda Maria Bravo Ururahy. *Canudos: subsídios para a sua reavaliação histórica*. Rio de Janeiro: Fundação Casa Rui Barbosa, 1986.

Nogueira, Ataliba. *Antônio Conselheiro e Canudos: revisão histórica*. 2d ed. Brasília: Editora Nacional, 1978.

————. "Centenário de Carlos de Laet." *Revista da Academia Brasileira de Letras* 74 (1984).

Nunes Leal, Victor. *Coronelismo, enxada e voto: o município e o regime representativo no Brasil*. Rio de Janeiro: Livraria Forense, 1949.

Novaes, José de Campos. "Os sertões." *Revista do Centro de Ciências, Letras e Artes* (Campinas) 2, no. 2 (1903): 45–55.

Ott, Carlos. *Vestígios de cultura indígena no sertão da Bahia*. Salvador: Secretaria de Educação e Saúde, 1945.

Otten, Alexandre H. "'Só Deus é grande': a mensagem religiosa de Antônio Conselheiro." 2 vols. Ph.D. diss., Pontifica Universitas Gregoriana, Rome, 1987.

Palacin, Padre Luiz Gomes, S.J., and Msgr. Francisco José de Oliveira. *História da diocese de Paulo Afonso*. Goiania: Diocese de Paulo Afonso, 1988.

Pang, Eul-Soo. *O Engenho Central do Bom Jardim na economia baiana: alguns aspectos de sua história, 1857–1891*. Rio de Janeiro: Arquivo Nacional/Instituto Histórico e Geográfico Brasileiro, 1979.

Parahym, Orlando. *O problema alimentar no sertão*. Recife: Imprensa Oficial, 1940.

Paraíso, Maria Hilda Baqueiro. "Os Capuchinhos e os Índios na Sul da Bahia: uma análise preliminar de sua atuação." *Revista do Museu Paulista*, n.s., 31 (1986): 148–96.

Peixoto, Demerval. *Campanha do Contestado: episódios e impressões*. Rio de Janeiro: N.p., 1916.

Peixoto, Eduardo Marques. "Questão Maurer, os Mukers." *Revista do Instituto Histórico e Geográfico Brasileiro* 68, pt. 2 (1907): 393–505.

Pena, Belisário. *Saneamento do Brasil*. Rio de Janeiro: N.p., 1918.

Petry, Leopoldo. *O episódio do Ferrabraz (os Mucker)*. 2d ed. São Leopoldo, Rio Grande do Sul: N.p., 1966.

Piccarolo, Antonio. *L'emigrazione italiano nello state di S. Paolo*. São Paulo: N.p., 1911.

Piedade, [Amaro] Lélis. *Histórico e relatório do Comitê Patriótico da Bahia*. Salvador: Typ. Reis, 1901.

Pinheiro, Irineu. *Efemérides do Cariri*. Fortaleza: Imprensa Universitária do Ceará, 1963.

Polícia Militar da Bahia. 3º Corpo do Regimento Policial da Bahia. 4ª Companhia. *Livro de assentamento de praças*. Ms., ca. 1897. Arquivo Geral do Quartel dos Aflitos, Salvador.

————. *Livro de registro de ordens do dia, 1889–1904*. Ms., n.d. Arquivo Geral do Quartel dos Aflitos, Salvador.

Portella, Eduardo. *Literatura e realidade nacional*. 2d ed. Rio de Janeiro: Tempos Brasileiros, 1971.

Prado, Eduardo. *A ilusão americana*. 1892; reprinted São Paulo: IBRASA, 1980.

Queiroz, Maria Isaura Pereira de. *O campesinato brasileiro: ensaios sobre civilização e grupos rústicos no Brasil*. 2d ed. Petrópolis: Editora Vozes, 1973.

————. "Classifications des messianismes brésiliens." *Archives de sociologie des religions* (Paris), no. 5 (January–June 1958): 111–20.

————. *La 'guerre sainte' au Brésil: le mouvement messianique du Contestado*. Boletim 187. São Paulo: Faculdade de Filosofia, Ciências e Letras da Universidade de São Paulo, 1957.

————. *O messianismo no Brasil e no mundo*. São Paulo: Alfa-Omega, 1977.

————. *Reforme et révolution dans les sociétés traditionelles: histoire et ethnologie des mouvements messianiques*. Paris: Anthropos, 1968.

————. "Tambaú, cidade dos milagres." In *Cultura, sociedade rural, sociedade urbana: ensaios*, 135–43. São Paulo: Universidade de São Paulo, 1978.

Queiroz, Maurício Vinhas de. *Messianismo e conflito social*. Rio de Janeiro: Civilização Brasileira, 1966.

Queiroz, Suely Robles Reis de. *Os radicais da república. Jacobinismo: ideologia e ação*. São Paulo: Editora Brasiliense, 1986.

Rabello, Dácio de Lyra. *O Nordeste*. Recife: Editora Farol, 1932.

Rabello, Sylvio. *Euclides da Cunha*. 2d ed. Rio de Janeiro: Civilização Brasileiro, 1966.

Rago, Margareth. *Do cabaré ao lar: a utopia da cidade disciplinar, 1890–1930*. Rio de Janeiro: Paz e Terra, 1985.

Ramos, Artur. *Loucura e crime*. Porto Alegre: Editora Globo, 1937.

Regimento Policial da Bahia. *Livro de registro de ordens do dia*. Arquivo Geral do Quartel dos Aflitos, Salvador, 3º Corpo do Regimento Policial da Bahia, 4ª Companhia, 1889–1904.

Regni, Pietro Vittorino. *Os Capuchinhos na Bahia*. Porto Alegre: Escola Superior de Teologia São Lourenço de Brindes, 1988.

Reis, João J. "A elite baiana face os movimentos sociais, Bahia: 1824–1840." *Revista de História* 54 (1976): 341–84.

*Relatório apresentado pelo Revd. Frei João Evangelista de Monte Marciano ao arcebispado da Bahia sobre Antônio Conselheiro e seu sequito no arraial dos Canudos*. Salvador: Typ. *Correio de Notícias*, 1895.

*Relatório da commissão especial nomeada para recolher as creanças sertanejas, feitas prisioneiras em Canudos*. Salvador, 1898.

*Relatório do Inspector do Thesouro . . . ao Dr. Governador do Estado em 12 de maio de 1896.* Salvador: Typ. *Correio de Notícias*, 1896.

Rodrigues, Carlos Brandão. *Os caipiras de São Paulo.* São Paulo: Editora Brasiliense, 1983.

Rodrigues, Edgar. *Socialismo e sindicalismo no Brasil, 1675–1913.* Rio de Janeiro: Laemmert, 1969.

Rodrigues, Raimundo Nina. "O animismo fetichista dos negros bahianos." *Revista Brazileira* 1 (April 15–September 4, 1896).

———. *As collectividades anormaes.* 1897; reprinted Rio de Janeiro: Civilização Brasileira, 1939.

———. "A loucura epidêmica de Canudos." *Revista Brazileira* (Salvador) 2 (October 1897): 129–218.

———. "Métissage, dégénérescence et crime." *Archives d'anthropologie criminelle* (Paris) 14 (1899): 477–516.

———. *As raças humanas: a responsibilidade penal no Brasil.* 1894; reprinted Salvador: Livraria Progresso, 1957.

Romero, Sílvio. *Estudos sobre a poesia popular no Brasil.* Rio de Janeiro, 1888; reprinted Petrópolis: Editora Vozes, 1977.

———. *O vampiro do Vaza-Barris: intermezzo jornalista em resposta ao vigário Olympio Campos. Complemento ao opúsculo "A verdade sobre o caso de Sergipe."* Rio de Janeiro: Impressora, 1895.

Saes, Décio. *A formação do estado burguês no Brasil (1888–1891).* Rio de Janeiro: Paz e Terra, 1985.

Saint-Hilaire, Auguste de. *Voyage dans les provinces de Saint-Paul et de Sainte-Catherine.* Vol. 1. Paris, 1851.

Sampaio, Consuelo Novais. "Da transição política da república ao movimento de Canudos." Paper presented at the seminar "A República e o Movimento de Canudos," Museu Eugenio Teixeira, Salvador, October 17, 1989.

Santos, Mário Augusto da Silva. "Sobrevivência e tensões sociais: Salvador (1890–1930)." Ph.D. diss., Universidade de São Paulo, 1982.

Saraiva, Antônio. *O discurso engenhoso.* São Paulo: Editora Perspectiva, 1980.

Sarmiento, Domingo Faustino. *Civilización y barbarie: vida de Juan Facundo Quiroga.* Buenos Aires, 1845.

Schupp, Ambrósio. *Die Mucker.* Paderborn, Ger.: Bonifacius Druckerei, 1900.

Secretaria da Agricultura, Viação e Obras Públicas. *Relatório apresentado ao Dr. Gov. do Estado da Bahia pelo Engenheiro Civil José Antônio Costa.* Bahia: Typ. *Correio de Notícias*, 1897.

Sena, Consuelo Pondé de. *Introdução ao estudo de uma comunidade do agreste bahiano: Itapicurú, 1830/1892.* Salvador: Universidade Federal da Bahia, 1979.

Sevcenko, Nicolau. *Literatura como missão: tensões sociais e criação cultural na Primeira República.* São Paulo: Editora Brasiliense, 1983.

Silva, Antônio de Moraes. *Diccionário da língua portugueza.* Lisbon: Typ. Lacerdina, 1813.

Silva, Eduardo. *Idéias políticas de Quintino Bocaiúva.* Vol. 1. Brasília and Rio de Janeiro: Senado Federal and Fundação Casa Rui Barbosa, 1986.

————. "Por uma nova perspectiva das relações escravistas." In *Sociedade Brasileira de Pesquisa Histórica, Anais da V<u>a</u> Reunião*, 141–47. São Paulo: SBPH, 1985.

Silva, Hélio, and Maria Cecília Ribas Carneiro. *O poder civil*. Rio de Janeiro: Editora Três, 1975.

————. *Os presidentes: Prudente de Morais. O poder civil, 1894–1898*. São Paulo: Grupo de Comunicação Três, 1983.

Silva, Maria Beatriz Nizza da. *Análise de estratificação social: o Rio de Janeiro de 1808 a 1821*. São Paulo: Faculdade de Filosofia, Letras e Ciências Humanas, Universidade de São Paulo, 1975.

————. *Cultura e sociedade no Rio de Janeiro, 1808–1821*. São Paulo: Editora Nacional, 1977.

Silveiro, Alfredo de Castro. *Pequeno dicionário de assuntos pouco vulgares, curiosidades e excentricidades da língua portuguêsa*. 3d ed. Rio de Janeiro: Livraria São José, 1960.

Sinzig, Frei Pedro, O.F.M. *Reminiscências d'um frade*. 2d ed. Petrópolis: Typ. das Vozes, 1925.

————. "Diário inédito d'um frade." *Revista Vozes* (Petrópolis) 69, no. 5 (June–July 1975).

Sobreira, Azarias. *O patriarca de Juazeiro*. Juazeiro: Editora Vozes, 1969.

Sola, José Antonio. *Canudos: uma utopia no sertão*. São Paulo: Editora Contexto, 1989.

Sousa, J. Galante de. "Algumas fontes para o estudo de Euclides da Cunha." *Revista do Livro* (Rio de Janeiro) 4 (September 1959): 183–220.

————. *Exposição comemorativa do centenário do nascimento de Euclides da Cunha, 1866–1966*. Rio de Janeiro: Biblioteca Nacional, 1966.

Souza, Eusébio de. *História militar do Ceará*. Fortaleza: N.p., 1950.

Süssekind, Flora. *Tal Brasil, qual romance? Uma ideologia estética e sua história: o naturalismo*. Rio de Janeiro: Editora Achiamé, 1984.

Tavares, Luiz Henrique Dias. "Duas reformas de educação na Bahia, 1895–1925." Centro Regional de Pesquisas Educacionais da Bahia, Salvador, 1968. Typescript.

Tavares, Odorico. *Bahia: imagens da terra e do povo*. Rio de Janeiro: José Olympio Editora, 1951.

Tejo, Limeira. *Brejos e carrascaes do Nordeste: documentário*. São Paulo: Scopus, 1937.

Theophilo, Rodolpho. *A secca de 1919*. Rio de Janeiro: Editora Imperial, 1922.

Torres, João Camilo de Oliveira. *Estratificação social no Brasil*. São Paulo: DIFEL, 1965.

Tostes, Joel Bicalho. "Cronologia de Euclides da Cunha." *Revista do Livro* (Rio de Janeiro) 4 (September 1959): 7–14.

Turner, Clorinda Matto de. *Aves sin nido*. 1889; reprinted Cuzco: Universidad Nacional del Cuzco, 1948.

Vannuchi, Ivo. "Tipos étnicos e sociais de *Os sertões*." In *Enciclopédia de estudos euclidianos*, edited by Adelino Brandão, 1:147–60. Jundiaí: Gráfica Editora Jundiá [*sic*], 1982.

Vargas, Augusto Tamayo. "Interpretaciones de América latina." In *América latina en su literatura*, edited by César Fernández Moreno, 441–61. Mexico City: Siglo Veintiuno Editores, 1977.

Ventura, Roberto. "'A nossa Vendéia': Canudos, o mito da Revolução Francesa e a formação de identidade cultural no Brasil (1897–1902)." *Revista do Instituto de Estudos Brasileiros* 31 (1990): 126–40.

Vianna, Francisco José de Oliveira. *Populações meridionaes do Brasil*. 4th ed. São Paulo: Editora Nacional, 1938.

Vianna, Hildegardes. "Breve notícia sobre acontecimentos na Bahia no início do século XX." Universidade Federal da Bahia, Centro de Estudos Baianos, Salvador, 1983. Typescript.

Warren, Donald, Jr. "A terapia espírita no Rio de Janeiro por volta de 1900." *Religião e sociedade* 11, no. 3 (December 1984): 56–83.

Wildberger, Arnold. *Os presidentes da província da Bahia, 1824–1889*. Salvador: Typ. Beneditina, 1979.

Wolff, Maria Tai. "Estas páginas sem brilhos: o texto-sertão de Euclydes da Cunha." *Revista Iberoamericana* 50, no. 126 (January–March 1984): 47–61.

"Wolsey" [César Zama]. *Libello republicano: acompanhado de commentários sobre a campanha de Canudos*. Salvador: Typ. *Diário da Bahia*, 1899.

Zanettini, Paulo. "Canudos, uma história incompleta." *Jornal da Tarde* (São Paulo), October 6, 1988, 21.

———. "Memórias do fim do mundo." *Revista Horizonte Geográfico* (São Paulo) 1, no. 3 (September–October 1988): 28–38.

# GLOSSARY

*Acaboclado(a)*: *Caboclo*-like. An uncommon racial term perhaps invented to describe children orphaned by the Canudos conflict and adopted by wealthy members of the coastal elite. It served to soften the stronger and pejorative racial term *caboclo* (q.v.).

*Afilhado(a)*: Godchild. The religious faithful of Canudos commonly referred to themselves as the *afilhados* of Antônio Conselheiro.

*Agregado*: One who lives by favor on another's land. The term was interchangeable with *morador*.

*Agreste*: The intermediate zone in the Northeast of Brazil, characterized by adequate rainfall and a pattern of small landholding.

*Aldeia*: A native settlement or village originally organized by Jesuit missionaries.

*Aldeiamento*: A village formed by the Jesuits that brought together Indians on the colonial frontier to facilitate religious instruction and make use of Indian agricultural labor for subsistence.

*Almas de confissão*: Term used to describe the Portuguese Catholic-born white communicant population in colonial census records.

*Almocreve*: Muleteer.


*Bacalhau*: Salted cod.

*Bacharel*: Holder of a university-level degree, in the nineteenth century most often in law or medicine. (Plural: *bacharéis*)

*Baiano*: A native of the state of Bahia. However, southerners use the term in a pejorative sense to refer to northeasterners in general, and the residents of Rio Grande do Sul in the extreme south of Brazil used it in the late nineteenth century to refer to all Brazilians north of their state.

*Bandeira*: A group of *bandeirantes* (q.v.).

*Bandeirante*: An adventurer who explored the Brazilian interior on Indian slaving raids and in search of precious minerals.

*Bandeirante de gado*: Adventurers who hunted and herded cattle on the frontier and laid permanent colonial trails into the interior.

*Beato(a)*: A lay ascetic of the backlands who lived as if a member of a religious order, consecrated in status by a curate.

*Belo Monte*: Name used for Canudos by Antônio Conselheiro and some residents, though not as commonly as chroniclers suggest.

*Bicha*: Nineteenth-century slang for intestinal parasites.

*Bico de pena*: Falsified voting roll using fictitious names. One of many terms invented to describe the corrupt voting practices that characterized the *coronel* system during the first republic.

*Boiada*: Cattle drive.

*Bóia fria*: Literally, "cold lunch." Refers to a day laborer, usually miserably paid, hired on a daily basis and driven by truck to a work site.

*Boitatá*: Spirit in African belief that can protect or destroy pasturage.

*Branco*: A white person.

*Branco de dinheiro*: Literally, "white by money." A term used to describe members of the elite whose skin tone and physiognomy were of African or Indian aspect.

*Brejo*: A pocket of land in the *agreste* (q.v.) and backlands with more rainfall than surrounding areas.

*Caapora* or *caipora*: A mounted demon of Amerindian legend.

*Caatinga*: Backland scrub prone to drought, characterized by desertlike conditions in times of low rainfall.

*Caboclo(a)*: Originally used to describe a civilized (that is, Christian) Indian, it later was generalized to describe mixed-race people of the backlands mostly of white and Indian blood, but also with some African features. Also used to denote any backwoodsman of north, northeast, or central Brazil. What writers about Canudos meant by *caboclo* was closer to the colonial-Brazilian usage of the term *cafuzo* (q.v.).

*Cabo verde*: Slang for a fat mixed breed.

*Cabra*: Mulatto.

*Cachaça*: A strong brandy made from sugar cane.

*Cadeirinha de arrurar*: A carriage borne by slaves in which members of the colonial and imperial elites were transported.

*Cafuzo*: An individual of half-Indian and half-African ancestry.

*Caipira*: Term used in the Center-South, especially in São Paulo, for a rustic. See also *Catingueiro*.

*Campesino*: Rural agriculturalist, usually working or squatting on someone else's property.

*Candomblé*: Cult religion that combines African spiritist cults with the Catholic devotion to saints. This term is used in Salvador, Bahia, whereas the terms *xangô*, *umbanda*, and *macumba* are used in Recife and southern Brazil to describe similar faiths.

*Cangaceiro*: An armed backland ruffian, often a bandit. Cf. *jagunço*.

*Canhembora*: A runaway Indian.

*Canudense*: A resident of Canudos.

*Canudo*: A reed of the *canudo-de-pito* plant, sometimes dried and smoked by *sertanejos* (q.v.).

*Capanga*: A henchman in the informal armed force of a *fazendeiro* (q.v.).

*Captaincy*: One of fifteen huge tracts of land averaging fifteen leagues in length and extending to the Treaty of Tordesillas line, granted between 1534 and 1536 to twelve donees by the crown.

*Carioca*: Native of Rio de Janeiro.

*Casa de caridade*: A house of charity constructed to care for orphans and other unfortunates in more prosperous backland communities and larger urban centers.

*Casamata*: A dual-purpose structure used as a barracks or for storing arms and supplies.

*Catimbó*: A type of white magic in Amerindian practices.

*Catingueiro*: An inhabitant of the backland *caatinga* region (q.v.). The term held mildly pejorative connotations, implying rudeness and rustic behavior.

*Cearense*: A native of the state of Ceará.

*Chapada*: A seasonal stream in the dry northeastern backlands.

*Charque*: Jerky or dried and salted beef.

*Chuço*: Cattle prod.

*Colono or colôno*: Inhabitant of an agricultural colony established in special government attempts to attract European settlers by distributing free tracts of land.

*Comarca*: A district of judicial jurisdiction, smaller than a *município* (q.v.).

*Compadrio*: A godparent system of more than symbolic importance that tied the interests of parents, child, and godparents together. Parents ideally sought a godparent of higher status to help insure the well-being of their child and family.

*Confederação do Equador*: A failed attempt at republican secession by a confederation of northern and northeastern states in 1825.

*Conselheirista*: A supporter or follower of Antônio Conselheiro.

*Conselheiro*: Only a few backlands *beatos* earned the title *conselheiro*, or counselor, as Antônio Maciel did. Considered wise counselors, *conselheiros* were highly respected lay religious leaders in the backlands, where most inhabitants rarely came into contact with clerics.

*Cordel*: Short for *literatura de cordel*, or "stories on a string," popularly produced verses accompanied by woodcuts and sold at outdoor marketplaces.

*Coronel*: A rural political boss. (Plural: *coronéis*)

*Corumbá*: Seasonal migrant who returned to his own lands when climatic conditions improved.

*Criado(a)*: A category that included servants and workers in public places.

*Crioulo(a)*: Ex-slave.

*Curandeiro*: An herbal medicinal faith healer.

*Curandeiro de rasto*: A folk veterinarian of the backlands who employed traditional remedies for the afflictions of animals, in particular cattle.

*Curuca*: "Old maid." Also connoted a harlot in backland usage.

*Desaparecido*: Literally, "disappeared." A term used in military records for soldiers unaccounted for after combat. It is presumed that some of the soldiers listed officially on casualty lists as "disappeared" either deserted or defected to the enemy.

*Diamba*: Slang for marijuana. Also known as *fumo d'Angola, maconha*, and *rafi*.

*Doutor*: A term of respect usually reserved for graduates of law and medical schools, but often ascribed to or adopted by graduates of the advanced military schools or by powerful members of the oligarchy who lacked higher education.

*Encilhamento*: Literally the act of girthing or mounting a horse, this term vividly describes the period of wild speculation that the fledgling and still-fragile republic had to ride out in the early 1890s. When the bubble of speculation finally burst, it left the new government in dire economic straits.

*Engenho*: Sugar plantation with a mill powered by water, steam, or carts drawn by oxen.

*Entrada*: A foray into the interior during the colonial period.

*Ermida*: A religious shrine.

*Ermitão*: A hermit linked to a religious shrine who lived on alms collected in return for special prayers and advice.

*Estanceiro*: The owner of an *estância* (cattle ranch). This term was used primarily in Rio Grande do Sul.

*Estrada de ferro*: Railroad.

*Fantasma*: Slang for a vote tallied for a person who had died or who did not exist.

*Farinha*: Flour, usually referring to a flour made from the cassava root, or *farinha de mandioca*.

*Fascículo*: A short chapbook, or pamphlet, often published in serial form during the late nineteenth and early twentieth centuries.

*Fazenda*: In the Northeast, a cattle ranch or farm engaged primarily in animal husbandry. The term was also used to refer to coffee plantations.

*Fazendeiro*: Owner of a *fazenda*.

*Feira*: Outdoor market, usually weekly.

*Feirante*: A professional costermonger who works the *feira* circuit.

*Feiticeiro(a)*: An individual who specializes in practicing witchcraft.

*Florianista*: A supporter of President General Floriano Peixoto. Most Florianistas also considered themselves *Jacobinos* (q.v.).

*Fluminense*: A resident of the province (later, state) of Rio de Janeiro.

*Foreiro*: Renter.

*Formação*: An ambiguous notion that embraced an individual's ancestry, upbringing, education, and manners.

*Foro*: Tribunal.

*Fósforo*: Literally, "match stick." A *coronel*'s client who dutifully delivered his vote out of loyalty to and fear of his patron.

*Freguesia*: A district of religious jurisdiction.

*Fumo d'Angola*: Slang for marijuana. Also called *diamba, maconha*, and *rafi*.

*Furriel*: An intermediate rank between sergeant and corporal in the Brazilian army.

*Gente decente*: The "respectable people" of the oligarchy.
*Gente de cor*: Nonwhites.
*Geração*: Generation.
*Grogotuba*: A soup or stew made from *farinha* (q.v.) and okra.
*Guasca*: A term, used mostly in the far South of Brazil, for a rustic. Cf. *caipira*.

*Inconfidência*: A conspiracy.
*Índio de curso*: A wandering Indian not under "white" auspices, whether clerical or secular.
*Intendente*: The top elected official of a municipality.
*Interventor*: Vargas-era administrator imposed in place of elected governors after 1930 Revolution or, during the 1930s, at the whim of the national executive. Mose of the interventors were army officers who had supported Vargas in 1930.
*Intruso*: Migratory squatter who invaded uncultivated private and public lands and whose willingness to work for low pay depressed local wages and earned the resentment of local agricultural workers.

*Jacobino*: Member of a radical wing of the Brazilian republican movement that sought to restructure the political system along nationalist lines. Strong supporters of President General Peixoto's dictatorial rule (1892–95), the Jacobins sought to batter the fragile administration of civilian president Prudente de Morais (1896–1900) by stirring up antimonarchist sentiments. As part of this effort, they interpreted Canudos as part of an international monarchist plot to overthrow the new Brazilian republic.
*Jagunço*: Pejorative term for the backland herdsmen who formed the bulk of Conselheiro's armed forces. Analogous in late nineteenth-century usage to *capanga*. The term probably came from Portuguese Africa, where *zarguncho* (or *zagunço*) was used for someone uncouth and quarrelsome.
*Jornaleiro*: Day worker, usually miserably paid.
*Juiz de direito*: Judge of law, or a circuit court judge not subject to local election or nomination.
*Juiz de paz*: Judge of the peace, elected or nominated at the municipal level.
*Jujú*: A type of countermagic used to combat spells cast by practitioners of black magic in African spiritist religion.
*Jurema*: A sweet orange berry distilled into a liquor (also called *jurema*) by Kiriri Indians.

*Ladeira*: A tortuous street common to the Brazilian cities nestled in hilly or mountainous regions.
*Latifundio*: A land tenure system in which large tracts of land are held by a tiny portion of the rural population.
*Lavrador*: A stock raiser who holds a small piece of land.

*Legenda áurea*: Golden Legend. A twelfth-century Catholic tradition asserting the intervention of saints in the world.

*Lei das terras*: The "law of lands" passed in 1850, requiring that land be acquired exclusively through formal purchase and thus nullifying the claims of renters and squatters.

*Maconha*: Slang for marijuana. Also called *diamba*, *fumo d'Angola*, and *rafi*.

*Macumba*: See *Candomblé*.

*Mameluco(a)*: Individual of Indian and Caucasian ancestry.

*Mandioca*: Cassava, whose root is ground into a flour (*farinha de mandioca*) that is the basic dietary staple of the Northeast. The *mandioca* root is poisonous unless carefully washed and dried.

*Maracás*: A rattle made from a dry gourd and used by Indians in religious and war ceremonies.

*Maracujá*: Fruit of the *Passiflori incarnata* (passion fruit), which produces a sweet and tangy juice.

*Maragabirigunço*: Composite word invented for satiric purposes to link President Prudente de Morais with the terms *jagunço* (q.v.) and *maragato* (q.v.).

*Maragato*: A partisan of the federalist side of the Rio Grande do Sul civil war in the early republic.

*Maragunço*: Composite word linking *jagunços* to the rebellious and monarchist *maragatos* of Rio Grande do Sul.

*Massapê*: A moist, rich soil common to the littoral regions of the coastal Northeast, ideal for growing sugar cane.

*Matuto(a)*: Literally, a poor farmer. The term also refers to a rural Portuguese immigrant, usually to Paraíba. In the late nineteenth century, the term was applied to men and women, typically of *caboclo* origin, who inhabited the countryside and who were considered rustics, like the *caipiras* of the South (q.v.).

*Meeiero* or *meiero*: A *campesino* who works within the *meiação* system (q.v.).

*Meiação*: A system of land tenure and labor relations in which a *campesino* (q.v.) is given the right to work a marginal piece of land in exchange for corvée labor performed for the landowner, usually during harvest and planting seasons.

*Meio-branco(a)*: "Part-white," a term used in reference to all baptized children of color who were not slaves.

*Milréis*: Unit of Brazilian currency during the late nineteenth and early twentieth centuries; equivalent to one thousand *réis*.

*Mineiro(a)*: A native of the state of Minas Gerais.

*Morador*: Renter who lives by favor on another's land. The term was interchangeable with *agregado*.

*Moreno(a)*: An individual of European and African ancestry whose physiognomy is predominantly European and whose skin is light brown. Often used in reference to people of African aspect as a palliative for the stronger terms *negro* and *preto*.

*Mulato(a)*: A person of mixed Caucasian and African origin.

*Município*: Municipality.

*Mutirão*: Festive communal labor performed in rural areas to complete a difficult and laborious task such as building a home or a water reservoir—similar to barn raisings in rural North America.

*Novela*: A serial novel popular in Brazilian newspapers of the late nineteenth and early twentieth centuries. (In contemporary Brazil the term refers to serialized television soap operas shown during prime time.)

*Ocioso*: A lazybones or vagrant.

*Ogan*: A sponsor of a spiritist cult.

*Ogun*: The warrior god of Nago-Yoruba religion commonly associated with Saint Sebastian in Bahia and Saint George elsewhere.

*Oiticica*: *Linconia rigida*, a tree native to the Brazilian *caatinga* (q.v.) and bearing seeds from which an oil can be extracted.

*Orixá*: An intermediary between heaven and earth in *candomblé* (q.v.), usually the leader in a local spiritist cult temple.

*Pajé*: A Kiriri Indian chief.

*Palafita*: A home built on stilts characteristic of the Amazon region.

*Parceiro*: A sharecropping tenant.

*Pardo(a)*: Dark-skinned mulatto.

*Pares de França*: The "Peers of France": the name of Charlemagne's guard, adopted by the millenarians of the Contestado community.

*Passoca* or *paçoca*: A backland dish composed of roasted nuts mixed with manioc flour, sugar, and salt.

*Patrão*: Patron, or "boss."

*Pau-a-pique*: Long wooden stakes used to make corrals.

*Paulista*: A native of the state of São Paulo.

*Pinga*: Slang for *cachaça* (q.v.).

*Posse*: Squatters' right to land.

*Posseiro*: Squatter.

*Povo*: Literally, the "people," but having a pejorative connotation to distinguish poor or common people from the *gente decente* (q.v.).

*Praia*: A beach. In Bahia, however, the word designates a geographic zone (see next entry).

*Praia-tabuleiro*: A steep-edged plateau forming a transitional geographic zone between the humid coast and the dry backlands of Bahia.

*Preto*: A black person; dark-skinned.

*Promessa*: A vow made directly to Jesus or to a saint on a quid pro quo basis, to fulfill a specific desire on the part of the votary.

*Quadrilha*: A bandit gang.

*Quartel*: Military barracks or compound.

*Quilombo*: Runaway slave community.

*Quimbanda*: Cult spiritism.

*Rafi*: Slang for marijuana. Also called *diamba, fumo d'Angola,* and *maconha*.

*Rapadura*: Raw brown sugar.

*Rapto*: Bride abduction. An aggressive challenge to patriarchal authority in the backlands in which the woman most often consented to her captor's actions. Once abducted, she was rendered unfit for marriage to her father's candidate because the loss of virginity meant that she could hope to marry only the man with whom she eloped.

*Recôncavo*: The site of Brazil's earliest sugar cane plantations.

*Rendeiro*: Sharecropper who lives on another's land and pays rent in cash or produce.

*Requerente*: A kind of unlicensed lawyer who aided citizens in simple court cases.

*Retirada*: A mud-brick residence at the edge of Salvador in which a poor family lived. Also called a *separada* (q.v.).

*Roçado*: A cleared field or pasture, sometimes planted with *mandioca* (cassava) or corn.

*Romeiro*: Pilgrim.

*Sábado dos caboclos*: Day on which missionary priests in the northeast interior allowed Indians to carry out their own rituals in the church, including the ringing of chapel bells in aboriginal rhythms.

*Sací* or *sacy*: Amerindian spirit who attacks belated travelers on Good Friday eves.

*Samba*: Popular music of Afro-Brazilian origins that emerged in Rio de Janeiro and remains the driving beat of Carnival there.

*"Se Deus quiser"*: "If God wills," an expression commonly used when departing or speaking of some hoped-for event.

*Senhor de engenho*: A sugar plantation owner who possessed a primitive mill for processing raw cane.

*Senhores de baraço e cutelo*: The "Lords of life and death," an epithet often used to describe the most powerful oligarchs of a backland region.

*Separada*: A house on the periphery of urban Salvador inhabited by poor people. Also called a *retirada* (q.v.).

*Sertanejo*: Backlander; inhabitant of the *sertão*.

*Sertão*: Backland region of northeastern Brazil, sometimes divided into "high" and "low."

*Sesmaria*: Colonial-era land grant bestowed by the crown, often three square leagues in area.

*Sítio*: A small agricultural property or farm occupied by coastal elites for recreation. In the nineteenth century, the term referred to a plot of arable land rented to sharecroppers.

*Sujeição*: Corvée labor.

*Tabuleiro*: Tableland; the intermediate zone between the coast and the *caatinga* in Bahia (q.v.).

*Termo de bem viver*: A written pledge of good behavior signed before a local judge, usually in answer to a specific offense such as vagrancy.

*Toque*: A cattle disease in which carbuncles broke out on the hides of animals, conditioned to the aridity of the high *sertão*, when overexposed to humidity during the brief rainy season.

*Tupi*: A Brazilindian tribe.

*Umbanda*: See *Candomblé*:

*Uricuri*: A type of shell commonly used as an offering at pilgrimage shrines.

*Usina*: A modern sugar mill, introduced in the 1890s, which quickly supplanted the less mechanized *engenhos*.

*Valentia*: Valor and prowess, the attributes most admired in backland men, who believed in an exaggerated sense of personal and familial honor that must be defended vociferously against all challengers.

*Vales*: Chits given to employees instead of wages for credit to buy food and goods at local stores.

*Vaqueiro*: Cowhand. A term more widely employed in the north of Brazil, while in the south the term *gaúcho* prevails.

*Varíola maior*: A virulent strain of smallpox.

*Vila*: A small town.

*Visão do litoral*: The "coastal perspective" of the educated members of the urban elite, which led writers such as Euclydes da Cunha to interpret Canudos as a dangerous revolt by misguided religious fanatics.

*Vivandeira*: A female camp follower who accompanied common soldiers to the battle front.

*Xangô*: The most important deity in the Umbandist hierarchy, the equivalent of Jesus Christ. Also, another name for *umbanda* (see *Candomblé*).

*Zona da mata*: Coastal strip of land characterized by ample rainfall and sugar cultivation on plantations.

# INDEX

Abbade, João, 150, 164, 166, 172
ABC chapbooks, 197
Academy of Letters, Brazilian: mentioned, 61; Paulista Academy, 209; racist attitudes of president, 110
Acarapé (Ceará), 211
Africa: Dahomey, 52; West Africa, 52
Afro-Brazilian culture: African ancestry disparaged, 91, 140, 207; Afro-Brazilian culture used to woo voters, 260n.150; alleged lack of messianic interest in, 232; Bantu religion, 107; Canudos considered example of, 208; "feminine" aspect of, 260n.151; foreign impressions of, 53; mentioned, 52–53, 203, 260n.148; religious cults and sects, 32, 52–53; saint equivalents in Afro-Brazilian worship, 52–53; Yoruba culture, 52–53, 107
Agassiz, Louis, 4
*Agregados* (retainers). *See* Land tenure systems
*Agreste* zone. *See* Pernambuco
Agriculture: animal power use in, 12; centralized sugar refineries, 99, 118, 135, 159; cruelty toward workers, 118; individual plantations attacked (1832), 219; land available to colonists, 106; sugar aristocracy, 135; sugar production, 56, 67, 92, 98–99

Agripino da Silva Borges, Vigário. *See* Borges, Agripino da Silva
Aguiar, Durval Vieira de, 85–86, 139, 145
Alagoa de Baixo (Pernambuco), 221–22
Alagoas: impact of republic on state, 59; lack of market town development, 269n.99; Maceió (capital), 67; markets attacked in, 90; Penedo, 67; plantation economy in, 12; rural roads, 83
Alagoinhas (Bahia): climate in, 78; Comité Patriótico in, 188; Conselheiro in, 131, 138; epidemics afflict troops in, 186; hospital in, 190; mentioned, 62, 85; railroad, 83; sends population to Canudos, 83, 191
Albuquerque, Dep. Antônio Joaquim Pires de Carvalho e, 143
*Almocreves* (muleteers), 118
Altamira, 78, *See also* Vila do Conde (old name)
Amado, Janaína, 8
Amazon region: influx of workers from Northeast, 102, 138, 210; Manaus (capital), 103; *palafitas* (stilt houses), 102; rubber plantations, 102
Amparo (Bahia), 141
Anabaptists. *See* Mucker uprising
Andarahí, 208
Anti-vaccination riots (1904), 28
Anzin, 59